MARINE ECOTOURISM: BETWEEN THE DEVIL AND THE DEEP BLUE SEA

Ecotourism Book Series

General Editor: David B. Weaver, Professor of Tourism Management, George Mason University, Virginia, USA.

Ecotourism, or nature-based tourism that is managed to be learning-oriented as well as environmentally and socio-culturally sustainable, has emerged in the past 20 years as one of the most important sectors within the global tourism industry. The purpose of this Series is to provide diverse stakeholders (e.g. academics, graduate and senior undergraduate students, practitioners, protected area managers, government and non-governmental organizations) with state-of-the-art and scientifically sound strategic knowledge about all facets of ecotourism, including external environments that influence its development. Contributions adopt a holistic, critical and interdisciplinary approach that combines relevant theory and practice while placing case studies from specific destinations into an international context. The Series supports the development and diffusion of financially viable ecotourism that fulfils the objective of environmental, socio-cultural and economic sustainability at both the local and global scale.

Titles available:

1. *Nature-based Tourism, Environment and Land Management*
      Edited by R. Buckley, C. Pickering and D. Weaver
2. *Environmental Impacts of Ecotourism*
      Edited by R. Buckley
3. *Indigenous Ecotourism: Sustainable Development and Management*
      H. Zeppel
4. *Ecotourism in Scandinavia: Lessons in Theory and Practice*
      Edited by S. Gossling and J. Hultman
5. *Quality Assurance and Certification in Ecotourism*
      Edited by R. Black and A. Crabtree
6. *Marine Ecotourism: Between the Devil and the Deep Blue Sea*
      C. Cater and E. Cater

MARINE ECOTOURISM: BETWEEN THE DEVIL AND THE DEEP BLUE SEA

Carl Cater

Department of Tourism, Hospitality and Sport
Griffith University, Queensland, Australia

and

Erlet Cater

Department of Geography
University of Reading, UK

www.cabi.org

CABI is a trading name of CAB International

CABI Head Office	CABI North American Office
Nosworthy Way	875 Massachusetts Avenue
Wallingford	7th Floor
Oxfordshire OX10 8DE	Cambridge, MA 02139
UK	USA
Tel: +44 (0)1491 832111	Tel: +1 617 395 4056
Fax: +44 (0)1491 833508	Fax: +1 617 354 6875
E-mail: cabi@cabi.org	E-mail: cabi-nao@cabi.org
Website: www.cabi.org	

A catalogue record for this book is available from the British Library, London, UK.

Library of Congress Cataloging-in-Publication Data

Cater, Carl.
   Marine ecotourism : between the devil and the deep blue sea / Carl Cater, Erlet Cater
      p. cm.
   Includes bibliographical references.
   ISBN 978-1-84593-259-6 (alk. paper)
      1. Marine ecotourism. 2. Marine ecotourism -- Environmental aspects.
   I. Cater, Erlet. II. Title
   G156.5.M36C38 2007
   910.9162--dc22

                                 2006101325

ISBN-13: 978 1 84593 259 6

Typeset by Columns Design Ltd, Reading, UK
Printed and bound in the UK by Biddles Ltd, King's Lynn

Contents

For our Family and Friends

Acknowledgements

We count ourselves as very privileged that we have been able to draw on such a wide range of expertise and support during, and indeed before, the writing of this book. At Reading our colleagues (who we actually shared for 18 months) as always have been generous with their advice and encouragement. Many staff and students at Griffith have provided support for the project, and encouraged our thinking throughout. Students of 3403EAS Marine Ecotourism Field Trip and members of the Griffith University Dive Club provided useful feedback and personal insights. In terms of technical support we were fortunate to call upon the skills of Erika Meller, who converted a number of colour slides and photographs to monochrome prints, while Heather Browning prepared the line drawings for Chapters 2 and 11. Thanks are also due to the publishing team at CABI, in particular Claire Parfitt, her predecessor Rebecca Stubbs, Rachel Cutts, Quentin Scott and Emma Brooks, who have guided us through the various stages of preparation of the final manuscript.

There are many other individuals who have contributed both indirectly and directly to our endeavour. While we hope that those who we do not mention will realize how much we value the inspiration they have given us, we should like to mention, in particular, David Weaver for his invitation to write this book and continued support, Ralf Buckley for much encouragement, Paul Cloke for sowing many seeds, Michael Lück for his role in positioning marine tourism centre stage in recent years and Ian Munt, whose suggestion that Erlet should attend the First Caribbean Conference on Ecotourism in Belize back in 1991 had more far-reaching consequences than either of us could ever have envisaged.

It is also important to us that we should acknowledge the influence of those working at the coal face: Hugh Somerville and Martin Brackenbury, as the tireless champions of sustainable tourism in the industry, have been very supportive over the years. In the preparation of the book we have met with unparalleled cooperation from Pete Raines (Coral Cay Conservation), Simon Berrow (Shannon Dolphin and Wildlife Foundation), Nigel Smith (Seaprobe Atlantis), Bruce Nicholls (Tall Ship/Whale Watching Gold Coast), Trevor Long (Sea World), Daniel Gschwind (Queensland Tourism Industry Council) and Cheyne Benjamin (Walindi Plantation Resort/Mahonia Na Dari), along with several others who kindly met our requests for up to date information without hesitation despite their busy schedules. Last, but not least, we should like to thank our family and friends who have been our anchoring points throughout our voyage of discovery.

Authors

Dr. Carl Cater is a Lecturer in Tourism at Griffith University, Queensland, Australia. His research centres on the experiential turn in tourism and the subsequent growth of special interest sectors. He is a fellow of the Royal Geographical Society, a qualified pilot, diver, mountain and tropical forest leader, and maintains an interest in both the practice and pursuit of sustainable outdoor tourism activity.

Dr. Erlet Cater is Senior Lecturer in Tourism and Development in the Department of Geography, The University of Reading. Joint editor of *Ecotourism: A Sustainable Option* (1994) and Advisory Editor for *The Encyclopaedia of Ecotourism* (2001), she is an advisor for the Society and Environment Forum of the RGS-IBG and Coral Cay Conservation and judged the British Airways *Tourism for Tomorrow Award* for several years. She has been privileged to have travelled the world for the past 40 years, but her heart lies in the Inner Hebrides of Scotland.

A note on the subtitle

It is likely that the phrase *'Between the devil and the deep blue sea'* has nautical origins, with *devil* not a reference to Satan, but to the seam which margins the waterways on a ship's hull. This seam would require periodic maintenance whilst at sea, but its inaccessibility made it a difficult and awkward job. There was very little space to get at this seam, since there is only the thickness of the ship's hull planking between it and the water. The phrase is first recorded in print in 1637 in Robert Monro's *His expedition with the worthy Scots regiment called Mac-keyes.* A similar term in the English language is 'between a rock and a hard place'. As such the idiom represents the contemporary challenges of achieving sustainable outcomes in the development of marine ecotourism.

1 Introduction

The Marine Realm

In many ways this book is our response to the powerful 'tug of the tide' so graphically described in Trevor Norton's delightful and informative evocation of the marine realm in *Under Water To Get Out Of The Rain*, subtitled 'A love affair with the sea' (Norton, 2005).

It is, perhaps, no coincidence that: both authors hail from an island state where nowhere is more than 100 km from the sea and where the shipping forecast is a national institution (Connelly, 2004); the elder of us spent the first 18 years of her life in what was then a small coastal town in the south of England; the younger has spent the most recent part of his on one of the most famous coasts in the world with its proliferation of experiences on and under the sea; with proximate Norwegian lineage, the blood of the Vikings courses strongly through our veins; and we have had the privilege of total immersion (sometimes quite literally) in the marine environment of the Inner Hebrides, Scotland, on innumerable occasions over most of our lives.

These immutable bonds cannot fail to endow a sense of wonderment and awe over what is arguably the most fascinating and yet tantalisingly under-researched component of our planet. Equally, they are bound to generate a profound concern for the health of the world's oceans and seas and the fundamental desire that others, near and distant, now and in the future, should not be denied the opportunity to both appreciate and benefit from their manifest richness.

This richness has spurred the growth of tourism that seeks to appreciate and respect marine life in all its forms. As such, marine eco-tourism has emerged as a significant industry, practice and development tool. A proliferation of new activities, increasing commercialization and numbers participating, has created new challenges for managing such activity. However, if managed sustainably, the diversity of this environment enables coastal and island destinations to maintain unique points of difference in a globally competitive environment.

This book seeks to document these trends and challenges and give a holistic perspective of the development of marine ecotourism. We use a broad lens to focus on activities that constitute and impact on this practice, for this is essential in understanding outcomes. This is perhaps representative of a growing maturity in ecotourism (Cater, 2005), which embraces a variety of disciplinary influences. Indeed we are not alone in our quest, and this book seeks to complement texts such as: Higham and Lück's *Marine Wildlife and Tourism Management* (Higham and Lück, (in press), which has greater emphasis on the management of marine tourism (examining issues such as visitor dynamics, interpretation and economics); that of Jennings (2006), which examines the breadth of water-based tourism; or Michael Lück's edited *Encyclopedia of Marine Tourism* (Lück, (in press), which will serve as a vital catalogue.

Whilst efforts are underway to exploit space as the 'final frontier' for tourism, it is clear that the penultimate frontier still offers much untapped potential. It is quite revealing that marine policy documents that we have accessed during the preparation of this book are often a far cry from their more turgid terrestrial counterparts. They are invariably peppered with facts and figures that serve both to convey and to further a sense of fascination but also one of frustration over the inadequacy of current knowledge and understanding.

The IUCN/WWF (1998) document *Creating a Sea Change*, for example, describes how the oceans are 'the engines that drive the world's climate, defining weather and storing huge quantities of solar energy in the process ... the liquid heart of the Earth's hydrological cycle – nature's great solar-driven water pump' (p. 7) and how the ocean currents – 'the blue planet's super highways transfer great quantities of water and nutrients from one place to another. The Gulf Stream, for instance, pushes more water than is carried by all the rivers on Earth from the Gulf of Mexico and the Caribbean across the Atlantic into northern Europe' (p. 7).

It describes the richness of marine biodiversity – that out of 33 animal phyla, 32 are found in the sea, 15 of which are exclusively marine, and how the oceans contain the world's largest (the blue whale) and smallest (meiofauna) animals. However, compared with 1.5 million land species, only 275,000 marine species have been identified and described, and yet it is estimated that coral reefs alone may harbour in excess of 1 million, with as many as 10 million in the deep ocean basins (IUCN/WWF, 1998).

It is no wonder that it has been claimed that, in the light of the fact that 'only around one-tenth of the 290 million km² of the seabed has actually been explored and charted' (p. 10), the IUCN/WWF report declares that 'We know more about the moon than our own ocean world' (IUCN/WWF, 1998, p. 10).

Consider this: as long ago as 1938, the UK Ministry of Agriculture and Fisheries recorded 10 cm-diameter sucker scars on sperm whale carcasses on a whaling ship emanating from the suckers of the giant squids of the deeps (Norton, 2005), and yet it was not until 2005 that a Japanese scientific expedition succeeded in photographing an individual of a total length (including tentacles) of over 8 m at a depth of 900 m with a robotic camera (Kubodera and Mori, 2005). Consider also that, despite the fact that an estimated 90% of all volcanic activity occurs underwater, so-called 'Black Smokers' were only discovered relatively recently, and yet 30 of these volcanic chimneys generate the same energy as the largest nuclear power reactors (*Horizon*, 1999; Dowdeswell, 2004).

Further evidence of our patchy knowledge is the fact that a 100 km-long coldwater coral reef was discovered off the Lofoten Islands of Norway only in 2002 (Schrope, 2005). This lack of knowledge, whilst serving as a call to action, also reminds us of the vast potential of the marine environment for ecotourism activity.

Our lamentable ignorance flies in the face of the fact that the oceans are indispensable to our life support, livelihoods and lifestyles. The

IUCN/WWF (1998) document records how the oceans contribute 63% (US$20.9 trillion) of the goods and services provided by the world's ecosystems, over half of which (US$12.6 trillion) originate from coastal ecosystems. Scottish waters generate £14 billion, or 21%, of Scottish GDP each year (SWT/WWF, 2005).

Oceans and coasts provide a myriad of products ranging from food to minerals, drugs and medicines, but also enhance our lifestyles in terms of opportunities for rest and recreation. As the former becomes increasingly corporatized and hidden, our divorce from this connection to nature spurs a need to reconnect through tourism and leisure activity. Millions of tourists are attracted to the sea every year by the proliferation of opportunities such as swimming, snorkelling, diving, water sports, boating, sailing, fishing and wildlife viewing.

Connectivity and openness

The open nature of the marine environment brings with it considerable problems of management. Marine systems differ from terrestrial systems in terms of a much higher degree of connectivity attributable to 'the sea's large size, enormous volume, continuity of habitats and ubiquitous currents' (Lourie and Vincent, 2004, p. 1005). The high degree of connectivity in the seas facilitates the transmission of substances and effects (Kelleher, 1999).

Sea currents carry sediments, nutrients, pollutants and organisms through, and beyond, a specific location. Consequently, actions taken in one locality, by whatever form of activity, tourism or otherwise, marine or terrestrial, may affect another hundreds of miles distant and often nations apart. This marine connectivity was graphically illustrated by the dispersal of 29,000 plastic bath toys originally shed from a container ship in a storm 2000 miles off the coast of Alaska in January 1992. The so-called rubber duck armada circled the entire north Pacific ocean in just three years, while others made their way northwards to even be trapped in the Arctic ice, some eventually to be spat out in the North Atlantic and to be washed up on beaches in New England, over 9000 miles from their origin, in 2003 (Simons, 2001; Elliot, 2003).

The issue of connectivity is not confined to the seas and oceans themselves, but is as vital a consideration at both the air/sea and the land/sea interfaces. Air pollution and run-off and point discharges from the land and rivers are estimated to account for around three-quarters of the pollutants entering marine ecosystems (World Resources Institute, 1996). The White Water to Blue Water Partnership (WW2BW), launched at the World Summit on Sustainable Development in 2002, recognizes the significance of land-based sources of marine pollution such as sewage, industrial pollution and agricultural run-off and aims to promote integrated watershed and marine ecosystem-based management. Measures will be taken to: (i) address marine pollution; (ii) promote sustainable fisheries, agricultural and forestry practices; (iii) prevent coastal degradation; and (iv) meet the challenges of tourism (NOAA, 2004). The first activity of WW2BW is a pilot project in the Wider Caribbean (Leeds Tourism Group, 2004).

It is interesting to note that traditional societies often recognize the inextricability of the land and sea. The indigenous people of South Pacific islands regard 'the land, its adjacent reefs and lagoons, and the resources therein, together with the people [as] ... a single integrated unity' (Sofield, 1996). Traditional clan territories in the Torres Strait Islands, Australia, by custom if not by law, comprise both land and sea territories that include adjacent home reefs as well as extended sea tenure over the waters, submerged reefs and sandbanks beyond (Zann, 2005). The residents of Mafia island, Tanzania, view the 'ownership' and use of both land and sea in related terms and fail to make an artificial distinction between the two, regarding terrestrial and marine activities as complementary. Walley (2004, pp. 153–156) describes how residents sometimes describe the work that they do on both land and sea as 'farming', as well as their view that the communal 'proprietorship' of *wenjeyi* over the land extends to the sea.

This notion of communal proprietorship brings us on to consider the whole question of ownership and access to marine resources. Whereas the seas and oceans have frequently been described as common property, and consequently subject to Hardin's 'tragedy of the commons', it is more accurate to describe them as a common-pool resource. A common property resource is one where the members of a clearly defined group have the legal right to exclude non-members from using that resource and, thus, it has been argued, there may be important social institutions that can effectively manage the commons.

Ostrom (2000) outlines how common-pool resources display two important characteristics. First, it is costly or difficult to exclude individuals from using the resource by physical or legal barriers, both of which are clear problems in the open marine environment. Secondly, the benefits consumed by one individual reduce the benefits available to others. Ostrom (2000, p. 338) describes how common-pool resources 'may be owned by national, regional, or local governments; by communal groups; by private individuals or corporations; or used as open access resources by whomever can gain access'.

Arguably, however, because of the open nature of the marine environment, all forms of 'ownership' usually result in open access. Despite designations of marine protected areas, or indeed of territorial waters, there are few physical barriers to accessibility. This renders coastal waters, particularly in more remote locations, notoriously difficult to police. Byrnes and Warnken (2003), illustrate the enormity of the task involved in monitoring compliance in Australia's Great Barrier Reef Marine Park (GBRMP), where policing by 74 patrol boats translates into one boat per 4730 km², pointing out that this is the equivalent of only one police car patrolling the whole of the greater Brisbane area! In

2001, at Bunaken National Park, Sulawesi, Indonesia, community members were enlisted to work alongside hard-stretched professional enforcement officers in a joint patrol system. Similar initiatives, which increase compliance, are reported from locations such as Jamaica and Tanzania (MPA News, 2003a).

Chapter 9 describes how The Law of the Sea Convention sets down the rights and obligations of states and provides the international basis upon which to pursue the protection and sustainable development of the marine and coastal environment, where the state may exercise sovereign rights over natural resources and jurisdiction over marine scientific research as much as 350 nautical miles from the baseline. When even full sovereignty over territorial waters, which extend only 12 nm (nautical miles) from baseline, is difficult to police as described above, it can be seen that effective monitoring and enforcement over much more extensive areas constitute an almost insurmountable challenge.

Walley (2004, pp. 153–156) describes how, on Mafia island, while there was a concept of proprietorship rather than ownership where fishers from outside in the past were allowed to fish Mafia's waters, 'they were expected to follow the same norms of appropriate behaviour including the same type of fishing gear ... [it seems] more accurate to view regional waters not as a common property resource but as a "commons" defined and governed by appropriate social behaviour'. However, in the light of increased pressure from outside, the residents had to turn to the Marine Park for assistance.

Young (1999, p. 586) describes how 'many of the same problems of managing common-pool resources encountered in fishing are now emerging in ecotourism'. We can see therefore, in these instances, and especially on the high seas, how marine resources can effectively be viewed as open access and that it is the 'tragedy of open access' (Lynch, 1999) that we are concerned with: there being a positive incentive for individual users to exploit the resource to the maximum, even if destruction of marine resources is the inevitable result.

Marine Tourism and Marine Ecotourism

Added to the fact that marine tourism takes place in an environment characterised by both high connectivity and open access, there are other distinctive features of marine tourism that have a bearing on prospects for sustainability. Marine tourism takes place in an environment in which humans do not live, and consequently in which they are dependent on equipment to survive (Orams, 1999). Whilst this dependence may engender a sense of humility and respect for the unfamiliar, it may, equally, result in serious physical damage from careless handling or inappropriate use of technical support and facilities.

Also, increasing interest in the marine environment has meant that the growth rate of marine tourism exceeds that of most of the rest of the tourism industry. Whale watching, for example, as described in Chapter 4, this volume, displayed average annual growth rates of around 10% during the 1990s (Hoyt, 2001). Dive tourism to Zanzibar more than doubled between 1990 and 1995, with a concomitant increase in dive operators from one to 11 over that period (Cater, 1995, unpublished BSc dissertation).

Delimiting marine ecotourism

While, as is described in Chapter 7, the sea is an enduring Western tourist attraction, with records of sea bathing, for example, going back to Greco-Roman times, it is important to make a distinction between marine ecotourism, marine-based nature tourism and marine-based tourism. As Wilson (2003) suggests, and as described in Chapter 2, this volume, there are intra-sectoral conflicts between marine ecotourism and other marine-based tourism segments. As she suggests, with few exceptions, the conventional tourism sector will prevail over ecotourism interests.

Examples of how marine nature tourism may compromise genuine marine ecotourism are described in this chapter. As Wilson again suggests, problems arise especially when 'the basic free-ranging marine wildlife resource may consist of the same animal groups and habitats for both forms of tourism, even if operating from different terrestrial locations' (p. 55). Young (1999, p. 600), for example, describes how the migratory range of grey whales, extending over 5000 miles, means that they 'are not the exclusive domain of any one group but instead are exploited by multiple users operating independently of one another throughout that range'.

That marine nature tourism may be destructive has been documented over time. Norton (2005) describes how the writings of Philip Gosse, including *A Naturalist's Ramble on the Devonshire Coast*, published in 1853, helped to precipitate the Victorian craze for collecting seashore creatures. The adverse impact on shoreline ecosystems was even documented by Gosse's son, who lamented that 'my Father, himself so reverent, so conservative, had by the popularity of his books acquired the direct responsibility for a calamity that he had never anticipated ... cost him great chagrin. No one will see again on the shore of England what I saw in my early childhood' (Edmund Gosse, cited in Norton, 2005). Of course, with the proliferation of opportunities for an ever-increasing number of participants to observe, and even engage with, marine wildlife in the present day, such impacts are even more profound and far-reaching.

Orams (1999) defines marine tourism as including 'those recreational activities that involve travel away from one's place of residence and which have as their host or focus the marine environment (where the marine environment is defined as those waters which are saline and tide-affected)'. As Orams includes all activities where the marine environment is either the 'host' or the 'focus', many coastal tourist activities, such as shore-based whale watching, are included in his definition. Marine-based tourism in general, therefore, embraces a multiplicity of activities, ranging from swimming and reef walking, through the use of recreational craft, to cruising on the high seas. It will also, therefore, inevitably embrace a multitude of sins in terms of a lack of environmental integrity, sociocultural responsibility and, ultimately, if these two are compromised, economic viability.

It therefore follows that our definition of marine ecotourism must embody the essential criteria of sustainability and that it is, in essence, as Halpenny (2002. p. 7) succinctly puts it, 'ecotourism that takes place in coastal and marine settings'. Halpenny defines the coast as generally starting 'at the point where the high tide reaches, and runs to the edge of the continental shelf under the water', so her definition, strictly speaking, would not include shore-based activities that have as their focus the marine environment (such as storm watching on Vancouver Island or interpretive centres such as the Norwegian Fishing Village in the Lofoten Islands, discussed in Chapter 5).

We are therefore inclined to follow Wilson and Garrod's (2003) broad definition of marine which encompasses the foreshore, offshore and coast zones. As they argue, 'In any case, there will be no clear distinction between these geographical zones in practice, these having a very close functional relationship in the marine ecotourism context' (p. 2).

Halpenny also broadens the definition of marine to include large inland lakes, which we will not do in this book. While we accept that many of the issues raised are equally relevant to inland, especially large, bodies of water, we will confine our attention to saline (70% of the surface of the Earth is water, and all but 3% of it is salt (IUCN/WWF, 1998)), and tide affected waters. Our working definition of marine ecotourism is therefore: marine ecotourism is ecotourism that takes place in saline and tidal coastal and marine settings. Of course, as with all definitions, there is a need to more explicitly spell out the requisite detailed criteria, and so, again we turn to Halpenny in order to itemize the essential elements of marine ecotourism which she lists as:

- Travel to a marine or coastal setting (this may include some cultural attractions) that benefits local communities, including involvement and financial returns.
- Travel that helps to conserve the local environment (both cultural and natural).
- Travel that minimizes its negative impact on natural environments and local communities.
- Travel that emphasizes learning and interpretation of the local environment to visitors.
- Travel that motivates visitors to re-examine how they impact the earth and how they can aid local communities and the environment (Halpenny, 2003, p. 8).

At first sight, her last bullet point might be modified to an evaluation of impacts on the marine environment but, as land and sea meet in coastal regions and, as discussed above, must be viewed as interconnected systems, her reference to 'the Earth' (albeit with a small 'e') and 'the environment' is all-embracing.

In nailing our colours to the mast, it is important that we also examine two of the most contentious topics in ecotourism in general, and marine ecotourism in particular. These are, namely, the issues of consumptive *versus* non-consumptive use and the issue of scale.

Consumptive and non-consumptive marine tourism

Conventional wisdom holds that non-consumptive nature tourism in terms of the viewing of wildlife is good: consumptive wildlife tourism in the form of hunting and fishing is bad. Not only is this a gross generalization, but also there are some essential paradoxes in this view. First, we have to accept that there is no such thing as non-consumptive wildlife tourism. Lück (2003a) cites Wilkes' indictment of the concept of the non-consumptive recreation user as a 'comfortable myth', because wildlife tourism involves spatial consumption in the form of: (i) infrastructural requirements; (ii) physical consumption by way of soil compaction, trampling and erosion; and (iii) visual consumption by way of disturbance of species.

Weaver (2001) adds to these the consumption of fossil fuels in the process of transit and when using vehicles and boats in the process of wildlife viewing. Transferring these to the marine realm, it is obvious that the various adverse impacts of marine nature tourism described in Chapter 2, result from the allegedly 'non-consumptive' use of marine resources and are thus every bit the 'comfortable illusion' to which Wilkes refers.

Secondly, there is no guarantee that ecotourism will divert local users from consumptive use of marine resources. Brandon and Margoluis (1996) argue that it may be a false assumption that poor households may switch from illegal, unsustainable and difficult activities to legal activities that generate equal revenue, such as ecotourism, and will remain happy to substitute the same amount of money from one activity to another. Their income needs are not fixed and they aspire to do better than just holding their own economically: they want to improve their income levels. They also highlight the frequently seasonal nature of ecotourism and question 'at what point will it act as an economic incentive – for the part of the year when the person receives the income or for the whole year? Or will the person work in ecotourism and undertake illegal and/or unsustainable activities during other times of the year?' (p. 6).

As Young (1999, p. 609) found in Baja California:

> Even if ecotourism provides a significant new source of income from an environmentally friendly, non-consumptive use of resources, it may not be sufficient to discourage local people from engaging in more destructive

(consumptive) use of resources. In the two study sites, the economic benefits of gray whale tourism are not sufficient to reduce extractive pressures on inshore fisheries. Furthermore, conflicts over access to marine resources have only intensified with the growth of ecotourism.

Not only may marine ecotourism fail to divert the local populace from unsustainable activities but, ironically, it may even in some cases serve as an impetus because it inevitably attaches a financial value to nature. Should it present an unattractive investment prospect because of market disincentives, or even fail because of 'unfair' competitive advantage (for example from eco-opportunists or from subsidized projects), there is the clear danger that marine ecotourism entrepreneurs will look towards other more financially advantageous investment options. Without policy intervention, these alternatives will ultimately outcompete ecotourism, due to the higher turnover possible with reduced consideration of environmental and cultural impacts.

Thirdly, the wholesale condemnation of consumptive wildlife use as destructive may not stand up to closer scrutiny. Zwirn *et al.* (2005) make a strong argument for recreational fishing to be viewed as sustainable, providing it is pursued responsibly and is confined to healthy populations that can support small-scale extraction in ways that will not diminish future population health. A major problem is of course that, given the open and interconnected characteristics of the marine environment described above, it is not as easy to determine sustainable off-take as it is for hunting on land where Buckley (2003a, p. 244) declares:

> If killing part of a local population for sport generates enough money to protect the remainder population from death by poaching or habitat destruction, sport hunting can arguably make a positive contribution to conservation. Paradoxical though it may sound, therefore, it is not completely illogical to consider whether hunting safaris should not be considered as ecotourism.

The proliferation of catch-and-release fishing across the globe, discussed in Chapter 4, muddies the waters still further, with several protagonists making a case for regarding this activity not only as non-consumptive but also as ecotourism. Zwirn *et al.* (2005) cite major advances in angler ethics such as the National Marine Fisheries Service Code of Angling Ethics, which was developed with the participation of both angling groups and conservationists (NFMS, 1999). This code limits catch to desired species and size, using techniques to minimize injury to fish when released. Halpenny (2002, p. 22) itemizes good practices in release fishing and examines how it helps promote conservation and economic opportunities in the Toledo district of Belize.

While the jury is still out on issues such as post-release mortality rates (Zwirn *et al.*, 2005, cite Hooton's estimates of 10% for bait fishing, 3% for lures and 1% for fly-fishing in steelhead fisheries in British Columbia, Canada; Holland *et al.*, 1998, report high survival rates for billfish), Zwirn *et al.* argue that properly managed and practiced recreational fishing might not only be environmentally sustainable, but also have the potential to contribute positively to conservation (by participating directly in monitoring of fisheries and research, as well as by incorporating educational and interpretive elements), and to contribute to local economies. By fulfilling these requirements of sustainable management they therefore put forward the case that the activity may be viewed as ecotourism.

Holland *et al.* (1998) make similar arguments for billfish angling in Costa Rica, the US Atlantic and Puerto Rico, where 61, 80 and 81% of billfish anglers, respectively, belonged to one or more fisheries conservation organizations. They argue that:

> It is not the type of activity per se but the specific nature of the human behaviours involved, the distribution of economic benefits, and the associated social and environmental impacts that should be considered when evaluating 'ecotourism' activities ... to the extent that anglers act responsibly to minimise their impacts and billfish angling remains sustainable as a result of their efforts, the ecotourism label seems appropriate for billfish angling.
>
> (Holland *et al.*, 1998, p. 111)

It can be seen, therefore, that the consumptive/non-consumptive dialectic is not only contentious but also convoluted. To clear the waters somewhat perhaps, we can turn to Fennell's suggestion that we need rather to view ecotourism activities, of whatever type, as being ranged 'along a continuum from hard path to soft path', recognizing that 'every outdoor activity has the potential for imposing some level of impact on the resource base' (Fennell, 2000). Weaver (2001) concurs with this view, citing Vaske's suggestion that activities fall along a consumptive/non-consumptive continuum, and that all activities actually incorporate elements of both.

The question of scale

The question of scale is one of the most contested characteristics of ecotourism. Pointers towards it being conceptualized as being primarily a small-scale activity include: the fact that early ecotourism was represented by a few, hardy individuals travelling alone or in small tour groups (Page and Dowling, 2002); smallness of scale is implicit if ecotourism is viewed as subset of alternative tourism (i.e. alternative to mass tourism) that is characterized by small-scale operations reliant on local inputs (Weaver, 1998); The International Ecotourism Society emphasizes the functional aspects, with the market segment concentrated on leading and accommodating small groups in natural areas in an educational manner using interpretive materials and local specialist guides (Epler-Wood, 2002).

However, confining ecotourism to small-scale participation not only brings the danger that enacting its principles in such confined contexts is tantamount to preaching to the already converted, but also that it is irrational to deny the designation of ecotourism to large-scale, nature-based tourism if it adheres to all the requirements of sustainable tourism. As Williams and Shaw (1998, p. 56) state: 'While sustainability is often popularly associated with "smallness" … the link between scale and sustainability has not been empirically (or theoretically) tested.'

Weaver (2001) also argues that it neither makes economic sense nor acknowledges the potent lobbying force constituted by increased participation. He observes that there is a two-way relationship. On the one hand, ecotourism can serve to strengthen the mass tourism product by offering opportunities for 'green' diversification as well as helping to impart an ethos of sustainability and environmental awareness to mainstream tourism. As Honey (1999, p. 53) suggests: 'The ultimate goal of ecotourism should be to infuse the entire travel industry with the principles and practice of ecotourism.' Lück (2003b) describes how Europe's largest package tour operator, TUI, and Germany's second largest charter airline, LTU, have a variety of policies and actions to minimize adverse environmental and social impacts in destinations.

On the other hand, mass tourism supplies a large market of soft ecotourists that helps position ecotourism as a significant stakeholder capable of lobbying on an equal footing with stakeholders in other sectors; in the case of marine ecotourism this would be with commercial fisheries, aquaculture, etc. Furthermore, mass tourism can introduce sophisticated environmental management strategies to ecotourism that are beyond the capability of most traditional small-scale operations. Weaver (2001), however, recognizes that the disparity in power between the two sectors will mean that the influence of mass tourism over ecotourism is likely to be much greater than vice versa, and, consequently, that mass tourism may effectively appropriate ecotourism for its own purposes.

The debate about scale again serves to illustrate the heterogeneity of ecotourism. It has become increasingly recognized that a spectrum of participation and involvement can be discerned from hard-core specialist groups, frequently undertaking scientific observation, such as coral reef monitoring, to more casual, natural resource-based activities, such as whale watching, providing they are sustainably managed.

Weaver (2001) identifies the latter as a 'soft' ecotourism market, which may largely consist of 'mass tourists engaged in such activities as part of a broader, multi-purpose vacation that often places emphasis in the 3S realm'. This of course is particularly pertinent to marine ecotourism, as activities such as snorkelling on coral reefs, visits to seabird or seal colonies and cetacean watching are increasingly popular as add-on activities in coastal destinations. Such a pragmatic view is adopted by Queensland, Australia, where three broad styles of ecotourism are distinguished: self-reliant, small group and popular ecotourism, with the latter involving the transport of larger numbers of visitors to, through or across the country's best known and most popular natural attractions (Page and Dowling, 2002).

Buckley (2003a) also tackles the issue of scale in ecotourism, arguing that 'There is nothing scale-dependent about a nature-based product, minimal-impact management, environmental education or contributions to conservation. In practice, however, big ecotourism seems rare.' He goes on to examine two possible models for increasing the economic scale of ecotourism without sacrificing its fundamental principles.

The first is characterized by high value and high volume such as reef and beach resorts in Australia and the Maldives; 'expedition' cruises in the Arctic, Antarctic and Amazon; and high-speed catamaran cruises to fixed pontoons on the Great Barrier Reef, all of which have a tendency to market themselves as ecotourism. Buckley examines these contenders for the title of ecotourism in turn. The environmental integrity of resort operations, he suggests, is driven more by the need for compliance with laws, statutes and development conditions as well as by the operational necessity to 'avoid fouling the immediate surroundings of the resort'. Only if the resorts 'can show a contribution to conservation proportional to their size', he suggests, should they be able to lay claim to the mantle of ecotourism. The expedition cruises, he feels, seem to fit the bill of large-scale ecotourism more closely, as appreciation of scenery and wildlife is a major driver; measures are taken to minimize impacts; the environmental education programme is expert and intensive; and the tours may help to generate political support for conservation.

The high-speed catamaran trips operated by companies, such as Quicksilver, again have the natural environment, the reef, as the principal attraction; systems are in place to manage environmental impacts on board ship and at the pontoons; information about the reef is provided through videos and printed material; and the operators collect the environmental management charge (see Chapter 3, this volume) which is paid by all visitors to the Great Barrier Reef Marine Park, so again this may be viewed as an example of large-scale ecotourism.

While Buckley cautions that, not only do the compulsory levies meet only a fraction of the direct management costs for the GBRMP, but also that there are inevitable environmental impacts from the catamarans and the reef pontoons, he suggests that the high-speed, high-volume catamaran tours are as deserving of the title of ecotourism as a small boat taking a few people snorkelling. However, it is important to note that, as highlighted by Mules (2004), and discussed in Chapter 3, the management costs of the park are more than met by the taxes contributed by operators and ancillary industries.

Buckley's second model for the commercial growth of ecotourism enterprises is that of a franchise or portfolio approach, whereby a wide range of individual tours are on offer by a company. Using the example of World Expeditions, he examines how large-scale revenue is generated through volume and variety, while each individual tour is characterized by small group size and able to adhere to the more conventional perception of ecotourism. In this case the picture is one of the sum of sustainable parts equalling a sustainable whole, and therefore qualifying as 'large-scale' ecotourism in aggregate.

Patterns and Processes

The first section of this book furnishes, as far as is possible, what could
be loosely termed the baseline for examining marine ecotourism. We use
this term with caution because it is probably, as may have been gathered
above, the most fundamental aspect of our deficient understanding of the
marine environment: we barely know what is there, let alone the
dynamics of what is going on. Chapter 2 sets the scene for the rest of the
book insofar as it highlights the complexities of the literally fluid inter-
connections and interchanges within and between physical, biological,
social, cultural, political and economic processes in the marine environment that will condition prospects for sustainable marine ecotourism.

Actions taken, wherever, whenever, will have ramifications for other
activities. Such is the complexity of these interactions, however, that
there are important considerations both spatially and temporally.
Spatially, the interconnectedness and openness of the seas and oceans, as
described above, has manifest implications for prospects for sustainable
ecotourism. Although it has been suggested by Craig-Smith *et al.* (2006)
that tourism impacts in coastal areas are generally localized, limited to
zones just a few kilometres from where the activity takes place and
within national boundaries and territorial waters, there are notable
exceptions such as adverse impacts on migratory species, in particular
from whale watching, and from cruise tourism. Temporally, not only do
current actions often have ramifications far into the future, but also, as we
describe, the frequency and intensity of such actions has undoubtedly
increased over the past two decades.

We examine the potentially deleterious effects of other economic
activities, both intra-sectoral (other tourism market segments) and inter-
sectoral, on marine ecotourism. The distinction between marine nature
tourism and marine ecotourism has been discussed above, with the
activities of the former potentially compromising the latter. More
obvious is the fact that the sustained popularity of tourism in coastal
areas, as well as the phenomenal growth of the cruise industry, depend
upon – and consequently impact on – the marine environment.

Craig-Smith *et al.* (2006) describe the impacts of coastal and marine
tourism in general under four headings: (i) coastal erosion (which is
frequently accelerated through the removal of mangroves or by the
blasting of access channels through coral reefs); (ii) habitat degradation
(arising from coastal development, marine- and shore-based activities
and discharge of effluents); (iii) pollution; and (iv) waste handling and
management (sewage and marine litter).

They examine the impacts of the burgeoning cruise industry on
coastal and marine habitats arising from port construction, dredging and
land-based infrastructure, and examine the need for responsible disposal
of waste as well as the exchange of ballast water, which may result in the
transmission of alien, possibly harmful, species (it has been estimated
that around 3000 species are transported around the world in all ships'

ballast water each day (WRI, 1996)). Although ships' discharges are regulated under the regulations of the International Convention for the Prevention of Pollution from Ships (MARPOL), there are frequent contraventions. Royal Caribbean, for example, was levied fines and penalties totalling US$33.5m to settle dumping complaints that occurred between 1994 and 1998 (surfrider, undated).

It is yet more obvious still that the activities of other sectors, such as commercial fisheries, aquaculture, port industries and offshore oil extraction (Wilson, 2003) may compromise the success – if not the very existence – of marine ecotourism. Indeed, Cohen (2001) suggests that the ecotourism industry must prohibit or restrict the activities of incompatible industries that may share a potential or actual ecotourism site. Wilson (2003, p. 55), however, suggests that this may be particularly difficult in a marine context and that it is unrealistic to insist that marine ecotourism must operate in an area free of incompatible industries, where even 'any *quid pro quo* alliance between marine ecotourism and the incompatible industry in question would not be a simple arrangement'.

We examine the complex web of interactions between marine ecotourism and other activities by way of two detailed examples: the impact of commercial fisheries on seabird viewing; and the impact of fish farming on the nature and quality of the marine tourist experience. Our examples also serve, however, to illustrate how we also need to consider the wider, global, context both in terms of global environmental change and the global political economy: not only is it relevant to consider the potential incompatibilities of individual sectors, but also we must recognize that these are cast in a dynamic world characterized by difference and diversity.

This dynamism not only applies to marine ecosystems themselves, subject to a multitude of perturbations such as coral bleaching as described in Chapters 2 and 3, but is also a feature of the continually changing mix of experiences on offer in marine ecotourism, for example the Swimming with Whalesharks Encounter at Ningaloo described in Chapter 3. Of course, the two are not mutually exclusive, as changes in either of these systems elicit transformations and adjustments in the other. For example, we examine problems associated with tourist visitation instigating behavioural changes among the stingrays of the Cayman Islands and of sharks through shark cage diving at varying locations across the globe. The impacts of Global Environmental Change are described in Chapters 2 and 3.

While there are significant threats to established destinations such as the Maldives, there may, ironically, be opportunities for areas currently 'off the map' due to a shift in species and habitats. It has been suggested, for example, that, as more areas of the ocean become warmer, coral reefs might actually expand their geographical range. The scandalous paucity of baseline data, also examined in Chapter 3, constitutes a major impediment to effective planning and management. As stated earlier, we barely know what is there in the marine realm, let alone what is going on, for example, regarding calcification rates of coral.

The changing mix of marine ecotourism activities is also attributable to technological change. The facilitation of underwater observation through SCUBA has to be the most significant development in relatively recent times, but the development of glass-hulled boats, semi-submersibles and tourist submarines, together with the construction of underwater observatories such as that at Milford Sound, New Zealand, facilitates ever-widening participation, as described in Chapter 4. This considerable increase in numbers able to experience at first hand and appreciate the remarkable diversity of the marine environment has the potential not only to spread environmental awareness to mainstream tourism and other activities but also, as described above, to help establish marine ecotourism as a significant stakeholder in the marine realm.

Primary Stakeholders and Interests

When we dedicated the second section of the book to an examination of the primary stakeholders involved in marine ecotourism, little did we realize that each of these chapters would take on a life of its own, as both their structure and content were dictated by the major driving forces behind those key interests. It became, perhaps, the most fascinating section of the book as we began not only to engage with, but also to attempt to identify with, the angle from which these key players were coming. In doing so we were drawn into a rich literature from a variety of disciplines and sub-disciplines that furnished the most appropriate frameworks within which to examine the salient issues.

This section focuses on four categories of stakeholder: coastal communities; marine ecotourists; marine nature; and the marine ecotourism industry. We consider these to be the primary stakeholder groups as they are ultimately affected in terms of benefiting or losing out from marine ecotourism. They may also be viewed as key stakeholders insofar as their activities can strongly influence the outcome of marine ecotourism.

However, there are obviously other key stakeholders who, although they may be viewed as secondary stakeholders insofar as they perform an intermediary role (such as governmental and non-governmental bodies and agencies at various levels), wield considerable power and influence over outcomes. These are considered in Part III of the book, which examines regulation, facilitation and collaboration.

It is, to us, logical that we commence the second part with an examination of coastal communities as primary, key stakeholders, as not only are they most immediately and enduringly affected by marine ecotourism but they are also major players in conditioning sustainability. The introduction to Chapter 5 describes how they display most of the criteria for stakeholder inclusion outlined by Borrini-Feyerabend (1996) and therefore play a central, vital, role in the planning and management of marine ecotourism. Coastal communities are concerned with not only making a living but also sustaining and even improving the various qualities of that living.

As discussed above, wholesale, unconditional, acceptance of ecotourism as a sole development strategy by local people is both unlikely and unrealistic. Poor households income needs are not fixed and they are likely to aspire beyond just holding their own economically. Consequently, they may divert to, or supplement with, other, less sustainable activities, particularly when the dimension of seasonality of tourism visitation is added into the equation (Brandon and Margoluis, 1996). In approaching marine ecotourism from the view of local communities, therefore, the sustainable livelihoods approach (SLA) offered a useful integrative framework as it facilitates a systematic appraisal of the impacts of marine ecotourism, both positive and negative, on the assets of coastal people. The classic 'pentagon' of assets that are drawn upon to build livelihoods (natural capital, human capital, physical capital, financial capital and social capital) is added to in this chapter by a consideration of cultural capital. Following other writers' arguments for the justification of the inclusion of cultural capital as a livelihood asset, we found it a useful construct for examining both its vulnerability and viability as a resource for marine ecotourism. While the chapter examines the various ways in which marine ecotourism may enhance the various assets (or capital) that are combined to constitute coastal livelihoods, it also highlights the ways in which it may detract from these. It is undeniable that the root cause of this detraction is the structural inequalities at play when the overall context in which marine ecotourism is cast as a process is considered. Communities are heterogeneous constructs, divided by ethnicity, class, gender and age: the benefits and costs of marine ecotourism are respectively skewed towards the haves and have-nots.

The recognition of heterogeneity is also important when we turn to examine another primary stakeholder group in Chapter 6, that of marine ecotourists. This chapter not only examines how individuals vary according to motivation, behaviour and reward, but also, importantly, points out that at any one time and place each individual may adopt a variety of guises, and thus gazes. We examine marine ecotourists' desires through a framework derived from Beard and Ragheb (1983), emphasizing education, esteem, expertise and escape as primary in the negotiation of experiences. To this blend we highlight how a desire for embodied experience must also be considered, especially when we consider the diversity of interactions detailed in Chapter 4, pausing to reflect that these may not always be pleasant. A case study of scuba-divers helps to illustrate the discussion.

Chapter 7 turns to the object of the marine ecotourism gaze: marine nature. Andersson *et al.* (2006, p. 296) argue that the formalization of the tourist gaze through ecotourism practices has actually 'served to reproduce the distance between nature and western culture' and, because nature and indigenous culture are positioned together in conservationist discourse, 'the scientisation of nature in tourist contexts has thus acted to dissociate tourists from nature and local culture, quite contrary to the general rhetoric. Nature has been objectified, a viewable thing' (p. 297).

However, in this chapter and as also described in Chapters 4 and 6, there has been a marked shift over the past few years in nature-based tourism representations and practices from nature as an object to nature as experience. We examine a 'third way', which would involve a more embodied relationship with nature; an emphasis on connection and kinship between the natural world and our own; and the recognition of existing relationships to nature.

However, Andersson *et al.* (2006, p. 301) describe how 'the formation of new touristic discourses and practices related to nature, where tourism operators are in the process of situating nature in a new global cultural economy' has resulted in 'conservation through commoditisation'. It is undeniable that marine tourism operators have a strong interest, which is commercially driven, in the future of marine ecotourism.

We therefore turn our attention to the tourism industry as a primary, key, stakeholder group in Chapter 8. As a major player in the tourism system (Holden, 2000), the industry has both a predominant interest and considerable influence in how marine ecotourism is shaped in a locality. While industry involvement is most likely to be motivated by profit, as tourism entrepreneurs invest in business (Hall and Page, 1999), financial viability may be appraised together with the level of engagement with environmental sustainability and social responsibility through the triple bottom-line approach.

This approach measures corporate performance, and thus sustainability, not only by profits but also in terms of ecological and social integrity. It offers a useful integrative framework to gain a holistic appreciation of the interplay between the marine ecotourism industry and other stakeholders and components of marine ecotourism, as well as enabling us to incorporate the industry view. Pragmatism dictates that we take on board Fennell and Dowling's suggestion that there is a need to move beyond the view of operators and service providers as a stakeholder group that must adhere only to policy and guidelines and to recognize that they should be regarded as 'not only active players in the operationalisation of policy but also shapers of policy' (Fennell and Dowling, 2003, p. 340).

As described above, there are many other key stakeholders in marine ecotourism who, although they perform a secondary, intermediary role, may be very influential in conditioning outcomes. Part III of the book turns therefore to examine regulation, facilitation and collaboration through planning agencies, institutional structures and networks and initiatives.

Regulation, Facilitation and Collaboration

The role of various agencies in planning and regulating marine ecotourism is considered in Chapter 9. As outlined in Chapter 2, planning for sustainable marine tourism is arguably considerably more complicated than that of the terrestrial environment. Not only are we faced with conflicting sectoral interests but, also, as described above with the complicating issues of: open access; common-pool resource use; connectivity between land, air and sea; and differing jurisdictions. In particular, the latter apply to not only often highly mobile resources but also to 'footloose' resource utilization.

In Chapter 9 we describe how, for example, Hall (2001, p. 605), cites Wood's description of cruise tourism as 'globalization at sea', with the corresponding phenomenon of deterritorialization. Visser (2004, p. 36) examines this phenomenon with regard to coastal areas, arguing that deterritorialization is a particularly relevant concept not only 'because of the mobility of maritime species and the fact that ecosystem boundaries cut across administrative boundaries' but also 'because of the fluidity of the coastal resources on regional and coastal markets' (obviously this applies as much to tourism as other resources) and because of 'the particular social, economic, and political conditions of the coastal population, who are among the least 'residential' members of civil society' (she is referring, in particular, to developing countries). Visser calls for an investigation of whether, or to what extent, theories and concepts developed and applied to a 'fixed land environment' have relevance to the fluid environment of the sea.

Hall (2000a, p. 145) describes how tourism, like the environment, constitutes 'a meta-problem, characterised by highly interconnected planning and policy messes', cutting 'across fields of expertise and administrative boundaries and, seemingly, ... connected with almost everything else'.

From what we have already written, and increasingly as the book progresses, it is manifest that nowhere is this more evident than in the field of marine ecotourism. It is not surprising, therefore that, faced with such an enormous challenge, 'specific and formal provisions for the planning and management of marine ecotourism are, in practice, either non-existent or only adopted sporadically and at the most basic level' (Wilson, 2003, p. 48). This is particularly ironic because, in the absence of effective planning and management, as described in Chapter 8, there is a danger that marine ecotourism may foul its own nest through unsustainable activities that adversely impact on coastal and marine resources, setting in motion a downward spiral whereby the compromising of visitor satisfaction through environmental degradation would result in reduction of tourist arrivals, questionable economic viability and jeopardization of locally accrued benefits.

Chapter 9 examines the various levels of government that have become increasingly engaged with the health of marine environments in recent years. Not all engage explicitly with marine tourism. Parker (2001, p. 509) describes how ecotourism in general and protected area management 'are also affected by the policies and operations of numerous other government agencies whose primary missions deal with different functions and whose main loyalties are thus found elsewhere'. However, there will be implicit ramifications for sustainable marine ecotourism, given that initiatives will shape the overall context of the seas and oceans in which it is set as a process.

This chapter also examines the roles of NGOs and research institutes in shaping policy. It is important to note that, in the light of the 'new post-sovereign multilayered governance architecture ... to which tourism is contributing and by which, in turn, it is affected' (Hall, 2005, p. 130), we need to recognize that other stakeholders are not only actively involved through the operationalization of policy, but also must be viewed as shapers of policy (Fennell and Dowling, 2003, p. 340).

Hall (2005, p. 130) cites the work of Kooiman, who argues that governance has become an inter-organizational phenomenon, best understood through mechanisms such as 'co-managing, co-steering and co-guidance'. In the planning and management of marine ecotourism it is evident, therefore, that we need to examine the agenda and influence of the primary stakeholders described in Part II, as well as the myriad of agencies, jurisdictions, protocols and laws with and within which marine ecotourism must operate, covered in Chapter 9. How these are translated and transposed to the sea in terms of marine management will, of course, be highly variable, contingent upon social, cultural, economic, institutional and political contexts that will condition prospects for sustainable outcomes.

The three principal marine management structures that should constitute facilitative, cooperative and integrative approaches are examined in Chapter 10. While each of these (community based coastal resource management, marine protected areas and integrated coastal zone management) will display varying degrees of collaboration, according to the various contingencies of place, there is now widespread recognition of the significance of collaborative efforts between levels, sectors and interests in order to ensure sustainable coastal and marine resource management. Chapter 11 turns to examine the plethora of initiatives at varying scale levels. Only a few are dedicated to marine ecotourism, reflecting the fact that tourism partnerships as a whole are relatively thin on the ground. Other collaborative ventures examined in this chapter are those concerned with marine environments as a whole. While they have a much wider remit, they again constitute the wider context that conditions prospects for sustainable marine ecotourism.

Setting Course

We offer no apology for the scattering of nautical terms throughout this book: the extent to which they have permeated our language is a graphic illustration of the pervasiveness of the marine realm in our everyday lives. It is justifiable from the point of view of areal extent alone, with the oceans covering 71% of the Earth's surface. Indeed, it has been argued that our planet should be called planet Ocean (NERC, 2005). The title of the 2001 BBC/Discovery series *Blue Planet: Seas of Life* bears testament to the enormous significance of the seas and oceans to our life support. The oceans perform a vital role in the Earth's carbon cycle: providing around a half of the oxygen we breathe through the photosynthesis of marine plants, as well as acting as a vital carbon sink (NASA, 2005).

An estimated 60% of the world's population lives on or within 100 km of the coasts, and by 2025 it is expected that 6.3 billion people will be living in the coastal zone, concentrated in coastal megacities (UNESCO, 2001a). By 2020, it is estimated that 90% of international trade will move by sea. As described earlier, we also not only depend on the oceans for sustenance and a wide range of products, but also they significantly enhance our lifestyles in terms of opportunities for rest and recreation. Hall (2001) describes how the ocean and marine environment is not only a 'new frontier' but also one of the fastest growing tourism market segments, citing the US National Oceanic and Atmospheric Administration's recognition of the fact that it is increasing, both in terms of volume and diversity, more than any other coastal activity. While it is impossible to estimate just how significant this is worldwide vis-à-vis the tourism sector as a whole, some indication of its importance may be garnered from individual examples. We discuss the economic significance of tourism to the Great Barrier Reef in Chapters 3 and 10.

The Nova Scotia Department of Tourism, Culture and Heritage, Canada, estimates that ocean tourism in the form of cruise tourism and saltwater fishing contributes Can$17.5 million to the GDP of the province. If coastal tourism activities such as whale watching, diving, kayaking, sailing and beach visitation could be added into the equation then it is undoubtable that a sizeable proportion of the total tourism expenditures of Can$1.3 billion in the province would be derived from coastal and marine activities (Fisheries and Oceans Canada, 2006).

It is also conceivable to argue that the attraction of developing small island states is largely attributable to their marine setting. The rapid growth of visitation to the Maldives, for example, is largely attributable to the attraction of the islands, which are surrounded by the largest group of coral reefs in the Indian Ocean, harbouring over 1000 species of fish and about 187 species of coral (UNDP, 2001). Although fisheries is the largest employment sector, tourism is the most significant to the economy, directly contributing almost one-third of GDP, and 60–70% if indirect impacts are considered (World Bank, 2005). Of the 615,000 tourists visiting in 2004, a significant proportion would have engaged in scuba, snorkelling and viewing of marine wildlife.

As the chapters of this book unfold we hope that it will become evident that we are attempting to advance both the conceptual and practical understanding of marine ecotourism and the physical, technological, ecological, economic, cultural, social, political and institutional contexts at varying scales in which it is cast as a process that may simultaneously disenable and enable sustainable outcomes for marine tourism. These contexts both shape, and are shaped by, the agenda and influence of the numerous stakeholders in the marine realm and so we also seek to highlight the various perspectives and roles of different stakeholders, whether they are beneficiaries or intermediaries, winners or losers, involved in or excluded from, decision making (Mosedale, undated). While the sheer scale and complexities of the issues alone dictate that we cannot possibly be comprehensive in our coverage, it is hoped that our elaboration of how, and why, marine ecotourism is precariously balanced between 'the devil and the deep blue sea' will contribute towards an appreciation of the particular challenges involved in this 'sink or swim' conundrum.

I Patterns and Processes

2   Marine Ecotourism in Context

A Complex and Dynamic Scenario

In Chapter 1 we have examined how the coastal and marine environment is highly interconnected, involving interchange within and between physical, biological, chemical, social, cultural, political, economic and legal processes. Actions taken, wherever, whenever, will have ramifications for other activities and localities over time. Consequently, our considerations must be temporal as well as spatial: not only do current actions often have ramifications far into the future, but also the frequency and intensity of such actions have undoubtedly increased over the past two decades. We witness a speeding up of events largely due to the relentless march of so-called human progress.

A case in point is the proliferation across the globe of blooms of toxic algae – harmful algal bloom (HAB), commonly known as red tides. In the last two decades certain types of red tide, which formerly occurred only in the waters of Europe, North America and Japan, are now regularly reported in South Africa, Australia, India, South-east Asia and other sites in the southern hemisphere (Gidwitz, 2002).

Anderson (2003) comments on the economic and societal impacts of such blooms, which have manifest impacts on tourism and tourism-related businesses as well as on mortalities of wild and farmed fish, shellfish, aquatic vegetation and coral reefs (which, in turn, also have implications for the natural resource base for tourism). He reports that, while three decades ago the problem was much more sporadic and scattered, virtually every coastal state in the USA is now threatened, and he makes a conservative estimate that the average annual economic impact of HABs in the USA, excluding multiplier effects, is in the order of US$50 million.

While increased reporting of red tides globally may be partially attributable to increased awareness, and spreading of harmful algae may be assisted by natural phenomena such as ocean currents and storms, Anderson (2003, p. 5) points to anthropogenic factors that are thought to have dramatically accelerated incidences. Of particular concern is 'the potential relationship between the increase in HABs and the accelerated eutrophication of coastal waters due to human activities'. Coastal waters are receiving massive and increasing quantities of industrial, agricultural and domestic effluents that increase the nutrient environment for certain HAB species.

Another underlying factor is the phenomenal increase in aquaculture activities across the globe. Red tides now plague the coastline of China where many of the salt marshes, mangrove swamps and wetlands have been uprooted for fish, shrimp and shellfish farms (Gidwitz, 2002). The transportation of toxic species across the globe in ships' ballast waters is thought to be a further human-induced factor in the global proliferation of HABs.

This example serves to illustrate the futility of considering marine ecotourism in isolation without considering the overall context in which it is set as a process, and the reason why the fragmented, sectoral planning of marine and coastal areas in the past has had such a poor record of success. As this and subsequent chapters will argue, it is imperative that we take a holistic approach, recognizing that the complexities of interrelationships within and between activities and components of the marine realm mean that there is a myriad of codependencies and interdependencies at work conditioning the prospects for marine ecotourism in any one locality.

To borrow the terminology of the Swedish economist, Gunnar Myrdal, whose theory of circular and cumulative causation (Myrdal, 1957) will be drawn upon in more depth in Chapter 8, there are marked spread (or positive) and backwash (or negative) effects between the various sectors, levels and interests (see Fig. 2.1). Indeed, as Cater and Cater (2001) point out, the relationships are not entirely unrelated to his overall thesis, as many of these interdependencies are bound up with centre–periphery relationships, as will be discussed in greater depth later in this chapter.

The spread effects from marine ecotourism include the raising of environmental awareness and disseminating an understanding of the coincidence of good environmental practice with advantages to business.

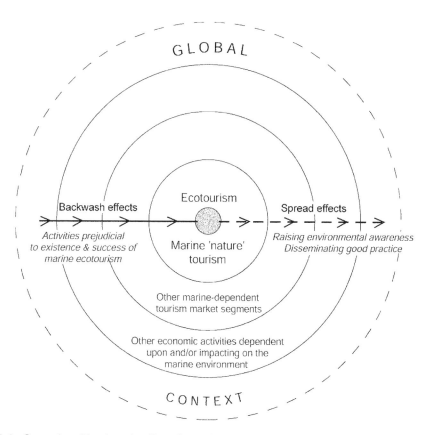

Fig. 2.1. Spread and backwash effects in marine ecotourism.

As we discussed in Chapter 1, the entire travel industry can learn from the principles and practices of ecotourism. The backwash effects hinge around the fact that other – often competing – activities are frequently prejudicial to the success, if not the very existence, of marine ecotourism. It is also vital to consider the overall, global context in which marine ecotourism is cast as a process. There are thus various scale levels to consider.

Marine ecotourism in the context of marine nature tourism

First, it is imperative that marine ecotourism is viewed in the context of marine tourism as a whole. Any one marine location is likely to host a variety of frequently incompatible recreational pursuits. Witness, for example, the conflict between scuba-diving and high-speed water craft. Even marine nature-based tourism may compromise genuine marine ecotourism.

Conscientious operators, such as the example of SeaCanoe – described in more detail in Chapter 4 – may find their efforts constantly thwarted by the unsustainable activities of other 'nature' tour operators whose businesses may be ecologically based, but far from ecologically sound. SeaCanoe began its kayaking operations in the tidal sea caves of Phang Nga Bay, Thailand, in 1989, winning a number of awards for its low environmental impact/high local benefits. However, the success of SeaCanoe spawned unscrupulous imitators and, inevitably, the caves have become degraded by these high-volume, environmentally unaware entries (Gray, 1998a,b; Buckley, 2003a).

Likewise, the increasing popularity of dive tourism has the outcome that irresponsible behaviour of often inadequately trained and environmentally unaware participants – as well as that of opportunist operators – results in the degradation of the marine environment. In Borocay, Philippines, it is possible to obtain PADI certification in only 1.5 days (see Fig. 2.2). At Langkawi, Malaysia, the local Nature Society voices concern over damage to the coral reef on Pulau Paya, declaring that: 'The beaches are crowded with divers who step on the coral … Diving operators are only thinking about profits and filling up their boats' (Khalid, cited in Sulaiman, 2005).

Another irresponsible behaviour utilized by opportunist marine nature tourism operators is that of 'chumming', usually using a 'soup' made of blood and fish scraps to attract fish for tourist viewing. At the very least, this distorts the natural food chain; for example, the Russian-owned and -operated tourist submarine, SADKO, at Larnaca, Cyprus, utilizes a diver to swim alongside the submarine and lure large quantities of fish with artificial feed (see Fig. 2.3). Of even greater concern, however, is the situation when such practices involve enticing sharks, particularly to facilitate close-quarter encounters with tourists lowered in heavy-duty shark cages (see Fig. 2.4).

Fig. 2.2. Diver certification in Borocay, Phillipines (photograph courtesy of E. Cater).

Such shark-cage diving experiences are on offer at a number of locations across the globe, and critics have attributed a number of recent shark attacks – for example in the Western Cape of South Africa – to a Pavlovian response whereby sharks associate humans with food, although studies examining this potential correlation have proved inconclusive (see Chapter 4, this volume). While operators defend their activities by claiming that they fulfil an educational purpose, the ethics of disturbing the natural balance and of conditioning behaviour must be under scrutiny, and several locations across the globe such as Florida, Hawaii, the Cayman Islands and the Maldives have placed bans on the feeding of sharks in the wild.

It is undeniable that the sharks are lured towards an orchestrated tourism encounter in shark-cage diving operations that employ feeding. As one operator in the Gansbaii area of South Africa describes this practice:

> It normally takes about an hour of chumming and baiting before the first great white hones in on the bait with deadly accuracy ... Great whites can smell the chum (crushed sardines) slick from a considerable distance. In addition, our crew plays tug-o-war, pulling the bait lines in to the boat to lure the magnificent creatures even closer.
>
> (White Shark Diving Company, 2006)

Fig. 2.3. Diver with 'chum' for the SADKO tourist submarine, Larnaca, Cyprus (photograph courtesy of E. Cater).

Fig. 2.4. Shark diving cage, Gansbaii, South Africa (photograph courtesy of E. Cater).

Marine ecotourism in the context of other tourism market segments

The second contextual level is that of marine ecotourism with respect to other tourism market segments that are dependent upon – and consequently impact on – the marine environment. The development and operations of coastal resorts, for example, have manifest implications for the success or otherwise of marine ecotourism, as indeed does the burgeoning growth of the cruise industry (see, for example, Craig-Smith *et al.*, 2006).

As Milne (1998, p. 47) suggests: 'In attempting to achieve more appropriate forms of tourism, it is also essential that we steer away from creating a dichotomy between "alternative" and "mass" tourism. Such a division serves little real purpose and diverts our attention away from the interlinked nature of all types of tourism development.'

On a positive note, the international Blue Flag eco-label awarded to around 3100 beaches and marinas in Europe, South Africa, New Zealand, Canada and the Caribbean in 2005, works towards sustainable use of the marine environment. Not only does it focus on water quality, but it also lays down criteria for environmental education and information, environmental management and safety and services (Blue Flag, undated). The scheme, therefore, has positive ramifications for marine ecotourism, although there are some concerns over a dominance of a *clean* over a *healthy* ecosystem approach, as discussed in Chapter 3.

One of the most extreme examples – certainly in terms of scale – of the potential conflict between coastal resort development and marine ecotourism is that of the construction of the three Palm Islands and The World projects off the coast of Dubai. The first of the former, the Palm Jebel Ali, is set to open in 2007, while the latter project, costing an estimated US$14 billion and consisting of 300 islands arranged to represent the shape of the land masses of the world, has a current estimated completion date of 2008. The largest of the four projects, the Palm Deira, recently slid its projected completion to 2015.

While environmental impact assessments were conducted, 'Most articles about the projects read like advertisements and do not question the depth of the company's professed environmental initiatives' (Holmes, 2004). The environmental impacts of this scale of development (all four projects are visible from space), however, are destined to be not only immediate but also long-term and far-reaching, despite claims to the contrary from the government-controlled corporation developing the islands, Nakheel, who have impressive plans for the alleviation and even reversal of some of the detrimental effects.

The Palm Jebel Ali is located in a former marine protected area that was reputedly one of the most biodiverse in the Gulf, the Jebel Ali marine reserve, the management of which was transferred from the Dubai Municipality Protected Areas Unit to Nakheel. The total amount of sand required by the projects has been estimated to be equivalent to building a wall 2 m deep and 4 m high around the equator (The Chief

Engineer, 2006). While sand and rock has been dredged from the Jebel Ali harbour canal, the majority of the sand was collected from a site 30 km distant.

The enormity of this dredge-and-fill exercise has inevitably affected neighbouring ecosystems, as well as altering hydrological and sedimentation patterns. Local scuba-divers record their frustration at reduced visibility and increased currents, which are also eroding existing beaches (Holmes, 2004). One of the most important coral ecosystems off the mainland coast was destroyed during dredging work, and oyster beds and sea grass fields have been covered with sediment. While the largest artificial reef in the world is being created as a substitute, WWF has expressed concern that the new coral community is artificial and will remain so (*Zee News*, 2006).

A further concern, when we consider the potential conflict between different types of tourism, is raised when we consider the question of ethnicity, an issue that is also raised in Chapter 5. Not only do the needs of visiting tourists and host populations frequently diverge, but also foreign and domestic tourists often have markedly different, incompatible agendas.

The danger of the ethnocentric bias inherent in Western-envisaged ecotourism is that it ignores the fact that there are 'multiple natures' constructed variously by different societies. As McNaghten and Urry (1998, p. 95) declare: 'There is no single "nature", only natures. And these natures are not inherent in the physical world but discursively constructed through economic, political and cultural processes.' Walley (2004, p. 14) draws attention to the dynamics of '... the ways in which ideas of development, nature, and participation are variously understood, appropriated, disputed and used'.

Lowe (2006, p. 9) describes how 'Any understanding of nature will always depend upon processes of representation and the subjectivity of those claiming or attempting to represent such nature'. She goes on to argue that: 'The knowledges, rationalities, and natures in Southern biodiversity conservation cannot be understood through the language of assimilation or adaptation in the tropics of a project that originated in more temperate climates' (Lowe, 2006, p. 14). Sofield (1996) describes how, in the Solomon Islands, 'The traditions of the Melanesian villagers are so interlinked with their forests, coastal reefs and associated habitats that these features are regarded as their most important social and economic resources' (Sofield, 1996, p. 176) and cites Baines' observations in Fiji that the land, adjacent reefs and lagoons – and the resources therein, together with the people – constituted a single, integrated entity.

In attempting to engage with different constructs of nature by different societies, Walley (2004) asked men on Chole island, Mafia, Zanzibar, what they believed about 'nature'. Most of them, having been fishers at some point in their lives, gave detailed descriptions of fishing gear, wind directions and types of fish. Although this practical knowledge did not convert easily into a conception of 'nature', she points out that this does not automatically mean that they do not appreciate nature, recording, for example, how local boat passengers registered excitement on viewing a school of dolphins.

However, Walley also records a divergence of views, as locals were 'puzzled by the penchant of *wazungu* (Euro-American) visitors to Mafia go to "deserted" places and to prize photographs of peopleless landscapes … In short, the people on Mafia did not share the romance for "nature" found among those who seek refuge from "modernity" in the natural environment' (Walley, 2004, pp. 140–144). In addition, those things that Mafia residents associated with poverty – for example, cloth sails rather than outboard engines – were instead perceived as valuable forms of 'tradition' by many visitors, attractive precisely because of their difference from 'modern development' (Walley 2004, p. 224).

A further example of differing perceptions is given by Rudkin and Hall (1996), who describe how the proposal to provide diving and snorkelling trips to the reef at Lauvi Lagoon in the Solomon islands 'was especially surprising given that local people will neither swim in the sea nor around Sahulu Island, just south of Lauvi Lagoon, because of the number of sharks in the water'. However, while it is tempting to focus on East–West or North–South distinctions in different constructs of nature, such generalizations may mask significant differences between and within individual nations.

Moscardo (2004), for example, found that there was greater variation between Chinese and Japanese visitors to the Great Barrier Reef than between these two groups and the other national cultural groups studied (from the UK and USA). In Taiwan, Hou *et al.* (2005) describe how the meaning and formation of attachment to a cultural tourism attraction in Taiwan differed between visitors of the same ethnic group as the hosts and other Taiwanese ethnic groups.

Marine ecotourism in the context of other forms of economic activity

Thirdly, with regard to the overall picture of sustainability, it is vital to consider the interactions that occur with all other forms of economic activity. As Butler (1998, p. 34) asserts: 'Tourism is part of the global system and cannot be tackled in isolation, spatially, economically or temporally.' It is vital that a move is made beyond a tourism-centric view, as it is 'inappropriate to discuss sustainable tourism any more than one might discuss any other single activity … we cannot hope to achieve sustainability in one sector alone, when each is linked to and dependent upon the others' (Butler 1998, p. 28). Garrod *et al.* (2001) list the sectors that may have a stake in, or impact upon, marine ecotourism (see Box 2.1).

The fact is that there are an enormous range of economic activities that impact either directly or indirectly on the marine environment. Marine ecotourism is thus inextricably linked with each of the activities

---

Box 2.1. Sectors that may have a stake in, or impact upon, marine ecotourism
(from Garrod *et al.*, 2001).

Agriculture
Coastal and ocean research
Dredge and spoil disposal
Fisheries
Forestry
Housing
Mariculture/aquaculture
Marine industry and power production
Military areas and facilities
Ocean engineering and technology
Oil and gas extraction
Ports/harbours/marinas
Protected areas
Shipping and navigation
Solid and hazardous waste disposal
Water pollution/pollution control
Water supply
Wildlife management and nature conservation

---

listed in the table. Consider, for example, the interplay with forestry:
destructive logging practices result in extensive run-off from the land,
with consequent siltation of coastal waters. This has serious
repercussions for marine life and, in turn, for marine ecotourism.

Turning to military activity, the harmful effects of naval sonar have
been recorded in several locations across the globe. Parsons *et al.* (2000)
present evidence that military sonar uses frequencies to which cetaceans
occurring in the Hebrides would be sensitive. Ritter (2003) records how the
mass stranding of beaked whales on the Canary Islands of Lanzarote and
Fuerteventura in September 2002 coincided with NATO military
manoeuvres conducted in the area. A recent report by the United Nations
Environment Programme confirms that the low-frequency sounds generated
travel vast distances, hundreds – if not thousands – of kilometres from the
source (Howden, 2005). The implications for the viewing of marine
mammals is thus obvious.

Frequently, a chain of events is set in motion that is often not only
circular but cumulative, given the complex web of interactions that
occur in the marine environment. Villena and Spash (2000, p.19) cite the
work of Kapp, who argues that: 'The principle of cumulative or circular
causation stresses the fact that social processes are marked by the
interaction of several variables, both "economic" and "non-economic"
which, in their combined effect, move the system away from a position
of balance or equilibrium.'

Kapp's recognition of the interdependence of natural–physical and social systems, that 'the causal chain is at the same time a physical and a social process ...' has been 'a constant among institutionalists [institutional economists] since ... and can be seen as a central argument in their approach to the environment' (Villena and Spash, 2000, p. 20). They go on to examine how social systems are so intertwined with natural systems that they co-evolve. In our list of activities perhaps none illustrates this better than the complex scenario with regard to the impact of fisheries on prospects for marine ecotourism. This is perhaps not surprising, given the fact that 10 years ago WWF declared that 'fisheries represent the greatest impact on the marine ecosystem today' (WWF, 1996).

Let us examine the complex web of interactions between marine ecotourism and fisheries by way of two examples, both drawn from the UK but, given the enormous pressures on the world's fish stock (Davenport and Davenport, 2006), with obvious relevance across the globe.

The first example examines the complex links between marine ecotourism and the fortunes of the humble sand eel. Populations of the sand eel have been subject to fluctuations over time, but the recent collapse in numbers has been attributed to two fundamental causes: industrial fishing and global climate change. Industrial fishing catches fish not for the table, but to be ground up into industrial products such as fish meal and fish oil, and accounts for more than 50% of all fish landed from the North Sea.

From the mid-1980s to the 1990s, sand eels constituted approximately two-thirds of the industrial catch (Greenpeace, undated). Sand eels are caught in huge quantities by Danish factory ships, which turn them into food pellets for fish, poultry and pigs. This is not the end of the story with regard to the impact of fisheries on sand eels, however. True to the circular and cumulative hypothesis outlined above, fisheries also have a knock-on effect: it has been estimated that the populations of scavenging birds in the North-east Atlantic exceed a natural distribution by the order of between 5 and 8 million (Holy, 2004). This population explosion has been brought about by readily available feed in the form of discards from the trawling industry, estimated to constitute around one-third of the entire catch. Too many scavenging seabirds place additional pressure on fish stocks – such as the sand eels – that other seabirds eat.

The present situation cannot, however, be blamed solely on fishing. Robards *et al.* (1999), while agreeing that depletion of sand lance stocks (as sand eels are known in North America) can be attributed to commercial fisheries in the North Sea and near Japan, caution that: 'It is uncertain that fisheries are solely accountable' (p. 24). In 2004, the Danish fleet caught only 300,000 t of its 800,000 t quota. The Shetland, UK, sand eel fishery was catching so few fish that it was voluntarily closed by local fishers as a precautionary measure in 2004 (Birdlife International, 2005). Scientists believe that the sand eels are disappearing in the surrounding

waters of the North Sea because the cold-water plankton upon which
they depend has moved further north. In the past 20 years, temperatures
in the North Sea have risen by 2°C, and research indicates that the
plankton has moved hundreds of miles northwards in response
(Wardlow, 2004).

So, what is the link between sand eels and marine ecotourism? The
fact is that is that the sand eel constitutes an important part of the diet
for over 100 species of marine wildlife, including 40 species of birds, 12
species of marine mammals, 45 species of fishes and some invertebrates
(Robards *et al.*, 1999). Many of these, such as puffins, skuas, tern, minke
whales, fin whales, humpback whales, white-beaked dolphins, grey seals
and Harp seals, are popular viewing for marine tourists (see Fig. 2.5).

The fortunes of the sand eel, the above species and marine
ecotourism are therefore intimately linked. It has been postulated that
the low sightings of minke whales off the west coast of Scotland in 2005
were due to the low stocks of sand eels. Over the past 3 years there has
been a catastrophic decline in the numbers of certain species of seabirds,
for which sand eels constitute the staple diet. In the south Shetland
Islands, where there were formerly over 1200 guillemot nests, all were
empty in the spring of 2004, and elsewhere on the Shetlands 24,000
arctic tern nests were almost entirely empty (Schulman, 2005). In the
summer of 2004, guillemots produced almost no young in Orkney and
Shetland, yet more than 172,000 breeding pairs were recorded in the last
national census, Seabird 2000. More than 6800 pairs of great skuas were
recorded in Shetland in the same census and yet only a handful of
chicks were produced in 2004 (McCarthy, 2004).

The spectacular seabirds of the Northern Isles are doubly important:
as well as their scientific value, they are of enormous significance to
Orkney and Shetland tourism, being the principal draw for many
visitors. Birdwatching in general is appealing to more and more people,

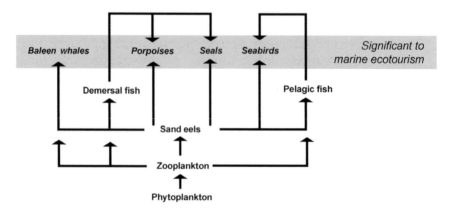

Fig. 2.5. The dependency of marine ecotourism on the marine food chain (adapted from Greenpeace, undated).

evidenced by the fact that membership of the Royal Society for the Protection of Birds (RSPB) in the UK doubled between 1987 and 1997, with the current figure at over 1 million. A staggering 3.5 million television viewers (15% of the total audience) tuned in to Bill Oddie's *Springwatch* on BBC TV in 2005, which featured seabird colonies on the Farne Islands (north-east England) and the white sea eagle on Mull (Inner Hebrides, Scotland).

The level of interest in seabird viewing in the UK is also indicated by the success of viewing centres such as the Scottish Seabird Centre, which opened in 2000 and had clocked its millionth visit by 2005. It should be noted, however, that this figure includes repeat visitation, as the centre is a significant local resource (L. Kelly, North Berwick, UK, 2006, personal communication).

One of the most charismatic species of seabird is the puffin, but considerable concern has been expressed recently over the decline in numbers in northern coastal locations, attributable to the dramatic fall in sand eel populations, so much so that this distinctive bird is now on the RSPB amber list of threatened species. On St Kilda, Western Isles, Scotland, for example, in 2005 there was 'a spectacular breeding failure for puffins, with only 26% of burrows producing chicks which compares to a normal figure of 71%' (RSPB, 2005a). The National Trust for Scotland reported that 'all indications seem to be that starvation was the major cause of chick death' (National Trust for Scotland, 2005).

However, there are still further factors to take into account. Global climatic change has yet another card to play in determining the fate of the puffin. There is evidence to suggest that the tree mallow is choking breeding sites on Scottish islands by covering the ground so thickly that puffins cannot burrow in the soil to make nests. Ironically, the puffins themselves make it easier for the seeds to take root as they break up the ground when burrowing. On Craigleith, near North Berwick, the numbers of burrows in which puffins breed had dropped from 28,000 in 1999 to 14,000 by 2004. Tree mallow grows mainly in Mediterranean countries, but has spread northwards as a result of global warming (McKie, 2005).

Our second example of the relationship between fisheries and marine ecotourism is presented by the fish farming industry, the fastest-growing sector in the world food economy (RSPB, 2006). Not only does this activity detract from the visual quality of a pristine setting – whether in the sea lochs of Scotland (see Fig. 2.6) or the fjords of Norway, British Columbia in Canada and Chile – but there are further concerns about its considerable environmental effects.

The fish farming sector is expected to account for 50% of fish meal and 80% of fish oil consumption by 2010 (RSPB, 2006), exerting yet further pressure on the fish species, mainly the Peruvian anchovy and the North Sea sand eel, as described above, from which these are derived. The extent of nutrient pollution from Scottish aquaculture was estimated in 2000 to be 7500 t of nitrogen, comparable to the annual

Fig. 2.6. Salmon farm, Skye, Scotland (photograph courtesy of E. Cater).

sewage inputs of 3.2 million people; and 1240 t of phosphorus, comparable to that from 9.2 million people (Cater, 2003). This has an impact on Highland and Island marine habitats such as seaweed forests, where resultant cloudiness of the water reduces the depth to which the forests can grow. While perhaps lacking the charisma of coral reefs, kelp forests are amongst the most beautiful and biologically productive marine habitats (Norton, 2005).

There is also a major economic threat posed by the proliferation of toxic blooms, as described in Chapter 1, this volume, attributable to the distortion of nutrient ratios. Apart from implications for commercial fisheries, an increase in toxic blooms has wider implications for wildlife, as these can be lethal to birds and sea mammals, for which Scotland has a significant international reputation (Berry and Davison, 2001).

A further consideration is that escapees from fish cages will lead to genetic dilution of the local wild salmon population, leading to a decline in the wild population and biodiversity in Scotland. As wild salmon is a protected species in Scotland, and the species is endangered in over 30% of the UK's historic salmon rivers, imagine the concern that was generated over the 731,000 fish reported lost in the severe storms in January 2005. Of these escapees, only 58,000 were confirmed mortalities. The potentially disastrous impacts for Scotland's wild salmon population and the lucrative fly-fishing tourism sector are evident (SWT/WWF, 2005).

Even more direct confrontation between the fish farm industry and marine ecotourism is evidenced by the shooting of seals. Mark Carter describes how the 'fisherman's clause' of the UK 1970 Conservation of Seals Act gives special dispensation for the shooting of seals where seals are actually causing problems to fishermen while fishing, but this refers to fishing nets, not to fish farm nets. He describes how a fish farm company based near Oban, western Scotland, slaughtered as many as 60 seals in and around a European Union Special Area of Conservation (SAC) in 2005 (Carter, 2005). This activity has manifest implications for the popular activity of viewing seals off the west coast of Scotland, graphically illustrated by the representations made by one marine tourism operator, based in Kyle of Lochalsh, also an SAC, in October 2005 concerning the operations of the fish farm based in Loch Alsh.

While accepting that, if a specific seal is causing damage, shooting is an option, Nigel Smith expresses concern that there is no means of controlling the number of seals shot and, 'As the farm can't identify the culprit seal their strategy appears to be shoot every seal that comes near their cages'. As the cages lie between where the seals feed and the islands where they haul out, 'The seals have no choice to go past the farm on the way to their feeding grounds'. During the last two weeks of October 2005, there were no seals in Loch Alsh to be seen by Smith's guests, whereas he estimates that there are normally around 20–40 on the rocks (Smith, 2005). While it is impossible to put a precise figure on the numbers of seals shot, as they often sink, Smith records that six dead and two wounded common seals were washed up on the beach (Smith, Kyle of Lochalsh, UK, 2006, personal communication). He is understandably concerned about his business if the end result is decimation of the seals in Loch Alsh.

Marine ecotourism in the global context

Global environmental change: the difference a degree makes ...

As Gössling and Hall (2006, p. 1) point out, global environmental change (GEC) threatens 'the very foundations of tourism through climate change, modifications of global biogeochemical cycles, land alteration, the loss of non-renewable resources, unsustainable use of renewable resources and gross reductions in biodiversity'. There are countless ways in which the coastal and marine environment is affected and, in turn, the under-pinnings for marine ecotourism are shaken.

Climate change, as has already become evident from this chapter, is probably the most important consideration as it both produces and is a production of the manifestations of global environmental change listed by Gössling and Hall. In 2003, the World Tourism Organization convened the First International Conference on Climate Change and Tourism in Djerba, Tunisia, which culminated in the Djerba declaration. One of the points of agreement was 'To encourage the tourism industry ... to adjust their activities ... in order to minimize as much as possible their contribution to climate change' (WTO, 2003, p. 2).

However, the industry tends more to emphasize the impact of GEC on the industry rather than vice versa, declaring that: 'Climate change will constitute an increasing risk for tourism operations in many destinations' (Frangialli, 2005). It is understandable, therefore, that Gössling and Hall voice their frustration that flying (often quite literally) in the face of the 0.7°C observed annual average warming trend over the past decade, and greater than expected ecological consequences over that period, the tourism industry seems fairly complacent.

The impact of global warming on seabird populations has been described above, but this experience is not confined to the UK. Concern has been voiced about the impact of anomalously warm sea-surface temperatures on the viability as a breeding site of Triangle Island, British Columbia, which contains the largest tufted puffin colony in Canada (Gjerdrum *et al.*, 2003).

Unprecedented deaths of seabirds were recorded all along the coast of North America, from central California to British Columbia, in the summer of 2005. These were also due to the disappearance of plankton, although the immediate causes differ from those experienced in the North Sea and its margins. The usual welling up of cold water from the sea bottom, rich in nutrients that feed phytoplankton, did not occur as water temperatures near the shore soared by 7°C. As a result, the amount of phytoplankton declined to one-quarter of its normal level, and this led, in turn, to a collapse in the zooplankton that it sustains, and which constitutes feed for fish, seabirds and marine mammals (Lean, 2005).

Variations in the amounts and distribution of the microscopic phytoplankton, as the base of the oceanic food chain, thus ultimately affect the numbers and distribution of marine species further up the chain (see Fig. 2.5). Paradoxically, the distributional variation may mean that certain marine creatures are being sighted further north than their usual range. In 2005, for instance, sightings increased of basking sharks, the largest fish to be found in the coastal waters of the British Isles, off the coast of Scotland (The Wildlife Trusts, 2005). Global warming has, however, significantly reduced overall phytoplankton numbers which, in turn, not only means fewer seabirds as described above, but also leads to a reduction in the numbers of marine wildlife that constitute an important ecotourism attraction, such as cetaceans, penguins and seals.

Of great concern is the negative feedback that is set in motion because phytoplankton, as the world's main photosynthesizer, produce an estimated 50% of the planet's free oxygen, simultaneously acting as a major sink for CO_2 (Schulman, 2005). Once again, the forces of circular and cumulative causation are set in motion and we can envisage a downward spiral in the biodiversity of the oceans and a concomitant loss of resources for marine ecotourism.

Another marine ecotourism resource, arguably the most significant in terms of economic gain as described in Chapter 3, this volume, which has been severely affected by global warming, is that of the world's coral reefs. The most publicized effect of global climatic change on the reefs has been that of coral bleaching when unusually high local water temperatures have killed off the algae that live inside the coral polyps. Existing coral reefs are also threatened by other factors such as: rising sea levels; storm damage from more frequent and intense tropical cyclones; and increased algal blooms resulting from increased run-off of sewage and fertilizers attributable to higher rainfall.

However, it may be the case that, as more areas of the ocean become warmer, reefs might actually expand their geographical range. Recent research also indicates that present coral reef calcification rates at various locations around the world are actually equivalent to pre-industrial levels, and that, given existing trends, these levels will be exceeded by the order of approximately 35% by the end of this century (McNeil *et al.*, 2004).

Although lacking the charisma of coral reefs, sea grass beds and mangrove forests are also affected. These constitute important habitats for species such as the manatee in the case of the former, and important feeding and breeding grounds for a large number of species in the case of the latter. The significance of mangroves for marine ecotourism was recognized as long ago as 1994, when Belize hosted the international 'Destination Mangroves' conference.

In Senegal, West Africa, the Parc National de la Basse Casamance, which is located close to the tourist centre Cap Skirring, contains over 200 species of sea birds and is a popular attraction for ecotourism in the form of photo safaris (afrol, 2000). Along with coral reefs, mangroves also act as a very important coastal barrier, and it has been surmised that the massive clearance of mangroves off the beaches of Thailand – as well as off Cancún, Mexico – removed the natural breakwaters, which may well have ameliorated the devastating impacts of the Asian tsunami of 2004 and hurricane Wilma in 2005. While the figure for extreme waves is unknown, it has been estimated that mangroves can absorb 70–90% of the energy of a normal wave (Kinver, 2005). The irony is that the construction of tourist resorts has contributed in a large part to the destruction of these natural shields, and yet they suffered massively from the results of that destruction.

The predicted rise in sea level resultant from global environmental change will obviously have the most severe consequences for low-lying countries, particularly when combined with other elements of GEC such as weather extremes. Small Island Developing States are particularly vulnerable (Gossling and Hall, 2006) and, as many of these earn considerable foreign exchange from tourism, the ramifications would be serious. In the Maldives, for example, around three-quarters of the land area is less than 1 m above mean sea level. Total tourism receipts were estimated to be US$478 million in 2004, with the direct contribution of the industry at around 31%, and an estimated 60–70% when indirect impacts are considered (World Bank, 2005).

While the reputation of the Maldives has been built around luxury resort development, it is heavily reliant on the health of its marine ecosystems, as a large number of visitors engage in snorkelling and scuba-diving. Rising sea temperatures are also therefore of concern as they jeopardize coral reefs, as described above: the Maldives experienced a major bleaching event in 1997, when around 90% of the reefs were affected (UNEP, 2002a).

The global political economy

It is not surprising, given the considerable backwash effects outlined above, that ecotourism often has yet to produce the hoped-for effects of either environmental improvement or social benefits for local residents (Zimmerer and Bassett, 2003). At the outset of this chapter we highlighted how many of the backwash effects that compromise successful outcomes for marine ecotourism are bound up with centre–periphery relationships inherent in the global political economy. These are framed by political and economic relationships of power that also condition 'accepted' knowledge. We need to ask ourselves, therefore, to what extent marine ecotourism across the globe is essentially Western-centric, insofar as it accepts as given an approach that is deeply embedded in Western cultural, economic and political processes.

The pervasive influence of Western-envisaged ecotourism needs to be viewed against the backdrop of the global political economy. To paraphrase Blaikie (2000, p. 1043), who is examining the reasons for the global dominance of the neo-liberal development agenda in general, 'the most powerful reasons why, in my view, are provided by political economy … Theories, narratives, policies and institutions – the global power–knowledge nexus – drive, and are driven by, global capital.'

Rudkin and Hall (1996, p. 223) describe how, in the Solomon Islands, 'The driving force for the promotion of ecotourism comes from foreign donors, investors, academic institutions, consultants and conservation groups … who perceive ecotourism as an opportunity to conserve biodiversity through the preservation process' and stress how there has been a failure to appreciate the role of social and political values within sustainable tourism development in the South Pacific.

Walley's study of Mafia Island Marine Park (the first marine National Park in Tanzania, which was gazetted in 1995) examines how Mafia residents were excluded from direct influence upon the Mafia Island Marine Park bureaucracy 'not only because they lacked the proper educational credentials to achieve formal positions of power within the bureaucracy, but also because of widespread assumptions about the kind of knowledge they possessed'. She observes how, within East Africa, Euro-American backgrounds were regarded as being of higher status, as more 'modern' and, often, as linked to 'science', while the popular knowledge of groups like Mafia's residents was often perceived as 'backward' or unsubstantiated.

Where attempts were made to incorporate popular knowledge, it was reduced to information 'to be slotted in to the pre-existing bureaucratic framework' (Walley, 2004, pp. 204–206). Lowe (2006) selected the

Togean Island project in Indonesia as her research field site because it was run entirely by Indonesian scientists and staff. She rejected Bunaken National Park and Taka Bonerate Park because they were managed by Euro-American consultants employing Indonesian field and office assistants, believing that:

> I would learn more from these Indonesian experts than I could from expatriate consultants with whom I shared a quite similar educational and social history. Although I could not predict what I would find, I assumed that there would be something 'different' about the Togean project as a result of its nationalization.
>
> (Lowe, 2006, p. 12)

We must not assume, however, that the imposition of 'conventional' wisdom in the form of scientific knowledge is confined to the experience of cases in the developing world. Walker (2003, p. 10) cites the work of St Martin in fishing communities in New England, which describes how dominant scientific narratives fail to value 'local' knowledge and 'traditional' systems of community resource management.

However, Walley points out that it is vital not to generalize and romanticize concepts of 'indigenous' knowledge. In the case of Chole island, Mafia, for example, popular knowledge is eclectic: a mix of personal knowledge and shared knowledge from diverse sources such as: coastal maritime traditions; seafaring practices derived from Arab, Portuguese and Indonesian sailors across history; and science-based knowledge conveyed through colonial and post-independence government officials and visiting researchers.

Similarly, Lowe describes how the Togean islands

> themselves collapse easy definitions of 'nature' when Indonesian scientists, Euro-American biologists, commercial traders, bureaucrats and diverse Togean people engage with Togean land and marinescapes in discontinuous ways producing the archipelago as contrastive and contested 'sites' ... the Togean Islands can be seen as a locality generative of cosmopolitan imaginings of science, nation, and biodiversity conservation.
>
> (Lowe 2006, p. 7)

It is important, therefore 'not to try to isolate environmental knowledge from the broader social dynamics of which it is a part' (Walley, 2004, pp. 211–216).

Walley's work serves to remind us that what we are witnessing is a working out of processes over a multitude of scales. Prospects of and for marine ecotourism at the local level are linked with multiscale politico-economic and ecological processes. It is vital, therefore, that we recognize the need to go 'beyond single geographical scale factors influencing land and resource use (e.g. the village) to consider the many regional, national and international dimensions' (Zimmerer and Bassett, 2003, p. 288).

Young makes the case for a political ecology approach for comparative assessment of local patterns of resource use with reference to marine ecotourism, declaring that 'As a multiscalar, contextual approach to understanding how markets, policies and political processes shape nature–society relations, political ecology provides a useful framework' (Young, 2003, p. 45). She highlights how 'A growing number of studies use a political ecology approach to examine the relationship between access conflicts in the commons and ecological change in aquatic habitats and wildlife, particularly in marine environments' (Young, 2003, p. 31).

Young's own study of marine ecotourism in Baja California examines how: 'The multi-million dollar whale watching industry there has become dominated by operators based in the USA ... In 1994, the Mexican Ministry of Tourism estimated that, in one weekend during the gray whale season, 30 planes of USA origin landed on the airstrip' (Young, 1999, pp. 601–602).

She also examines the national scale, revealing how the two main Mexican federal agencies – which are legally empowered to both monitor tourism activities around grey whales and enforce laws that restrict such activities – are, as discussed in Chapter 9, this volume, overcentralized, and how government decision-makers (based in Mexico City) are unfamiliar with local ecological and social conditions. Young also points to the fact that 'insufficient funding for field personnel, facilities and equipment impede effective regulation of local activities in both areas' (Young, 1999, p. 609).

The multiscalar approach of political ecology is, therefore, of value in reminding ourselves that: 'The narrative of globalization downplays the importance of national dynamics, failing to adequately address the symbiotic relationship between national and international institutions and elites' (Walley, 2004, pp. 262–264). Richter (1989) examines how many nation states in Asia have used tourism as a tool to elevate their status in international relations and, as Teo (2002, p. 470) argues: 'In the discourse on global–local dynamics, it is propitious to ask whether such a view overlooks the role that national economies have moulded for themselves within the global capitalist framework.' Rudkin and Hall (1996, pp. 203–204) describe how ecotourism development in the Solomon islands has 'primarily been driven by Western consultants ... operating in conjunction with the local business and political elite'.

A pertinent but poignant example of this interplay was seen in the month immediately following the catastrophic tsunami that hit the coastlines of the Indian Ocean on 26 December 2004; the significance that the region and individual countries affected attach to international tourism became immediately evident. Not long after the disaster, the president of PATA declared: 'If you want to help us, book your trip now', while the chairman of the Sri Lankan Tourist Board, launching the tourism 'Bounce-Back' campaign, announced less than 1 month later: 'The country is open for business in a big way' (Sri Lanka Tourism, 2005).

If anything, however, these overtures serve to highlight the extent to which individual nation states are enmeshed in the global tourism industry. The Sri Lankan government's proposed US$80 million redevelopment of Arugam Bay on the east coast has met with resistance from local villagers. A local guest house owner declared: 'We don't want mass tourism with luxury hotels. We would rather promote community-based tourism' (Raheem, quoted in Tourism Concern, 2005).

There is also concern that affected coastal populations throughout the region, faced with a loss of traditional livelihoods, may also be faced with being moved from where they have lived to make way for tourism development as reconstruction proceeds (Tourism Concern, 2005). Hoogvelt's pointed observation that 'We may try to understand and improve the conditions of life of those who live within our world system, we cannot even think about those who live outside it' (Hoogvelt, 1985) is sadly relevant.

A Can of Worms

Inspired by our case study of the relationship between the sand eel and marine ecotourism, this heading for our conclusion to this chapter reflects the complexities of the interlinkages and interchanges that exist between physical, biological, chemical, social, cultural, economic, political, legal and technical processes that operate in the marine realm and, in turn, condition the prospects for – if not the very existence of – marine ecotourism. How do we begin to try to unravel the intricacies of what is going on? From this, the preceding and subsequent chapters it is evident that we need not only to adopt an holistic approach but also, in doing so, to extend our thinking – spatially, temporally and topically – beyond the confines of singular disciplines, to embrace varying conceptualizations of the human–nature interface.

Thus, we can learn from the institutional economists outlined above who 'more recently have claimed that a holistic systems approach to environmental problems must start with the recognition that social systems co-evolve with natural systems' (Swaney, cited in Villena and Spash, 2000, p. 20). In unpicking the relationships in each of these in this chapter, the contributions from political economy and political ecology – as well as social anthropology – have also furthered our understanding. As the book progresses, invaluable insights will be gained from other subdisciplines so that, hopefully, we move towards a greater understanding of the complexities of the challenges faced by marine ecotourism.

3   Marine Ecotourism Resources

Diversity and Change

The oceans of the world contain vast resources, and have an importance far beyond that of tourism. However, the contemporary growth of marine ecotourism can, in part, be explained by a similarly recent awareness of what aquatic resources are actually available for interactive experiences. The sheer diversity of the marine environment makes it impossible to catalogue all of the resources used for ecotourism activity, and the authors acknowledge that many are being added to the list every day.

We cannot hope to predict what new forms of marine ecotourism will emerge in the years to come. For example, the existence of giant squid is now confirmed, as discussed in Chapter 1, and, judging by the numbers that turned out to see a preserved example at London's Natural History Museum in March 2006 (*The Observer*, 2006), could prove a popular attraction, but this as yet is not a viable ecotourism resource. However, we can safely assume that participation in those activities we observe today will continue to increase as long as the resource base itself is maintained.

Herein lies the crux of the challenge for marine ecotourism in the years to come. Increasing participation, which this book documents, leads to increasing pressure on resources, which are exacerbated by the Hardinian nature of the open ocean, as discussed in Chapter 1. This is magnified when we consider that the most resource-rich areas of the ocean are those that are the most valuable for both extractive and non-extractive uses. The 'vital areas' to marine ecosystem health are identified by Miller and Auyong, 'consisting of coral reefs, kelpbeds, shellfish beds, grass beds, drainageways, wetlands, vegetated tidelands, tideflats, dunes and beachfronts, barrier islands, breeding areas, nursery areas, wintering areas, feeding areas, and migration pathways' (Miller and Auyong, 1991, p. 78).

However, it is no surprise that these regions are those holding most interest for tourists and the fishing industry alike. Furthermore, despite the fact that, in theory, the size of the marine environment should mean that most of its resources are renewable, 'Efficient management and sustainable exploitation have been the exception rather than the rule' (Davenport and Davenport, 2006).

Managing a wide variety of different resource users is, however, vitally important if we are to achieve sustainable outcomes. An awareness of the complex contextual background detailed in the previous chapter is therefore central to this task. Economics has an important role to play in this process, particularly realistic interpretations of the value of marine resources, for both tourism and other uses. Situations such as that identified by Davenport and Davenport (2006), in which global fish production was estimated to cost US$124 billion whilst providing only US$70 billion in revenue, cannot be allowed to continue. Such reassessments are far from easy, as Davis and Gartside have shown:

Although there has been considerable development of both economic theory and biological models as they apply to the management of marine natural resources over the past 50 years, policy development for the marine environment is particularly complicated compared with that for many land-based resources. Despite development of increasingly sophisticated and complex policy frameworks, biological, economic and social outcomes often have been poor. Complications range from wider questions of sovereignty at both international and state levels to the difficulty of defining ownership of free-ranging or migratory resources like fish stocks. Establishing property rights in ways that result in the generation and fair distribution of economic rent, along with sustainable utilization of resources, has proved to be extremely difficult.

(Davis and Gartside, 2001, p. 224)

In order for us to achieve such noble goals, we must have an accurate picture of marine resources and how they link to interspecies livelihoods at a variety of scales. In this chapter, then, we discuss some of the biomes in which marine ecotourism takes place. This is neither a biological inventory nor an economic balance sheet, for this is left to those far better trained in these important tasks. What we do present, however, is an insight into the diversity of environments in which these activities take place, the status and threats to the continued existence of these resources and examples of where marine ecotourism can be used as a force for resource sustainability instead of indiscriminate exploitation.

Coral Reef Resources

Perhaps the most obvious marine ecosystem that has become both the focus of much marine ecotourism and the cause célèbre of the environmental movement is that of coral reefs. As defined in the United Nations Environment Program-sponsored 2001 World Atlas of Coral Reefs: 'Coral reefs are shallow marine habitats, defined by both a physical structure and by the organisms found upon them' (Spalding *et al.*, 2001, p. 15).

The hard calcite structures that are built up by coral species over hundreds of years are literally the bedrock on which these communities are founded. Reefs can take a number of structural forms, including fringing, patch, barrier, atoll or bank. It is only relatively recently that the diversity of these environments has become apparent. Varying estimates of the number of species that inhabit reefs illustrates this lack of knowledge. Conservative estimates put the number of reef species at 100,000 but, as Spalding *et al.* (2001) suggest, the actual number of coral reef species may be between 0.5 and 2.0 million. This species distribution is also highly concentrated, as there are only an estimated 284,000 km^2 of reef worldwide. Because reefs only develop in tropical areas, in shallow seas of consistent temperature and shelter, they cover only 1.2% of the continental shelf and a mere 0.089% of the oceanic sea floor (Spalding *et al.*, 2001). Furthermore, this distribution is geographically concentrated, with 91.9% of all reefs in the Indo-Pacific region. This is reflected in largely separate faunas to the more limited Atlantic reef populations.

Tourism is only a newcomer to coral reef resource use, as the concentration of species on reefs has ensured their use as a food source for millennia. This has brought tourism into conflict with consumptive uses of the reef. One also needs to recognize the historical importance of reef builders in creating habitats above the waterline. Many coral atolls, popular for both eco- and mass tourism, are the result of thousands of years of coral manufacture, creating islands for terrestrial species.

In many coastal and island communities, coral has also been used as a natural building material, its high calcite content making it suitable for the purpose. Such use may have been sustainable in the past, but growing populations mean that this is no longer the case. In the Maldives, the lack of any other building resource has meant that it has been long used for this purpose (Spalding *et al.*, 2001, p. 53).

A resource use that has emerged somewhat in parallel to tourism is that of the pharmaceutical potential of reef ecosystems. Similar to rainforests, the sheer species density of reefs renders them ideal locations for prospecting for new medical compounds.

There is a wide range of threats to coral reefs; indeed, in a recent report the World Resources Institute estimates that 58% are under medium to high risk (Spalding, 2001). It is interesting to note that, like all marine environments, reefs are highly dynamic ecosystems, and localized changes may be common. Indeed, as Spalding (2001) suggests, the huge diversity in terms of species composition may be a direct result of frequent disturbances. Thus disturbance should not necessarily always be cast as a wholly negative force.

However, at the same time it is important to note that humans have brought on extreme changes that exceed those naturally occurring in an oceanic context. Pollution is an important factor to consider, particularly that of oil spills and eutrophication caused by terrestrial chemical use. The latter has been implicated in harmful algal outbreaks and also pressures from the notorious 'Crown of Thorns' starfish, which feeds on live coral.

Related to chemical discharges is the increase of sedimentation as a result of coastal development. Increased run-off from agricultural and building uses can smother reef ecosystems and cause rapid demise of the scleractinian communities. In Northern Queensland's Daintree region, there was controversy following the building of a development road in the mid-1980s, as sedimentation on adjacent coral reefs increased more than sixfold in comparison with undisturbed catchments in the same area (Hall, 2001, p. 608). Because all reef species rely on corals as a keystone species, ecosystem collapse may ensue.

Land reclamation can also smother reefs; for example in the resort town of Hurghada on the Egyptian coast, the gradual encroachment of hotels eventually destroyed all of the fringing reef (Spalding *et al.*, 2001, p. 53). Today, tourists have to catch boats to snorkel on offshore reefs, whilst they sleep metres from the location of once-thriving reef communities.

Despite their importance as a food source, increasing pressure on reefs from booming coastal populations – and indeed, coastal tourism – may also threaten the reef through unsustainable fishing practices. This is particularly true in the more harmful non-selective practices such as dynamite and cyanide fishing. Despite moves to curb these strategies, many developing countries still struggle to control their use. In the Philippines, for example, many of these fishermen are agricultural farmers who have been evicted from their lands, and resort to these destructive practices as they have little knowledge of traditional or more sustainable methods (Norton, 2005).

As described in the previous chapter, rising sea temperatures brought about as a result of global climate change may also have a significant impact on reefs. Coral polyps are extremely sensitive to even minor changes in sea temperature. It is estimated that corals on the Great Barrier Reef will experience between 2 and 6°C increases in sea temperature by the year 2100 (WWF, 2003a, p. 3). Such a rise causes the coral polyps to eject the algae that give the coral structures their colour, leading to so-called 'bleaching'. The coral polyps can continue to survive for a period without the algae but, unless they return and their nutrient provision is regained, the polyps and hence the coral colony itself will die.

While bleaching events in the first half of the 20th century were small in scale and linked to local factors, they have become global in scale and much more frequent as a result of global environmental change. The 1997–1998 major bleaching event attributable to the El Niño–Southern Oscillation (ENSO) affected corals in all the world's coral oceans, removing an estimated 16% of the world's coral, with some regional estimates as high as 46% (Hansen, 2004).

In the subsequent major event of 2002, of all the reefs surveyed across the whole Great Barrier Reef Marine Park, 60–95% were bleached to some extent. Around 5% of reefs have been severely damaged, and 50–90% of corals on these reefs are dead (WWF, 2003b). In relation to the Great Barrier Reef specifically, the Intergovernmental Panel on Climate Change stated that it faces significant death or damage from coral bleaching of medium to high certainty over the next 20–50 years (WWF, 2003a). In addition, the increase in storms and wave action, as a result of climate change, also pose a threat to the future stability of the reef (WWF, 2001).

Furthermore, there is very little that can be done to control coral bleaching at a local level. Some recent work suggests that corals may be able to partially adapt to sea temperature change through altering their relationship to the algae (Buddemeier and Fautin, 1993). However, this evidence comes from areas used to greater variability in sea temperatures, and should not be relied upon as a reef resilience strategy.

Lastly, physical damage is clearly of significant threat, since the reef structures are, to a large extent, the habitat for all these species. Although there are some natural causes of physical damage, the majority are human induced. Anchoring over reefs has caused significant damage in the past, which may take hundreds of years for recovery. A move to fixed moorings and anchoring off the reefs has reduced this impact for both tourist and non-tourist practice. Smaller-scale damage, such as that caused by divers and snorkellers, may be less apparent in the short term, but their longer-term threat to the reef may be just as severe.

Indeed, tourism is clearly implicated in many of the threats discussed here, ranging from the direct to the indirect. Direct impacts such as those from physical damage, fishing practice and pollution are compounded by indirect threats from resort development and climate change contributed to by long-distance air travel, for example. With the growing legions of tourists wanting to see the myriad colours of the reef, it may literally be a case of loving the reefs to death.

Case Study: Great Barrier Reef, North Queensland, Australia

Tourism to the Great Barrier Reef

As the largest biological feature on earth, the Great Barrier Reef is arguably the world's most famous marine tourism attraction, stretching more than 2300 km along the north-east coast of Australia from the northern tip of Queensland to just north of Bundaberg. Aside from the coral reefs, the region also contains a wide variety of other habitats and an extraordinary diversity of plant and animal species. Its popularity as a destination has been somewhat in parallel with increased political and scientific interest in the marine environment since the 1950s.

Technological advances that enabled access to this environment – particularly the invention of the aqualung – had no small part to play in significant increases in visitors right through the 1970s and 1980s. At that time, forecasts were being made of continued growth for the foreseeable future, and thus a concern with the potential impacts of these tourists lead to the founding of the Great Barrier Reef Marine Park Authority (GBRMPA) in 1975 and World Heritage listing in 1981. The rapid increase in numbers of tourists and development of tourism infrastructure on the reef, which caused great concern in the 1980s, have stabilized since 1995.

As befits a destination such as the Great Barrier Reef, the scope and range of tourism activity within its boundaries is truly diverse. Figures suggest that tourism is far and away the largest commercial activity in the Great Barrier Reef region, generating over Aus$4.1 billion per annum (BTR, 2003). As a consequence, the marine tourism industry is a major contributor to the local and Australian economy. In 2004 there were approximately 730 permitted tourism operators and 1500 vessels and aircraft permitted to operate in the Park. Tourism attracts approximately

1.8 million visitors each year (GBRMPA, 2004). Recreational use of the GBR region by coastal residents is also high and, in many circumstances, the impacts of recreational users can be impossible to separate from those of commercial tourism activities (Harriott, 2002).

Some of the principal tourist activities that take place within the marine park include boat trips, snorkelling, scuba-diving, fishing, whale watching, island resorts and cruise ships. Harriott (2002) takes a structural approach to the division of tourism facilities operating within the park, listing the major sectors of the Great Barrier Reef marine tourism industry as being:

- Structure-based tourism operations. Tourist pontoons are used as a base for day passengers. Other structures include underwater observatories, and a floating hotel that operated briefly in the 1980s. Larger day trip operations to pontoons represent the largest single component of the industry.
- Vessel-based tourism operations. These carry from less than 10 to over 400 passengers, may be site-specific or roving and may operate to islands or moorings.
- Extended vessel-based tourism operations. Vessels carry between six and 160 passengers on trips of several days to weeks, generally stopping at more than one destination.
- Bareboat charter. Primarily based in the Whitsunday Islands, yachts are available for charter with or without crew for operation within a restricted area.
- Cruise ships. Large (> 10,000 t) cruise ships pass through and anchor overnight in the Marine Park.
- Aircraft-based operations. Conventional aircraft, seaplanes and helicopters are used for sightseeing and transfers.
- Resort and shore-based operations. There are 27 island-based resorts within the Marine Park, and a number of mainland resorts adjacent to the Marine Park.

However, it is important to note that this tourism activity is highly concentrated. Some 85% of all visits take place within the Cairns and Whitsunday sections of the park, which represent less than 7% of the total area (CRC Reef, 2003). Data from Environmental Management Charge (EMC) returns (see below) suggests that visitation to the Great Barrier reef from Cairns has been largely static over the past decade. In stark contrast to the Cairns planning area, the Whitsundays region has seen significant growth in visitation. Although the region seems to have suffered a slight stagnation and downturn in visitors in the late 1990s, the four years 1999–2002 saw an increase in visitation from 335,459 to 687,436 total visitor days, an increase of 105% (Cater, 2004).

Managing tourism to the Great Barrier Reef

Managing tourism activity in this huge marine area (the park is bigger than the area of the UK, Switzerland and Netherlands combined) is far from simple. Under the World Heritage listing, the Australian government is responsible for ensuring a delicate balance between reasonable human use and the maintenance of the area's natural and cultural integrity. As a UNESCO report states:

> The enormity of this task is compounded by the sheer size of the GBRWHA[1], its economic importance, the political and the jurisdictional complexities determined by Australia's system of Federalism, the close proximity of rural and urban populations to the coast, the range of users and interest groups whose use patterns frequently compete and displace each other, the need for equity and fairness in access to resources, and the ecological diversity of the region.
>
> (UNESCO, 2002a, p. 10)

Management has been primarily achieved using a spectrum of multiple use zones ranging from General Use Zones, where most reasonable activities can occur, through to National Park Zones (no-take zones providing opportunities to see and enjoy the diversity of the Reef but where no fishing or collecting are allowed), to Preservation Zones (reference areas which are off limits to virtually everyone except for limited scientific research).

The GBRMPA takes the lead role in DDM (day to day management) of the region in conjunction with Queensland Parks and Wildlife Service. This activity is funded by both the Commonwealth and state governments, who provide matching funds primarily for enforcement, surveillance, monitoring and education/interpretation. In order to provide additional funds for these activities, an Environmental Management Charge was introduced in mid-1993, payable by all visitors to the reef on commercial operations. From April 2007, the daily charge for individual visitors is Aus$5.

EMC logbooks and charging returns are provided by the GBRMPA to all commercial operators at the beginning of each calendar year or when a new permit is granted. Operators are required to keep a logbook of operations and supply charging returns on a quarterly basis. Penalties exist for commercial operators who do not maintain records or pay the required EMC. EMC data from the logbooks are used for the purposes of charging, but also provide valuable information to the GBRMPA relating to tourism use of the Marine Park.

Policy context

The policy context in which the Great Barrier Reef exists is almost as diverse as the reef itself. In addition to the World Heritage Convention, a

[1] Great Barrier Reef World Heritage Area.

number of other international conventions discussed in this chapter – as well as in Chapter 9 – apply to the GBRWHA or parts of it: for example, the 1971 Ramsar Convention; the Convention on International Trade in Endangered Species of Wild Fauna and Flora (CITES, 1973); the Convention on Conservation of Migratory Species of Wild Animals (Bonn Convention 1979); the Convention on the Law of the Sea (UNCLOS 1982); the International Convention for the prevention of pollution at sea (MARPOL); and the Convention on Biological Diversity (CBD 1992) (UNESCO, 2002a).

At a national level, the most important legislation is of course the Great Barrier Reef Marine Park Act, which was enacted in 1975 'to provide for the protection, wise use, understanding and enjoyment of the Great Barrier Reef in perpetuity ...'; in other words, to protect the area's outstanding biodiversity whilst providing for reasonable use.

However, a plethora of other Commonwealth acts are also relevant to its management, for example the Environment Protection & Biodiversity Conservation Act (1999) and the Environment Protection (Sea Dumping) Act 1981. Within the Australian federal system, Queensland State legislation is also relevant. For example, almost 50% of the state islands within the GBRWHA are national parks under the (Queensland) Nature Conservation Act 1992. In some areas within the GBRWHA, the tidal lands and tidal waters are declared as parks under State Marine Park legislation (Marine Parks Act 1982) to complement the provisions of the adjoining Commonwealth Marine Park. Additional state legislation that is important includes:

- Coastal Protection and Management Act (1995).
- Environmental Protection Act (1994).
- Fisheries Act (1994).
- Integrated Planning Act (1997).
- State Development and Public Works Organisation Act (1971).
- Transport Infrastructure Act (1994).

In 2003–2004, The Great Barrier Reef Marine Park was rezoned as a result of implementing the Representative Areas Program. This was instigated by a recognition that the previous zoning of no-take or green zones, which made up < 5 % of the park, did not adequately protect the entire range of plants and animals, and should be revised. In addition, there was a number of inconsistencies between the management of state waters, extending to 3 nm offshore and the federal zone beyond. As a result, a selection of 70 bioregions was identified, being 'representative' examples of all of the different habitats and communities in the GBRWHA. Each bioregion contains plant and animal communities, together with physical features, that are significantly different from the surrounding areas and the rest of the GBRWHA (GBRMPA, 2005). A high degree of public consultation was encouraged throughout the planning process.

These representative areas join the existing network of green zones in forming a greater area that restricts extractive activity. Approximately one-third of the total area of the park is now afforded this higher level of protection. Many non-consumptive tourism activities, such as swimming and snorkelling, are still permitted within these zones.

By and large, the planning and management of tourism to the Great Barrier Reef has been very successful. In many cases the region is upheld as an example of world-class planning practice, with significant recognition of the issues of connectivity and consultation relevant to such a large natural area. It is important that this planning is adaptive to future threats and opportunities, especially that of global warming and resultant coral bleaching, which occurred on a significant scale in 1998 and 2002. In addition, certain commentators have suggested that federal and state governments see the Great Barrier Reef as a tourism 'cash cow' (Mules, 2004). Without fair reinvestment of the significant returns from tourism to the region, adequate planning for the future may be jeopardized.

Artificial reefs

An alternative resource that is seeing increasing intervention and development in order to reduce pressure on natural reefs is that of artificial reefs. The term artificial reef is deliberately vague, and takes into account a broad variety of artificial structures that may have been placed in the aquatic realm either deliberately or by accident. Wrecks, jetties, beach erosion barriers, walls, groynes and a variety of other structures are testament to human endeavour in the marine environment, but they soon become colonized by marine creatures and form attractions in their own right.

Artificial reefs aggregate fish and other mobile marine organisms very quickly after deployment and, given time, also host fixed life forms like algae, barnacles, mussels, sponges and soft and hard corals. In fact, 'established' artificial reefs have the potential to sustain a greater density and/or variety of biota (particularly fish species) than nearby natural reefs (Stolk et al., 2005). In the last decade four ex-navy destroyers have been deliberately sunk around the coastline of Australia to form scuba-diving attractions for tourists. An abandoned 1.8 km jetty in Busselton, Western Australia, was restored in 2001 specifically for its recreational potential (Stolk et al., 2005).

The economic 'value' of these artificial marine resources can be significant. Research undertaken in south-east Florida estimated that spending associated with artificial reefs, as a recreational resource, was approximately one-third of all expenditure related to reefs in the region (Johns et al., 2001). In a state so reliant on marine tourism resources, this slice of the pie is considerable. This same report estimated that south-east Floridian reefs accounted for US$873 million of residents' annual expenditure. Fishing constituted a US$499 million dollar industry, snorkelling US$167 million and scuba-diving was worth US$207 million annually. Furthermore, users would be willing to pay some US$26.7 million annually to invest in and maintain new artificial reefs.

Island Resources

It should come as no surprise that island tourist locations are heavily dependent on their marine surroundings as recreational resources. The growth of nature-based tourism has considerably strengthened this potential for archipelago nations; indeed Weaver and Schlüter (2001, p. 175) highlight the 'inherent suitability of island settings for ecotourism related activity'. Many Pacific islands, for example, have a small resource base with 'weak economies, minimal manufacturing bases, and distance from source markets' (Sofield, 1994, p. 207). However, the size of many of these destinations means that they are not suited to mass tourism, and so small-scale environmentally and culturally sensitive tourism is more appropriate.

Whilst the potential for marine-based tourism is great in these regions, it is important to pay regard to the impacts on precariously balanced local communities, as well as to consider the skills base required to develop tourism. In the Maldives, for example, Sathiendrakumar and Tisdell (1989) found that the much-touted employment benefits of tourism development rarely trickled down to the indigenous fishing communities. The majority of managers, diving instructors and some chefs were non-Maldivians, and indigenous employment at resorts was generally limited to non-skilled labour such as room boys, gardeners and cleaners. Although somewhat dated, this research points to the problems in island nations where there is 'little or no indirect employment effect from tourism for the villagers outside of the main tourist areas' (Sathiendrakumar and Tisdell, 1989, p. 264).

Although island tourism development is mostly small-scale, and thus lends itself to marine ecotourism, it is important that resource information is maintained at all scales. As Hall (2001) maintains, much of the data on island tourism development are highly fragmented. There is a particular lack of knowledge about the baseline status of island locations, or about the condition of the natural environment prior to tourism development. Volunteer marine ecotourism organizations such as Coral Cay Conservation (see Chapter 10, this volume) work to address this gap.

In addition, there is also a need for more comprehensive information gathering to interpret regional tourism impacts. This is especially true when we consider that many of the threats to island states are actually global, such as coral bleaching and sea-level rises. As Hall suggests: 'Within the context of the South Pacific, an area which is highly dependent on marine and coastal tourism for its economic wellbeing, there has been no systematic study of the environmental impacts of tourism over the region as a whole' (Hall, 2001, p. 604).

Littoral Resources

Estuarine resources

It is now recognized that, although of limited scenic value, mangrove ecosystems are among some of the most important littoral environments. They act as natural filters and remove many pollutants, as well as acting as a nursery for many ocean species. Sadly, they are also an ecosystem under significant threat, primarily as a result of the value of coastal land. For example, in the last three decades, Mexico has deforested more than 60% of the original coverage (1.5 million ha) of the mangrove forests in the coastal region (Yañez-Arancibia *et al.*, 1999, p. 335).

Whilst this has brought temporary gains in fish production and logging, there has been a simultaneous loss of these nurseries, flood protection and increased coastal erosion. Using integrated coastal models, Yanez-Arancibia *et al.* estimated that, far from being non-productive land, the true value of each hectare of mangrove in the Campeche region was approaching US$5000, based primarily on its value in sustaining shrimp populations in the Gulf of Mexico.

Tourism has been complicit in much of this resource attrition, as mangrove swamps have been removed for tourist development in many countries, including Australia, Hawaii, Vanuatu and Fiji. In the latter, the construction of the Denarau resort in 1975 involved the clearance of 130 ha of mangrove forest to construct an 18-hole golf course and create an artificial marina (Hall, 2001, p. 607).

This example is relatively benign when compared with the example of Cancún in Mexico. Prior to development, the 17km long Cancún island fringed a shallow, mangrove-lined lagoon that was home to a variety of marine life and was an important nesting site for seabirds and sea turtles (see Fig. 3.1). Following extensive development and construction of causeways linking the island to the mainland, the flow of water to the lagoon became restricted and the sand supply to the beaches has been substantially altered (Davenport and Davenport, 2006). In its place is one of the world's most extreme examples of mass-tourism development, with over 3.4 million visitors every year (see Fig. 3.2).

Despite this destruction, mangroves are belatedly becoming recognized as a resource for ecotourism activity. Much of this is admittedly terrestrial, with boardwalks as the main experiential infrastructure. However, many marine ecotours often incorporate mangrove ecotourism as part of the experience, either in transit or as the focus of the marine experience. Kayaks, for example, enable close penetration of this environment and observation of the significant wildlife that inhabits this ecosystem. At Couran Cove resort in Australia, kayak tours into the

Fig. 3.1. Cancún in the 1970s (photograph courtesy of A. Carballo-Sandoval).

Fig. 3.2. Cancún in the year 2000 (photograph courtesy of A. Carballo-Sandoval).

surrounding mangrove forests enable ecotourists to view six different
mangrove species and the wide range of marine and terrestrial organisms
that inhabit this environment.

Preservation of these resources for tourism may rely on much bigger
schemes than those provided in the industry. In Florida's Everglades
region, host to a wide variety of estuarine ecotourism activity, a recent

federal and state government scheme to rehabilitate the region may be a last chance to save an entire ecosystem. Human settlement and agricultural use have dramatically altered the hydrological flow that created the Everglades; indeed, it is estimated that the sea and mangrove swamps are advancing inland at the rate of 12 feet (3.66 m) per year (*The Economist*, 2005).

The Comprehensive Everglades Restoration Plan (CERP), first proposed in 2000, was suggested as a plan to restore some of the flow and ensure the long-term viability of the Everglades region. In the wake of Hurricane Katrina's damage to New Orleans in 2005, observers suggested that wetlands might have a vital role in flood and storm protection, and so such schemes take on a new dimension. However, it would appear that, like all such grand schemes proposing environmental clean-up, it has become bogged down in partisan politics, and may not come to fruition.

Perhaps the key in such schemes is to maintain their local relevance, as Yáñez-Arancibia *et al.* suggest: 'The experience in coastal resources management in developed nations suggests the need for an integrated multi-sectoral approach in developing plans which provide a course of action usable in the daily management of the coastal areas' (Yáñez-Arancibia *et al.*, 1999, p. 339).

Intertidal resources

Perhaps the most readily accessed marine ecotourism resource is that of the foreshore. Admittedly, not all visitors may consider themselves 'ecotourists', with easy access to this zone ensuring a wide range of recreational users. Nevertheless, these are zones that encourage a great deal of curiosity about the marine environment, and also host a variety of managed and commercial ecotourism attractions. An excellent review of the impacts that such activity can have in foreshore regions is provided by Davenport and Davenport (2006).

For example, beaches are an enduring tourist attraction, but impacts on dunes from human activity are significant. Walking through dunes to access the beach often removes vegetation cover, which is vital to the dune stability. Experiments carried out in Jutland, Denmark, demonstrated that dune trampling in heavy-use areas removed 98% of vegetation, creating very unstable dune structures, with a corresponding reduction in insect life (Hylgaard and Liddle, 1981, cited in Davenport and Davenport, 2006). Without boardwalks, visitors tend to avoid the most well-used section of a track, creating a number of new paths. Managers of such sites call this 'braiding', as eventually these coalesce into a broad trail that significantly erodes the sand dune.

Ironically, the European 'Blue Flag' initiative for clean beaches, discussed in Chapter 2, may not necessarily be wholly good for beach ecosystems. Although, clearly, the removal of non-organic material is undoubtedly positive for a beach, the fact that 'rubbish' does not distinguish natural beach detritus may be important. Organic material is actually very important to sand communities, raising water content and the level of organic nutrients in the soil.

The impact of humans on beach areas is also magnified by the increasing use of vehicles in these regions. As Buckley (2004) suggests, off-road vehicles (ORV) typically cause a range of environmental impacts including: (i) soil erosion and/or compaction; (ii) damage to vegetation and soil animals; (iii) road-kill and noise disturbance to birds and other wildlife; (iv) air and water pollution; (v) introduction of weeds and pathogens; (vi) slopewash and similar impacts from ORV tracks; and (vii) secondary impacts through increased number of visitors.

Off-road vehicles cause many times as much damage as pedestrians. Typically, ORV tyres exert ten to 100 times as much pressure as a boot, especially if the vehicle is turning or braking, and cause five to 30 times as much damage to vegetation (Buckley, 2004). Barros (2001) found that beaches in Australia with high levels of ORV use had far fewer ghost crabs than more remote beaches, and suggested that 100 passes could kill 98% of ghost crabs. As access to the beach is usually through sand dunes, damage to these can be significant.

Human activity on beaches may also have reduced a major marine ecotourism attraction, that of nesting turtles. In Florida, disturbances to sea turtles and their nests is prohibited not only by the US Endangered Species Act of 1973 but is also enshrined in Florida law (see Fig. 3.3).

As Davenport and Davenport (2006) suggest, Mediterranean sea turtles of the green, loggerhead and leatherback varieties were once common,

Fig. 3.3. Sea turtle protection in Florida (photograph courtesy of E. Cater).

breeding on beaches in North Africa, Southern Europe and many of the islands. Today, green turtle breeding is now limited to Cyprus, while declining loggerhead populations are confined to small areas of coastal Greece and Turkey. Leatherback breeding is virtually absent, with occasional reports in Israel and Syria. Coastal development has undoubtedly been the major reason for these population crashes, with roads replacing sand dunes and towers placing beaches in shade, thereby lowering temperatures. Sand compaction from high levels of use makes it difficult to dig nests, and may damage eggs in existing nests. Artificial lighting is also a major issue, as light is used by both mothers and hatchlings as a navigational aid. Light pollution from cars, street lights and airports (for example, on the island of Zakynthos, Greece, where the end of the runway is within 1 km of key nesting beaches) upsets hatchlings in particular which, by instinct, seek the brightest part of the horizon. Naturally this would be over the sea, but in many Mediterranean locations there may be roads and areas of coastal settlement.

At Mon Repos, just north of Bundaberg in Queensland, the threat of coastal development prompted the state government to set up a conservation park to protect the site for nesting turtles in the 1980s. The reputation of the site has developed from a research and conservation focus to a major ecotourism attraction, with 27,940 people visiting the information centre at Mon Repos during the turtle season between November 2003 and March 2004 (EPA, 2005a).

This has created some challenges for the parks and wildlife service, and basic research facilities have been replaced by an interpretation centre that provides visitors with an understanding and appreciation of turtle biology, behaviour and management (see Fig. 3.4). During the nesting season, staff conduct education programmes and nightly guided walks for hundreds of visitors. Visitor movements to the beach are highly controlled to ensure there are no negative impacts on turtle breeding success at the site, and a management fee of Aus$8.50 goes towards providing these facilities. Such measures go towards protecting species under significant threats (Wilson and Tisdell, 2001).

Rocky foreshores may not have the recreational appeal of beaches, but they are popular zones none the less. Just walking in these areas can cause damage to flora and fauna. Damage to barnacles, mussel beds and foliose algae is apparent in areas that have been trampled, and the effects are usually long-lasting (Brosnan and Crumrine, 1994, cited in Davenport and Davenport, 2006). A study of coach parties visiting wave cut platforms in New Zealand found a reduction in algal cover of 25% after as few as ten tramples, and a reduction of up to 90% in high-use areas (Schiel and Taylor, 1999, cited in Davenport and Davenport, 2006).

Loss of this protective algal cover then led to the loss of a number of other species that rely on its presence. Ironically, the growth in interest in the foreshore may be its biggest threat, as tourists and educational groups can cause significant damage. Davenport and Davenport cite the example of Purbeck Marine Wildlife reserve in Dorset, UK, as evidence of such a

Fig. 3.4. Mon Repos visitor centre, Queensland, Australia (photograph courtesy of C. Cater).

phenomenon. The setting up of the reserve in 1978 has virtually guaranteed a stream of casual visitors and school and university groups. Easily accessed areas show severely impacted limpet populations and reduced cover of large branched seaweeds (Davenport, 2006, p. 283).

Exploring rockpools and collecting species may also have impacts, particularly if boulders are removed and not placed in their original orientation and position. 'Boulders have markedly different fauna and flora on their upper and lower surfaces, so this human activity causes degraded habitat stability and reduced biodiversity' (Davenport and Davenport, 2006, p. 283).

Additionally, some emerging adventure tourism activities may have impacts in rocky areas. The recent development of coasteering, a marine version of canyoning, where tourists jump and abseil from cliffs and scramble over rocky ledges, may have significant impacts. Equipping participants with protective suits and gloves may cause them to be less cautious as they 'jump into water-filled gullies and brush against fauna and flora whilst swimming, pull on kelps to get out of water, and trample on coralline turf, barnacles, etc. when climbing out of surf' (Davenport and Davenport, 2006, p. 289).

A recent paper by Gössling *et al.* (2004) looked at tourist behaviour regarding shell collection and purchase in Zanzibar, Tanzania. They found that 39% of the tourists surveyed had collected shells and 7% had bought shells, contributing an estimated US$136,000 to the local economy. Whilst shell collecting is frowned upon by a 'leave only footprints' ecotourist ideology, many tourists identify shells with a souvenir of marine paradise to take home (see Fig. 3.5).

Gössling also points to the problems of the so-called 'souvenir hinterlands' that may provide such artefacts for popular tourist centres. This leads to contradictions in legislation and practice. For example, in Queensland, Australia, although the spectacular triton shell is subject to export control under the Australian Wildlife Protection Act of 1982 and the triton is a protected species in state legislation, hundreds of tritons are annually imported to the state for sale in popular tourist centres. Thus, areas with weaker environmental protection, which invariably are those with greater economic problems, end up supporting developed countries, which can then have the luxury of promoting their own environmental stewardship (Gössling *et al.*, 2004, p. 2636).

Nearshore resources

A variety of nearshore biomes are used as marine ecotourism resources, including kelp forests and seagrass meadows. Tasmania makes much of its giant kelp forests in marketing its dive tourism portfolio. These plants are one of the fastest growing organisms in the world and, under optimum conditions of sunlight, nutrients and temperature, growth can reach 0.5 m per day, providing a renewable food source and home for up to half a million invertebrates per plant (Kelpwatch, 2004). However, surveys suggest that there has been significant decline in the coverage of these kelp beds over the past 30 years, to perhaps only 5% of their former extent.

Fig. 3.5. Shell seller, Zanzibar, Tanzania (photograph courtesy of E. Cater).

Seagrasses are submerged plants (angiosperms) found in shallow water along coasts (Osbourne, 2000, p. 310). They are unique, as seagrasses are the only marine flowering plant (Green and Short, 2003). Seagrass meadows are widely distributed over the world's shores, occurring in sheltered locations where human activity is often prevalent, such as shallow bays, lagoons and estuaries, with many different species found in both temperate and tropical regions (Barnes and Mann, 1980, pp. 58–59). They are highly productive ecosystems providing a habitat and food for many fish varieties, invertebrates, turtles and dugongs (sea cows) (Osbourne, 2000, p. 310).

In common with mangroves discussed above, seagrasses are important nursery areas for fish, with 'as many as 70% of pelagic fish spending at least part of their juvenile life in seagrass beds' (CRCReef, 2005). Over the last 30 years, however, seagrass habitats have declined as a consequence of human activity. Degrading factors include dredging, sediment input, water pollution, construction of jetties, coastal development, water sports and tourist activity (CRCReef, 2005).

Polar Resources

Although not exclusively marine, Polar tourism is dominated by marine ecotourism products. Polar tourism has been subject to a range of academic scrutiny in recent years in parallel with its growth. Despite the differences between Northern and Southern Polar regions, they do have a range of similarities in characteristics. As Hall and Johnston point out, in their seminal text on polar tourism, their 'harsh climate and physical environment, the high degree of endemism among flora and fauna, an extremely sensitive environment and the increasing attraction of these harsh landscapes have created a number of common elements in the management of these regions' (Hall and Johnston, 1995, p. 6).

There are some obvious differences, particularly the longer history of human occupation and the lack of a continental land mass in the North. Nevertheless, both regions have a long history of natural resource use, especially that based on whaling, sealing and fishing.

Arctic tourism is undoubtedly less confined to the maritime environment, with much taking place in northern regions of the USA, Canada, Scandinavia and Russia, although there is still a significant marine component. Partly this is supply-driven, as many polar tourism operators run 3- or 4-month seasons at either end of the globe, maximizing the use of their vessels and staff.

However, the lack of a continental land mass at the North Pole also encourages maritime access. Indeed, as Stonehouse (2001) describes, polynyas – pockets in the ice sheet free of frozen material – tend to concentrate life and offer good wildlife viewing opportunities. The opportunities for small-scale balanced ecotourism here may offer more sustainable alternatives to other forms of tourism. As Hall cautions: 'A study of cruise tourism in the Canadian Arctic concluded that given the environmental fragility of much of the region and the vulnerability of small, remote, largely aboriginal communities to impact, great care should be exercised in using the area for cruise tourism' (Hall, 2001, p. 605).

The vast majority of visitors to the Antarctic are 'ship-borne adventure travellers' (Stonehouse and Crosbie, 1995). Of the 30,232 tourists who visited Antarctica in 2004–2005 (IAATO, 2005), over 90% were ship-borne visitors, and some 17% were on cruises that did not land their passengers; hence the marine component is dominant in these experiences. Operators typically run short cruises of between 10 and 20 days with perhaps 5–14 of these spent in Antarctic waters. The spectacular scenery and the relative proximity of the Antarctic Peninsula to South America means that the majority of cruises visit this portion of the continent, along with significant island groups in the region such as South Georgia.

In 2004–2005, this region was host to 96% of all seaborne visitation (IAATO, 2005). These cruises have traditionally followed the 'Lindblad' pattern of visiting the continent: named after the first Antarctic tourism entrepreneur, this involves boats of up to 140 passengers guided on vessels and ashore by experienced staff. The emphasis is on an exploratory and educative tour, with a high priority placed on appropriate behaviour in this fragile and remote environment. Visits ashore are usually conducted in parties of ten to 15 people in special boats called Zodiacs (see Fig. 3.6).

Fig. 3.6. Exploring by 'Zodiac' (photograph courtesy of D. Filby, reproduced with permission of IAATO).

Recently, there has been a change in the character of these trips, brought about mainly as a result of increasing demand and larger cruise vessels being used. The educative nature of the Lindblad pattern, with its strong emphasis on group exploration, has given way to more traditional 'cruising' such as that seen in Alaska. Furthermore, this growing fleet of seasonal visitors has put stress on a small number of popular sites.

At present, the majority of visitors visit the continent with an operator who is affiliated to the International Association of Antarctic Tour Operators (IAATO), and comply with the strict codes of conduct outlined by that organization (see Chapter 11, this volume). For example, the by-laws of IAATO state that no ship of over 500 passengers is allowed to land its tourists ashore, and that any ship with over 200 passengers is restricted to specific sites and must comply with stringent environmental controls (IAATO, 2005, p. 3).

However, in 2004–2005, two vessels operated by non-IAATO members, the *Marco Polo* (passenger capacity 800, operated by Orient Lines) and the *Discovery* (passenger capacity 650, operated by Discovery world cruises), landed some 4088 tourists during the season. Although these represented only 15% of Antarctic visitors, the growth in these mass visitations, without IAATO oversight, is somewhat troubling.

Antarctic tourism is ostensibly managed by the provisions of the Antarctic Treaty, signed in 1959. Although designed primarily to deal with territorial and environmental concerns, tourism is mentioned in a number of the Treaty's articles. The regulatory framework for tourism is provided by a combination of Treaty articles and national legislation. Thus, legislation outside the Treaty may provide the specific terms by which the intent of the Treaty is enforced. For example, in protecting marine wildlife, the Treaty works with legislation such as the Convention for the Conservation of Antarctic Seals (CCAS) and the Convention on the Conservation of Antarctic Marine Living Resources (CCAMLR) (Enzenbacher, 1995, p. 181).

However, the peculiar nature of this continental management means that self-regulation and unofficial codes have been just as important to date. Nevertheless, as Enzenbacher (1995) suggests, with increasing numbers visiting the region and the growth of adventure products, a more proactive approach will be needed in the future. Ironically, it may be that the continent's major drawcard is also its biggest threat. As Stonehouse and Crosbie (1995) suggest, the pristine nature of Antarctica is its biggest pull, with the often-touted promise of 'treading where no human has done so before'. However, this is clearly not a sustainable attraction, and the continent's association with a notion of 'virginity' is a problem that needs to be addressed (Stonehouse and Crosbie, 1995).

Indeed, the Antarctic has a significant history of human endeavour, and its other main attraction apart from the scenery and marine wildlife is that of human settlement. Historic huts and whaling stations have become popular tourist sites and have belatedly become protected, to preserve their historical character. There are many more of these sites on subantarctic islands, related to both their milder climates and their proximity to the Antarctic convergence. This is defined by biologists as the region where cold waters of polar origin disappear under warmer subtropical waters, separating distinctive suites of species (Stonehouse, 2001). It also creates a zone of mixing that is incredibly rich in wildlife, and a rich resource for marine ecotourism. Additionally, it is substantially closer to centres of population, and therefore is a rewarding but less expensive destination for cruise visitors.

New Zealand's subantarctic islands comprise five groups in the Southern Ocean. As Sanson (1994) describes, the potential for marine ecotourism in these island groups is significant, featuring:

- The world's largest breeding populations of royal albatross on Campbell Island and wandering and shy albatross on Auckland Islands.
- Among the greatest diversity of penguin species in the world: four breeding species (two endemic) and ten visiting species.
- Giant subantarctic megaherbs including the *Pleurophyllum* genus, which is found nowhere else in the world.
- The endemic Hooker's sealion, with its principal breeding ground on Auckland Islands.
- Four endemic species of land birds.
- The spectacular rata forests of Auckland Islands and the southernmost tree ferns in the world.
- The Snares Islands (only 328 ha) are estimated to have over 6 million breeding seabirds, comparable to the total number of seabirds around the entire British Isles.
- 120 species of birds and 200 species of plants.
- The world's rarest cormorant, duck and penguin species.
- One of the world's largest rodent-free islands (Adams Island).
- A fascinating history of exploration, shipwrecks, sealing, whaling, farming and early scientific expeditions (Sanson, 1994, p. 344).

All of these islands are managed as national nature reserves, which makes them popular for nature-based tourists. However, as Sanson describes, these island communities are highly fragile and, being so isolated, require stringent quarantine procedures to ensure that no new species are introduced. Clearly polar and subpolar marine ecotourism is a very significant growth area, and sustainable management of these fragile resources will require some proactive strategies.

Pelagic Resources

The open ocean is a marine environment that is only recently being tapped for its ecotourism resource potential. It is somewhat hampered by the cost:benefit ratio of large distances and lower densities of attractions. However, sites such as deep-sea vents, described in Chapter 4, are seeing increased use. Historically, the major tourism users of these regions have been cruise vessels, and a marine tourism sector that is witnessing significant growth. In particular, there has been growth in both the large- and small-scale operations in recent years.

At the top end there has been a trend towards ever-larger vessels, with over 5000 passengers and crew onboard at any one time. Simultaneously, there has been the growth of so-called expedition cruising, with smaller vessels undertaking boutique tours (Halpenny, 2001, p. 240). However, all of these vessels produce substantial quantities of garbage, wastewater and sewage that are often discharged untreated into pristine marine habitats. The International Maritime Organization estimates that each passenger on a large cruise ship produces 3.5 kg of garbage and solid waste per day. In addition, a typical cruise ship discharges around 1 million l of 'black water' (sewage) during a 1-week voyage (Davenport and Davenport, 2006).

Animal Resources

Much of marine ecotourism is based around encounters with large marine animals or charismatic megafauna. The reasons we are attracted towards species of our size and larger are discussed in Chapter 7, and is perhaps captured by the I-to-eye encounter described by Bulbeck (2005). As Constantine (1999) documents, in New Zealand it is possible to watch and/or swim with, on a regular basis, five species of dolphins, six species of whales and two species of pinnipeds (seals). All marine mammals are protected under New Zealand's Marine Mammals Protection Act 1978 and Marine Mammals Protection Regulations 1992.

However, as this report points out, this is not easy, given the paucity of data on the 'population size, habitat use, home range and behavioural ecology of the target species' prior to the establishment of tourism operations. Successful resource management of these populations therefore depends on much better information as to their extent and impacts that tourism may have. Shackley (1998, p. 334) echoes this concern in her discussion of the emergence of 'Stingray City' in the Cayman islands, where hundreds of tourists feed these animals each day. In particular, the long-term impacts, whereby young rays are 'taught' how to behave by older generations, could have major consequences for the future existence of this resource in a way that is not wholly dependent on humans.

Great white sharks, also known as white pointers, have captured public interest through their size and reputation, and a number of operations provide viewing of this species in the wild. Internationally, great white sharks are listed as 'vulnerable' on the IUCN Red List of threatened species (IUCN, 2006), as well as being protected in South Africa (1991), Namibia, the Maldives, Florida and California (USA) and Malta. Despite an awareness of population decline, accurate figures on the actual status of this particular species are very hard to come by. This is related to very poor knowledge about the sharks' stock structure and migration patterns, and piecemeal records of fishing by catch and beach net trappings. As discussed in Chapter 2, there are some concerns that the practice of 'burleying' or 'chumming' by tourism operators in order to attract the sharks may alter shark behaviour and also have impacts on their prey relationships:

> Certainly allowing many people to see sharks *in situ* is good publicity for these animals and helps to dispel the 'man-eater' stereotype. But are entrained sharks performing on cue really exhibiting any more natural behaviour than we see in trained circus animals? Does swimming in circles and gnawing on a frozen 'chum ball' or taking bait fishes off a spear or out of the hand or mouth of a human constitute 'sharks in the wild'? Public aquaria offer basically the same view of sharks without fostering the 'eating machine' image enhanced by frenzied feeding.
>
> (Burgess, 1998, p. 1)

Indeed, Topelko and Dearden (2005) question whether the increase in shark-based tourism across the globe is a sufficient economic incentive to encourage a reduction in fishing pressure on sharks. They conclude that, while the shark-watching industry may generate sufficient income to act as incentive to conserve some species in some locations, as an estimated 100 million sharks are caught each year worldwide, it will provide limited impetus to providing adequate protection globally. However, tourism may offer some potential for finding out more about these animals, as 'regular viewing trips when properly managed offer good opportunities for data collection' (Commonwealth of Australia, 2002, p. 41).

In South Australia the permitting authority, the Department of Environment and Heritage (DEHSA), has made it a permit condition that licensed shark cage dive operators fill out a logbook that records sightings of sharks, and this is passed on to government marine resource research organizations. Data collection in this manner, leading to a greater awareness of the status of marine resources, has been very successfully used in whale shark population monitoring in north-western Australia. A controlled interaction procedure and cooperation between operators and conservation authorities has created a good example of sustainable marine ecotourism.

Case Study: the Whale Sharks of Ningaloo

The elusive whale shark is the largest fish in the ocean, and yet very little is known about these animals, which can grow up to 12 m in length (Colman, 1997). However, reasonable numbers of juvenile males regularly visit the reefs of north-western Australia between April and June each year, coinciding with the coral spawning season. They come to the surface periodically for up to 20 min, before diving to feed. Predictably, the opportunity to swim with these behemoths has, in recent years, been a significant factor in a booming tourist industry in the North-West Cape, centred on the town of Exmouth and Ningaloo reef. The reef is Australia's largest fringing reef, stretching some 290 km from North-West Cape to Red Bluff in the State of Western Australia.

Dive charters have been offering the chance to encounter whale sharks in their natural environment since the early 1990s, although the first dedicated operator did not commence until 1993. During that season, 14 boats handled approximately 1000 visitors, increasing to over 2000 by 1995 (Davis *et al.*, 1997). It is estimated that some 500 interactions with sharks take place each year, although it is likely that many of these are with the same individuals. Activities surrounding this highly specialized marine ecotourism experience are estimated to contribute Aus$12 million to the local economy (B. Fitzpatrick, Exmouth, Western Australia, 2004, personal communication).

Despite their size and a remarkable camouflaging, combined with the fact that, unlike true whales, they do not need to breach the surface, sighting the whale shark is far from easy. Consequently, spotter planes are used to assist with the location procedure and, on sighting an animal, tourist boats are directed to intercept. Typically these boats will hold up to 20 tourists with snorkel gear, who will be split into waves and enter the water with a guide from the company in the path of the shark. These groups then split to allow the shark to travel, whilst the snorkellers swim alongside for up to 5 min. In some cases another wave will be dispatched from the boat to replace that already in place, or another operator will arrive to deposit their charges. The rare nature of these interactions means that operators are able to charge a significant premium, with most day outings costing over Aus$300.

The increased popularity of the experience led the Western Australian Conservation and Land Management (CALM) agency to introduce management of the operators. As most of the interactions take place within the Ningaloo Marine Park, established in 1987, the agency was able to license the operators from the outset. Initially these licences were issued for only 1 year, but from 1995 this term was extended to 3 years for 13 operators based in Exmouth. In the same year, an Aus$15 levy per person was introduced to allow CALM to meet the costs of bringing their own vessel, crewed by Wildlife Officers, to Ningaloo Marine Park in order to monitor the industry (Davis *et al.*, 1997). Unlike other taxes, for example on the Great Barrier Reef, tourists are made aware of this contribution through the provision of a high-quality souvenir validation pass. This fee currently stands at Aus$20. In addition, licences must be used a minimum of 50% of the time, to ensure that a cartel cannot emerge through operators sitting on their licences.

Comprehensive guidelines have also been developed by CALM in order to ensure that the whale sharks' natural behaviour is not disturbed (see Fig. 3.7). The most significant of these is that only one boat is allowed to be 'in contact' at any one time. It is worth noting that this is likely to be safer for tourists as well as less stressful for the animal. In 1995, swimmers

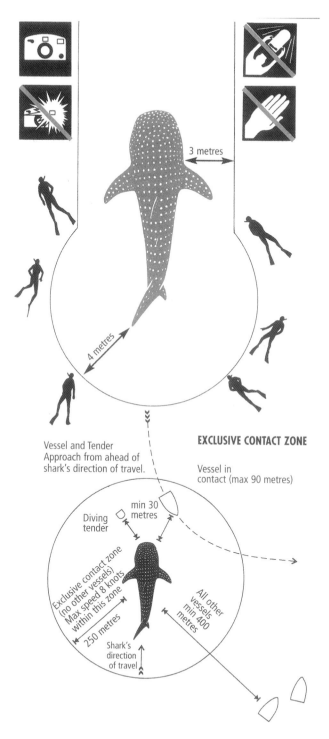

Fig. 3.7. Whale Shark Approach Guidelines (image reproduced with permission of Department of Environment and Conservation).

were required to maintain a minimum distance of at least 1 m from the head or body of a shark and 4 m from its tail (Davis *et al.*, 1997). The minimum distance from head or body has now been increased to 3 m, principally to avoid accidental contact with the shark (B. Fitzpatrick, Exmouth, Western Australia, 2004, personal communication).

This is an example of impacts largely being managed by the operators, although they are still under the regulations set and enforced by CALM. The author observed that there was a high level of cooperation between operators to provide the best experience for visitors. For example, although the CALM guidelines allow one boat to be 'in contact' for up to 1.5 h, in practice several boats may stagger their interactions by leapfrogging each other, allowing for more efficient trips. Furthermore, tourist operators have provided a great deal of recent knowledge on the animals, particularly through a logbook that is pro-vided by CALM, in which statistics for each interaction are recorded including sex, estimated size and behaviour (see Fig. 3.8).

Scientific analysis through this record suggests, for example, that the average size of whale sharks visiting the reef is declining, and also has informed us that the visiting population is mostly male. To date there is no suggestion that the industry has impacted severely on the whale sharks. However, whilst 500 interactions may not sound a lot, within a compressed 3-month timescale, this is actually nearing capacity, a fact

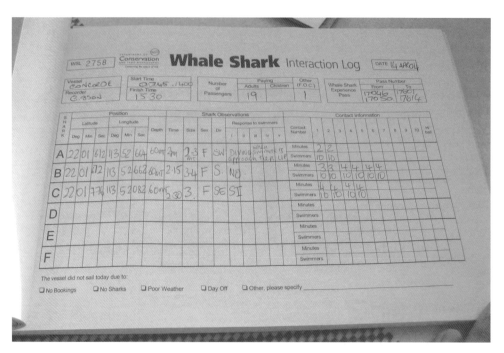

Fig. 3.8. Interaction log filled out by the whale shark operator after each encounter (photograph courtesy of C. Cater).

borne out by CALM observers (B. Fitzpatrick, Exmouth, Western Australia, 2004, personal communication).

Davis *et al.* (1997) suggest that, in the late 1990s, a large number of tourists engaging in the experience were Japanese (some 40% of the sample); the authors' own observations in 2004 would suggest that this figure is not currently representative. It is acknowledged that the survey figure may have been skewed by the fact that the operators surveyed did target the Japanese market, although an alternative explanation may lie in the overall drop in Japanese visitors to Australia in the new millennium. However, the global reputation of the site means that a majority of participants are still international. On individual trips to visit the whale sharks, there are likely to be a large number of repeat visitors, as frequently they are not sighted at all, particularly in the shoulder periods. Most operators offer a free second trip in this case, signifying that on the observed outing approximately 50% of all individuals were repeating.

It is important to set the whale shark operations within a booming tourism industry context in the North-West Cape. The pristine nature of Ningaloo reef itself, the only extensive system anywhere to fringe the west coast of a continent (Collinsa *et al.*, 2003), brings increasing numbers of tourists, not all of them ecologically minded. Controversy raged in the late 1990s over a proposed marina resort to be built at Mauds Landing at the southern end of the reef (Morton, 2003). Public resistance and astute political capital garnering by the incumbent government eventually stopped the construction of the resort, which would have had disastrous consequences for the health of the reef. Nevertheless, the threat of such developments remains.

Rezoning of the marine park in 2004 (CALM, 2004a) sought to tighten up the management of the Cape's recreational opportunities. There are a large number of diving and snorkelling opportunities in the marine park, including that at Navy Pier, part of the support structure for a US military listening post. The fringing nature of the reef itself allows drift snorkelling opportunities directly off the beach, unavailable in sites such as the Great Barrier Reef. Whilst clearly being very popular, as they do not require the hiring of boats, management of increasing numbers of visitors becomes a problem. To date, marine tourism activities seem to have been managed sustainably at Ningaloo, but the growing reputation of the region for world-class experiences, coupled with increased access opportunities to what is a very remote location, will put stresses on this fragile environment.

Cultural Resources

Marine ecotourism resources are not solely natural, and there are a variety of anthropological resources above and below the waterline that may form significant attractions. The density of shipwreck remains in

English waters may be the highest in the world, with over 40,000 recorded sites, whilst Northern Ireland has 3000, South Africa 2500, Australia 6000 and Canada 9000 (DEFRA, 2002a). In 2002, the National Heritage Act in the UK extended English Heritage's remit to include archaeological sites of all types in or under the seabed to the 12-mile limit around England in recognition of the nation's rich maritime history (Roberts and Trow, 2002).

Similarly, the Caribbean island of St Kitts is host to hundreds of historic shipwrecks as a result of its trade importance, battles between the English and French and the incidence of hurricanes (Spooner, 2003). Since 2001, the Anglo-Danish Maritime Archaeology Team (ADMAT) has been working to preserve these wrecks. There are a number of threats to these resources, particularly from cruise ship prop wash and treasure hunters, but the ADMAT programme proposes to catalogue, excavate and preserve these wrecks for heritage purposes. These wrecks can then form tourist attractions both above the waves – with salvaged material placed in museums, and below the surface – with protected wrecks becoming important dive sites.

Malaysia is also waking up to the potential of its underwater heritage, promoting the maritime importance of destinations such as Malacca (Mustapa, 2005). It is worth considering that some of this cultural heritage is potentially far more fragile than the natural environment in which it is placed. 'Unlike many biological communities that have some degree of resilience to recover from degradation, once they are damaged, underwater historic and cultural resources usually cannot recover' (*MPA News*, 2003b). Protection for these tourism resources is thus a priority.

A variety of cultural resources such as artefacts – including built heritage, visual and performing arts, crafts, literary traditions and lifestyle; knowledge and skills; and beliefs and values are detailed in Chapter 5. For example, in 2005 a new tourist experience was proposed by Galapagos Island fishermen representatives: the opportunity for tourists to experience for themselves how artisanal fishermen work and live. Not only would this reduce fishing pressure on the Marine Reserve by generating an additional means of livelihood, but it would also provide a link between local fishers and tourists, with the former still retaining their rights to fish in the reserve (Galapagos Conservation Trust, 2005a).

More recently, a holistic appreciation of the cultural interpretation of the sea has emerged through the concept of seascapes. A joint Welsh-Irish project was launched in 1999 to 'develop and test methods for assessing seascapes so that decisions on coastal and marine development can be informed to the same extent as land based development decisions have been in recent years through the process of landscape assessment' (DETR, 2000).

Resource Management

The growing popularity of marine ecotourism experiences means that the resources detailed in this chapter are in increasing demand. As Mark Orams has highlighted:

> More and more people are now able to access more and more of the marine world. Whether it be through submarines, boats, scuba, sea kayaks, yachts, personal water craft ('jet-skis'), underwater hotels, floating pon toons or whatever, increasing access means increasing use, which in turn implies increasing pressure on the quality of marine resources.
>
> (Orams, 1997, p. 116)

This pressure from users undeniably brings the opportunity for greater conflict between different user groups, between ecotourism and waterbased-tourism and between ecotourism and more consumptive users of the sea, as discussed in the previous chapter. The only way that these conflicts can be resolved is through effective resource management. However, such a goal may be far from easy to achieve, and some of the challenges for policy and planning in the marine environment are discussed in Chapter 9.

In some cases, prior experience of resource management may be a hindrance. We highlight the not always helpful legacy of terrestrial planning protocols in Chapter 9 after Timothy (2002). These work on very different principles than can be applied in the sea. One example is that of fishing in relation to agriculture. As Spalding *et al.* (2001) point out, our notion of 'harvesting' on the land is largely based on significant environmental modification. In contrast, maintaining a harvest from the sea relies on keeping the ecosystem as it is. 'If this harvesting is turned to mining, sustainability is lost, and with it food, jobs and entire economies' (Spalding *et al.*, 2001, p. 66). We should also be aware of exporting resource management philosophies from one location to another. Orams has discussed the dangers of 'the ethnocentric approach taken by many agencies with regard to decision making on coastal and marine resource management' (Orams, 1997, p. 116).

The key to managing marine resources for tourism and other users is dynamic information gathering. Unless we know the true extent to which human activities impact on these environments we cannot hope to manage their use effectively. As Constantine suggests for marine mammals:

> Issues such as the impacts of noise produced by vessels, boat handling practices, numbers and proximity of boats and humans, effects of swimmers in the water, continual disturbance *vs* sporadic disturbance, differences in responses of different species, age classes, sexes, individuals, or seasonal changes are not known.
>
> (Constantine, 1999, p. 7)

This is largely true for marine resources as a whole. The need for this is especially acute in developing nations, which have little capacity for documenting their present resource base, although we should be wary of neocolonialist approaches such as those just mentioned. In this regard, organizations such as Coral Cay Conservation (see above) should be lauded for their ability to provide baseline data collection on host communities' own terms. This is only a small slice of a much bigger task, but comprehensive research has a vital role to play in determining what may constitute sustainable resource use. The health of marine ecotourism resources will depend upon it.

4 Marine Ecotourism Attractions and Activities

Marine-based Activity

A truly bewildering array of activities is possible in the marine environment, some as a result of technological development, but many of which have evolved from long-popular pursuits. A good proportion of the latter significantly predate the term ecotourism, even though at their heart they may be all about sustainable interaction with the marine environment. Therefore, most people experiencing the marine environment through these activities may only weakly associate them with the principles of ecotourism. As such, it is important to situate marine ecotourism activities first within a recreational context.

Our recreation has a strong marine focus as a result of geographic trends, for a large proportion of the world's population resides in coastal regions. For example, although coastal states make up only 11% of the contiguous USA in land area, they are home to over 50% of the population (Cordell, 2004). In Australia the situation is even more pronounced, as over three-quarters of the population live within 40 km of the coast, and one-quarter are within 3 km. It is no surprise then, that recreational activities are likely to make heavy use of the marine environment. The USA National Survey on Recreation and the Environment gives some indications of popular marine-based activity (see Table 4.1).

Although these figures underscore the high significance of traditional forms of marine interaction, such as visiting beaches and swimming in Western societies, they also acknowledge the appreciable numbers involved in less popular activities such as surfing, scuba-diving and kayaking. Also of note is the manner in which fishing continues to attract large numbers of participants. Observing wildlife – which may constitute some form of independent ecotourism – is also highly significant,

Table 4.1. People aged 16 or older participating in saltwater-based activities in the USA, 2000–2001 (from Cordell, 2004).

Activity	Population engaging in activity on at least an annual basis (%)	Approximate number (million)
Visiting beaches	30.03	64.0
Swimming	25.53	54.4
Saltwater fishing	10.32	22.0
Viewing/photographing scenery	9.19	19.6
Birdwatching	7.17	15.3
Motorboating	7.11	15.2
Viewing other wildlife	6.45	13.6
Snorkelling	5.07	10.8
Sailing	2.98	6.3
Surfing	1.59	3.4
Scuba-diving	1.35	2.9
Kayaking	1.33	2.8

particularly for birdwatching. The majority of these pastimes are non-consumptive in nature, which creates an interesting paradox, as Cordell suggests that 'Recreation management is often focused on consumptive activities' (Cordell, 2004, p. 171). Although the figures above are for participation at least once per year, the report also notes that viewing/learning activities displayed significantly higher average annual days of participation than did the other activities. Mean days participating in viewing/photographing scenery and birdwatching were both reported as over 40 days per year.

It is worth noting a bias in participation along race and gender lines that should also be considered in an ecotourism context (see Table 4.2): (i) there is a very significant difference between white and black participation in water-based activity that should be recognized; and (ii) although smaller, there is also a minor gender bias towards males participating in these activities.

Clearly, these figures are related to a highly developed leisure society, and would have less application in less developed settings or in other cultural backgrounds with differing views of the marine environment. There has been very limited work on the race (with the exception of Moscardo, 2004) and gender dimensions of ecotourism participation, but these figures and author observations would suggest an area ripe for enquiry.

Through this recreational context, the diversity of activities that must be considered in this chapter soon becomes apparent. In a commercial context this diversity is extended through the provision of experiences that would be unlikely to be taken by individuals. The authors have opted for a broad perspective here, as a narrow identification of marine ecotourism activities is of limited benefit. As described in Chapter 8, whilst eco-labelling may be advocated by some ecotourism industry players, any text that seeks to understand the development and extent of marine ecotourism must appreciate the fluid interpretation of the term in the public realm. This proactive approach should also consider activities that are on the fringes of even the loosest definition of ecotourism, and these are covered at the end of this chapter.

Activities that should be considered are best divided by the degree of interaction with the marine environment. We begin with those that are most interactive, and take place within the water. These are followed by activities requiring less effort on the part of the individual – although

Table 4.2. Estimation of numbers of persons aged 12 or older in the USA who had participated at least once in the previous 12 months, by activity, race and gender, 2000–2001 (from Cordell, 2004).

Activity	White (%)	Black (%)	Male (%)	Female (%)
Swimming in natural waters	50.5	19.8	45.5	40.5
Motorboating	31.2	8.4	29.4	20.7
Kayaking	15.3	3.6	14.6	9.9

they are still active in the pursuit of an experience – and finally examine those activities that take place within a marine ecotourism context but are largely passive in terms of interaction.

In the water

Swimming and snorkelling

Perhaps the most basic marine ecotourism activity is that for which we are well equipped – that of swimming. Although usually practised in a recreational context as discussed above, it may also be significant in ecotourism activity. The chance to enter the marine environment, and to experience it as its more adapted inhabitants do, fulfils a basic and popular need. The use of simple equipment such as a mask, snorkel and fins enables more efficient interaction with this environment, and generally, has a low participation cost.

Indeed, a study by Park *et al.* (2002) indicated that trips by snorkellers to the Florida Keys were not statistically linked to household characteristics such as age and household income. The same study found that snorkellers were relatively dedicated to their pursuit, 'engaging in a focused set of activities, suggesting that these recreationists may not shift expenditures to other sites or other recreation activities in the Florida Keys when confronted with increased access costs for the snorkelling experience' (Park *et al.*, 2002, p. 312).

As commercial activity, swimming and snorkelling may involve doing so in coral reef environments, or with significant wildlife. The opportunity to swim with a range of larger mammalian species – for example, seals, dolphins and whales – has become popular in recent years. As discussed in the previous chapter, at Ningaloo reef in Western Australia, the opportunity to swim with whale sharks has become a significant tourist attraction over the last decade. Recently, an industry has developed on the Great Barrier Reef based on swims with dwarf minke whales whereby mermaid lines are deployed to enable snorkellers to drift behind the boat (Valentine *et al.*, 2004). The whales are free to approach the snorkellers, and may often do so for lengthy periods of time. Shackley suggests that 'Snorkelling is a far less intrusive activity than scuba-diving' (Shackley, 1998), particularly relating to her work on manatees (1992) and stingrays (1998).

The whale shark experiences in Western Australia opted for a snorkelling experience for the reason that these would minimize the chance that tourists would swim underneath the animal and effectively cut off its ability to dive. However, the authors would be wary of such a claim in all marine environments. The number of snorkellers at any one location at any point in time is likely to be higher; little or no training is required and snorkellers are rarely given guidelines about responsible behaviour; snorkellers' activities are not normally monitored by either the presence of a co-diver (buddy) or divemaster (see below); and snorkellers are far more likely to come into physical contact with reefs, either through treading water or resting. Indeed, Western Australia's Conservation and Land Management Agency encourages snorkellers to abide by the following simple code of conduct to mimimize their impacts:

- When touch means 'ouch!'.
- Choose sand to stand.
- No need to feed.
- Leave and let live (CALM, 2004b).

Scuba-diving

Scuba-diving as we know it today owes its origins to the pioneering work carried out by Jacques Cousteau in the 1940s. Replacing the highly cumbersome diving suits of the time with tanks of compressed air enabled much greater freedom in the water: 'To swim fishlike, horizontally, was the logical method in a medium eight hundred times denser than air. To halt and hang attached to nothing, no lines or air pipe to the surface was a dream. At night I had often had visions of flying by extending my arms as wings. Now I flew without wings' (Cousteau, 1953, p. 16).

Many might argue that the scale of the scuba-diving industry, with estimates ranging from 5–7 million (PADI, 2005) to as high as 14 million divers worldwide (Viders, 1997, cited in Shackley, 1998), means that it cannot be considered as a true form of ecotourism. Indeed, diving is often an example of what may be considered 'mass ecotourism', since many of the participants are actually on a 3S (sea, sand and sun) format holiday.

However, if we are to treat ecotourism as a method of tourism practice rather than of scale as Weaver (2001) suggests, scuba-diving may be considered one of the original ecotourism practices. Schuster (1992, p.45) contends that ecotourism is neither a new word nor concept in diving, since: 'From the beginning dive travel has been a form of ecotourism since diving involves observing nature.' This contention, however, assumes responsible behaviour, which is by no means automatic.

There has been significant growth in the number of qualified divers over the last 30 years. The world's largest diving organization, the Professional Association of Diving Instructors (PADI) has issued in excess of 13 million certifications since 1967, with 951,470 new certifications in 2004 (576,125 were the basic Open Water Classification) (PADI, 2005). Most of these qualifications were taken in the Americas and the Asian Pacific (see Fig. 4.1), although it is important to note that many of these individuals will take this qualification whilst on holiday, so this does not give a clue to divers' actual residence.

PADI trains about half of divers worldwide, whilst the other major global diving organizations include BSAC, NAUI and SSI. The

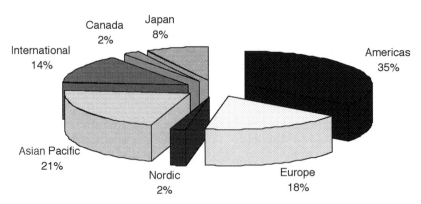

Fig. 4.1. PADI certification worldwide (from PADI, 2005).

Recreational Scuba Training Council of Europe estimates that there are 3.2 million active European divers, and an estimated 825,000 of these tend to travel to their diving destinations whilst on holiday each year, although many will not take a diving holiday every year (RTSC Europe, 1997). According to RTSC, the expenditure from this travel may amount to US$3 billion alone.

Statistics from PADI show that 80% of newly qualified open-water divers have a college education, but this is not to say that they may be more ecologically aware. Instead, it is more likely to illustrate the fact that diving is an expensive hobby, as suggested by Orams (1999). He contends that marine activities are patronized more, relative to land-based activities, by upper socio-economic groups, due to the significant cost of such pursuits. A typical open-water training course might cost up to US$200, and a day diving about US$50, adding considerably to the cost of a holiday (see Chapter 6).

The fact that scuba training is necessary to practise the sport means that, unlike other marine-based activities, it is much easier to educate in terms of sensitive environmental behaviour. One of the most important elements of diver training is that of buoyancy control, meaning that the diver can rest at any point in the dive without either rising or sinking in depth. Whilst ensuring that the divers are able to control themselves underwater, it is also stressed, during the training, that this may minimize contact between the diver and any sensitive marine life. Research suggests that environmental briefings before a dive can substantially reduce contact with coral (Medio *et al.*, 1997).

In addition, all the large dive agencies have environmental education programmes, which are integrated into the dive training: for example, PADI's Project AWARE (Aquatic World Awareness, Responsibility and Education). Sometimes divers may be an early warning of ecological crisis, as they are in a unique position to observe the environment at close hand, and are encouraged to report anything unusual to local environmental protection agencies.

Diving procedures mean that divers always dive in pairs as 'buddies'. This is primarily for safety, but also influences diver behaviour. The advantages when observing a marine environment are clear, as two pairs of eyes working together will find a greater number of interesting things than one pair. In addition, the continual monitoring of another person does reduce the opportunity of damage to marine environments, as buddies may be able to warn each other of unintentional harm that an action might cause to that environment. Examples might include hitting the reef with a fin or oxygen tank, as it is difficult to know how much further both of these extend outside the body space. Author observation also highlights both the buddy-to-buddy disapproval and the individual guilt that such an incident provokes within the diving fraternity.

Scuba-divers tend to follow a path, perhaps similar to Pearce's travel career ladder (Pearce, 1982), whereby an initial desire to see the big stuff is gradually supplanted by a fascination with smaller underwater inhabitants. The most experienced dive instructors are more often than not more excited by the most colourful nudibranch (a small underwater slug) or miniature seahorse than by sharks or turtles (see Fig. 4.2).

In addition, most divers now demand a sensitive environmental operation from the dive companies themselves. With forces from above and below, most successful companies will have sound environmental policies, such as the establishment of shared permanent moorings off a reef between different dive operators. Whilst positive for the environment, this also make business sense, as operators can advertise their eco-credentials, often to significant effect, as well as ensuring the long-term sustainability of the resource.

Fig. 4.2. Nudibranch, Kimbe Bay, Papua New Guinea (photograph courtesy of C. Benjamin).

Despite increased ecological awareness present within the diving community, the careful management of divers is extremely important. Although aware of the fragility of the underwater environment, an underwater holidaymaker still has human curiosity and the desire to make the half-hour experience as worthwhile as possible. Research suggests that underwater photographers have a higher incidence of contact with the substrate, as their concentration is focused on the task of taking pictures. Independent work by both Rouphael and Inglis (2001) on the Great Barrier Reef and Barker and Roberts (2004) in St Lucia suggests a contact incidence for photographers of approximately four times that of divers without cameras. Charismatic wildlife may also be harassed, as in the instance reported at Sharm el Sheik, Egypt, in March 1999 where an estimated 30 divers were chasing one turtle. Clearly, the potential stress caused by such an incident must be avoided wherever possible, but the relative invisibility of such an occurrence to all but the participants makes it difficult to police.

The most obvious method for doing so is to limit the numbers of divers at any one site, but this requires the establishment of thresholds. Dixon *et al.* (1993) showed how diver thresholds have been set for the marine reserve of Bonaire in the Netherlands Antilles. Results from interviews with divers, together with data on coral cover and species diversity, suggest that the threshold stress level for any one dive site at Bonaire is between 4000 and 6000 dives per year. Multiplying by the number of individual sites gives an upper limit of maximum theoretical capacity within the park. This would still, however accommodate unacceptably high visitation levels at the more popular sites, so this upper limit is then halved to give a more realistic threshold. However, each location will have different capacity levels, meaning that these calculations need to be tailored to the individual case, as shown by Hawkins and Roberts (1992).

In addition, Bonaire is fortunate in that it has been a reserve since the early 1980s and there is a historical record of the condition of the reefs. In many of the emerging ecotourism destinations of the less developed countries, there is little scientific record of the marine environment, and marine parks are often being set up well after the diving operations have been in place.

One of the most extreme measures taken in setting thresholds for a dive site is that taken at Palau Sipadan off the eastern coast of Sabah, Malaysia. In early 1998, the Malaysian Ministry of the Environment and Tourism introduced restrictions to the numbers of visitors, many of them divers, allowed on the island. Effective limits were set at 25% of the previous peak daily number (Cochrane, 1998; Musa, 2003). Restrictions have been enforced, ostensibly to reduce the impacts that divers were having on this tiny island's population of turtles and a dwindling supply of fresh groundwater, although some commentators suggest that the radical action may be more related to a territorial dispute over the island between Malaysia and Indonesia. Irrespective of the exact reason, the plan should have important implications for the local marine environment, although the island now has a further degree of exclusivity, with diver operations raising their prices to over 1 thousand US dollars for 5 days' diving.

Some marine parks pay for their management through the use of fees, although this is still a relatively untapped source of potential revenue, as discussed in Chapter 10. Evidence suggests that divers are willing to pay extra levies to ensure the continued preservation of the reef ecosystems that they enjoy. The work carried out by Dixon *et al.* (1993) showed that divers would be willing to pay, on average, US$27.40 for a year's permit in Bonaire, and more than 92% were happy with the existing US$10 charge. Results calculated by Sloan (1987) found that divers to Heron Island would be willing to pay Aus$44 per year.

A willingness-to-pay survey conducted in Zanzibar yielded comparable findings, with 82% of divers prepared to pay US$10 for visitation to an individual marine site (Cater, 1995, unpublished BSc dissertation). Nevertheless these data quite clearly show that divers are willing to part with significant amounts of money to ensure the continued preservation of the reef ecosystems.

It is important to note that the large majority of dive schools are owned and staffed by Western dive instructors. Frequently, this is not a question of ability, but of cost and difficulty of getting the right training. As a dive operator in Zanzibar, who admitted he would like to train local staff, lamented: 'PADI don't produce a training manual in Swahili' (C. Golfetto, Zanzibar, 1995, personal communication). However, whilst not overt, in an activity such as diving where personal risks may be higher, trust is likely to be an issue. Western tourists are likely to feel safer with a Western instructor. Although this picture is changing, it is important when considering the local socio-economic impacts of a dive operation in relation to other ecotourism ventures, as discussed in the community focus of the following chapter.

There are, undeniably, still far too many causes of degradation of marine environments attributable to over-visitation and insensitive behaviour in dive tourism. A further problem is the fact that the vast majority of diving occurs within only 0.025% of the marine environment, that around coral reefs (see Chapter 3). However, it is suggested that scuba-diving is at the forefront of changing attitudes and a more responsible ethos, hopefully with the result that scuba-divers may be proud to call themselves ecotourists.

On the water

Whale watching

Whilst whale watching as a commercial activity began in 1955 along the southern Californian Coast, there were still only around a dozen countries conducting commercial whale-watching activities by the early 1980s. This form of marine observation really took off during the 1990s, so that by 2002, 10 million tourists went whale watching worldwide, generating over US$1 billion in revenue (Mendoza, 2002). It has been estimated that currently 87 countries host whale watching (Hoyt, 2001). Even destinations that are still involved with hunting whales have recognized the tourist value of the animals.

A 'whale route' established in the Lofoten islands in Norway means that different ships hunting the whales for meat and for photography depart from the same ports. In the summer of 2006, this juxtaposition resulted in a boatload of 80 whale-watching tourists witnessing the harpooning of a whale in front of them (Associated Press, 2006).

Locations such as Kaikoura, New Zealand and Puerto Piramides in Argentinian Patagonia registered a 15–20-fold increase in visitation during the 1990s (see Table 4.3). Whale watching has undoubtedly brought an economic turnaround for small coastal settlements, such as for the 90 residents of Puerto Piramides (Orri, 1995) and the 3000-strong town of Kaikoura. Indeed, in 2005/2006, the total number of visitors to Madryn, gateway to Puerto Piramides, was over 100,700 and Whale Watch Kaikoura carried approximately 95,000 whale watchers (P. Gill, Kaikoura, 2007, personal communication; S. Vinas, Puerto Madryn, 2007, personal communication).

Table 4.3. Growth in whale watching in Peurto Piramide, Argentina and Kaikoura, New Zealand, 1987–1998 (from Orri, 1995; Vinas, 1999, personal communication; Whale-Watch, 1999).

Year	Whale-watching visitors (n)	
	Puerto Piramides	Kaikoura[a]
1987	5,214	
1988	10,519	
1989	12,336	3,500[b]
1990	16,524	n/a
1991	17,446	[c]
1992	29,121	25,000
1993	33,772	n/a
1994	44,829	n/a
1995	n/a	n/a
1996	n/a	40,000
1997	72,000	50,000
1998	79,481	60,000

n/a, not available.
[a] Approximate figures only.
[b] Kaikoura Tours.
[c] Whale watch established.

However, it is undeniable that such a rate of growth has brought with it considerable problems of management, and there are reasons for concern in many areas. Duffus and Dearden (1993) describe the scientific uncertainty and institutional inertia surrounding killer whale viewing on the north-east coast of Vancouver Island, Canada.

In the case of Kaikoura, the situation is being closely monitored. The town was badly hit by recession during the 1970s, and post-1984 restructuring resulted in the loss of 170 jobs in the town (McAloon *et al.*, 1998). Commercial whale watching began as a result of a partnership between an American researcher and a local fisherman, which established Naturewatch in 1988. The venture offered a range of whale-watching products from 2-hour trips to 3–10-day packages. In 1989, local Maori began trading as Kaikoura Tours. Whilst the two operators worked well together, Naturewatch sold out to Kaikoura in 1991, and the award-winning Whale Watch was born, which to this day holds the monopoly of sea-borne whale viewing in the area (Horn *et al.*, 1998). The operation has evolved from an initial small-scale operation to large-scale, carrying 60,000 passengers by 1998.

This scale of operation has brought undoubted economic benefits for Kaikoura. A recent survey found that a one-quarter of respondents worked either full- or part-time in tourism, and that 80.6% of respondents felt the 'community as a whole' benefitted from tourism (Horn *et al.*, 1998). Furthermore, through a range of tourist developments in Kaikoura, including Whale Watch, local Maori moved from a position of a relatively powerless, low socio-economic status to become a major employer and economic force in the community (Horn *et al.*, 1998). It has been estimated that 70% of Maori in Kaikoura have been involved in tourism (Simmons and Fairweather, 1998).

The level of visitation, however, inevitably raises the question of environmental change, but whale watching at Kaikoura is regulated and closely monitored by the New Zealand Department of Conservation (DoC). They use the precautionary principle of not issuing any further whale-watching permits at Kaikoura, and Whale Watch are also not allowed to increase the number of trips per day that they operate. Four other operations, however, offer scenic flights to view whales and dolphins along the Kaikoura coast. A strong regulatory framework is in place, as all marine mammals around New Zealand are fully protected under the Marine Mammals Protection Act 1978, amended in 1990 to introduce regulations specifically for the control and management of marine mammal watching.

These regulations were reviewed in 1992 when the Royal New Zealand Navy provided technical advice on the impact of noise on whales and dolphins. As a result, a minimum set of conditions were established: (i) boats are required to approach a whale from a direction parallel to, and slightly to the rear of, the whale; (ii) no more than three (including airborne) vessels are allowed within 300 m of a whale at any one time; and (iii) sea vessels are required to travel at a 'no wake' speed inside this distance. A minimum approach distance of 50 m has also been set, and vessels are required to keep out of the path of any whale (Baxter and Donoghue, 1995).

Whale watching at Kaikoura is not wholly without problems, however. Residents recognize the negative impacts that tourism brings, the most commonly cited being pressure on existing infrastructure including water, sewage disposal and car parking space (Horn *et al.*, 1998). The extent to which tourism can remain under local control as it grows has also been brought into question. Some feel that outside investment is inevitable but this, in turn, implies outside control. It is essential to maintain local ownership and management of key facilities and retain local control in decision making (Horn *et al.*, 1998; Simmons and Fairweather 1998).

In terms of impact on the whales themselves, the cumulative impacts of this burgeoning activity have, perhaps, yet to be realized. DoC recognize that many questions remain unanswered about the long-term effects of marine mammal watching. Driven solely by conservational objectives, and not required to balance commercial development against the protection of marine mammals, the department is likely to continue to err on the side of caution. It is not difficult to perceive a state of economic vulnerability on behalf of the resident population.

The influence of legislation on marine ecotourism is discussed in detail in Chapter 9, but is demonstrated in the example of whale watching in Queensland, Australia. In this state, the settlement of Hervey Bay has traded on a reputation as a humpback whale playground since the mid-1980s, now hosting over 75,000 whale watchers a year (Hervey Bay City Council, 2005). There are strict controls over the numbers of permits issued by Queensland Parks and Wildlife Service (QPWS), limited to 20 within the Hervey Bay area and three in Moreton Bay, with none from Moreton Bay south to the border with New South Wales.

Despite these controls, it is possible to see whales all the way up the east coast during their annual migration, a fact utilized by many New South Wales operators. However, as described in the Great Barrier Reef example in the previous chapter, state waters extend only 3 miles offshore. In 2005, boat operators on the Gold Coast realized that there were no restrictions to whale watching, as long as it was conducted outside of the state zone in Commonwealth waters, leading to the sudden emergence of this activity in Australia's foremost beach resort destination (the Gold Coast receives over 4 million visitors a year). Despite high court challenges, state bodies were powerless to stop the new operators, and by 2006 there were three successful whale-watching companies operating.

Although these involve a somewhat unusual trek out to sea (with whales often sighted, but passed in the exclusion zone), this has developed a new product for the destination. Whether this muscling in on Hervey Bay's position will erode its reputation still remains to be

Fig. 4.3. Whale watching, Hervey Bay, Australia (photograph courtesy of C. Cater).

seen, but it does emphasize the political influence on ecotourism activity. As Hall reiterates: 'Planning is not rational. It is highly political. The goal of sustainability is not a given. It is a contested concept that we need to be arguing for' (Hall, 2000b, p. 205).

Feeding of marine wildlife

A wide variety of commercial activities may engage in feeding of marine wildlife to encourage higher levels of tourist satisfaction. Often marine species have been fed, in defiance of codes of conduct, in order to maximize the chances that tourists will see an animal. As discussed below, tourist submarines are often accompanied by divers who 'chum' the water to achieve higher levels of fishes. The use of feeding to facilitate interactions with marine life occurs also in cases such as the Cod Hole, located in the northern Great Barrier Reef, where the feeding of giant potato cod and moray eels by divers became popular after the site was discovered by recreational scuba-divers in 1972 (Davis *et al.*, 1997). Material covered in the PADI Underwater Naturalist course encourages divers to bring their own feed so that existing wildlife is not harmed and to frequently change site so that animal behaviour is not adversely affected.

Determining whether feeding initiates behavioural change is often difficult because of the lack of baseline studies in many popular locations. Some of the difficulties of this 'catching-up' are highlighted by Shackley (1998) in her discussion of the world-famous Stingray City in the Cayman Islands. At present there are no controls over the high visitation levels to this site where divers may hand feed stingrays, as the area is outside present marine reserves. There are few data, beyond those observed at the site, on how the feeding may have influenced the natural behaviour of the stingrays. Nevertheless, the high visitor numbers, estimated at 80,000–100,000 per year to this one location, are likely to have a major impact on the local ecosystem. Shackley states that: 'At any one time up to 25 boats can be anchored at Stingray City, each with up to 30 people in the water ... it is not unusual to see 300–500 people in the water at any one time' (Shackley, 1998, p. 334).

DOLPHINS   Tourist feeding of dolphins has developed as an activity in Monkey Mia in Western Australia and Tangalooma on Moreton Island in Queensland (see Fig. 4.4). The former has a longer history, spanning over 30 years, but has become a popular tourist attraction, with over 100,000 visitors per year (Davis *et al.*, 1997), and CALM has recently introduced a webcam for people to watch the feeding over the Internet.

Dolphin feeding at Tangalooma originated from a particularly sociable individual that began accepting hand-held fish from fishermen in 1992. The dolphins visiting the provisioning programme come predominantly

Fig. 4.4. Feeding the dolphins at Tangalooma, Moreton Island, Australia (photograph courtesy of C. Cater).

from a pod of about 12 dolphins, with the occasional casual visitor. As there are estimated to be over 300 dolphins in Moreton Bay, they make up a very small proportion of the wild population. In comparison to Monkey Mia, the dolphins spend only a limited time at the beach (less than 1 h daily, one feeding session only per day, with provisioning time restricted to 20–30 min), are fed only at night, there is no touching, and no swimming with the dolphins is permitted (Neil and Brieze, 1996).

There have been concerns over the health of dolphins as a result of such programmes. Wilson (1994, cited in Neil and Brieze, 1996) identified high infant mortality, low juvenile (post-weaning) survival and changes in behaviour resulting from the provisioning of wild dolphins at Monkey Mia. Orams (1995) examined similar behavioural changes at Tangalooma, particularly the incidence of aggressive behaviour by dolphins towards humans. His findings contributed to better management of the dolphin-feeding programme at Tangalooma, so that the process is now tightly controlled. Participants are given an extensive briefing that includes the following measures:

- How to conduct themselves around the dolphins.
- What to expect of the dolphins.
- The need to disinfect their hands prior to the provisioning (disinfectant is provided for the purpose).
- A prohibition on provisioning the dolphins if the participants are suffering from colds or flu.
- Prohibition on insect repellants and suntan lotions.
- Prohibition on smoking in the provisioning area.
- The need to remove any sharp hand jewellery, etc., to avoid any injury to the dolphins.
- Prohibition on touching, stroking or patting the dolphins.
- The reasons for the short duration of their time in the water (Neil and Brieze, 1996).

Undeniably, Tangalooma is assisted in regulating this activity by the fact that it is an island resort, and therefore can impose much stricter controls on the feeding regime. It has been suggested that there are significant educational benefits to be gained out of such programmes if they are properly managed. Orams (1999) suggests that the educational briefings and visitor centre at Tangalooma encouraged tourists to change their behaviour and become more environmentally responsible. Notably, when the author visited the programme in 2005, the experience was also being used as a vehicle to encourage petition signatures against the resumption of commercial whaling.

SHARKS   Feeding of sharks to encourage sightings has generated a great deal of debate in recent years. Experiences are available with either significant protection (cages or chain mail suits (see Fig. 4.5)) or no protection, where only guides wear protective equipment and safety is based on behavioural understanding.

George Burgess, the curator of the International Shark Attack File, which catalogues worldwide shark attacks, is deeply sceptical of shark-feeding operations:

> My reservations about feeding-type dives are based on four interrelated factors: the safety of the divers; the likelihood for negative publicity directed at sharks if a shark bites a diver during one of these dives; the possibility for ecological disruption; and potential negative impact on multi-user recreational use of the feeding area.
>
> (Burgess, 1998, p. 1)

Growing evidence that the fears outlined by Burgess were being realized, including over a dozen injuries in the Bahamas, prompted Florida, Hawaii and the Cayman islands to outlaw shark feeding in 2001–2002. Despite this, a self-styled shark 'expert', Erich Ritter, suffered a serious leg injury in the Bahamas in April 2002 (CDNN, 2002), where the activity is still available, as it is in southern Fiji at Beqa Lagoon. Western Fiji's most famous shark feeding at the 'shark super-market', near Mana Island, became a major attraction in 1989 when a local spearfishing chief, Apisai Bati, began tours based on behavioural understanding, even hugging the sharks as a display of his mastery over the animal.

Despite running for 15 years there were concerns with the tour, and divers not on the feeding trip reported unusual shark behaviour whilst on normal dives, with the shy animals coming closer than would normally be seen (Blue Oceans, 2005). Increased concerns from clients following the unrelated death of Bati in 2000, and the subsequent

Fig. 4.5. Shark cage, Kaikoura, New Zealand (photograph courtesy of C. Cater).

handover of the feeding to his son, Aku, forced a reassessment of the practice. Notably Aku maintains that it was environmentally aware American and Japanese visitors who were most perturbed by the feeding (A. Bati, Aqua Trek, Mana Island, 2007, personal communication).

Thus, in 2004, the feeding was suspended, and the dive began to be marketed as a 'shark encounter' as opposed to shark feeding. Whilst visiting the site in 2007, the author observed significant numbers of sharks still present on the reef, and less timid than would be normally the case, so it may be that the behavioural impacts of feeding will continue to have some legacy.

The opportunity to view the notorious but elusive great white has spawned a significant industry in South Africa. This was initially started at Gansbaii on the Western Cape in 1990, spreading to Mossel Bay in 1993 and, most recently, to False Bay in 1996. There are an estimated ten operators serving some 4000 divers annually, and estimates indicate that activities related to cage diving contribute about 5 million Rand (US$885,000) to the local economy (Kroese, 1998).

Concerns with the cowboy nature of the industry, which was confirmed by the authors' visit in 1999, led to the establishment of a permit system and a code of conduct. The code of conduct makes recommendations on the level of technical training operators need, equipment standards in terms of cages, and safety gear. The specific chum types, quantities allowable per day (no more than 25 kg), bait presentation and shark handling are also outlined (South African Collaborative White Shark Research Programme, 2005).

However, there is growing evidence that the practice is significantly altering the behaviour of the sharks. In late 2004, one of the operators was bitten on the foot and in March 2005 a British tourist narrowly escaped an aggressive shark that caused serious damage to the cage which was supposed to protect him. The welfare of the sharks, which are a protected species in South Africa, is clearly of limited concern as 'The captain had a big metal pole and was hitting it on the head and trying to push it off, but it was just making it worse' (BBC News, 2005a). It is likely that, following a fatal attack on a skin diver in June 2005 (CDNN, 2005), there will be renewed calls for the industry to be discontinued. Similar tours continue in Australia and New Zealand.

Sea kayaking

Sea kayaking is potentially the most environmentally benign of all marine tourism as, providing waste is taken back, it is non-polluting: 'A canoe across water leaves no trace' (SeaCanoe, 1999). The self-powered nature and good manoeuvrability of these craft means that they are less intrusive to wildlife: birds and animals tend to be curious rather than frightened (N. Johnson, North Uist, UK, 1999, personal communication). As the infrastructural demands are low, it also offers the potential for much greater local input and consequent benefits. Manufacturers have produced a wide range of lightweight but durable products, ranging from moulded, sit-on single-seaters to double sit-in touring models. As a result, kayaking has seen huge growth worldwide; for example, *Sea Kayak* magazine, which has been in print since 1984, lists over 200 sea kayaking organizations in 22 countries, from Greenland to Japan (2005).

The situation facing an operation that has achieved a degree of notoriety in ecotourism circles is the case of SeaCanoe in Thailand. The company won a number of awards for its low environmental impact/ high local benefits cave kayaking experiences in South-east Asia. SeaCanoe began its kayaking operations in the tidal sea caves of Phang Nga Bay, Thailand, in 1989. The caves are home to significant tropical wildlife, including swiftlets that make nests prized for delicacies like birds' nest soup (Shepherd, 2003).

John Gray, the founder of SeaCanoe, recognized the unique nature of the caves and began exclusive inflatable kayaking operations to visit them. Following a stringent environmental code, the company limited the number of kayaks on any one trip, and attempted to involve the local population in the operation. Local people were trained to staff, and eventually own, the local operations (SeaCanoe Thailand is now majority owned by local people and employs over 50 staff). It is estimated that 90% of SeaCanoe's budgets stay in the host communities and their human resources programme provides full benefits to all employees, including training and education (SeaCanoe, 1999).

In Thailand, however, the very success of SeaCanoe in an unregulated scenario inevitably spawned less scrupulous imitators, of which there were 11 by 1998. Cave visitation grew to four-figure levels per day, with dozens of kayaks waiting in line to beat the tide. Inevitably, the caves have become degraded by these high-volume, environmentally unaware entries (Gray, 1998a, b). The mass tourism business system prevalent in Phuket, with holiday 'reps' often booking tours through companies providing the highest commissions, also eroded SeaCanoe's position relative to its competitors (Shepherd, 2003).

In 1998, SeaCanoe's problems intensified, as the monopoly that had the right to harvest the birds nests forged an alliance with a group of operators to charge for every tourist entry to the caves. SeaCanoe refused to pay the charge on the basis that the bay was a national park, which allegedly led to the non-fatal shooting of one of the company's managers in late 1998. Gray eventually set up his own operation, John Gray's SeaCanoe, in 2001. Shepherd suggests that: 'Despite central government rhetoric, in developing nations, understanding principles of environmentally sensitive tourism at a local level is very hard to get across, especially in the light of potential business opportunities' (Shepherd, 2003, p. 145). It is important to recognize that in this lax regulatory scenario, conscientious operators such as SeaCanoe may find their efforts constantly thwarted by the unsustainable activities of other 'nature' tour operators whose businesses may be ecologically based, but far from ecologically sound.

In Abel Tasman National Park on the South Island of New Zealand, the activity has gained enormous popularity to the extent that in the summer months almost as many people visit the park by kayak as they do on foot (see Fig. 4.6). As much of the natural beauty of the park is based on the water, kayaking is an ideal way to experience it. Commercial operations commenced in the late 1980s, and grew to over five operators by the mid-1990s. As has happened in other areas of the tourism industry in New Zealand, Maori business concerns have been instrumental in acquiring controlling stakes in many of these operations. In 2003, Wakatu Incorporation, made up of four local Iwi, bought the two largest, oldest sea kayaking companies in Marahau, Ocean River Kayaks and Abel Tasman Kayaks.

Annual visitor numbers to the park are around 200,000, with 30,000 staying overnight at campsites or huts in the park in the year ending June 2004 (DoC, 2005a). Research suggested that, in 1998–1999, there were over 18,000 kayak visits per year (DoC, 2005b). In peak season there are about 2000 people entering the southern part of the park per day. Of those, about 500 walk in, but 1500 use boat access, which would include kayaks, as many kayaks are rented one way or 'bussed in'. A survey conducted by Cessford (1998) suggested that kayak use in 1994 was at 'high normal' levels, as 60% of the visitors surveyed felt a degree of crowding. It is suggested that these levels may now be much higher, as

Fig. 4.6. Kayaking, Abel Tasman National Park, New Zealand (photograph courtesy of C. Cater).

the global reputation of the park has increased and the activity has become the 'must do' way to experience it.

A positive development out of the popularity of sea kayaking in New Zealand has been the formation of a voluntary industry organization called SKOANZ, in 1992. At that time, the industry was seeing significant growth and there were as yet no guidelines or conventions in place that would establish minimum standards of operation (SKOANZ, 1993). The principal objectives of the organization were to promote both 'the interests of sea kayak operators within a framework of the highest possible standards of safety, environmental care and social responsibility' and 'the development of sea kayaking skills and standards within the industry' (SKOANZ, 2005). The former objective has evolved into a comprehensive (17-page!) code of practice covering operational, safety and environmental requirements, whilst a structured guide certification programme represents the latter.

Boats and cruising

Increased interest in the marine environment and access to boating opportunities is responsible for putting many more people on the water. Although much boating is undertaken in a recreational context, it is a significant user of the marine environment, particularly for fishing (see below). There is potential for introducing significant changes to ecosystem function as a result of impacts of small boats; in particular, there have been concerns as to the impact of anti-fouling paints. A recent study by Warnken *et al.* (2004) demonstrates significantly higher copper concentrations at popular anchorage sites for recreational boats in South East Queensland.

Lück (2003c) documents the switch in Western societies of large ships from a means of transport to a form of tourism in, and of, itself in the 1960s. Although clearly not ecotourism, cruise ships visit many popular ecotourism destinations, such as the Great Barrier Reef. However, Douglas and Douglas (2004) detail how cruise ship companies use their economic power to bully small island communities into providing staged experiences, with limited flow back into the host population. Although there is a trend towards bigger and better-equipped vessels, simultaneously there has been significant recent growth in boutique or 'expedition' cruises that are able to access more remote locations in a more intimate setting.

In north-west Australia, such vessels have become popular for exploring the Kimberly region, promising the 'adventure experience of a lifetime' (Coral Princess Cruises, 2005). Some boats can take on a more explicit ecotourism focus. A number of tallship ventures have emerged in recent years, including South Coast Eco-Adventure Voyages in Western Australia and the (sadly unsuccessful) Earthship in the Grenadine Islands, Caribbean.

Underwater observation

Underwater observatories

Technological change has facilitated relatively passive means of viewing the diversity of marine life below the surface. The Milford Sound Underwater Observatory in Harrison Cove in Milford Sound, New Zealand, was opened in December 1995. The north side of Milford Sound, where the observatory is located, was gazetted as a marine reserve, with World Heritage status, in 1993. The observatory consists of a cylindrical, 450 t viewing chamber that is completely submerged beneath a main reception area. Comprehensive environmental impact assessments were conducted between 1987 and 1995 prior to permission from the various authorities being granted to the facility.

The whole ethos behind the observatory is one of educating the visitor about the complex ecology of the fjord environment. An interpretation centre in the reception area is complemented by clear species keys above each viewing window and visitors receive a talk from a marine scientist. As the observatory is in a marine reserve it complies with the strict environmental regulations laid down in that designation. In the first 3 years of its operation, the observatory received between 41,000 and 55,500 visitors per year (Hamilton, 1999, Milford Sound, New Zealand, personal communication). Owned by a group of South Island business people and managed by Milford Sound Red Boats, the observatory is accessible only by boat.

Glass-bottomed boats and submarines

Underwater viewing of marine life is also possible from glass-bottomed boats or from larger vessels with specially constructed underwater viewing galleries. The Kyle of Lochalsh (Scotland)-based 'Seaprobe Atlantis', Britain's first such craft, began operations in July 1998. It took up to 24 passengers at a time on a variety of excursions ranging from short, 35-min trips to see seals and kelp forests to extended tours at certain times of the year to view dolphins. Two thousand passengers were carried in the few summer months of operation in 1998 but, prior to the 1999 season, the craft was chartered for a special exercise in community education by the Loch Maddy Marine Special Area of Conservation (SAC), North Uist, Scotland (N. Smith, Kyle of Lochalsh, Scotland, 1999, personal communication).

The management scheme for the SAC is being developed by the local community and government agencies, and special legislation gives locals the opportunity to influence how the status can benefit them in terms of opportunities to develop business ventures such as ecotourism. As part of this programme of involvement, 281 local residents were taken on half-hour trips in March 1999 to view the underwater ecology of this sea loch (A. Rodger, North Uist, 1999, personal communication).

However, the degree of local interest was initially disappointingly low, illustrated by a lack of participation of local schools in the Kyle area (N. Smith, Kyle of Lochalsh, 1999, personal communication). The importance of such raising of awareness is highlighted by Nigel Smith, the proprietor of Seaprobe Atlantis, who reports that, while local interest is slowly improving, with most of the local primary schools and schools on Skye now having been carried, there is still an entrenched belief that 'There is nothing to see down there' (N. Smith, Kyle of Lochalsh, 2006, personal communication).

In 2005, the original Seaprobe Atlantis was replaced by a larger craft accommodating 55 passengers on 1 h trips to view seals, seabirds, the occasional otter and the magnificent kelp forests of Loch Alsh, which also now has SAC designation. The increasing popularity of such excursions with visiting tourists is revealed by the fact that there are now around 15,000 participants annually (see Fig. 4.7).

Underwater observation from semi-submersibles, such as Le Nessee in Mauritius, or from tourist submarines, is also rapidly growing (see Table 4.4). Tourist submarines have been operating since the mid-1980s and today there are over 50 operations worldwide. Most examples carry approximately 50 passengers and crew and can reach depths of up to

Fig. 4.7. Glass-bottomed boat tour, Kyle of Lochalsh, Scotland, UK (photograph reproduced with permission of Seaprobe Atlantis).

Table 4.4. Tourist submarines operating worldwide (from US Submarines, 2005).

Tourist submarines: historical operating locations and vehicle count			
Location	Number	Location	Number
Switzerland	1	Aruba	1
Grand Cayman	5	Sint Maarten	1
Bahamas	2	Spain	3
Barbados	1	Florida	1
Rota	1	Indonesia	1
St Thomas	1	France	2
St Croix	1	Monaco	1
Saipan	1	Taiwan	1
Canary Islands	2	Malta	1
Hawaii	7	Martinique	1
Bermuda	1	Mexico	1
South Korea	1	Italy	2
Guam	1	Columbia	1
Japan	1	Fiji	1
Okinawa	1	Scotland	1
Egypt	1	Brazil	1
Israel	1	Refit/retired	7

100 m. As the average price of a dive is between US$65 and 85, underwater sorties are accessible to an increasing number of tourists (Newbery, 1997).

One of the largest operators, Atlantis Submarines International, has submarines in Grand Cayman, Barbados, St Thomas, Aruba, Guam, Cozumel and on the Hawaiian Islands of Kona, Maui and Oahu. They have taken over 7 million passengers on undersea adventures since 1985. In 2004, the organization employed approximately 450 people, operating 11 tourist submarines at 13 locations around the world, taking over 750,000 people on undersea tours (Atlantis Submarines, 2005). There are also submarines in Lanzarote, Tenerife, Saipan, Bali and Phuket, many of which originated in Finnish shipyards.

The Thai submarine was originally based for 13 years at Eilat on the Red Sea, but has been replaced by a semi-submersible, which indicates that there is probably a marketing trade-off between vessels that are true submarines – and the extra technological costs involved in operating them – and semi-submersibles. The Eilat product is also based at an aquarium, which underlines the importance of these facilities being used as a springboard for other marine ecotourism activities (see below).

The environmental impact of these vessels is likely to be quite variable. Some operators claim that their low speed whilst underwater minimizes impacts on wildlife, although the presence of such vehicles, many of which weigh over 100 t, is hardly likely to go unnoticed. Some have diesel engines, but many are entirely non-polluting, with battery-powered electric thrusters that emit no effluent. They also arguably promote environmental stewardship: observing and appreciating marine life in its natural setting will motivate an increasing number of people to protect the marine environment (Newbery, 1997).

However, the practice of underwater feeding to attract fish ('chumming') by scuba-divers swimming alongside the *Atlantis*, Lanzarote and Larnaca (see Fig. 2.3) tourist submarines undoubtedly impacts on the marine ecology. Operators at Eilat, however, are proud that their vessel operates within a reserve, which consequently has no feeding or fishing. Nevertheless, the very considerable capital costs of entry (a minimum of US$4.5 million for a tourist submarine), coupled with stringent maintenance and safety requirements, put this form of entrepreneurship way beyond the realms of truly local involvement.

At the extreme end of submarine experiences is that offered by Deep Ocean Expeditions, a company founded in 1998, who own and charter research submarines for tourism purposes. They offer a range of trips to significant shipwrecks, such as *Titanic* and *Bismarck*, and the deep-sea hydrothermal vents in the mid-Atlantic ridge. In a similar marriage to early Antarctic expeditions, the tourists are normally part of a broader scientific expedition, as the trips normally include a number of research scientists seeking to undertake investigations at the operating sites. The company feels this is of benefit because: 'In addition to doing their research work, these experts also offer the expedition participants a rich resource for teaching and lecturing about the places being visited. Many of expeditions also have scientists, filmmakers and adventurers all working alongside to record the action as it happens' (DOE, 2005).

Indeed, the two main submersibles used, which are technically owned and operated by the Russian Academy of Sciences, were also used in a number of projects for Hollywood director James Cameron. These vehicles can operate up to a depth of 6000 m, and are two of only five that can venture lower than 3000 m. The company espouses a strong environmental ethic, as stated on their website:

> The founding principles of Deep Ocean Expeditions are simple: offer unique expedition experiences for the adventurer; educate lay people about the world's deep oceans, help support scientific research and to offer remote location support logistics. In addition, the company is deeply concerned with marine conservation observing the best and highest standards for its operations. Nothing is disturbed, touched or removed. The only things taken away are photographs and memories.
>
> (DOE, 2005)

A typical Deep Ocean Expedition trip would last for two weeks on a support vessel and include one deep dive during that time, which may last up to 10 h. The submersible carries one pilot and two passengers. Clearly, this is a very exclusive market, with a trip to *Titanic* in 2005 costing US$36,650. Tourists are encouraged to see themselves as explorers and scientists (see Chapter 6), and are advised to take 'a notebook and pen to record your observations, and a small tape recorder to record your impressions' (DOE, 2005), as well as the obligatory video and camera equipment. Marine life is rare at the depths involved, but forms a highlight of the trip, including swordfish, hammerheads, squid, nautilus, lantern fish, siphonophores and deep-sea fangfish.

Longer periods in the marine environment may be facilitated by current and planned underwater facilities. Jules Undersea Lodge, which uses the shell of an ex-research laboratory, operates in Key Largo, Florida, USA (see Fig. 4.8). Whilst accommodating only two couples, the facility provides for a unique experience. Qualified scuba-divers enter the hotel through a pressurized wet room in the base of the structure, and can take meals prepared by a 'mer-chef' who dives down to serve them (Jules Undersea Lodge, 2005). A Hilton resort in the Maldives opened a 14-seater underwater restaurant in 2005 (see Fig. 4.9).

The manipulated nature of these environments is shown by the fact that here, resort management is intending to 'plant a coral garden on the reef to add to the spectacular views of the rays, sharks and many colourful fish that live around the reef near the restaurant' (*E turbo News*, 2005). Future developments may take this format to a whole new level, as luxury underwater hotels are being planned for Dubai and the Bahamas. The latter will have a planned 220 suites, all sitting on the Persian Gulf floor 20 m below the surface (Hydropolis Hotel, 2005).

These developments could potentially have major impacts in their local ecosystems, as 'There will be controls in each room that guests can use to adjust the lighting of the underwater worlds outside their windows and to release food for fish swimming just outside' (Poseidon Resorts,

Fig. 4.8. Jules Undersea Lodge, Key Largo, Florida, USA (photograph reproduced with permission of Jules Undersea Lodge).

Fig. 4.9. Hilton Ithaa underwater restaurant, Maldives (photograph reproduced with permission of Hilton).

2005). Historically, tourist hotels in the marine environment have not been very successful: a floating hotel on the Great Barrier reef that was completed with a thorough impact assessment in 1988 lasted only 18 months before it was removed for financial reasons (Harriott, 2002).

By the water

Intertidal walking

A number of tourist authorities worldwide have developed walking trails in the intertidal environment, and these are also included as part of many commercial marine tours. Whilst some of these locations are resilient enough to withstand large numbers of tourists, other sites – particularly coral reefs– are clearly susceptible to major damage. Early studies on the impacts of reef walking on the Great Barrier Reef demonstrated a major reduction in coral cover as a result of this activity (Woodland and Hooper, 1977; Kay and Liddle, 1984). The Great Barrier Reef Marine Park Authority stipulates the following guidelines for reef walking:

- Be careful not to step on coral or living matter.
- Follow marked trails and avoid straying.
- If there is no marked trail, locate regularly used routes or follow sand channels.
- Use a pole or a stick for balance; take care not to poke animals.

- Learn about the reef environment and what to look for before reef walking.
- Observe animals rather than handle them. Handling some animals may be dangerous.
- If you pick up anything, living or dead, always return it to the exact position where you found it.
- Do not pick up animals or plants that are attached to the reef flats (GBRMPA, 2005).

Ancillary activities

Fishing

Although not perhaps thought of as an ecotourism activity, the heritage and position of recreational fishing in the marine environment means that to ignore this activity would be very short-sighted. Many recreational fishermen have a high appreciation of the natural system, and are often advocates for maintaining environmental quality. Holland *et al.* (1998) make a convincing case for considering Atlantic billfish (marlin and sailfish) operators who practise catch-and-release as fulfilling the pragmatic criteria of ecotourism, as discussed in Chapter 1, this volume.

Recreational fishing can certainly have significant adverse impacts in marine environments, however, if it is poorly managed. For example, recent research in the Ningaloo Marine Park by Westera (2003) showed evidence of trophic cascades that are likely to have resulted from the removal of 'top-end' predators targeted by recreational fishermen. This finding reinforces other national and international studies, which demonstrate the ecological implications of removing 'top-end' predatory fish on the surrounding ecosystem.

Initiatives in the Cairns, Australia, charter boat industry documented by Gartside (2001) attempt to reduce these impacts. Here, catch-and-release techniques and support for enhancing angler awareness of environmental issues and responsibilities are setting new standards that other sectors of the industry may find valuable. An effective move has been in the provision of trophies for anglers who catch and release large game fish, which in the past would have been landed.

Surfing

Another activity that is on the fringes of what may be termed ecotourism although may be very strongly aligned philosophically – is that of surfing. Surfing is a global activity, with estimates of over 10 million surfers worldwide, and potentially constituting a US$10 billion industry (Buckley, 2002a). Although often thought of as a sport, surfing involves 'purposive interaction of the participant with the natural environment ...

where the outcome of the activity rather than the competition, is of prime importance' (Fluker, 2003, p. 6).

Thus surfers are clearly nature-based users of the marine environment, seeking high-quality natural experiences in pristine environments. Indeed, one of the biggest issues in surfing is that of crowding, as the activity tends to funnel participants to the 'best' waves, which can normally only be ridden by one surfer at a time. The environmental impact of their activity should be minimal, and many surfers are allied to environmental groups such as 'Surfers against Sewage'.

However, the natural focus of the activity does challenge its positioning as ecotourism. 'In particular, it is almost completely tied to highly specific features of the natural landscape; it is largely disjunct from the cultures of host communities' (Buckley 2002a, p. 405). Additionally, the presence of large numbers of surf-tourists in fragile environments does pose significant environmental challenges. In particular, on 'small reef islands, growth in tourism carries risks to drinking water and subsistence fisheries' (Buckley 2002b, p. 425). These risks are easily overcome, but only if appropriate waste and sewage management technologies are installed.

The importance of these tourists in 'opening up' many tourist destinations to ecotourism and even mass tourism has been highlighted by Dolnicar and Fluker (2003). Coastal destinations 'such as Bali, the Mentawai Islands, Fiji, the Maldives, Tahiti and South Africa' (Dolnicar and Fluker, 2003, p. 186) are just some of the locations that have based much of their initial tourist development on surfing. Although major tourist destinations, the islands of Oahu and Maui in Hawaii, and the coastline around Rio in Brazil, also rely on surfing as a significant economic generator of visitors (Buckley, 2002a).

The Mentawai islands off western Indonesia are 'currently flavour of the month amongst cash-rich, time-poor surfing tourists who are willing to pay a premium to surfing tourism operators to surf high quality waves in the absence of large numbers of their sporting peers' (Ponting, 2001). A significant surf-tourism industry of over 30 live-aboard charter boats has developed in the region, which may be approaching maximum capacity without resulting in downmarket competition forces, as has happened at other surfing destinations such as Bali (Buckley, 2002b). A variety of management options have been suggested for the chain, including allocation of rights to particular breaks to specific operators, development of syndicates and a regulatory authority (Buckley, 2002b; Ponting, 2001).

The development of small-scale, shore-based resorts may encourage the development of tourism to the islands that is less dependent on the surf-tourism industry and take some of the pressure off the increasingly crowded breaks. This would also encourage broader community benefits, which at present are rather limited, although an NGO – Surf Aid International – has improved healthcare opportunities in the region (Ponting, 2001).

Marine aquaria

An activity that is unlikely to be thought of as part of ecotourism, but which is vital to consider alongside our discussion, is that of visiting marine aquaria. These are undeniably mass tourism facilities and are big business for their operators. For example, Busch Entertainment Corporation, operator of the three US Sea World attractions, recorded over 20 million visitors and an operating profit of US$163 million in 2003 (Anheuser-Busch, 2005). However, as a tool for raising awareness of the marine environment, and potentially acting as a motivator for other activities listed in this chapter, their importance cannot be underrated.

For example, Planet SOS, a '4D' 45-min presentation that highlights the plight of rainforest and polar and marine environments is shown several times a day at Sea World in Australia. The film, which was funded by the World Wide Fund for Nature (WWF), was originally made for a Dutch theme park and combines entertainment with a strong environmental message. This is a controversial area, for education is often used as an excuse to keep large marine animals such as orcas in captivity, whilst opponents point out that it is more about entertainment (see Chapter 7). Certainly, marine parks are likely to portray animals in a performative and anthropomorphic sense, with 'trainers riding, kissing, hugging, patting and flying off the heads of orcas' (Williams, 2001, p. 50). At least 134 orcas have been taken into captivity from the wild since 1961, and 106 have died, many prematurely.

A great deal of negative publicity surrounded the treatment of sharks in captivity prior to the opening of the 'Shark Bay' exhibit at Sea World in Australia in 2004. One previously injured shark was humanely euthanased and two sharks were released, as an RSPCA inspector deemed the holding tanks too small.

Despite this, many marine parks do contribute actively towards conservation; indeed, the Australian Sea World Research and Rescue Foundation has funded a total of 55 research projects into marine life. They are also involved in a significant number of marine mammal rescues resulting from beaching or netting each year. The importance of captive breeding programmes for endangered populations should also be recognized.

The educational potential may also be larger than is recognized by the parks themselves. In an awareness study undertaken at a marine park in Canada by Jiang (2004, unpublished report), respondents indicated that 'to learn about the natural history of the marine wildlife on display', 'educational opportunities' and 'information on conserving the natural environment' were much more important reasons to visit than factors such as 'petting dolphins or whales', 'feeding dolphins or whales' and 'facilities of the aquarium or marine park'. A recent development has been the growth of more interactive experiences with the marine creatures of the facilities, which may relieve pressure on wild populations (see case study, below).

Case Study: Animal Adventures

In recent years, some marine aquaria have recognized that visitors desire an experience that goes beyond the visual and entertainment encounters that categorize the majority of their offerings. In a survey carried out by Saltzer at Sea World Australia in 2001, the most commonly suggested improvement was to increase the level of animal–human interaction, prompting the introduction of a number of programmes under the banner 'Animal Adventures' that allow just such an experience (see Fig. 4.10).

Opportunities to swim and interact with dolphins, seals and even sharks have become immensely popular since their introduction, with over ten different programmes now on offer. Such programmes are highly structured and, as such, the welfare of the animals engaged in the experience is closely monitored. However, these interactions open up a whole new realm of performance management for these organizations, coordinating a range of actors from tourists, wildlife trainers and the animals themselves.

Participants in these experiences surveyed by the author in 2004 indicated a strong wildlife orientation, as over 85% responded that viewing wildlife was an important factor in their choice of destination. Therefore, such tourists are heavily nature based, even if they may not be classified as pure 'ecotourists'. The importance of 'getting closer' was slightly complicated, as although over 50% identified this as a major

Fig. 4.10. Animal Adventures at Sea World, Australia (photograph courtesy of C. Cater).

reason for participating in the experience, only 7% wanted to touch the animal. Despite this, after the experience, > 50% said that contact had been a definite highlight.

The educative aspect of the experience is clearly strong, as, when asked if they could list a new fact about their chosen animal, only 16% of participants were unable to do so. The majority listed facts related to the animals' anatomy, life cycle and behaviour. Although a minority, it is significant that > 40% felt that their attitudes to the animal had changed as a result of the experience. One of the researchers felt that, in particular: 'Those engaged in the dolphin activity seemed to learn more from the experience and were highly talkative' relative to other programmes.

A Marine Smorgasbord

It would seem clear from the diverse inventory of pursuits detailed in this chapter, which is by no means exhaustive, that there is a vast array of ways through which to experience the marine environment. Indeed, we have shown how a number of marine-based tourism activities not considered ecotourism in a 'traditional' sense are vital to the understanding of our interactions with the ocean realm. As described in Chapter 2, not only do these often compete for the same resources, but they form a portfolio of activities for the tourist that are largely indistinguishable from one another in terms of motivations or experiences, a point explored in more detail in Chapter 6.

As a result, we cannot afford to ignore this diversity if we hope to achieve sustainable outcomes. An important part of this process is an appreciation of how activities can interface with, and build on, existing community resources, which is where we now turn.

II Primary Stakeholders and Interests

5 Coastal Communities

Coastal Communities as Key Primary Stakeholders

The focal event of the UN-designated International Year of Ecotourism 2002 was the World Ecotourism Summit held in Quebec, Canada. Conceivably, the most significant recommendation outlined in the Quebec Declaration on Ecotourism emerging from this summit (UNEP/WTO, 2002, p. 3.) is the need for participative planning mechanisms that 'allow local and indigenous communities, in a transparent way, to define and regulate the use of their areas at a local level, *including the right to opt out of tourism development*' (authors' italics).

Clearly, there is a moral obligation to involve the local population in the projects that affect them, but there are other, powerful, reasons for recognizing coastal communities as key, primary, stakeholders in marine ecotourism; as Miller and Auyong (1991, p. 78) put it: 'Traditional small-scale maritime and coastal communities merit special consideration on most coastal management agendas.'

Borrini-Feyerabend (1996) distinguishes among stakeholders in the management of protected areas according to the following criteria. While marine ecotourism is not confined to protected areas, coastal communities are likely to display many – if not all – of these characteristics, which therefore vindicate their central, vital role in its planning and management:

- Existing rights to land or natural resources.
- Continuity of relationship as opposed to other stakeholders (for example, residents versus tourists).
- Unique knowledge and skills for the management of the resources at stake.
- Losses and damage incurred in the management processes.
- Historical and cultural relations with the resources.
- Degree of economic and social reliance on the resources.
- Degree of effort and interest in management.
- Equity in the access to the resources and the distribution of benefits of their use.
- The compatibility of the interests and activities of the stakeholder with government conservation and development policies.
- Present or potential impact of the activities of the stakeholder on the sustainability of the resources base.

So, in the same way that Bramwell *et al.* (1996) widened the net of sustainable development beyond the classic 'trinity' of economic, social and environmental criteria, to embrace cultural, political, managerial and governmental dimensions, we also need to recognize the multi-dimensionality of the involvement of coastal communities as stakeholders in marine ecotourism.

Coastal livelihoods

When it is considered that approximately one-half of the world's population, 3 billion people, live within 200 km of the sea, a figure that is set to double by 2025 (UNESCO, 2001a; Creel, 2003); that over 1 billion people, most of whom live in the developing countries, depend on fish as their main source of animal protein; and that there are around 400 million fishers and fish farmers across the globe (95% of them in developing countries), the significance of coastal and marine areas to local populations worldwide can be appreciated.

It is obvious that, not only will coastal populations have a strong vested interest in access to marine resources (although their economic and social reliance on these will vary), but also their activities will impact on the coasts and seas. In turn, they must be considered as key stakeholders in marine ecotourism not only because of its implications for sustainable coastal livelihoods but also because their activities have a strong bearing on the state of coastal and marine resources. Furthermore, Borrini-Feyerabend's (1996) criterion, outlined above, of continuity of relationship with marine resources vis-à-vis other stakeholders is clearly met.

It is suggested that the islanders of Ono, Kadavu Province, Fiji, were more amenable to the concept of a no-take zone in the establishment of a marine protected area because the proposed community-based management system reflected their customary ownership rights. Amongst their options was the return to the *tabu ni qoliqoli*, the traditional practice of reserving a traditional fishing ground in order to increase the fish population for a traditional ceremony (WWF, undated).

Sustainable coastal livelihoods

The Sustainable Livelihoods Approach (SLA) offers a useful integrative framework for examining the impacts of tourism, both positive and negative, on people's assets (Ashley, 2000). Although the SLA was developed during the 1990s as a new approach to poverty reduction (Carney, 1999) – indeed, it has been central to the focus on the emphasis on 'pro-poor tourism' in recent years (Ashley *et al.*, 2001), and most of the examples used in this chapter are drawn from the developing countries – it will be seen that it facilitates a systematic appraisal of the various ways in which tourism in general, and marine ecotourism in particular, impacts on coastal livelihoods.

The approach is people-centred, designed to be participatory and has an emphasis on sustainability. Also, as Cahn (2002, p. 3) suggests, it 'is positive in that it first identifies what people have rather than focusing on what people do not have. The SL approach recognizes diverse livelihood strategies, it can be multi-level, household, community, regional or national, and can be dynamic.'

At the heart of the SLA lies an analysis of five types of asset upon which people draw to build their livelihoods (Sustaining Livelihoods in Southern Africa, 2002). These are: (i) natural capital (the natural resources stocks upon which people draw for livelihoods); (ii) human capital (the skills, knowledge, ability to labour and good health important to be able to pursue different livelihood strategies); (iii) physical capital (the basic enabling infrastructure such as transport, shelter, water, energy and communications); (iv) financial capital (the financial resources available to people such as savings, credit, remittances or pensions, which provide them with different livelihood options); and (v) social capital (the social resources such as networks, membership of groups, relationships of trust upon which people draw in pursuit of their livelihoods).

It has been suggested, however, that to this classic pentagon should be added cultural capital, which can be defined as the cultural resources (heritage, customs, traditions) that are very much a feature of local livelihoods (Glavovic *et al.*, 2002; Sustaining Livelihoods in Southern Africa, 2002). Following Ashley (2000), who examines the positive and negative impacts of tourism in Namibia on livelihood assets, and adding in cultural capital, let us examine specifically how marine ecotourism affects people's access to these different assets.

Natural capital

Marine ecotourism, as a competing use, will directly affect coastal people's access to marine resources as well as indirectly affecting the way that marine resources are managed. As Ashley (2000) points out, resource competition takes many forms. A major concern is that occurring when residents may lose access to key resources when areas are designated for tourism/conservation. Such an example in marine ecotourism is the designation of no-take areas for fishing in marine protected areas. This move has been resented and resisted by fisherfolk, dependent on fishing for sustenance, livelihoods and recreation, in many locations around the world.

Emerton and Tessema (2001) describe how the opportunity costs of fishing activities foregone through the designation of the Kisite Marine National Park and Mpunguti National Reserve in Kenya (some US$172,000) overshadow the estimated US$39,000 in local benefits accrued in 1998. The banning of all commercial and recreational fishing boats from one-third of the Great Barrier Reef (up from only 4.5%) in 2004 was heavily criticized by the fishing industry, which declared that hundreds of jobs would be lost (CNN, 2003). Similarly, the call by New Zealand's Conservation Minister for 10% of coastal waters to be designated as marine reserves, in which fishing would be banned, was countered by the fishing industry, which declared that New Zealand's EEZ was already protected by the Fisheries Act, with its focus on sustainability and restriction on catches (Thomas, 2002).

The Galapagos Islands are probably the most graphic example of the conflict between conservationists, marine ecotourists and fishermen (Buckley, 2003a). In the year 2000, islanders took giant tortoises hostage in protest against the designation of a marine reserve 40 miles offshore, restricting their lucrative catch of sharks and sea cucumbers. Shark fins fetch as much as UK£66/kg in Asia, while Galapagan fishermen, who could sell as many as 2000 sea cucumbers at UK60p apiece, were 'doing as well as a dope dealer selling cocaine on the mainland' (McCosker, cited in Bellos, 2000). As the Galapagos Islands received 90,500 tourists in 2003 (Galapagos Conservation Trust, 2005b), to appreciate the marine and island ecology of this world-renowned destination, the environmental damage as well as the adverse publicity being generated by the fishermen was of considerable concern.

An example of the resolution of these types of conflict is that of the island of St Lucia, Caribbean, where fishermen complained of severe declines in their catches as a result of the designation of no-take zones within the Soufrière Marine Management Area. As a result, they were compensated the equivalent of US$150 per month for 1 year, and part of one reserve was reopened for pot fishing. The year's compensation allowed for a period of adjustment while fishermen became more knowledgeable about the benefits of the reserves (*MPA News*, 2002).

Another example of conflict over marine resources is that tourist divers may cause damage to fishing equipment. At Apo island in the Philippines, local fishers reported damage to fishing traps, also claiming that fish had been driven away from fishing grounds (Raymundo, 2002). There may also be conflicts over access to natural resources between marine tourism and ecotourism operators. Chapters 2 and 4 describe the situation in Thailand when eco-opportunists imitated the highly successful operations of SeaCanoe (Gray, 1998a, b).

Young (1999) looks at the competition between whale-watching operators in two small fishing communities in Baja California, Mexico. She examines whether the economic benefits of recreational whale watching reduce resource conflicts and promote stewardship of marine resources. On the surface, it makes a significant contribution to local livelihoods, contributing as much as 50% of individual household income. However, Young identifies two major problems. The first is that outside tourism companies, who organize the activity and also often use outside whale skiff drivers, are the main beneficiaries, with as little as 1.2% of revenues accruing locally. The second is that she comes to the conclusion that many of the same problems of managing common-pool resources encountered in fishing are emerging in marine ecotourism. Even with the organization of a local tourism cooperative in one of the villages there is the problem of inequitable distribution of benefits.

One of her respondents declared: 'The president of the cooperative is managing it as if he were the owner. [People who rent out their privileges as whale-skiff drivers to others] should give those privileges away to other families who really need the money ...' (Young, 1999,

p. 604). Young also describes how tensions flared during the 1994 season, when a new group of 31 aspiring skiff guides challenged the capacity of the cooperative to manage local whale-watching activities.

In terms of indirectly affecting the way that natural resources are managed, when community-based tourism is developed within the broader framework of Community Based Coastal Resource Management (CBCRM), then it can give the necessary impetus to, and strengthen, the process as the benefits are realized. In the case of Olango Island in the Philippines, described in more detail below, the benefits to the community from the Olango Birds and Seascape Tour Project have meant that local fishermen are dissuaded from destructive fishing practices.

Human capital

Marine ecotourism can enhance human capital in a number of ways. Through education and training programmes, new knowledge and skills gained by employees or committee members can be transferred to other activities. Young (1999) describes how, in Puerto Adolfo Lopez Mateos, Mexico, general awareness of the ecological significance of coastal wetlands was raised. A course was also created to teach local guides how to enhance passenger safety and minimize gray whale disturbance.

The Toledo Institute for Development and the Environment (TIDE), a grassroots, community-based organization in the south of Belize, ran an environmental educational programme to raise the community's awareness of the need to preserve and protect marine life, in particular the habitat of the endangered manatee. As a result of intensive lobbying by the community, with TIDE's help, the no-take Port Honduras Marine Reserve was designated in January 2000. By mid-2001, TIDE had trained 50 former fishers and hunters to serve as tourism brokers in flyfishing, kayaking, scuba-diving, snorkelling and other activities (*MPA News*, 2001).

In Zanzibar, the Chumbe Island Coral Park project, which is discussed more fully in Chapter 10, runs an environmental education programme for secondary school pupils, students, government employees and other interested guests. Since 1998, the project has informed around 2000 pupils and 160 teachers about the biodiversity of the island and the coral reef during free day trips.

Health is another important aspect of human capital, as it has a marked effect on labour availability and efficiency (Potter *et al.*, 2004). As described in Chapter 10, the initial community-run Marine Management Committee at Apo Island allocated a proportion of the revenue from visitor fees to a monthly health clinic. When the Protected Area Management Board (PAMB) took over in 1994 this ceased, but the proposal was that part of PAMB income should be allocated to a health team. Recommendations have also been made on the treatment of wastewater, with seasonal contamination being monitored on a monthly basis (Raymundo, 2002).

The question of inequitable distribution of the impacts of marine tourism also arises in the case of human capital. Stonich *et al.* (1995) used a political ecology approach to examine the relationships between tourism development, water and environmental health in the Bay Islands, Honduras. They concluded that the adverse effects of tourism development were not distributed evenly, with the islands' impoverished ladino immigrants and poor Afro-Antillean residents being the most vulnerable to environmental health risks emanating from those activities.

Physical capital

Marine ecotourism may act as a catalyst, providing the incentive for the improvement of infrastructure that will benefit not only the tourists but also the local population, in the issues of electricity, safe water supply and improved roads. On the island of Manono, Western Samoa, homestay visitation by American elderhostelers prompted the construction of wharves on the shore as it was too difficult for older people to wade and climb the rocks. Flush toilets and showers, a new concept to the families concerned, were also necessary in the households visited.

There is the clear danger, however, that enhancing one livelihood asset – in this case increased access to physical capital – may mean a concomitant erosion of another. In the case of Manono, there would have been the problem of the reduction of financial assets should the islanders have had to provide and finance improved sanitation. This was circumvented by public works providing a design complete with a septic tank built by the families themselves. The necessary appliances were financed by a revolving fund from Australia (Ala'ilima and Ala'ilima, 2002). A further consideration is that, however low-key and small-scale the marine ecotourism development, the question of access frequently means that physical capital is enhanced at the cost of natural capital. De Haas (2002) describes the situation of small-scale ecotourism on the island state of Niue in the South Pacific, where concrete tracks – which clearly detracted from Niue's natural resources – were built across the island to allow for easy access to coastal areas.

Financial capital

It is important to recognize that coastal communities in the developing countries undertake a variety of income-generating activities, in particular fishing, and that marine ecotourism must take its place alongside them, viewed as a complement or a supplement, not as an alternative. There are many examples across the world of where marine ecotourism has proved a valuable supplement to the financial assets of coastal livelihoods, in particular where marine ecotourism has occurred within a CBCRM programme.

One of the most successful CBCRM projects is that of the award-winning Olango Birds and Seascape Tour (OBST) Project in the Philippines. Faced with severely depleted fish stocks (the average daily fish catch having dropped from around 20 kg per fisher in 1960 to less than 2 kg by 2000), Olango fishermen turned to cyanide fishing to supply the aquarium trade as a source of income (oneocean, 1999). The women stayed at home to make shellcraft, but their income was minimal and their livelihood threatened by an over-saturated market and a dwindling supply of shells. OBST, owned and operated by the Suba, the Olango Ecotourism Cooperative, was initiated in 1998 with the help of the Philippine Coastal Resource Management Programme.

The villagers provide tours, such as canoeing through an island seascape, snorkelling and diving in a protected marine sanctuary, visiting seaweed farms, interacting with the community and guided birdwatching in the Olango Island Wildlife Sanctuary (a RAMSAR site of international significance because of its high biodiversity and critical feeding and roosting site for tens of thousands of shorebirds).

The men, who are mainly involved in paddling the day visitors and guiding, formed a Paddlers' Group. They set and implemented guidelines for accrediting, orienting, assigning and monitoring paddlers for each tour. The roles of the women's group include cooking, purchasing, physical arrangements, cookery and shellcraft demonstration and bookkeeping. The villagers, as owner-manager-operators of this venture, and therefore economic beneficiaries of the project (community service fees, product sales and profit margins account for 20–50% of the tour price), consequently appreciate the value of the Coastal Resource Management Project (Flores, undated).

Whereas a wide section of the community benefits in Suba, there are examples of where attempts to develop community tourism have either exacerbated or caused conflicts. It is naïve to think that all in the community will benefit equally. Coastal communities are highly heterogeneous, their members sharply differentiated by demographic and socio-economic characteristics. Borrini-Feyerabend's (1996) criterion of equity in access to the resources and the distribution of their benefits outlined above may remain an unattainable ideal, with elite capture of the benefits from marine ecotourism being a frequent phenomenon. Indeed, it has been argued that ecotourism may even exacerbate, or even create, divisions. Entus (2002) describes how:

> Many projects which have set out to be community-based ... have, at some point or another in their evolutionary cycles, engendered or exacerbated pre-existing internal divisions of power, and led to the formation of new business elites who represent but a small fraction of the 'local community', so that they end up catering primarily to those interests rather than those of the community at large, leaving the latter to pay the costs of development without also sharing worthwhile benefits.

This concern illustrates a manifest power differential not only between the different stakeholders but also within the local community itself; it is far from a homogeneous construct and, as Burkey (1993) argues, there is a need to demystify the harmony model of community life. Community members are differentiated by ethnicity, class, gender and age.

In terms of ethnicity, we need to recognize that, while members of the coastal community may be local residents they may be 'outsiders', either in the sense that they are economic migrants or that they are outside investors. In both instances, qualities are imported that 'do not and cannot stem from the group itself' (Taylor, 1995, p. 488). Stonich *et al.* (1995) describe how, in the Bay Islands, Honduras, desperately poor ladinos (Spanish speakers) from the mainland seeking a better life migrated to the islands, where the rapid growth of tourism had brought increased prosperity. These migrants helped escalate the local population to the level at which the islands' fresh water supply, food and land resources became jeopardized. At Sandy Bay, they lived in a 'shabby ghetto of small wooden structures built on stilts, above a lagoon filled with human waste and other garbage' (Stonich *et al.*, 1995, p. 22).

A similar situation occurred at Ambergris Caye, off the coast of Belize, where the rapid construction of hotels and condominiums in the late 1980s and early 1990s caused low-paid and unemployed migrants (again predominantly Spanish speaking) to move to San Pedro from the mainland of Belize and the rest of Central America in search of employment. Adequate accommodation and infrastructure were not available, and so generally substandard housing was built on infilled mangrove swampland (McMinn and Cater, 1998).

In both cases, the indigenous islanders were better placed to take advantage of new economic opportunities provided by the growth of the tourist industry, even if the poorest received only marginally better benefits. Shah and Gupta (2000) distinguish between poor, unskilled migrants seeking employment in tourism and outside entrepreneurs with better access to skills and capital than the locals. With respect to these outside entrepreneurs, Place (1991) describes how the rapid increase of visitors to view the nesting sites of the green turtle at Tortuguero, Costa Rica, actually had the net effect of reducing the opportunity for villagers to be involved in the business other than as menial employees. The pace of outside investment, in particular from the capital, San José, was too fast to permit villagers to accumulate sufficient capital to invest in the construction of tourist facilities.

A different slant on ethnicity is provided by the example of Kaikoura, New Zealand, as discussed in the previous chapter. Through a range of tourist developments in Kaikoura, including the award-winning Whale Watch, local Maori moved from a position of relative powerlessness and low economic status to become a major employer and economic force in the community. However, the monopolistic nature of Whale Watch operations has been criticised as being unfair. Maori use their position as Maori to defend their monopoly which, unfortunately, adds a political and racial dimension to this strategy, whereby any criticism of this position is construed as racist (Horn *et al.*, 1998).

Often closely allied to the question of ethnicity is that of social class. There is, unfortunately, no substantiation with hard facts to guarantee the claim that ecotourism generally contributes to a more equitable distribution of tourism income and a reduction in poverty. At both Tortuguero, Costa Rica (Place, 1991) and in the Bay Islands, Honduras (Stonich *et al.*, 1995), those members of the community who did benefit from tourism were those who started out wealthier than most and who could, therefore, take advantage of emerging opportunities because they had sufficient income to invest in tourist-related enterprises. In both these examples the divisions have, as Entus suggests, consequently been exacerbated.

Not only are there marked divisions between those in the community with privileged status and the poor but, even amongst the poor, lines of division are sharply drawn according to access to resources, markets and employment, whether formal or informal. In the case of coastal fisheries in the developing countries, for example, the situation may be similar to that described by Ellis and Allison (2004) for the African lakes and wetlands, where wealthier households own assets related to fishing (boats, nets, traps), as well as coastal land and businesses, and may have control over the best fishing areas. Middle-income households often own land, but have not generated sufficient capital to own substantial fishing-related assets, although they may share these. Lower-income households may have access to land for subsistence cropping but have access to fishing opportunities only as crew labourers on boats owned by others. It is obvious, therefore, that similar groups in coastal areas will be differentially placed with regard to the impact of marine ecotourism on their livelihoods.

There are also clear divisions within communities attributable to gender. Flintan (2003) describes how the collection of natural resources is gender differentiated. While fisheries tend to be male dominated, women are becoming increasingly involved in the processing of natural resources as opportunities are opened for diversification of livelihoods. Off the east coast of Unguja, Zanzibar, for example, the overwhelming majority of seaweed farmers are women (Pettersson-Löfquist, 1995). While the men may benefit from both supplying fish and by acting as guides and boatmen for tourists, the women face a scenario of conflicting use: seaweed cultivation is not the most visually aesthetic resource use (see Fig. 5.1). Flintan (2003) suggests that, in integrated conservation and development projects, already existing gender inequalities may be increased as a number of opportunities have been opened up for men but not for women.

One of the ways in which marginalized sections of the community – including the elderly and disabled – can share in the capture of ecotourism revenue is through the sale of tourist merchandise. Healy (1994) summarizes the advantages of home- and village-based handicraft production under five headings: (i) compatibility with rural activities; (ii) economic benefits (particularly a more equitable distribution); (iii) product development; (iv) sustainability; and (v) tourist education.

Fig. 5.1. Seaweed farming in Zanzibar, Tanzania (photograph courtesy of E. Cater).

However, careful thought needs to go into the choice of product. In commenting that soap production by women at Olango has a limited domestic market that might be enlarged to the tourist market if packaging included information on the bird sanctuary, Schuler *et al.* (1998) highlight the failure of a basket-weaving project at a coastal village in Indonesia. Here, women perceived basket-weaving as a high-labour cost, low-value work that would not raise their living standards in the long term and, as a consequence, all the nipa trees in the village were cut down.

Sometimes, the choice of product and source of material might not be the most obvious. At the Kiunga Marine National Reserve Conservation and Development Project in Kenya, women are engaged in 'eco-friendly' handicraft production. Old flip-flops washed up on the shore are crafted into keyrings, necklaces, bracelets, cushions, mosaic pictures and other innovative items. The income from this handicraft production is seen as a welcome source of supplemental income but, importantly, it is not viewed as an alternative or replacement (Flintan, 2002).

In addition to direct, indirect and induced earnings from employment related to marine ecotourism, the financial assets of local livelihoods may be enhanced through allocation of user fees (as discussed in Chapter 10, this volume), as well as through donor funding for projects that include a marine ecotourism component. In Vietnam, the Global Environment Facility and DANIDA (Denmark) are funding an MPA pilot project of Hon Mun in Nha Trang City, which includes marine ecotourism as an alternative income-generation activity. The project will assist each village in establishing a micro-credit loan facility in the form of a community development fund, which is to be managed by the village women's union (Lan, undated). On the occasion of the International Year of Microcredit 2005, The World Tourism Organization (WTO) advocated micro-credit as a source for both venture capital and operating costs for tourism micro-, small and medium-sized enterprises (SMEs) (Yunis, 2004).

However, Flintan (2002) cautions that, while the social capital of women as a target group in particular may be enhanced through increased self-esteem and pride, there are problems with micro-credit. She suggests the following outcomes: the poorest of the poor are likely to miss out; banking principles and their application are often impractical and alien to many people; economic impacts are often not very positive; and livelihood integration and conservation of resources must be linked to the savings and credit scheme.

Social capital

As Ashley (2000) suggests, some of the strongest and most positive impacts of tourism on social capital have occurred when tourism is developed by communities within the Community Based Natural Resource Management (CBNRM) programme. In the case of marine ecotourism, there are many instances where it has been developed within Community Based Coastal Resource Management (CBCRM). Several examples are given in this chapter, but the reader is referred to Chapter 10, where CBCRM is discussed in greater depth as a management strategy.

Social capital, when seen alongside natural, human, physical and financial capital, may seem a simple concept, but it is, as Glavovic *et al.* (2002) suggest, critical to the way in which many societies manage natural resources. Indeed, lack of social cohesion may prejudice sustainable outcomes. Myers (2002) attributes the shortcomings of the Jozani-Chwaka Bay Conservation Area (JCBCA) in Zanzibar to economic, political and educational differences in the community.

Amongst the aspects of social capital examined by Glavovic *et al.* (2002) is the case of communal 'ownership' of natural resources that 'requires particular understandings and protocols concerning when and how such resources can be used and by whom' (Glavovic *et al.*, 2002, p. 5). In particular, as far as marine ecotourism is concerned, an appreciation of the issues of open access and common-pool resources are essential, as described in Chapter 1. Young (1999) examines the case of grey whale-watching in Baja California, Mexico, where marine ecotourism involves the use of common-pool resources.

Glavovic *et al.* (2002) also point out that understandings of social capital should focus not only on horizontal societal linkages, but also recognize vertical linkages with individual groups having different levels of power and resources: strong regional or national organizations could help communities defend their rights. Hall (2000a) suggests that such collaboration, various forms of which are examined in Chapter 11, has the potential to contribute to the development of more sustainable forms of tourism in that it creates social capital.

However, it is important to recognize that, while community-based tourism planning may enable communities to communicate their priorities to outside influences in this way, it may indirectly disrupt the relations of power within the community, bringing changes in the social organization that are too rapid for supporting institutions to arise. The net effect then may be that 'outside' institutions are imposed and begin to undermine existing knowledge structures (Wearing and McDonald, 2002).

Cultural capital

Glavovic *et al.*'s (2002) exploration of the role of social capital in sustainable livelihoods leads them on to consider the wider role of culture. They argue that cultural practices help to preserve and build social capital, citing Bebbington's claim that they 'enable, inspire and indeed empower', by fostering identity and particular patterns of interaction (Glavovic *et al.*, 2002, p. 6). They make a strong argument for the consideration of cultural capital within the livelihoods framework, suggesting that 'preserving the culturally familiar and strengthening cultural diversity … should rank alongside the preservation of biodiversity and increasing incomes as a goal of sustainable livelihood strategies' (Glavovic *et al.*, 2002, p. 6).

It is important to consider cultural diversity, as there is a need to appreciate that each culture articulates and deploys a particular view of nature and how it ought to be used. In the majority of cases of marine ecotourism across the globe, it may be argued that we are faced with a situation where the dominant, Western-centric, environmental imagination has given rise to what Vivanco (2002) calls ecotourism's 'universalistic and self-serving vision'. The danger of this ethnocentric bias is that it ignores the fact that there are 'multiple natures' constructed variously by different societies, as also discussed in Chapters 2 and 7. It fails to recognize, or downplays, the fundamentally divergent values and interests between the promoters and targets of marine ecotourism.

The dominant ideology behind ecotourism of conservation-for-development may, quite often, not resonate with other, non-Western, societies. As a North American indigenous person declared: 'That is not necessarily consistent with our traditional view of guardianship and protection' (Taylor, cited in Vivanco, 2002, p. 26). Wearing and McDonald (2002, p. 199) describe how:

The concept of conservation originates from a western world that is indeed very different from village life, and as such it represents a new time – new ways of thinking about the environment – that is foreign to the communities. The concept implicitly suggests that the environment should be thought of in terms of scarcity, or threats to scarcity; this being an understanding of the environment which is foreign to communities who have traditionally lived in an ecologically sustainable manner.

They go on to cite Flannery's observation that western notions of conservation often appear to be completely nonsensical to the local people in Papua New Guinea, where 'The Melanesian world-view incorporates humans and animals, the seen and unseen, the living and the dead, in a way that is vastly different from the European outlook'. Alternative views, arising from a 'generally holistic (or cosmovision view) of nature held by indigenous peoples' (Colchester, cited in Mowforth and Munt, 2003, p. 154), mean that not only will there be a fundamental difference between how nature tourism – and hence ecotourism – is constructed in different societies, but also that indigenous communities may have a real problem with the effective commodification of marine nature through marine ecotourism.

Also, with the burgeoning domestic and regional tourism in developing and transitional economies, it is increasingly evident that nature tourism is variously constructed by different societies and, therefore, that there are multiple 'nature tourisms'. Thus, it can be seen that the construction of nature by different ethnicities may result in markedly divergent tastes and demands that do not conform to Western views of ecotourism. While, as Weaver (2002) suggests, the extent to which Asian markets will be influenced by Western models of ecotourism participation is unknown, he argues for peculiarly 'Asian' models of ecotourism that, for cultural reasons, deviate from the conventional Western-centric constructs.

One of the very few examples worldwide of attempting to introduce an expressedly non-Western system of environmental protection into a threatened conservation area is the Misali Ethics Pilot Project of the Misali Island Conservation Programme, Zanzibar, Tanzania. The Misali fishing grounds support more than 10,000 people and, additionally, its reef wall is a renowned scuba-diving location. In the light of the fact that mainstream environmental education was having little or no impact on the illegal fishing practices of local fishermen – which were causing irreparable damage to the marine environment – the Islamic Foundation for Ecology and Environmental Sciences is laying down the foundation of Islamic environmental practice in Misali.

Appropriate institutions are being established, based on the holistic *Sharia* code of living, which stresses that, in Islam, there is no separation from any one aspect of creation and the rest of the natural order (Khalid, 2004). The aim is also to produce an educational guide book to popularize the Islamic approach to environmental protection amongst Muslims, as well as to inform the international community of the breadth of the Islamic contribution to human welfare (IFEES, 2003).

Two examples of alternative marine tourism development from Samoa also show how tourism development that is sympathetic to traditional cultural practices holds more appeal to local communities. Scheyvens (2002) describes how the enormous growth of budget beach *fale* accommodation, owned by local people, reflects the fact that around 81% of land is held in customary tenure. She suggests that this type of low-key tourism is more likely to respect the traditional way of life, or *faaSamoa*, of Samoan people by taking a more cautious approach to tourism development. On Manono island, western Samoa, the conducting of monthly visits of North American Elderhostel groups since 1994, according to the traditional So'o (village exchange) format, has also been more in tune with local cultural practices (Ala'ilma and Ala'ilima, 2002). The North American Elderhostel company provides not-for-profit educational trips for senior citizens

An associated problem with Western-envisaged ecotourism is that of the inevitable commodification of nature and culture whereby a financial value is attached to natural and cultural resources. As Hinch (2001, p. 347) suggests, indigenous people have a much deeper connection with the land than non-indigenous people and, consequently, 'because they do not treat land as a possession, they are very wary of treating it as a commodity, even in the purportedly benign context of ecotourism'.

The same argument can be applied to marine resources. The knock-on effect is that, once a financial value has been attached in this way, should ecotourism fail, the expectations that are thus raised might push local populations into other, less sustainable, livelihood options. This again indicates the importance of recognizing that, where ecotourism is being pursued as a strategy for development, it should take its place alongside a range of livelihood options for the community, rather than superseding these other activities (Scheyvens, 2002, p. 242).

Heritage, customs and traditions can also be viewed as vitally important resources for marine ecotourism. While it can be argued that certain, charismatic, species – such as the whale sharks of Ningaloo, Australia or right whales of Hermanus, South Africa – have a unique 'pulling power', many of the resources for marine ecotourism – such as coral reefs, kelp forests or seal grounds – are replicated at multiple locations across the globe. Cultural resources are therefore vitally important in marine ecotourism as they differentiate the marine ecotourism product, as well as emphasize the inextricability of natural resources and cultural practices.

Three types of cultural resource may be distinguished: (i) artefacts, including built heritage, visual and performing arts, crafts, literary traditions and lifestyle; (ii) knowledge and skills; and (iii) beliefs and values (Mani, undated). Arguably, these are under-capitalized in the majority of marine ecotourism locations across the globe, but in several locations they not only offer a fascinating insight into traditional livelihoods but also serve to reinforce and maintain cultural identity, engendering a sense of pride and thus empowering and facilitating the preservation and building of social capital, as argued above.

The Maori war canoe at Waitangi, New Zealand, the Chinese fishing nets at Cochin, India (see Fig. 5.2.) and the fish-drying racks of the Lofoten Islands, Norway, are all examples of artefacts that signify varied local cultures and impart a sense of uniqueness to their locations.

While the art of scrimshaw carving (carved or etched items traditionally made from whales' teeth, whalebone or walrus tusks, but now using more sustainable sources such as antlers or fossilized walrus tusks) was a traditional leisure pastime of whalers, with examples found from locations as far flung as Patagonia and Tasmania, it is likely that it owes its origins to Inuit carvings made to show their respect to the Inua spirits who were believed to be the owners of nature (Lundberg, undated).

The roles of literature and the cinema are examined in Chapter 7 but, apart from certain exceptions such as the snake boat races in Kerala, India, it could be argued that the performing arts are an especially neglected dimension of cultural capital in marine ecotourism interpretation. We have only to think, for example, of how few are aware of the fact that different sea shanties were sung at different posts onboard ship to fit the rhythm of the physical exertion required to turn capstans, haul sails, lanyards, etc.

The incorporation of indigenous knowledge in marine ecotourism is vitally important. Not only can it present an alternative approach to environmental management, often constituting a more holistic overview, but also it can constitute an important resource for marine ecotourism.

Fig. 5.2. Chinese fishing nets, Cochin, India (photograph courtesy of E. Cater).

Barker and Ross (2003, p. 290) call for the need 'to move beyond economic and species-specific dominated strategies towards ecosystem and adaptive management strategies to include indigenous knowledge'.

One of the cases in an ongoing UNESCO project on indigenous people and protected areas involves working with the Moken sea nomads of the Andaman Sea, Thailand. The traditional ethnobotanical knowledge of the Moken regarding plants as a source of sustenance and for medical use is being incorporated into existing information researched and documented by the Surin Islands National Park Authority. Activities include the setting up of an exhibition hut and distribution of publications, including material for elementary school children (UNESCO, 2001b).

There are examples of marine ecotourism locations that successfully convey the significance of cultural capital at interpretive centres and with the use of guides. The significance of coastal and marine areas to aboriginal people has been recognized in Australia, where indigenous people in Western Australia, the Northern Territory and Queensland identify cultural sites offshore. Such sites are known up to 80 km off the coast in the Northern Territory. Many groups of indigenous people identify with the coastal and marine environments, calling themselves, for example, 'salt water people' or 'white sand beach people' (DEH, 1993).

At Couran Cove in Queensland, the visitor is introduced to aboriginal myths and legends, as well as to traditional practices such as the use of dolphins to herd sea mullet. In pre-colonial times, aboriginal elders would call dolphins by hitting their spears on the surf, requesting their assistance. Dolphins would then guide the mullet into the net and were rewarded with the best of the fish (Barker and Ross, 2003). Couran Cove's Alcheringa, or Dream Time trail, introduces the visitor to traditional aboriginal use of coastal resources, such as the multiple uses of the mangrove.

The Norwegian Fishing Village at Å, Lofoten Islands, Norway, not only disseminates an understanding of the coastal culture by way of exhibitions, demonstrations, active participation, the sale of culturally 'correct' souvenirs and various events, but also has a declared aim 'to work in close collaboration with the local community to work towards achieving the sustainable management of our cultural and natural resources – in order to help preserve our way of life and identity' (lofoten-info, undated).

In the UK, the Comann na Mara (Society of the Sea) at Lochmaddy, North Uist, Scotland, carries out marine science research for fishermen, fish farmers and other sea users. Central to its objective of fostering sustainable development of the marine environment by encouraging its sensitive stewardship is that not only should its proposed marine interpretation centre constitute a visitor attraction but, more fundamentally, it should act as a 'drop-in' local resource centre for fishermen as well as providing a catalytic role for visiting students and marine scientists. Two interpretation panels about Lochmaddy Bay, partly in Gaelic, are already in place (J. Mcleod, North Uist, 2002, 2005, personal communications).

Conclusions

While this chapter has shown how marine ecotourism may enhance the various assets (or capital) that are combined to constitute coastal livelihoods, it has also drawn attention to how it may detract from these in various ways. It is undeniable that the root cause of this detraction is the structural inequalities at play, when we consider the overall context in which marine ecotourism is cast as a process. Church and Coles (2006) highlight how relationships of power have been relatively neglected in tourism research in general.

We have seen above how communities are divided by ethnicity, class, gender and age, and how both the benefits and costs of marine ecotourism are respectively skewed towards the haves and have-nots. The danger is that the situation will be self-perpetuating because of the relationships of power that both reflect and reinforce this scenario.

As Jamal and Getz (2000) suggest, it is not only a case of stakeholders in the community having a variety of needs and desires, but also having differing abilities to influence the agenda and scope of investigations. They voice a concern that the interests of 'other', less affluent, less visible segments of the community might not be adequately considered, or indeed that they are even kept informed about the process. They argue that 'Greater effort needs to be directed towards bringing the marginalised voices of hybridised cultures from in-between spaces into the public sphere of community-based collaborations for destination planning and management' (Jamal and Getz, 2000, p. 179).

Quite clearly, there is a question of empowerment and capacity raising: goals that are not achieved overnight. In our oft-quoted example of Apo island in the Philippines, the Marine Conservation and Development Program was formally implemented in 1984 following 5 years of preliminary activities. One of the lessons learned from Apo was that community-based coastal resource management is a long and never-ending undertaking (Calumpong, 2000) requiring sustained commitment. This finding is echoed by Hoctor's observations of West Clare's marine ecotourism project in Ireland. Utilizing the typology of participation outlined by Pretty (1995), she suggests that there was a need to move beyond the consultative to the self-mobilization level to ensure the long-term sustainability of the project. This she recognizes as being a long-term process requiring the sustained commitment of all the actors involved (Hoctor, 2003).

As well as the question of empowerment, however, there is the consideration of actual representation. As Jamal and Getz (2000, p. 176) put it: 'Participatory democracy is both a matter of *right* and *capacity* to participate.' Barker and Ross (2003, p. 290) urge that a move needs to be made beyond viewing the local, indigenous community as 'just another stakeholder'. They argue that there is a need to recognize the local community as a group of people with a variety of rights and responsibilities to resource management rather than as 'a single stakeholder', and that representation on the relevant committee should reflect this fact to avoid subjugation to the stronger lobbying presence of other, more powerful, stakeholders.

While this is morally defensible, in the case of marine ecotourism this is easier said than done. This is because existing, more powerful, stakeholders resist what they perceive as a threat to their agenda. As Selin (2000, p. 140) states: 'Conservative resource managers fear collaborative initiatives will lead to a loss of agency power and influence while representatives of national environmental groups are loathe to see hard-fought environmental laws circumvented by community-based collaboration.' Also, there may be covert resistance on the part of governments anxious to keep tourism revenue flowing.

Apprehension concerning the potential situation where, as McClosky (cited in Selin, 2000, p. 140) puts it: 'Small local minorities have the power to coopt the collaborative process or veto actions that may be in the national interest' may lead to the engineering of an outcome where community participation remains tokenist. Mowforth and Munt (2003, p. 214, citing Taylor), lament that local participation may not be working because 'it has been promoted by the powerful and is largely cosmetic ... but most ominously it is used as a "hegemonic" device to secure compliance to, and control by, existing power structures'.

6 Marine Ecotourists

The Draw of the Sea

We begin this chapter with a question. Why do tourists wish to experience the marine environment and what do they hope to find when they are there? The marine environment is arguably one of the least hospitable environments on earth for humans. We cannot survive for very long without specialized equipment, and it is one of the few environments still containing a significant number of other species that will kill us.

From this perspective it may seem strange that we would want to enter it at all. Of course, enter it we do, for the multitude of leisure and tourism experiences detailed in the previous chapters. It is the purpose of this chapter then to explain why this is so. We begin with a brief overview of societal changes that have shifted our gaze seaward, and then move on to the level of the individual and discuss what such experiences may offer them.

The history of the sea

The sea is an enduring attraction in the Western tourist imaginary, but this is not to say that its existence is static. The constant ebb and flow of the tides reflects the dynamic, contested and contradictory spaces that the sea represents. The seashore is first and foremost a boundary, a boundary between the land where we live and the sea where we came from. Despite an early Greco-Roman affinity for the sea, with highly ritualized bathing (Lencek and Bosker, 1998), for much of history the sea has been characterized as a wild, inhospitable place, useful only as a means of transport and as a resource for fishing. This utilitarian view of the sea is demonstrated in Urry's (1990) example of Ravenglass in the Lake District, UK, where houses were built with their backs to the sea, because the sea was for fishing, not gazing upon (see Fig. 6.1).

Unlike the land, where the surface can be seen and tamed, the infinite depths of the sea for centuries bred myth and fear. Such a perception is visually represented in Copley's famous 18th century illustration *Watson and the Shark*, based on a real shark attack in Havana harbour, Cuba, at the time (see Fig. 6.2). The painting became somewhat of a novelty at the time for its gruesome depiction, although artistic licence seems to have been used, particularly in relation to the size of the shark itself.

Ironically, it is out of the otherness and terror of the sea that emerged what may be regarded as its genesis as a site of leisure. In 18th century Britain, the popularity of the seaside as a site of medicine was associated with subjection to various degrees of trauma, in the belief of the health-giving properties of seawater. The shock that cold saline administered to the nervous system was thought to revitalize the organism, soothe anxieties, help restore harmony between body and soul and revive vital

Fig. 6.1. Seafront houses, Ravenglass, Lake District, Cumbria, UK (photograph courtesy of C. Cater).

Fig. 6.2. *Watson and the Shark*, 1778, John Singleton Copley (1738–1815) (photograph used with permission of the National Gallery of Art, Washington, DC, USA).

energy. In order for this to happen, as Urry suggests: 'Some considerable development in the health-giving properties of "nature" must have occurred' (Urry, 1990, p. 20).

Lencek and Bosker tie this to a period in which enlightenment philosophies and humankind's technological advance had created enough of a chasm between culture and nature for the former to become nostalgic for the latter. 'First we had to grow radically alienated from nature, by paradoxically, gaining systematic and wide-scale mastery over it' (Lencek and Bosker, 1998, p. 26).

Although the seaside was developed as a site of 'medicine' rather than 'pleasure' (Urry, 1990, p. 17), it was always going to be difficult to segregate the latter from muscling in, especially as the idea of a holiday began to find its place in everyday language. Gradually, the seaside developed a medicinal value, which fostered the growth of seaside resorts, and a host of infrastructure to support these practices. The requirement for entertainment when not engaged in the specific purpose of bathing seems to have underpinned the character of the seaside resorts.

The sea as a site of leisure then, owes much to the British invention of cold bathing, the steam engine and the Industrial Revolution. Without the latter two it is unlikely that sea bathing would have ever reached such popularity. Although we are clearly concerned with activities that have moved long beyond this genesis, it can be convincingly argued that this sea-as-leisure philosophy is a major underpinning of all contemporary marine based pursuits.

A marine playground

With this reversal of attitudes the gates were opened for tourism operators to exploit this new tourist frontier. Indeed, it is interesting to note that glass-bottomed boats were introduced in Florida in the late 19th century to allow tourists to 'view beneath magic waters teeming with wildlife' (George, 2004; Fig. 6.3).

It would seem that attitudes to that wildlife would take some time to change however, as the marine environment was seen as a curiosity, but one in which a consumptive ethic took priority. It is worth noting that commercial whaling was continued until relatively late in countries now strongly opposed to it, with hunting still allowed in the UK and Australia in the early 1960s. The two illustrations below (Figs 6.4 and 6.5) show images that would be culturally unacceptable in contemporary society, but indicate that there was nothing unusual about such a view of marine wildlife at the time. Certainly, the development of ecotourism as a practice and a set of principles would require some important societal changes from those prevalent here.

Fig. 6.3. Glass-bottomed excursion boat *Eureka II*, Miami, Florida, USA, 1926 (photograph used with permission of the State Archives of Florida).

Marine ecotourists

It is only relatively recently that we have begun to label a wide variety of existing activities and a number of emergent ones as constituting ecotourism. Eagles and Higgins (1998) suggested three significant influences in the 1980s that created the sector we now acknowledge as ecotourism. These were significant changes in environmental attitudes, a development of environmental education and the development of an environmental mass media (Page and Dowling, 2002, p. 91). As Page and Dowling (2002, p. 88) suggest, early writing on ecotourism seemed to favour the idea that ecotourists were a new breed of environmentally aware traveller as a 'distinct and identifiable group'. This was undoubtedly allied to a number of authors at the time suggesting the emergence of a 'new tourist'; for example, Poon describes how:

> Old consumers were homogenous and predictable. They felt secure when travelling in numbers and took vacations where everything was pre-arranged and pre-paid. New tourists are spontaneous and unpredictable. They are hybrid in nature and no longer consume along linear predictable lines. The hybrid consumer may want to purchase different tourism services in different price categories for the same trip. New consumers want to be different from the crowd. They want to assert their individuality and they want to be in control.
>
> (Poon, 1993, p. 90)

Fig. 6.4. Children playing on a beached whale, Florida, USA, 1960s (photograph used with permission of the State Archives of Florida).

It is clear that tourism has undergone a significant evolution, and to this end we would not wish to deny powerful changes within the industry, many of which have been the catalyst for this book. A 'democratisation of travel' (Urry, 1995, p. 130) has certainly led to growth and ease of choice in tourism experiences. Societal organization of these offerings has been as important as technological advances, as Lash and Urry (1994, p. 253) highlight. Nevertheless, the reality is that the tourists are the same as they always have been, although their ability to engage and negotiate these new experiences and new environments is vastly heightened. Indeed, as Adler has suggested: 'Any travel style, no matter how seemingly new, is built on earlier travel traditions' (Adler, 1989, p. 1373).

One thread within Poon's argument that is vital for us to consider is the manner in which contemporary tourists are able to wear very many hats. Indeed, it may be argued that the most under-researched facet to so-called special-interest tourism (Weiler and Hall, 1992) is its interface

Porpoise, St. Petersburg, Fla.

Fig. 6.5. Men with a dolphin, 1911 (photograph used with permission of the State Archives of Florida).

with allied activities and with the general tourist experience as a whole. As Cloke and Perkins point out: 'Forms of "mass" or "niche" tourism are by no means mutually exclusive' (Cloke and Perkins, 2002, p. 523). There are examples where this is the case, particularly in holidays having an overall theme of adventure travel, for example Antarctic cruises or sea-kayaking expeditions. However, the increasing norm is that special interests form the selective part of any tourist experience, and the move towards independent travel encourages this.

It is thus important to realize that our 21st-century tourist is a creature of multiple identities, because of the fact that they can be. Thus, the 'marine ecotourist' that this chapter seeks to uncover may be that for only a day or even afternoon, the next they may be an adventure tourist, then a 'sun, sand and sea' tourist for several days, and maybe then culturally and heritage-based before going home. Lusseau and Higham illustrate how this may happen in a marine ecotourism context with dolphin watchers in Doubtful Sound, New Zealand: 'Whales and dolphins will often attract tourists to one location and keep them there for several days and during that time tourists may engage in other forms of tours (e.g. scenic flights, fishing charters, pelagic bird tours)' (Lusseau and Higham, 2004, p. 659).

This is only the tip of the iceberg, as it is likely that for many less remote locations many of the activities will not come under the marine ecotourism banner. Failure to grasp the multiplicity of desires that are part of the touristic experience leads to an inadequate account, and this should be borne in mind. What many of the activities we are concerned with do share, however, is a degree of personal satisfaction that has been termed self-actualization.

Self-actualization

Many of the marine tourism activities discussed in previous chapters have an element of self-actualization. This term is one developed by Abraham Maslow to explain why humans could be observed to supplant needs for safety and security with situations that would be the very opposite, which is of clear relevance in the marine environment. Central to Maslow's theory is the concept of 'being' psychology, or the fact that we are all motivated by certain values. Although they clearly differ between individuals: 'These are values that are naturally developed by healthy human beings and are not imposed by religion or culture' (Maslow, 1987, p. xxxv). Maslow suggests that there is a point in our personal history where we are responsible for our own evolution, and become self-evolvers: 'Evolution means selecting and therefore choosing and deciding, and this means valuing' (Maslow, 1973, p. 11).

In a sense, our own evolution mirrors that of the species, as Giblett suggests: 'This process of sublimation can be construed in psychoanalytical terms via the way in which individual development repeats the development of the species as a move out of the swamps of the conscious into the tilled fields of the surface of the earth/body' (Giblett, 1992, p. 149). It can be convincingly argued that the estuarine swamps are where we evolved from, and will always have a powerful draw because of this.

Maslow's theory of motivation centres on a basic hierarchy of needs. Physiological needs, such as thirst or hunger, are primary, and dominate behaviour if they are unfulfilled. If these are satisfied, then higher and more complex needs emerge. Needs are split into those that are deficiency- or tension-reducing motives and those that are inductive or arousal-seeking motives (Cooper *et al.*, 1993, p. 21; Fig. 6.6).

Of particular interest is the recognition by Maslow that, although the hierarchy dominates behaviour, there is flexibility within the scale, so that it can 'be modified, accelerated or inhibited by the environment' (Cooper *et al.*, 1993, p. 21). For example, the second level of safety needs is concerned with striving for stability and preferences for the known, but healthy humans can cope with disruption to this need in order to satisfy higher levels, as long as it can be returned to.

This acknowledgement has clear applications in the practice of pursuits like diving, where security is momentarily replaced by trepidation in order to achieve self-esteem and self-actualization in the process. At these higher levels, sublime experiences are representative, as 'the values that self-actualisers appreciate include truth, creativity, beauty, goodness, wholeness, aliveness, uniqueness, justice, simplicity and self-sufficiency' (Maslow, 1987, p. 147).

LOWER   1.   *Physiological* – hunger, thirst, rest, activity

              2.   *Safety* – security, freedom from fear and anxiety

              3.   *Belonging and love* – affection, giving and receiving love

              4.   *Esteem* – self-esteem and esteem for others

HIGHER   5.   *Self-actualization* – personal self-fulfilment

Fig. 6.6. Maslow's hierarchy of needs.

The Ecotourism Spectrum

Transplanting Maslow's theories of motivation into explanations of touristic desires, however, requires some modification. In research originally conducted for airlines, Plog (1974) attempted to identify a spectrum along which tourist personalities could be identified. At one end of the continuum are *allocentric* tourists, who are adventurous and seek to explore remote and 'untouched' destinations. The other end of the scale is represented by *psychocentric* tourists who dislike destinations and facilities without a high degree of familiarity and security.

Relating to Maslow's model, it is suggested that the psychocentric is driven by safety needs, whilst the allocentric has higher levels of motivation towards self-actualization. From this observation, and as shown by Ryan's (1997, p. 60) research, it is apparent that satisfaction in marine tourism is largely as a result of the fulfilment of Maslow's higher order, or self-actualization requirements (fantastic scenery, educational commentary), whilst dissatisfaction is dominated by the failure to meet lower-order physiological needs (bad food, poor weather).

Plog's identification is not without its criticisms, however. It has been suggested that the model is based overly on the US situation, where it was developed, and is less accurate when applied to other cultures. In addition, it has little room for dynamic change, either within societies or within individuals. As Cooper *et al.* (1993, p. 23) contend, tourists may differ in travel motivation on separate occasions, seeking more allocentric or psychocentric vacation experiences depending on the type of holiday sought. Indeed, this balance may change from day to day during a vacation, as discussed above.

Later amendments (Plog, 1974) have improved the model, notably the suggestion that tourism products can move down the spectrum as they become more accepted and have a wider appeal. This has obvious applications in the realm of ecotourism products, with allocentrics being the first to pick up new practices, and then improving their recognition, so more psychocentric practitioners lose their apprehension and participation is widened.

At first glance it would seem that marine ecotourists are predominantly allocentric, seeking new stimulating experiences in an unfamiliar environment, often at the expense of safety needs. As Page and Dowling suggest: 'Depending on their motives, some ecotourists are often more tolerant of primitive conditions and unfamiliar territory' (2002, p. 92). However, one could convincingly argue that diversification of the ecotourism product has reduced this perspective, as many psychocentric travellers are able to access a multiplicity of activities with the minimum of fuss. In addition, a significant media interest in the marine environment (see Chapter 7) probably means that we are more familiar with its unusual inhabitants than were previous generations.

It is inadequate for us to hypothesize self-actualization without determining what it actually means. A useful division of motivation for leisure pursuits is that suggested by Beard and Ragheb (1983), which can easily be applied to ecotourism activity. These authors identified four possible areas for leisure motivation: intellectual, social, competence-mastery and stimulus avoidance. Each of these corresponds to opportunity for self-actualization.

Education in the marine environment

An *intellectual* requirement for leisure is an interesting proposition, as humans clearly possess a level of curiosity that is satisfied through mental stimuli such as 'learning, exploring, discovering, creating or imagining' (Beard and Ragheb, 1983, p. 225). Certainly, a significant motivator for seeking marine ecotourism experiences is that of education about the marine environment, as tourists are after more than just a good time (Orams, 1999). However, it is important to note that, in a tourism context, the opportunities for education are generally less formalized. As Lück (2003d) points out, there has been recent recognition of the distinct differences between interpretation and education. Indeed, as Hammitt (1984, p. 11) states: 'Environmental education often involves a formal approach to educating while environmental interpretation is almost always informal. It is sometimes said that: "Environmental education involves students while environmental interpretation involves visitors"'.

The majority of marine ecotourists will be in the latter category. Often, the need for education as an underpinning of ecotourism is also reflected at a policy level. For example, one of the conditions of a commercial whale-watching licence in New Zealand is that of an educational component (Lück, 2003d, p. 944).

Certainly, an educative dimension is significant in the spectrum of ecotourism activity, and is even present at the softer and ancillary end of the industry. As described in Chapter 4, research by Jiang (2004, unpublished) on visitors to marine aquaria demonstrated that educational motivations of visitors outweighed concerns with facilities. Corresponding research carried out by Saltzer (2001) at Sea World on Australia's Gold Coast indicated that visitors felt they had learnt a moderate amount about the wildlife on display with an average score of 7.6 out of 10 (on a scale where 0 = learnt nothing at all and 10 = learnt a great deal). Interestingly, this rating was higher than in samples of more classic 'ecotourists', those visiting the Great Barrier Reef and the Far North Queensland rainforest, who gave average scores of 6.2 and 5.9, respectively, for the same question.

Of course, this is a slightly problematic comparison, as it is related to the perception of the visitors towards learning, although it does indicate an educative bent. It also worth noting that education at marine aquaria is often used as an excuse to justify the keeping of large animals in captivity (Jiang, 2004, unpublished). The oft-cited argument goes that, although these individual animals may not be happy, the benefits gained for conservation through education about the marine environment outweigh concerns for their welfare.

Modes of interpretation are clearly highly varied, ranging from commentary, interpretative displays, videos, and literature to direct interaction. Newsome *et al.* (2002, p. 250) divide techniques into publications and websites, visitor centres, self-guided trails and guided touring. However, in the same way that tourist information channels overlap, interpretative facilities can transcend these boundaries. Formats need to be designed with the type of marine tourism experience in mind. For example, boat-based activities such as whale watching and ecocruises have a highly captive audience. In addition, there is usually a significant travel time involved, which may be one when educational videos are played and an onboard library may be accessed.

However, existing work and personal observation would suggest that the best method will always remain that of personal contact, having a tour guide who is able to answer questions and adapt commentary to the particular group's needs.

All of this begs the question, however, as to individual operators' capacity to educate, also explored in Chapter 8. Many will not have had a specific training in either the marine environment or education and interpretation. In some cases, such training is a requirement of the job (for example, diving instructors) and the drive towards accreditation often involves greater standardization of training for guides (see, for example, the discussion on SKOANZ in Chapter 4).

Nevertheless, in the majority of cases, capacity is likely to be less than is often required. A major cause of dissatisfaction on ecotourism trips is a lack of environmental knowledge by the guides (see, for example, Almagor, 1985). In related work on adventure tourism, Cater highlights the way in which participants expect guides to be 'typically active, outdoorsy, knowledgeable and larger than life' (Cater, 2001, unpublished PhD thesis, p. 197). This is also emphasized by Crang, who suggests that guides act as the 'exemplars of the bodily habitus expected of and desired by tourists' (1997, p. 151). Indeed, in Lück's (2003a) study of three swim-with-dolphin operators in New Zealand, the greatest educational satisfaction came with the operator that was deemed to have the most enthusiastic and knowledgeable guide.

It is perhaps better to consider principles for interaction that cover the spread of individual methods that can be applied. Newsome *et al.*, identify five key mantras for interpretation (2002, p. 240), which we examine with regard to marine ecotourism, as follows.

1. *Interpretation should centre on a theme and associated messages*: Having a clear theme to interpretation assists visitors in organizing a significant amount of new information in a logical format. For example, PADI divers taking an underwater naturalist course are asked to identify relationships in the underwater environment through observing symbiosis and predator/prey interactions.

2. *Interpretation entails active involvement and the engagement of first-hand experiences*: There is clearly no substitute for 'being there', and the educational potential for marine ecotourism rests on this very principle. Lück (2003d) refers to the work of Forestell and Kaufman (1990), who highlight that a 'direct guided' experience – or one in which there is simultaneously both guide interpretation and natural interaction – will be the most effective. For example, a guide explaining a whale's immediate behaviour over the loudspeaker as it happens will have the greatest impact.

3. *Interpretation facilitates maximum use of the senses*: Educational theories point to the significance of utilizing all of the senses in the interpretive process. Tourist demand is increasingly driven by the desire for experiences that tap into the multisensual nature of the human body. This desire for embodiment is discussed later in the chapter.

4. *Interpretation seeks to foster self-discovered insights*: Insights that are discovered by the tourist are likely to have greater impact than those are merely absorbed from an external source. Again it is up to planners, operators and guides to encourage tourists to find out things for themselves. The design of underwater snorkelling trails is an example of how such insights can be fostered. Marine aquaria often have a variety of touch pools where visitors can learn about the selected wildlife through such processes.

5. *Interpretation is of relevance to the visitor and clients find the imparted knowledge and insights useful*: Such a principle recognizes that not all visitors may have the same needs and requirements, and may also be interested in different things to the facilitator. An effective guide discusses these with a group prior to the experience and determines areas of particular interest. It is also important to layer the knowledge so that it can be accessed by different types of participants. This especially applies to children, who may not be able to understand complex explanations, but should be involved in the process nevertheless.

It is important to consider that an educational motivation is highly variable and dependent on individual circumstances, which is perhaps why it has a lower reliability ranking in Beard and Ragheb's research (1983, p. 226). In addition, it is worth moving away from the stereotype – prevalent in much tourism research – that intellectual drives are split along educational or aspirational lines. As May has shown: 'Some kind of informational value is important to a whole range of tourists enjoying a number of different kinds of holiday' (May, 1996, p. 731).

Esteem in the marine environment

The *social* component assesses the extent to which individuals engage in activities for social reasons, and includes two basic needs. The first is the need for friendship and interpersonal relationships, while the second is the need for the esteem of others. The dual components of the social motivation are interesting to examine, as they are defined as not only the importance of a period of bonding with old friends as making new ones, but also the gaining of esteem in others' eyes.

This demonstrates how important tourist practice is to a definition of self. We know who we are not solely in terms of our individual delimitation, but also in terms of comparison with others and the way that others see us (or how we perceive they do). Holidaymaking is a fundamental foundation of these determinants, particularly because of the fact that: 'When compared to regular leisure activities, travel has greater prestige potential because it is not "sandwiched" between the ever present necessities of day-to-day living' (Riley, 1995, p. 631). Travel experiences are seen as a true expression of individual identity because of the very fact that they are separate from everyday life. As Ryan playfully suggests: 'It would appear that in contemporary society we are not only who we are, but also where we have been' (Ryan, 1997, p. 30).

The social element to these experiences is illustrated in motivational research on marine ecotourists. A survey of artificial reef scuba-divers in Texas (Ditton *et al.*, 2002) indicated that 56% of participants pursued this activity with friends, and 21% with a combination of family and friends. Over 60% listed 'being with friends' as either very important or extremely important reasons behind their diving trip. Of interest is the manner in which, although some marine ecotourism activities may be family based, especially those taken on vacation, scuba-diving is probably less so due to the need for qualifications, which may be held by only one family member.

On disaggregating the results, the same study indicated that only 13% were diving with family members and nearly 30% felt that 'family recreation' was not at all important on their trip. Although it has been largely overlooked in existing research, the opportunity for social interactions is clearly an important part of ecotourism experiences, especially the ability to bond with like-minded individuals during an activity. Indeed, as Miller suggests, marine ecotourism may be studied as 'symbolic interaction fostering social solidarity' (Miller, 1993, p. 181).

Esteem also comes through the stories that we are able to tell others, and more importantly ourselves, about who we are. Narrative psychology recognizes the important social capital that is garnered through such processes. This narrative capital is discussed by Schiebe (1986), who suggests that adventurous tales form the basis of life stories that, in turn, are foundations of individual identity:

> The value of such action is that the consequences of having enjoyed such thrilling experiences flow beyond the bounds of the occasion. One tells stories about these events, 'dines out' on them, elaborates and embroiders on successive retellings. In this fashion, the life story of the participant is enriched.

(Schiebe, 1986, p. 136)

As she goes on to detail, the construction of tales is a complex process, but their creation sustains the importance of travel as a commodity. Indeed, as Schiebe rather bluntly puts it:

> The cash value of adventures, after all, is only partly enjoyed at the time of their occurring or being suffered, but realizes itself later as the survived adventure becomes the stuff for enriching one's story. Travel to remote or foreign places is partly done for the intrinsic pleasure of beholding the strange and unfamiliar. But without the possibility of redeeming the travel by showing photographs and souvenirs, and telling stories to interested friends of how it was – without these possibilities the traveller is cheated of the major value that can be realised from the trip.

(Schiebe, 1986, p. 145)

What is debatable in Schiebe's thesis is whether, as she suggests, the collection of narrative capital still maintains the rewards to collective society (Schiebe, 1986, p. 147) in the increasingly individualist 21st century. Certainly, As Mowforth and Munt claim, there is a powerful force towards establishing ones individual identity through travel, and 'doing' things that may distinguish one from the average 'tourist', or 'traveller' for that matter, so the experience can be presented as 'more than just a holiday' (Mowforth and Munt, 1998, p. 146). In order to claim the desired cultural capital, the experience 'must be sufficient in distancing itself from supposedly inactive or inert forms of tourism' (Mowforth and Munt, 1998, p. 146).

Undoubtedly significant status is attached to seeing rare or distinctive species, and this is no less prevalent in the marine environment than it is in the terrestrial. Research by Norton on visitors to the African savannah identified dissatisfaction when they were unable to see the 'big five', and several commented on the elusiveness of certain animals, which had been depicted in the brochures as being abundant (Norton, 1996, p. 367). The popularity of whale shark tours in Western Australia, discussed in Chapter 3, is an example of this phenomenon.

Certainly, many marine ecotourism experiences are prohibitively expensive, and may exclude certain groups on the basis of this alone (Mowforth and Munt, 1998, p. 133). Indeed, all of the activities we have detailed thus far involve a considerable outlay in terms of commercial participation, and many may require the purchase of specialized equipment. An average whale-watching trip may cost upwards of US$50.

Scuba-diving training costs, on average, US$200, and individual dives from then on are likely to be around US$50. A study of scuba-divers in the western Mediterranean found that > 50% were in the 31–45 age group for the suggested reason that this activity 'requires a certain level of purchasing power not always within reach of younger people and a physical fitness that is not always found among older persons' (Mundet and Ribera, 2001, p. 505). Those experiences that have more status are, by association, more expensive. For example, diving with whale sharks in Australia costs around US$200, and a trip to the Antarctic will cost upwards of US$3000.

Some writers have taken a rather cynical approach to this factor in ecotourism, with the label 'egotourist' applied to those who seek such experiences merely for the status that comes with them (see, for example, Wheeller, 1994). There may be an element of self-righteousness involved in the process, as 'Egotourists believe that their travel is beneficial and that they are certainly not part of the mass' (Page and Dowling, 2002, p. 90). Such a debate is linked to well-trodden discourses in academia and the public realm about the differences between travellers and tourists. Indeed, as Mowforth and Munt (1998, p. 155) suggest, ideas of sustainability can be seen to be as much a method of ensuring the exclusivity of certain travel experiences encouraged by middle-class values as the environmental preservation they purport to be.

However, it is also easy to forget that ecotourists are also tourists, and perhaps we should be wary of expecting too much of them. To deny holidaymakers the opportunity for enjoyment and a bit of hedonism misses the fundamental point of taking a vacation, and is also dangerous for any tourist product that wishes to maintain long-term viability.

Expertise in the marine environment

The extent to which individuals engage in leisure activities in order to achieve, master, challenge and compete is assessed by the *competence–mastery* component. In Beard and Ragheb's original scale, competence and mastery was associated particularly with motivations of a physical nature. However, it is also clear that competence and mastery can also apply to items of a more intellectual dimension, as discussed above. A variety of writing on adventure tourism and ecotourism has discussed this nexus as it relates to physical rigour and degree of commitment by distinguishing between hard and soft forms of activity (see Fig. 6.7). Fennell (1999), for example, articulates how ecotourism activities may sit on an axis of these attributes.

The letter B identifies a harder ecotourism experience based on a more difficult ecotourism experience, and also shown by the ecotourist relative to the interest in the activity relative to A. In this market segment it may be suggested that A may be characterized by an activity

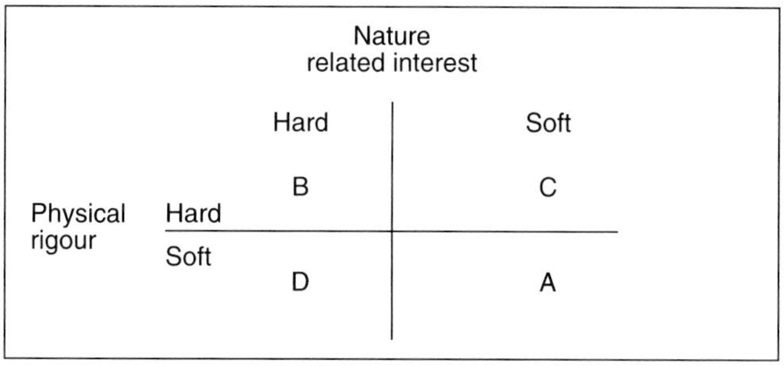

Fig. 6.7. The ecotourism spectrum (after Fennell, 1999, p. 35).

such as whale watching, whereas for the majority of participants the nature-related interest is limited to seeing the cetaceans in the wild, but interest in them is probably minimal and all creature comforts are maintained.

Coastal birdwatching may be classified as D, in which the commitment to spotting species can be high, although again physical rigour may be minimal. Scuba-diving would, in many cases, occupy the space B, where physical commitment and natural interest are both high. An example of an activity having high physical commitment but only minimal natural interest may be that of surfing, although it should be noted that environmental symbolism for surfers is articulated in some very different, but strong, forms (Buckley, 2002a, b).

It is important to note that these classifications are not all-encompassing, as both physical activity and environmental commitment are characteristics that are largely dictated by the individual. High levels of exertion for one person can be relatively easy for another, identified as the 'adventure spectrum' by Swarbrooke *et al.* (2003, p. 19). Similarly, a person does not have to be a marine biologist to show a high level of interest in the functioning of marine ecosystems.

The desire for challenge is clearly linked to the satisfaction gained from self-actualization. However, the concept of flow developed by Csikszentimihalyi (1975) helps to explain why intellectually or physically based pursuits can be inherently rewarding in and of themselves. He endeavoured to show that, when there is a balance between the skill required and the challenge inherent in an act, positive feedback occurs in terms of satisfaction.

Although originally developed to describe activities such as chess or mountaineering, competence required by marine ecotourism activities – for example, sea kayaking or snorkelling – has a similar immersion. The experience of flow is defined as 'one of complete involvement of the actor with his activity' (Csikszentimihalyi, 1975, p. 36) and is characterized by feelings of fusion and fluidity with that activity. Indeed, as Ryan has suggested: 'The experience of ecotourism lies in the intensity of interaction with the site' (Ryan *et al.*, 2000, p. 158).

Csikszentimihalyi identifies seven possible indicators that would suggest the conditions for flow (Ryan, 1997, p. 33):

- The perception that the challenge offered by an activity and personal skills to meet that challenge are in balance.
- The centring of attention.
- The loss of self-consciousness.
- A clear feeling of feedback from the activity.
- Feelings of control and mastery over actions and environment.
- Loss of anxiety and restraint.
- Intense feelings of enjoyment and pleasure.

However, for the flow experience to be felt, there are some important prerequisites:

- That participation is entirely voluntary.
- That the benefits to participation in an activity are perceived to derive from factors intrinsic to participation in the activity.
- A facilitative level of arousal is experienced during participation in the activity.
- There is a psychological commitment to the participating activity.

Of particular importance, then, is the manner in which, for flow to occur, the activities must be freely chosen. Hence flow is, by its nature, more likely to be found in leisure and tourism activities, as these are held to be, at least in perceptual terms, areas of unhindered personal selection.

Flow is an important concept because it gives theoretical manoeuvre for *enjoyment* in experience (Johnston, 1989, p. 34, unpublished PhD thesis). It is of particular application to the study of ecotourism activities because, as has been highlighted by others (Johnston, 1989, unpublished PhD thesis, Morgan, 1998), they carry little in the way of tangible rewards. It is only through closer study of the experience, via a flow framework, of the notable facets of feelings of harmony, satisfaction and the loss of a conscious self that the true treasures become clear.

Despite this, indiscriminate application of the concept is not appropriate, as it is important to recognize that the concept of flow is extremely generalized, and that its application requires significant qualitative insight in order to give situational relevance to any example. Given this condition, there is the potential to move towards 'a broader concept of experience in sociological analysis, as well as empirical studies of the contextual frames of different variants of flow experiences' (Bloch, 2000, p. 43).

In the commercial ecotourism sphere there needs to be consideration as to the level of competence transferred by the operator to the tourist. Often, a significant deal of trust is placed in the operator, which introduces further elements to the axes suggested by Fennell, above. An attempt to illustrate this is shown in Fig. 6.8. The broad spectrum of activities discussed in previous chapters offer widely ranging attributes in the manner of skill required, reliance on others and the level of natural interest. Indeed, there is significant variation in these three factors, and the sketch in Fig. 6.8 shows a suggested tripolar axis for a few selected marine ecotourism activities.

It is important to note that this is not definitive, as the levels of balance between the factors will depend to a large degree upon both the individual and the specific context of the activity. However, it is suggested, for example, that dolphin feeding would require a degree of natural interest, reliance on others to facilitate the process but virtually no 'skill'. In contrast, snorkelling would require less reliance on others but some skill and interest in the marine environment. Scuba-diving might require all three attributes in equal measure, as there will be a significant interest in the underwater environment, a requirement to use the skills gained in previous certification, along with a reliance on the skills of the dive leader to guide around an unfamiliar location. Whilst these categories are not definitive, they do highlight that there is considerable variation within the activities that characterize the marine ecotourism experience.

Escaping to the marine environment

Beard and Ragheb's final motivator is that of *stimulus avoidance*, and this can be interpreted in a number of different ways. For some individuals,

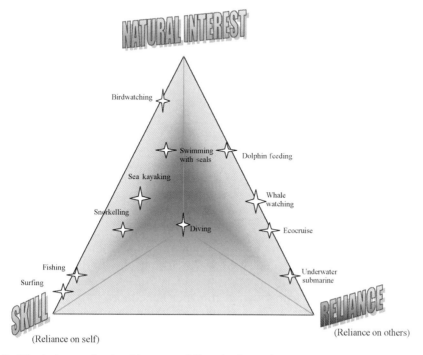

Fig. 6.8. The balance of natural interest, skill and reliance in marine ecotourism.

the drive to escape may manifest as 'the need for some individuals to avoid social contacts, to seek solitude and calm conditions; for others it is to seek rest and to unwind themselves' (Beard and Ragheb, 1983, p. 225). It is clear that themes of escape are strong in any holiday motivation and many commentators associate this need for escape with stimulus avoidance (e.g. Iso-Ahola, 1982).

However, Beard and Ragheb (1983, p. 227) tentatively hint at the possibility that the avoidance may be merely of those stimuli associated with the workplace and that escape takes the form of a need to 'rest and unwind'. More importantly, Ryan (1997, p. 32) highlights 'to rest and unwind' does not necessarily mean 'to relax physically'. This fact is of clear relevance to a study of this nature, given that the ecotourist is engaging in often strenuous practice whilst notionally being 'on holiday'. However, as Ryan quite rightly demonstrates: 'The very action of physical exertion can itself be mentally restful even while, paradoxically, the mind is focused on a specific task' (Ryan, 1997, p. 32).

Stimulus avoidance can also be interpreted as escaping to an environment different to that normally experienced. The very fact that the sea is an environment in which we are not designed to live is one that stimulates curiosity. The function of the beach as the last frontier emphasizes the liminality of this space, as Urry notes: 'Beaches are complex spaces, anomalously located between land and sea, nature and culture' (Urry, 1990, p. 38). Indeed, the move 'beyond the beach' was somewhat inevitable given the pressure on these spaces illustrated by Hall (2001, p. 601).

When we are in the marine environment we have crossed this boundary and entered a world that is largely alien to us. We make sense of this liminal space through narratives that make sense to us. For example, Besio *et al.* (2003) illustrate the way that ecotourism operators in New Zealand, through themes of sexuality and maternity, commodify dolphins.

Embodiment in the marine environment

It is important to note that these previously listed motivations can be concurrent, so that the competence and mastery of the activity is paralleled by an intellectual absorption of the unfamiliar marine environment, as well as social interactions that define the experience and the individual. However, not all interactions with the marine environment are negotiated through the mind. Recent writing on the embodied nature of tourist experience helps us understand the highly sensual context of the majority of marine tourism experiences.

Tourists increasingly want to experience more than sights: they want action, to be able to 'participate with their own skins' (Moeran, 1983, p. 94). This is an important trend within the tourism industry as a whole, with the emergence of the 'high-tech' but 'high-touch' ethic described by Poon (1993, p. 119). Sharing a breath with a whale from an observation boat, hearing dolphins communicating underwater whilst diving or feeling the warmth in one's arms after kayaking are all experiences that are situated within the body.

Partly, this desire to 'feel' the natural environment has come about through changes in society. It has been suggested that we are increasingly moving towards what Turner (1996, p. 1) calls a 'somatic society', in which 'the body is now part of a self-project within which individuals express their own personal emotional needs through constructing their own bodies'. As a result, 'The individual body is connected into larger networks of meaning at a variety of scales. [Embodiment] refers to the production of social and cultural relations through and by the body at the same time as the body is being "made up" by external forces' (Cresswell, 1999, p. 176).

One significant reason for this development has been the change in the place of the body in society more generally. Whilst in early capitalism there was a close connection between the body and work, this has been eroded in postmodern times, with the reduction of physical work leading to 'an entirely different and corrosive emphasis on hedonism, desire and enjoyment' (Turner, 1996, p. 4) as the focus for embodied concern. The reduced role for the active body in many workplace settings means that we frequently seek it out during leisure and tourism experiences. Therefore, in examining marine tourism activity, we need to take a broader perspective of tourist motivation than is presently adopted by those responsible for managing it. The need for a broad range of deeply felt embodied experiences is undeniably an important trend behind these active experiences.

However, Cloke and Perkins (1997) cite Veijola and Jokinen's observation 'that the body is absent from the corpus of the sociological studies on tourism' (Veijola and Jokinen, 1994, p. 149). Active pursuits such as diving or snorkelling are 'fundamentally about active recreational participation, and they demand new metaphors based more on "being, doing, touching *and* seeing" rather than just "seeing"' (Cloke and Perkins, 1997, p. 189).

Furthermore, it is important to grasp that embodied experience is the whole experience, so that all the senses should be considered. It is easy to *see* (the metaphors of our language reveal a lot) why vision is traditionally the dominant sense, because we rely on it more than the other senses, and the eye is (rightly or wrongly) endowed with a host of notions of objectivity. Wilson (1992, p. 122) discusses how the eye 'provides access to the world in a particular way, and while it gives us much, it also conceals'.

Embodied experience or the experience of *being* there relies on all of the senses: 'Is the gaze really detachable from the eye, the eye from the body, the body from the situation?' (Veijola and Jokinen 1994, p. 136). In order to better understand the experience, 'We must have a more fully embodied concept of the tourist, expanding the notion of the "tourist gaze" to include other embodied aspects of experience (movement, sound, touch and so forth) both in the physical and imaginary realms' (Desmond, 1999, p. xxi).

Part of the attraction of getting to know one's body lies in the fact that it has the ability to surprise us. We can never really know how our body will respond to the hostile environment in which it has been placed, although this mystery is undeniably part of the attraction. As Radley (1995, p. 5) contends: 'By virtue of being elusory, the body is empowered to configure the realms of experience.'

Indeed, quite often the experiences are not actually pleasant. Anyone who has been on or in the water can vouch for the pain and discomfort that comes with the territory. We may get seasick, we may be cold, biting sealice may irritate us, we may have pain in our sinuses as we descend beneath the surface, the salt gets in our eyes, barnacles may cut us. Even things that we would expect to control on firm ground may elude us in the water. Scuba divers constantly have to adjust buoyancy, and it is deeply frustrating for novice individuals to find that they have difficulty staying in one place, as the following example demonstrates.

The life aquatic: the scuba-diving experience

Scuba-divers exhibit a significant number of the characteristics discussed in this chapter. Beard and Ragheb's (1983) motivational classifications of intellectual and social competence and stimulus avoidance are all present in the majority of dive experiences. In addition, the experience is one that is profoundly embodied, often requiring a significant amount of discomfort to achieve the sensations and feelings that are sought by participants. A number of unstructured interviews were carried out aboard a 3-day live-aboard dive trip to the Great Barrier Reef in April 2005. The insights given by the respondents demonstrate the significance of these attributes to the marine ecotourism experience.

Education

The intellectual motivations to engaging in scuba-diving are clear, with parallel tracks of learning about how to dive and learning about the underwater environment. These educational stimuli can extend beyond the dive experience, as was suggested by one respondent who felt this had influenced her later choice of degree programme:

> My first introductory dive was in 2001, that was amazing! I got hooked, it actually got me really interested in marine biology and science, and so I ended up doing that at Uni.
>
> (Jess, Sweden, 3 years' experience)

All of the divers felt that their knowledge of the underwater environment had increased during the time they had been diving. However, some divers pointed to significant disparities in the level of education provided by different operators and the satisfaction with the experience that resulted:

> I think PADI do their best, but there are always dive companies that I have been with that are not really you know that good at explaining what is going on with it. The first snorkelling I did up in Cairns they were really, really good, explaining why you can't touch that thing or that thing. The second time we went out they didn't even mention it, even though there were people snorkelling for the first time, I don't know – how would they know that you can't step on the coral.
>
> (Claire, USA, 6 months' experience)

Esteem

The social nature of diving is clearly an important part of the experience. The 'buddy' format of scuba-diving, discussed above, is felt to be an integral part of the activity, as high levels of trust between individuals need to be built upon:

> I am always relaxed. Especially if I am diving with a good buddy – I am diving with Roger now, it's easy to dive with him, because I know he is on my shoulder anyway. Its always a bit more stressful when you are diving with someone new, because you don't know how they behave.
>
> (Jess, Sweden, 3 years' experience)

Respondents indicated that it was not just the underwater experience that was important, as the opportunity for bonding as a group through the activity – particularly through discussing the adventures afterwards. This is probably heightened in the dive experience, as there is little opportunity for direct communication whilst underwater:

> A lot of fun. It's a sport and an adventure. Every time you go out you see new things. It's also a social activity, I like to go out with a group, and we all go diving and we have a few drinks after.
>
> (Jess, Sweden, 3 years' experience)

The opportunity to practice the activity with friends was also deemed important, emphasizing the research conducted by Ditton *et al.* (2002) and discussed above:

> I think diving will always be important to me, it depends on friends and stuff like that. I don't think I'd quit completely ever, but how much I do depends on people I know and stuff like that. I like to dive in big groups like this, its always fun to get to know new people.
>
> (Freddy, Norway, 1 year's experience)

As well as the status that can be gained through moving up the hierarchy of certification, there is clearly status to be gained through having 'ultimate' diving experiences. The desire to see big fish – especially sharks – is a significant motivator for these ecotourists wishing to gain travellers' tales:

> I'd like to dive with sharks, whale sharks would be cool.
>
> (Roger, Norway, 7 years' experience)

> First I like seeing big stuff, just because I am new at diving, so seeing sharks and really big fish is fun.
>
> (Matt, USA, 6 months' experience)

Expertise

Linked to the educational perspective is the nature of competence with the skills of being a scuba-diver. A number of respondents felt that there was a spectrum of development as a diver, which is undoubtedly encouraged by diving organizations like PADI having certification hierarchies (See Chapter 4, this volume):

> The more you do it the easier it gets. Like your first dive I was so nervous; 'where is my buddy? I don't want to lose my buddy', and you have just got to practice everything and know what you are doing I guess, like in advanced.
>
> (Claire, USA, 6 months' experience);

> Especially for each dive, I have only dived on three different boats and the last dive was always ten times better than the first dive, because once you get in there you get used to the equipment, its just nice and relaxing and you are comfortable and you are confident.
>
> (Matt, USA, 6 months' experience);

> After this trip I feel pretty comfortable. I think tense whenever you start. For me a little bit tense when it's been a few weeks between dives. Yeah but this one here after a few dives you feel pretty comfortable.
>
> (Jeff, Canada, 1 year's experience)

Having mastered the skills as a diver enables one to get more out of the underwater experience, particularly in terms of observing what goes on beneath the waves:

> I think I have developed on this trip, just doing the advanced diving course as well, more control, everything, buoyancy, and then you can check out more stuff too, because you know that you are not going to crash into the coral, you can go a bit closer and not lose control.
>
> (Jess, Sweden, 3 years' experience)

> I think it goes from more than a novelty like to um, when you start to recognize things down there, yeah. When you can recognize things, it makes it a bit more meaningful, when you see fish that you understand. You just notice a lot more stuff I guess, I guess when you first start diving you are more concerned with your equipment and making it through, whereas now you are more observant as you get more comfortable with your equipment. I think that's what's mainly changed, you see more fish and that, understand what species are going on.
>
> (Jeff, Canada, 1 year's experience)

These feelings of competence in the water contribute to significant feelings of self-actualization, which are a primary motivator for repeated activity. In addition, the loss of conscious self lends itself to feelings of flow and, in turn, provides a relaxing experience.

Escape

The liminal nature of the underwater environment is a defining facet of this branch of marine ecotourism, and almost all respondents emphasized the alien nature of this world:

> The best bit is being, you know, somewhere you are not supposed to be, rather than swimming around on the surface, you are twenty metres below. You feel like an intruder, an explorer, that's so cool. It's like an alien world, especially on a night dive.
>
> (Roger, Norway, 7 years' experience)

> I would have to say that it is more unlike anything that you have done really. You know it's really hard for them to know what to expect until they do it because it is so different from anything they are used to. But its like weightlessness almost you know. Yeah it's like completely another world down there. It's pretty sweet. It's like walking on the moon.
>
> (Jeff, Canada, 1 year's experience).

Embodiment

The scuba-diving experience is also profoundly embodied, entailing a wide range of sensations and feelings, many of which may be new to the first-time diver. Participants pointed to the strange experience of being able to breathe underwater, especially at the start of their diving career:

> Breathing underwater was so cool. I actually think that was my coolest dive, because it was so new. I have had lots of fun since, but I guess that was the coolest one.
>
> (Freddy, Norway, 1 year's experience)

> It freaked me out a little bit to be honest, I had a bit of a claustrophobic reaction I think. Yeah it was weird. Just breathing only though your mouth – I had trouble getting used to that.
>
> (Jeff, Canada, 1 year's experience)

The feeling of being weightless was also felt to be one that they would define to non-divers if explaining the activity. Most also identified that they felt relaxed when they were underwater:

> You feel relaxed. Because you have to concentrate on staying neutral and breathing, so you are very relaxed when you are down there, have a look at everything.
>
> (Roger, Norway, 7 years' experience)

However, there is a paradox here in that the scuba experience is simultaneously relaxing and physically demanding. This emphasizes the points made by Ryan (1997) above and further underlines the presence of Csikszentmihalyi's flow experience at work:

> It's an adrenalin rush and a completely relaxing thing at the same time. It relaxes me because of the deep breathing and the slow movements but then you will see something in the shadows and it gets your heart pumping- – you go up there to see what it is and it's a really big fish or something like

that. On the night dives that was a really good blast, because you couldn't
see anything except what was right in front of you. Like I saw a couple of
green eyes glowing back at me so I went over and checked it out and it was a
lobster. But if it was during the day I never would have seen it.

(Matt, USA, 6 months' experience)

It is clear that many of the attributes discussed in this chapter apply
to scuba-diving. Although this is only one selected activity, it is
suggested that different levels of these attributes will be found in all
other marine ecotourism experiences. What is also apparent is the
significance that such activity can have for individual people. Such
experiences may be highly valued and fulfil a wide variety of purposes
in the definition of self:

I just think its important to me, because I have a very stressful life,
especially at the moment I do so many things that I just get to relax and not
think about anything. The combination is so good, because you get to learn
something every time you are down there, learn something new, see
something new, you get a bit of exercise, and everything that is around it, the
social and that. It's cool. Love it.

(Jess, Sweden, 3 years' experience)

Immersion in the Marine Realm

This chapter has served to illustrate how immersion in the marine realm
by marine ecotourists – whether partial and relatively passive, in terms of
viewing species or total and active, in terms of literal bodily immersion in
the sea – offers considerable opportunities for self-actualization. This is
achieved not only through the elements of education, esteem, expertise
and escape – as suggested by Beard and Rahgeb (1983) – but also
increasingly through embodied experiences whereby 'techniques and
tools extend the body outwards into nature and where temporary
moments of ecstasy or "flow" are experienced' (Franklin, 2003, p. 177).

It is apparent that, through the tourist body, the three 'E' travel
motivators of the 21st century suggested by Newsome *et al.* (2002, p. 8)
are articulated: 'Entertainment, Excitement and Education.' Certainly, as
Page and Dowling (2002, p. 97) suggest, the 'tourist experience is a
complex combination of factors which shape the feelings and attitudes of
the tourist towards their visit'. Marine ecotourism has the potential to
facilitate a variety of the attributes discussed above in significant
amounts. Indeed, as Franklin suggests, while there are a wide range of
activities that enable this type of encounter: 'Many of these focus on
water, beach or ocean' (Franklin, 2003, p. 177).

However, these activities rely to a large degree on nature being
complicit in the experience. Thus, in order to explore the implications of
the proliferation and escalating popularity of more embodied
relationships with marine nature we need to examine our place within
it, and its place within us, and it is to this task we now turn.

7   Marine Nature

Back to Nature

This chapter will expand a thread from Chapter 6 that we feel has received minimal attention in the study of ecotourism to date. Namely, it is to understand the role of 'nature' in ecotourism beyond the dominance of purely scientific and management approaches. It is a curious lacuna, for the existence of ecotourism is based fundamentally upon the presence of nature above all else. It is certainly a 'difficult' question, for it involves a host of complex relationships that have developed over millennia.

However, we would argue that the popularity of ecotourism gives humanity an opportunity to re-examine our relationships with nature at the coalface, rather than fall into the routines that dominate contemporary practice. As such, we would advocate an open discourse that seeks to critically engage with debates over how we relate to nature.

An important acknowledgement is that 'nature' is a cultural construct, evidenced by its many uses in language. However, these meanings are not static, and have been renegotiated over time. Indeed, far from slowing down, in an age of debates surrounding genetic engineering, discourses about what nature actually 'is' are livelier than ever. Much of this debate takes place within the popular media, and certainly our understandings of the marine environment are coloured by such discussions. Influences on how we 'see' oceanic creatures are diverse, and include documentaries, films (even animated ones!), books and marine ecotourism's 'ugly sister', marine aquaria.

We conclude the chapter with a question that we feel has been ignored in contemporary discussion of ecotourism, relating to the agency of ecotourism animals. These 'stars of the show' are often fundamental to the experience, and yet they have received little attention that acknowledges this beyond numerous 'impact studies'. Partly, this is a result of 'the thoroughly modern instrumental rationality that characterizes contemporary human–animal dependency that has rendered animals both spatially and morally invisible' (Wolch and Emel, 1998, p. 22). In beginning to appreciate animal agency, however hard that might be, we hope that a more balanced standpoint may result. Through a consideration of our powerful but rooted place in the natural world, hybrid cultures open the door to new understandings.

The Great Divide

It is beyond the scope of this book to attempt to provide a history of human relationships with nature. However, in the context of our discussion, it is important to recognize that marine ecotourism is based fundamentally on this relationship. The desire to interact with nature drives the entire industry, and so we need to understand our place within it. As Franklin (2003) suggests, Western tourism has a long track record of visiting natural places, but this was largely dominated by an aesthetic need rather than a desire to interact with that nature itself.

Indeed, as he describes: 'Although most people today would find the notion of natural beauty and the implicit attractiveness of natural landscapes unproblematic, or even self-evident or normal, it is important to understand that this was not always so; that is far from inevitable or "natural" or even in leisure terms, stable' (Franklin, 2003, p. 14).

So where is it that this understanding comes from? One of the most fundamental 'truths' that viewing nature – and indeed the entire ecotourism industry – is founded upon, is that nature constitutes an 'other' to ourselves. The roots of this go back to the very evolution of our species but, in philosophical terms, it has been an ongoing dialectical tension constantly negotiated down the centuries. The ancient Greeks, in creating a civilized urban society and tamed *pastorale* countryside, were among the first to create such a separation. Indeed, as Robert Pirsig argues in *Zen and the Art of Motorcycle Maintenance*, this Athenian division went further than that between human and nature, creating philosophical junctures between 'mind and matter, subject and object and form and substance' (Pirsig, 1974, p. 373), which simply did not exist before. In his reasoning, many of the ills of contemporary Western society are derived from this false separation, a theme that has been picked up by contemporary popular philosophers such as Alain de Botton. The connections we discuss in this book would seem to be partly a cure from this inheritance.

However, it is important to note that this divide has been revisited many times over the years, including the scientific advances of the Renaissance and the Enlightenment, both of which served to drive humans and nature apart, and movements such as the Romantic, which sought to articulate the ever-present spiritual connections between them. Poets such as Wordsworth are often held up as pioneers of a romantic view of nature, and still influence Lake District pilgrims today. However, as Franklin points out, his poetry was about aesthetic appreciation of *all* environments, natural and man-made, for he wrote of the view from Westminster Bridge in London: 'earth has not anything more fair.' This appreciative mode of passive interaction with the landscape is one that has dominated tourism and natural area management until very recently.

Much of the discourse that we describe here is the relationship to nature as 'land'. This should come as no surprise, as the land is 'our' environment. Of course the marine environment is far less tameable, although in our search for wilderness this is partly its very attraction. Discussing the sea as a site of experiencing nature in the 19th century, MacNaghten and Urry highlight its attributes: 'especially its wild, untamed and immense quality; it seemed to be nature in a quite unmediated and directly sensed fashion' (MacNaghten and Urry, 1998, p. 13).

Soon, however, the lookouts that would enable one to take in the aesthetic qualities of the landscape were replicated through the construction of piers, such as that completed in Margate, UK, in 1815. The practice of promenading and visual appreciation of the sea followed suit (Macnaghten and Urry, 1998, p. 113). Despite the wild and fluid nature of the marine environment, our desire to tame and manage in the same way that we have achieved over the land dominates our mindset. For example, many marine parks are managed along principles developed for the land, although their borders are significantly more permeable. Dictionary definitions of a park emphasize enclosure, which is clearly impossible in a marine environment, especially one the size of the Great Barrier Reef Marine Park (see Chapter 3, this volume).

Indeed, the creation of national parks is an interface that informs us much about how we relate to nature. The idea of a protection of nature is clearly very closely dependent on the separation discussed above. Of course, this highlights perhaps the greatest contradiction in protected area management and the meaning of wilderness. By protecting, and bringing that environment within the bounds of human management, we have already changed what 'wilderness' is supposed to be about. We should be somewhat careful about inscribing these values on all, as clearly there are significant variations between cultures in our relationship to nature. For example, in the UK, national parks have always been 'living' places (Dale, 2000).

In contrast, national parks in settler societies, such as Australia and the USA, are perceived as being 'untouched' wilderness (although this is clearly a myth in itself). Whilst protected areas in Japan and China have been more recently gazetted, they are often organized around communal appreciation of nature. For example, at the World Heritage-listed Huangshan Mountain, which receives over 1.3 million visitors per year (UNESCO, 2002b), the experience is characterized by following a set route of concrete steps and paths that criss-cross the mountain peaks in the company of a significant number of other tourists (see Fig. 7.1). Huangshan also has strong literary links for the visitors, with particular sights/sites drawing on a long history of landscape poetry.

Indeed, as Bulbeck (2005) suggests, many Eastern cultures find photographs of landscapes without people boring. Chinese translations of nature are *da-ziran*, literally 'everything coming into being', reflecting a more organic connection of all modalties of being (Sofield and Li, 2001). The separation of humans and nature is thus not as apparent. Similarly, the equivalents to 'wilderness' and 'wildlife' have much more negative connotations, being empty or threatening, respectively. Although this poses problems, a concept of Confucian harmony is one from which the West could learn. In addition, rapid urbanization in Asian countries is simultaneously promoting a 'resurgent solace' amongst many (Bulbeck, 2005).

Although such a shifting perspective on humans relationship to nature requires a Khunian view of society and masks individual interactions with nature, it does help explain the priorities of different ages. As described in Chapter 6, one of the most influential recent movements in our

Fig. 7.1. Tourists at Huangshan Mountain, Huangshan Province, China (photograph courtesy of C. Cater).

relationship to nature – and underpinning the growth of ecotourism – has been that of the environmental cause. As Bulbeck contends, the 'late 1970s were a watershed, during which trends shifted from anthropocentric to zoocentric, non-sentimental to sentimental and from animals posing a risk to humans to animals being at risk' (Bulbeck, 2005, p. 109).

As described in the previous chapter, a move towards more embodied modes of experiencing nature has also shaped this relationship in recent years. The reflexive, decentred tourist described by a number of authors is key to this movement (Lash and Urry, 1994; Franklin, 2003). Indeed, these embodied practices help to solve the contradiction in the separation of humans and nature described by Franklin (2003). A Romantic view of being in nature is posited as sublime, whereas a Darwinian standpoint emphasizes the benefits to individual health. However, an embodied perspective recognizes both. To be *using* the body is Darwinian, whilst at the same time our experience of nature can lead us to be *moved* in a spiritual sense.

In considering our relationships to marine nature, it is important that we are not constrained purely by an ecotourism lens. Our relationships to nature are mediated by a host of societal and cultural influences, and coloured by our previous experiences, particularly those of captive animals. As described previously in this book, although ecotourism is about the experience of 'nature in the wild', all of our other desires for viewing nature are mirrored in visits to zoos and aquaria. Whilst these captive facilities have had to adapt to changes in acceptable and dominant discourses over time, their enduring popularity with all but a minority ensures that their existence as a kind of 'fake' ecotourism will continue.

Furthermore, it is perhaps better to consider our interactions along a spectrum from captive to wild, the latter being increasingly rare. For example, where should we place the growing number of artificial reefs, such as the HMAS *Brisbane*, scuttled off its home town in 2005 (EPA, 2005b)? Structures like these are rapidly colonized by 'wild' species, but their very existence is owed to human intervention.

Consequently, attitudes to marine nature are equally well observed in the history of aquaria as a history of the sea. Jarvis (2000, p. 79) provides evidence that fish species were kept in ponds by the Chinese, Egyptians and Romans, and the first evidence of an aquarium dates to mid-1800s England. Melbourne, Australia, set up a public aquarium in 1885, and the New York aquarium dates from 1914. 'As with museums and zoos, the development of public aquaria has been associated with a desire to classify and domesticate nature within a context of imperial scientific exploration and the emergence of leisure time in industrializing societies' (Jarvis, 2000, p. 115). Consequently, marine nature has been packaged primarily as a form of entertainment.

However, although Jarvis suggests that aquaria utilize marine nature for the emphasis of 'entertainment and distance over education and intimacy' (2000, p. 87), it can be observed that the recent touristic search for interaction encourages parks like SeaWorld to put on intimate experiences.

An interesting discussion by Hughes (2001) highlights changing attitudes towards the keeping of marine mammals in captivity. Following the release of the film *Flipper* in 1963 and the allied television series, the dolphinaria industry expanded massively in the UK, predominantly in seaside resorts and existing animal parks. By the mid-1970s there were 25 dolphin shows and 41 permanent or temporary sites where dolphins were on display. However, a swift change in public attitudes, examined by Hughes in the discourses surrounding a facility in Morecambe, Lancashire, meant that by the mid-1980s there were only six captive displays, and by the time of his study there were no longer any captive dolphins in the UK.

Such a shift in the attitudes to marine mammals is illustrated with delicious irony on Moreton Island near Brisbane, Australia. At Tangalooma, a former whaling station has been converted to a popular tourist resort that has become famous for its dolphin-feeding encounters. One of the major structures of the site is the flensing deck that was once used for the processing of the whales. Today, it serves as the leisure centre for the resort (see Fig. 7.2). Furthermore, visitors to the daily dolphin-feeding experiences are encouraged to sign petitions to the International Whaling Commission (IWC) to maintain the ban on commercial whaling.

Anthropomorphing the Ocean

In seeking to know the 'other', it is understandable that we should attempt to do so on our own terms. As we understand each other through relationships and narratives, it comes as no surprise that we transpose these identities on the natural world. The result is a somewhat rampant anthropomorphism that pervades many of our interactions with the natural world, especially animals. It is here that we promote animals – and, in particular, large and 'sexy' ones. The draw of seeing the 'big five' whilst on safari is mirrored in the marine environment by the dominance of whales, dolphins, sharks, turtles and dugongs over jellyfish, sea slugs, clams, lobsters and sea urchins, for example.

Bulbeck (2005) points to the dominance of fluffy/sexy animals in ecotourism experiences, and particularly the provenance of the 'baby releasers'. This maternal discourse has a long history, as evidenced in the root of early anti-vivisection movements in 19th-century Britain such as the Royal Society for Protection of Children and Animals, which combined concerns for the welfare of both (Wolch, 1998).

Fig. 7.2. Flensing deck (as was) now used as a leisure centre at Tangalooma, Moreton Island, Australia (photograph used with permission of Tangalooma Wild Dolphin Resort).

Indeed, in Besio *et al.*'s (2003) examination of the narratives surrounding swim with dolphin operators in New Zealand, maternal and sexual themes were prevalent. They suggest four reasons why the maternal discourse dominates: First, it cements a protective (and patriarchal) relationship over the dolphin mothers and calves, which is required for the long-term sustainability of the industry; second, it reinforces the notion that maternal bodies 'belong' to nature, for 'the natural (and 'normal') female human and non-human body is widely considered to be one that bears offspring' (p. 11); third, it encourages the idea of an interspecies connection sought by participants, which is particularly strong in dolphin-based ecotourism. 'Dolphins *per se*, especially swimming with 'wild' dolphins in their 'natural habitat', are thought to offer opportunities for inter-species connections and maternity is seen to cement this inter-species bond even more strongly' (p. 12); last, this maternal discourse both reinforces, and is reinforced by, a latent anthropomorphism, whereby dolphins and their calves become mothers and children, and behave in human 'ways'.

Of course this anthropomorphism, particularly of the 'nice' animals, brings a range of dilemmas. One only needs to examine the number of charismatic species that are used to champion environmental causes. It can be argued that this demotes a range of equally important but less influential creatures. As Bulbeck (2005, p. 173) argues, drawing on an earlier argument by Leach, the dominance given over to 'sexy' species in documentaries has the rather strange affect in contemporary society that we may know more about dolphins, for example, than chickens. In terms of our understanding of animals, pets and charismatic megafauna become constructed as 'near' to us, whilst those we know little about as the 'others'.

In a global political and economic sphere increasingly dominated by neo-liberal approaches, there is a danger in this dominance, with the potential that 'only the animals that can pay their own way can stay' (Wolch and Emel, 1998, p. 12). This process may be more underway than we realize. As Katz argues: 'As a scratch almost anywhere on the transnational landscape will reveal, preservation and restoration facilitate the privatization of nature and space that have become the hallmark of global neo-liberalism' (Katz, 1998, p. 58).

Certainly, privately operated marine theme parks commodify nature and reinforce the anthropomorphic processes. Desmond shows how the shows involving killer whales and dolphins in the USA rely heavily on family values, whereby human and non-human animals are seen to share common characteristics, such as child raising. Much is made of the ways that both humans and marine mammals 'bear, nurse, and raise young as we [human animals] do, breathe the same air as we do, their warm-blooded bodies covered with smooth skin just like ours' (Desmond, 1999, p. 23). Visitors to Sea World in Australia are encouraged to 'bring your family to meet ours' (see Fig. 7.3).

The extent of this anthropmorphism can be seen in the interactive experience visitors to Sea World, Australia, discussed at the end of Chapter 4. As part of this study, visitors were asked to identify three words that they would associate with the animal in question. These metaphors were completely unprompted and freely chosen. For those undertaking activities with dolphins, which were of course the most popular (71 from the sample), there is a remarkable convergence of similar opinions, given the range of potential responses (see Table 7.1).

Even more interesting is the dominance of character attributes that are transposed on to the animals that shared the experience. Some 41.2% of all the metaphors suggested were attributes that we would associate primarily with humans. Most scientists would have difficulty in accepting the ability for these animals to show these characteristics, and yet, so strong is our anthropomorphic desire, these human understandings of nature come out on top.

Although there is some variation in percentages here from the study of everyday SeaWorld visitors carried out by Saltzer in 2001, where all animals were categorized as either intelligent/smart (37%), large/big (22%), beautiful (19%), graceful (19%) or playful (14%), it is interesting to note the metaphorical 'bag' being used. Furthermore, the fact that the interactive participants were more, not less, likely to anthropomorphize

Fig. 7.3. Family values extolled at Sea World, Australia (photograph courtesy of C. Cater).

Table 7.1. Metaphors used to describe dolphins by Animal Adventure participants, Sea World, Australia.

Category	Metaphors (n)	Proportion of total (%, n = 187)
Awe	Amazing (6), majestic, (2), magnificent (1), fantastic (1), exciting (2), wonderful (1)	7.0
Attributes	Big (2), spongy (1), rubbery (6), soft (6), smooth (5), squishy (1), smelly (1), fishy (1)	12.3
Character	(i) Cheeky (5), happy (3), friendly (15), playful (15), fun (4), smiley (1)	23.0
	(ii) Kind (1), affectionate (3), loving (7), gentle (8)	10.2
	(iii) Serene (1), peaceful (3), tranquil (2), calming (1), relaxing (1), spiritual (1), sensual (1), sensitive (1)	5.9
	(iv) Trainable (1), obedient (1), cooperative (1), responsive (1)	2.1
Beauty	Beautiful (14), attractive (1), adorable (1), cute (8), cuddly (1), graceful/gracious (10), elegant (2)	19.8
Intelligence	Intelligent (14), clever (1), curious (4), fascinating (1), intriguing (1), human (1), smart (1), informative (1), different (1)	13.4
Power	Energetic (1), powerful (4), strong (3), noble (1), agile (1), fast (1), aggressive (1)	6.4

their encounters sheds light on how these are contextualized. Certainly, the park narratives themselves have a strong role in this process, as Desmond suggests for Marine World USA:

> The overriding impression that one gets from spending time at the park and reading the program booklet is that most of these animals are beautiful, charming, intelligent, inquisitive, often playful and dying to meet us. They come across as just the sort of people we would like to have as friends: trustworthy, fun, clever, responsive and good looking.
>
> (Desmond, 1999, p. 194)

It seems clear that anthropomorphic tendencies undoubtedly owe a great deal to the cultural influences on our natural understandings. When the same exercise was repeated with whale-watching participants on Australia's Gold Coast in 2005, similar results were found. From 99 responses, over half commented on size of the mammal and the awe of seeing it in the wild. There were still a number of anthropomorphisms, mostly relating to the 'stubborn' nature of the elusive whales. Interestingly, there were no discussions of intelligence, which seems surprising given the high profile this attribute is given in whale-hunting debates. This may be the result of the absence of very close encounters on the trips surveyed, with no eye contact between species.

'Finding' Nemo

In a process that began with landscape poetry, our appreciation of the marine environment is undoubtedly mediated by a wide range of cultural constructs. Indeed, as Wilson has argued: 'Our experience of the natural world ... is always mediated. It is always shaped by rhetorical constructs like photography, industry, advertising, and aesthetics, as well as by institutions like religion, tourism, and education' (Wilson, 1992, p. 12).

In particular, film and television have 'come to dominate the ways in which the "wild" is construed in contemporary cultures ...', even 'cartoon representations of wild animals ... [are] used by audiences as sources of "knowledge" about the real thing' (Beardsworth and Bryman, 2001, p. 86). As Whitmore (2003) found in her study of safari tourists in South Africa, many were embarrassed to admit that everything they 'knew' about lion behaviour had come from the Disney film *The Lion King*.

One of the most popular marine characters of recent years, and claimed by many to have increased interest in reef observation in particular, is the barrier reef anemone fish (*Amphiprion akindynos*), which featured as the title in Disney's 2003 film *Finding Nemo*. The story tells of a father's quest to find his only son, who has been kidnapped for the aquarium trade, travelling the length of Australia's East coast to rescue him. Disney films are probably one of the most influential factors in anthropomorphizing wild creatures, and this synopsis indicates that Nemo is clearly no exception.

Nevertheless, it cannot be denied that the film raised a great deal of awareness about the Great Barrier Reef in particular, and various agencies and operators seized on this opportunity. The Great Barrier Reef Marine Park Authority (GBRMPA) collaborated heavily with the film's producers, indeed the GBRMPA Communications and Marketing Manager Barry Duncan stated: 'Nemo is really going to help put the Great Barrier Reef in the hearts and minds of the whole world' (GBRMPA, 2003).

Queensland used this coverage to extensively promote its marine tourism product, and the Australian Tourist Commission has been using the film heavily in overseas promotions campaigns, particularly in the USA and Japan. At the launch, film, media and tourism industry representatives joined the State Premier and Tourism Minister for an early morning tropical 'Breakfast at Nemo's Place', on Green Island off Cairns (Queensland Government, 2003).

Operators reported a significant boom in reef-based tourism, with some resorts reporting occupancy levels up to 80% above normal (Allen, 2004). Nemo even went so far as to become immortalized as an official state emblem. After a public consultation and voting process, the anemone fish was adopted as Queensland's aquatic emblem in March 2005 (see Fig. 7.4). Admittedly, Nemo was up against some rather less charismatic opposition, including brain coral, spiny crayfish and cod.

However, in a case of truth imitating fiction, it seems that the film's popularity may pose some threat to reefs through the growth of the

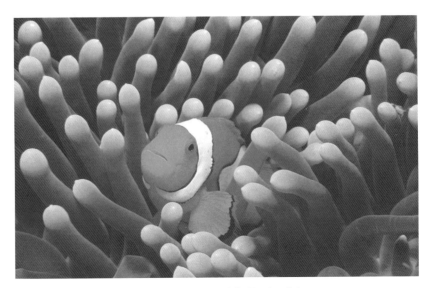

Fig. 7.4. The 'real' Nemo (photograph courtesy of C. Benjamin).

aquarium fish trade. The UN estimated 20 million fish worth US$500 million would be caught in 2004 for this purpose. In Vanuatu, in the Pacific, where a lack of regulation has spawned a significant industry, dive operators and marine biologists suggest that there has been a dramatic decline in the number of high-value species on the surrounding reefs (ABC, 2004). Firms such as Sustainable Reef Supplies, a subsidiary of the large US multinational Seagrest, have taken an industrial approach to fish collection, bringing in live-aboard vessels with up to ten divers at a time. A 2004 documentary by the Australian Broadcasting Corporation highlighted allegations of corruption and bribery, alongside a fisheries agency moribund due to a lack of funds (ABC, 2004).

Despite this, the importance of films such as this for raising awareness of the marine environment cannot be ignored. Indeed, it may be that Nemo has also had educational value in less developed countries, where many have not previously had access to the underwater world. A marine biologist working in Vanuatu suggests: 'They love watching Nemo. The village kids here don't really have an intimate contact with the reef. It's just not in their traditional nature to love the reef and to love fish and love animals and so that film really did show them the different side of the reef' (ABC, 2004). Similarly, IMAX features such as *Planet SOS*, mentioned in Chapter 4, do much to raise awareness of the marine environment.

Reporting the reef

In a study that examined potential factors influencing visitation to the Great Barrier Reef (Cater, 2004), links were examined between newspaper coverage of environmental damage and visitor numbers. Specifically, articles on the crown of thorns starfish and coral bleaching were sourced from selected Australian and UK newspapers. Crown of thorns starfish are not a new phenomenon, indeed they have been present on the Great Barrier Reef for at least the last 7000 years (CRC Reef, 2001).

However, they are a threat to the reef because once the starfish reach maturity, at about 6 months, their primary diet is live coral, and they may live up to 7 years. Sections of reef can support small numbers of the starfish for long periods without any significant reduction in coral cover. However, when populations of the starfish grow beyond a certain level, their impact can be dramatic. During a severe outbreak, there can be several crown of thorns starfish/m^2, and they can kill most of the living coral in an area of reef, reducing coral cover from the usual 25–40% of the reef surface to < 1%. Such a reef can take 10 years or more to recover its coral cover (CRC Reef, 2001).

Although tourists are highly unlikely to be aware of the *actual* levels and locations of starfish outbreaks, media coverage of starfish outbreaks is relatively common. Table 7.2 shows the number of articles in newspapers that discussed the crown of thorns starfish problem between 1994 and 2004.

As might be expected, there were increased levels of coverage in the years following significant outbreaks, and also an overall increase in recognition of the problem over time. However, there were no significant correlations between the media coverage of crown of thorns starfish outbreaks and visitation to the Great Barrier Reef, either at reef-wide or section level.

Table 7.2. Media coverage[a] of crown of thorns starfish on the Great Barrier Reef, 1994–2004 (from Cater, 2004).

	1994	1995	1996	1997	1998	1999	2000	2001	2002	2003	2004[b]
The Australian	0	2	2	3	2	1	11	1	6	4	0
Daily/Sunday Telegraph (NSW)	0	0	3	2	0	1	4	2	1	2	5
Sunday/Herald Sun (Victoria)	0	0	1	0	2	1	4	2	4	3	2
Sunday Mail (South Australia)	0	0	0	0	0	0	0	0	0	1	0
Courier Mail (Queensland)	3	8	8	3	1	10	13	11	9	12	10
The Times (UK)	0	0	1	1	1	0	1	0	0	0	1
The Guardian (UK)	0	0	0	0	0	0	0	1	0	0	0
Total	3	10	15	9	6	13	33	17	20	22	18

[a] Articles (*n*).
[b] To date.

As for the experience itself, 85% of visitors to the reef surveyed in late 2001 described the overall environment as being good or very good (Saltzer, 2002). This clearly indicates tourist satisfaction with the quality of the marine environment, although Gössling and Hall (2006, p. 19) caution, in a study of Mauritian reef quality, that 'Only few of the tourists have the knowledge to judge whether environmental conditions are good ... and reefs healthy ... it remains unclear when environmental conditions reach a state that no longer appeals to tourists'.

Coral bleaching as a result of rising sea temperatures was another 'popular' media story on the Great Barrier Reef. Table 7.3 shows the number of articles in the same newspapers that discussed the coral bleaching problem between 1994 and 2004. Again, there was limited evidence of any correlation between media coverage of coral bleaching events and changes in visitation, although what is interesting to note is a peak in media interest in the year following a major bleaching event (see Fig. 7.5).

As for the experience itself, 79% of visitors to the reef surveyed in late 2001 described the coral as being good or very good (Saltzer, 2002), inferring that coral bleaching had not yet had a major impact on tourist satisfaction. It can be argued that, perhaps, whilst the media coverage of environmental threats to the Great Barrier Reef was not a barrier to visitation, it was likely to raise awareness of its existence and issues. Although very difficult to measure, it may be that some tourists view their trip as a chance to 'see it while you can', a message that has been encouraged by a number of doomsayers in the press.

Table 7.3. Media coverage[a] of coral bleaching on the Great Barrier Reef, 1994–2004 (from Cater, 2004).

	1994	1995	1996	1997	1998	1999	2000	2001	2002	2003	2004[b]
The Australian	0	0	1	0	5	7	7	5	5	13	1
Daily/Sunday Telegraph (NSW)	0	0	1	0	4	7	5	2	4	4	7
Sunday/Herald Sun (Victoria)	0	1	0	0	0	1	4	1	4	4	0
Sunday Mail (South Australia)	0	0	0	0	0	0	0	0	0	0	0
Courier Mail (Queensland)	4	0	2	0	8	15	9	6	15	15	2
The Times (UK)	0	0	0	0	2	1	1	2	1	0	0
The Guardian (UK)	0	0	0	0	0	4	2	3	3	4	1
Total	4	1	4	0	19	35	28	19	32	40	11

[a] Articles (n).
[b] To date.

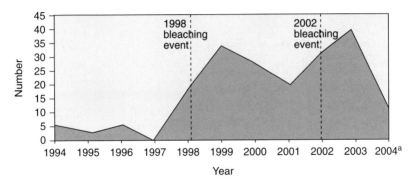

Fig. 7.5. Number of newspaper articles concerning coral bleaching, 1994–2004 ([a] to date).

The whale story

Alongside dolphins, equal attention is paid – in both ecotourism experiences and cultural discourses – to the whale. From Melville's *Moby Dick*, perhaps emblematic of an earlier age where whales were lumped into the dangers and mysteries of the deep, to contemporary Western discourses of whales under threat, these leviathans have captured the public imagination.

As Bulbeck (2005, p. 62) notes, every winter the Australian media play out the contemporary story of the whale to coincide with their annual migration up the eastern seaboard. Regular characters such as 'Migaloo', a rare albino humpback, receive particular attention in the media, with the usual anthropomorphic tendencies (*Sydney Morning Herald*, 2004). A past where the West hunted these creatures is swept under the carpet, and instead one may witness the championing of our 'enlightened' postmodern stance towards protecting these animals, despite the fact that many die in shark nets each year.

This is contrasted with the 'primitive' behaviour of the Japanese and Norwegian whaling fleets. Furthermore, in a relationship with the oceans mediated by the tension between rationalism and romanticism, it is interesting to see how these countries' catches are justified by the IWC as 'scientific'. As such, these practices are categorized as morally wrong, but situated within a rationalist use of marine resources. With reports on IWC meetings focusing on which country bought which out, it becomes apparent that the story is as much about politics as it is about the fate of cetaceans. This only further emphasizes that we must take into account the politics of the management of marine resources, as shown by Hall (2000b), and echoed in Chapter 9.

Certainly, there are now significant tourism interests who wish to see the whales protected and increase in number. Whilst whales are a long way off ever reaching population levels that predate human slaughter, we might be wise to consider the ethical and practical debates that have surrounded unsustainable levels of 'protected' South African elephants in recent years (BBC News, 2005b). As detailed in previous chapters, whale watching is a significant global industry, and thus represents a number of interests. In Hervey Bay, Australia, the annual Aus$15 million injection from 75,000 whale watchers leads to estimates that each whale is 'worth' Aus$100,000 to the local economy (Bulbeck, 2005; Hervey Bay City Council, 2005). Other estimates put the national significance of whale watching in 2003 at over Aus$300 million, up from Aus$46 million in 1991 (Club Marine, 2005).

The economic picture is, of course, blurred, but dominates the thinking of those who exercise power, even in those who are responsible for management. In Hervey Bay, operator licences for tourism and whale watching can amount to Aus$5000, and a 'whale tax' on each passenger contributes approximately Aus$120,000 each year (Marine Parks Regulation, 1990). These whales seem expensive. Contrast this with a local celebrity, 'Vic Hislop', who runs a museum based on fomenting fear of sharks (see Fig. 7.6). Flyers for the facility show the owner proudly displaying his latest catch. Some might think the sharks were getting a raw deal. Of course, we are not arguing for a whale-hunting position but, as Bulbeck (2005) suggests, we are perhaps a little myopic in our views.

Fig. 7.6. Display at Vic Hislop's Great White Shark Exhibition, Hervey Bay, Australia (photograph courtesy of C. Cater).

Experiencing the 'other'

The previous chapter attempted to explain what it is that we gain from engaging in marine wildlife experiences. However, there is also a philosophical desire that backs up these interactions. Partly, it is the chance to experience difference, or the 'indescribable, mysterious, deliriously pleasurable other' (Bulbeck, 2005, p. xix). Desmond makes much of our desire to experience other, radically different bodies from our own: 'The pleasures produced by these experiences are based on our calibration of relative size, scale, body structure and function between the animal and ourselves' (Desmond, 1999, p. 264). However, some have suggested that there is a higher level to this need, and echo Edward Wilson's (1993) concept of 'Biophilia', the need to be close to nature. Bulbeck (2005) makes much of the desire to look nature in the eye, through such connections with marine megafauna.

Indeed, there is an increasing body of medical work that suggests that we are also hard-wired to appreciate natural interaction. A variety of research supports our need for such contact. Recent research suggests that swimming with dolphins may alleviate depression (Antonioli and Reveley, 2005). In this study, one group of clinically depressed participants were allowed to swim with and 'care' for Honduran dolphins over a 2-week period, whilst a second control group engaged in snorkelling on the Honduran reef. Whilst both groups showed a positive outcome in the form of reduced depression, the group who swam with dolphins achieved significantly higher improvement in their condition. The interactive nature of the experience may explain its efficacy, the researchers suggesting that: 'The echolocation system, the aesthetic value, and the emotions raised by the interaction with dolphins may explain the mammals' healing properties' (Antonioli and Reveley, 2005, p. 1233).

In the case of sharks, we also probably want to look the predators of our past in the eye. The media hype that surrounds fatal shark attacks – for example, that of a 21-year-old student off North Stradbroke Island, Australia, in January 2006 – stirs up a frenzy not unlike that of the sharks. We are reminded, perhaps primevally, of Bruce Chatwin's discussion of *Dinofelis*, the leopard-like creature which, it would appear, hunted our ancestors in Africa, the Australopithecines, some 1.2 million years ago: 'Could it be, one is tempted to ask, that *Dinofelis* was Our Beast? A Beast set aside from all the other Avatars of Hell? The Arch-Enemy who stalked us, stealthily and cunningly, wherever we went? But whom, in the end, we got the better of?' (Chatwin, 1987, p. 253). Chatwin, and many academics, have argued that overcoming our primary predator was a major step in our evolution, even though *Dinofelis* fossils have been found around the world: *D. abeli* (China), *D. barlowi* (Africa), *D. diastemata* (Europe), *D. paleoonca* (North America) and *D. piveteaui* (South Africa).

Finally, humans were masters of the terrestrial world around us, although we still carry fear of the dark as a marker of this previous association. In the marine environment, however, the 'beasts' are still present, and these emotions are stirred up every time there is a fatal attack, although of course there is no longer a threat to the future of our species. However, the general consensus seems to gravitate towards a greater respect for such creatures. Indeed, Chatwin also argued that there was a sense of sublime intimacy with our predators, that there was, in some senses, a 'nostalgia for the Beast we have lost' (Chatwin, 1987, p. 254) that surely drives a desire to experience these animals in the wild.

Disappointment

There is significant room in the marine ecotourism experience for nature not to live up to expectations, and we would argue that encounters are rarely as good as anticipated. First, there is the need to get up close and personal, shown to be important in Chapter 4. Although Orams (1995) suggests that whale watching is not just about seeing whales, proximity is a significant measure of satisfaction. Describing the subdued attitudes of dissatisfied dolphin watchers on the Moray Firth, Scotland, and whale watchers at Hervey Bay, Australia, Bulbeck shows that 'closeness can be everything' (2005, p. 101). The specks on a photograph are rarely desired proof that one has seen the animal in the wild.

Secondly, there is the desire for connection. In the large number of marine tourism experiences the authors have engaged in prior to, and during, the writing of this book, most animals have been characterized by an overwhelming indifference to human observers: dolphins not caring that you are there, turtles mildly irritated at being disturbed from slumber or whales that disappear as soon as the humans show up. All are characteristic of ecotourism interactions, but where was that cross-species communication that we so desired? It is the norm that 'we look at them but they do not look at us, ignorant of or ignoring our presence (or so it seems)' (Desmond 1999, p. 188). Indeed, it is interesting to note that, in Bulbeck's research, she suggests that: 'Visitors to animal encounter sites did not consider they had an "interaction" when they observed animals that ignored them' (Bulbeck, 2005, p. 7), although if they were able to pet or hold them, this would suffice.

This disappointment has a number of causes. Certainly we are spoiled by the technical wizardry of the modern documentary, which takes us closer than we could ever achieve in an ecotourism experience. Tour operators and marketers are also likely to sell us false expectations. The best professionally taken photographs – and guarantees of sightings (although no mention of proximity) – are essential for business, but are unlikely to be repeated. In addition, ecotours themselves are usually regimented, because they have to be. Franklin, drawing on work conducted by Markwell (2001), suggests that operators 'promise close contact but the structuring of the tour ritually and technically serves to create a distance between the tourist and the wild' (Franklin, 2003, p. 240).

All of this does not mean that we are bound to be dissatisfied, just that we would perhaps be better off if we had fewer false expectations. Some might argue that it is inherently sustainable for the industry, as it leaves us always wanting more, and thus wanting to come back, as well as not adversely affecting the species. However, a value change, as part of a broader appreciation of the natural environment, would certainly do us no harm. More enlightened operators should be seeking to encourage more appropriate expectations, as this is more representative of the environment with which they are associated.

Do not disturb

We would not want to deny the significance of impact studies on the understanding of ecotourism's impacts on marine nature. Indeed, this vital research often tells us how our desire to see nature impacts on animal behaviour. Many studies have examined the impact of wildlife watching on resting, as it is 'a fundamentally important behavioural state to the health of many species of animal' (Constantine *et al.*, 2004, p. 304). These authors studied the resting behaviour of dolphins in New Zealand's Bay of Islands. The amount of resting decreased significantly with an increase in the number of boats carrying out dolphin tours. Resting was observed during only 0.5% of the observations when there were more than three boats associated with a school. They also provide an excellent review of a number of other studies of marine animals in ecotourism encounters.

Dolphins have been observed to engage in less resting behaviour elsewhere in New Zealand (Lusseau, 2003), Ireland (Ingram, 2000) and Portugal (Harzen, 1998). Similar behaviour has been observed on the St Lawrence river in Canada in the presence of tourist boats for both harp seal pups (Kovacs and Innes, 1990) and harbour seals in Quebec (Henry and Hammill, 2001).

The review carried out by Constantine *et al.* (2004) shows that it is not just resting behaviour upon which ecotourism activity impacts. Pacific spinner dolphins have been shown to engage in less of the aerial activity that they are named for when boat traffic is higher (Forest, 2001; Ross, 2001). Animals may also seek to change their habitat if repeatedly disturbed. Dolphins may seek deeper water or different locations (Wells, 1993; Allen and Read, 2000). Humpback whales (Corkeron, 1995), and killer whales (Jelinski *et al.*, 2002) have also been shown to alter their travel paths in the presence of vessels.

Not all animals demonstrate disturbance, however; in fact, marine iguanas in tourist areas have been shown to be less stressed than ones having little human contact (Romero and Wikelski, 2002). However, the authors suggest that this may in fact be a form of habituation, and that the reduced ability to respond to stressful situations could be detrimental in the long term. Disturbance is clearly a major issue in ecotourism, and harks back to our desire to explore the world. Indeed, perhaps this disturbance of animals is the source of the 'guilty pleasure' described by Bulbeck (2005).

It should come as no surprise that tourist behaviour has a bearing on the response elicited from marine animals. Whilst a simple acknowledgement, this does highlight that the interaction is to some extent cooperative and, although power relations are not equal, both the animal and human are actors in the experience. Research carried out by Cassini with South American fur seals showed that: 'Calm people were able to approach the members of the colony almost with no disturbance' (Cassini, 2001, p. 341). Couples were invariably the best at this. However, there was a threshold of about 10 m that elicited a strong response from the seals. This does, therefore, emphasize the importance of managing ecotourism interactions, and particularly the use of effective behavioural education through guides and guidelines.

In New Zealand, Kaikoura operators comply with a voluntary Department of Conservation code not to swim with dusky dolphins between 12 and 1pm, as research has shown this to be a major resting time for the natural animals (Lück, 2003d). Habitat protection is also important and, as Lusseau (2003, p. 1785) suggests: 'The delineation of multi-levelled marine sanctuaries may be an effective approach to managing the impacts of tourism upon marine mammals.'

Animal geographies

It is widely acknowledged that tourism is largely about the performance of 'place myths' (Anderson, 1991; Shields, 1991), which become reinforced through touristic practice. Indeed, 'As accessibility and transport costs have declined a much wider geography of muscular tourism has developed, with activities specific to single sites operating as a draw card rather than generalized activities around a particular region or country' (Franklin, 2003, p. 225). The art of placemaking beloved of destination marketers is about encouraging performances that reinforce a destination's reputation for a particular touristic experience. Through this commodification of place, certain destinations emerge as being 'the opening of a space of places at which activities can intelligibly be performed' (Thrift, 1999, p. 311).

Ecotourism has not been immune from this, and it is apparent that the 'nature myths' on which the practice is predicated are some of the most powerful. Certain places have been very successful at establishing a reputation for seeing a particular animal or phenomenon. Many of these are described in this book and are inscribed within popular cultural knowledges. In Australia, for example, the equations Hervey Bay equals humpback whales, Ningaloo equals whale sharks, Mon Repos equals turtles and Monkey Mia equals dolphins, are all powerful touristic forces. However, the dominance of these places is based on effectively managing the desire to see these animals in the wild. Should the animals leave, the product is lost, and we should not ignore the potential for other places to become established. As Thrift suggests: 'Like societies, places can be made durable, but they cannot last' (1999, p. 317), and nowhere is this more true than of tourist destinations.

So long and thanks for all the fish

The final question that we began this chapter with was a consideration of animal agency or, as Wolch and Emel contend, the ultimate 'animal question'. As they discuss, the major shortcoming in an approach that maintains that most human understandings of nature are culturally produced leaves very little room for the animals themselves. By 'denaturalizing nature and treating geographic places as cultural productions, the agency of nature and especially animals has been denied' (Wolch, 1998, p. xv).

Ecotourism in particular – and this is perhaps where the split from trained and retrained marine park animals comes in – is dependent on the appearance of wild animals. Undeniably skilled operators who have knowledge of animal behaviours and habitats are likely to achieve high levels of success, but it is ultimately the animals which have to be complicit in putting on a show. As Whitmore points out: 'Wild animals are not privy to the demands of tour schedules and cannot be relied upon to provide sought after photographic opportunities' (Whitmore, 2003, p. 185). In her discussion of seal ecotourism in the USA, Jane Desmond underlines this animal power: 'Ultimately it is the animals that hold the final card ... at least in the short run, their agency gives them the upper hand in setting the limits of contract between seer and seen' (Desmond, 1999, p. 191).

This narrative is often used by ecotourism operators, particularly as it helps to explain 'no-shows'. On Moreton island we are told: 'The dolphins that visit Tangalooma are totally wild. They *choose* to come into the shallows to interact with us and take a few fish from our hands' (Tangalooma Wild Dolphin Resort, 2005).

In these interactions there also appears an issue of who is watching whom, a point often echoed by ecotourism commentary. Whilst this may seem overly romantic, we must acknowledge that, at least to some extent, the animals in ecotourism experiences are seeking to find out about us as much as we are finding out about them. This subjective approach recognizes that: 'Animals as well as people socially construct their worlds and influence each others worlds ... animals have their own realities, their own worldviews; in short, they are subjects, not objects' (Wolch, 1998, p. 121).

Clearly, the power of animals has a reach beyond ecotourism, and contemporary writers have discussed the political economy of animal bodies. The adoption of Nemo as a state symbol for Queensland, as discussed above, is mirrored in a host of other locations that rely on particular animal bodies as a source of ecotourism. In Hughes' (2001) discussion of dolphin watching in the UK, he describes how the town of Nairn in Scotland changed its logo to include a dolphin. These moves reinforce the idea of a place 'for' an animal and link to the discussion above.

The agency of animals is allied to the power of physical nature to control the experience. In a marine context, weather conditions are probably at their most influential over the ecotourism product. In the more adventurous forms of marine ecotourism, this may pose a real risk to the participants. The ocean environment is not a theme park, and cannot be predicted with such accuracy. On a far more common level, natural conditions can still determine the enjoyment of the experience, especially seasickness. These scenarios demonstrate that nature has an agency manifest in the ability to 'push back' (Thrift, 2001; Franklin 2003).

Hybrid Natures

A number of contemporary writers have discussed strategies for negotiating the human–nature divide and its manifest complexities. We feel that in ecotourism, an industry built on this fault line, there are perhaps as many opportunities as any to map out this relationship further. Of course, there are also multiple situations where conflicts arise as a result of this proximity. However, a hybrid approach acknowledges that the divisive categorizations that have been handed down to us are a false rationalism that impedes the long-term sustainability of our mutual relationships.

We could learn much from Eastern philosophy that has developed without such a division, instead promoting a 'middle way'. As Sofield (2005) has shown, Confucian ideals emphasize 'an avoidance of extremes combined with a blending of both ends'. This would seem to answer calls from academics – such as Burns (2004) – searching for a 'third way'. This holistic approach should prioritize three complementary strategies.

A more embodied relationship with nature is a first step. Moving away from a rationalist discourse towards a non-representational approach recognizes that the human body and other natural objects do not stand as separable bits. Instead, we should be looking for 'a closer sensual knowledge of nature through having direct contact with its sonic, textual, olfactory and visual presences' (Franklin, 2003, p. 220). Encouragement is not an issue, as this is a trend that is already sought by a wide variety of ecotourists (and almost-ecotourists), as evidenced by the number of interactive experiences detailed in this book. Of course, our narratives rarely do justice to the importance of these embodied experiences as a direct result of this representational trap: 'knowing our descriptions were dust in our mouths by comparison with what had vibrated through our bodies' (Bulbeck, 2005, p. 151).

Secondly, we must seek to emphasize connection and kinship between the natural world and our own. Monbiot calls for us to 're-examine our involvement with the natural world and reawaken, hard as it now may be, some interaction with animals more meaningful than our visits to pets' corners or burger bars' (1995). Whilst anthropomorphism has been largely vilified for allowing a false discourse to dominate, perhaps we should not be so quick to detract from such narratives. Whilst these descriptions may be scientifically wrong, Wilson (1992) suggests that an enlightened anthropomorphism can also be used as a strategy for blurring the dividing line between different species. This may also be a tool for recognizing that nature still has a strong hand in the negotiation of the ecotourism experience. As we have described in this chapter, it is clear that the ecotourism experience is highly mediated, but some of that mediation comes from the marine animals themselves.

Thirdly, we must seek to acknowledge existing relationships to nature, particularly those of local communities, many of which underlie the examples described in Chapter 5. As Hughes demonstrates in his discussion of dolphin operators in Scotland, a top-down, science-led, regulatory approach is rarely successful. Instead, he calls for an 'alternative approach which relies more on local lay understanding or folk knowledge and a trust in the self-regulatory powers of the community' (Hughes, 2001, p. 328).

Such moves are not always easy, and a fundamental reorientation of our relationship to nature is unlikely to occur overnight. Certainly, it challenges a number of powerful interests that are based on the continuation of such a harmful divide. However, if we do not make some fundamental changes, the long-term consequences – not just to the ecotourism industry – could threaten *all* of nature. Chilla Bulbeck summarizes our contemporary dilemma perfectly:

> Humans need to see ourselves neither as totally separate from and superior to nature, the perspective of modernism, nor as totally immersed in and undifferentiated from it, the perspective of premodernism. Instead we need to forge a postmodern relationship with the non-human world, one which recognizes the vast imbalance of power and destructive potential between humans and the wild world and also notes the epistemological difficulty of seeing the world from the perspective of wild others.
>
> (Bulbeck, 2005, p. 184)

8 The Marine Ecotourism Industry

Circular and Cumulative Relationships

The tourism industry is patently a major stakeholder in marine ecotourism. This is because there is a symbiotic relationship between the industry and the natural and cultural resources that constitute the marine tourism attraction. To borrow the terminology of the Swedish economist Gunnar Myrdal (Myrdal, 1957), this relationship is not only circular but also cumulative, as emphasized in Chapter 2, this volume. It is circular in the sense that the industry has a strong vested interest in a healthy marine environment but, simultaneously, there is a danger that it may foul its own nest through unsustainable activities that adversely impact on coastal and marine resources. It is, however, also cumulative, in the sense that such an outcome would set in motion a downward spiral whereby the compromising of visitor satisfaction would result in reduction of tourist arrivals, questionable economic viability and jeopardization of locally accrued benefits.

It is evident, therefore, that a holistic appreciation must be gained of the interplay between the marine ecotourism industry and other stakeholders and components of marine ecotourism. Such an understanding can be facilitated, if only partially, by a framework introduced during the 1990s to measure corporate performance, and thus business sustainability, along three lines: profits, environmental sustainability and social responsibility. This triple bottom line approach is therefore, as Slavin (1998) puts it, about 'people, planet and profit – the idea being that environmental quality and social equity are just as important as black ink at the bottom of the ledger'.

The Triple Bottom Line

Buckley (2003b) makes a special case for ecotourism in terms of achieving the triple bottom line of sustainability, arguing that, while other industries may take steps to reduce their operational environmental impacts, their environmental bottom line is still negative. He suggests that:

> It is only in tourism that there is a realistic opportunity to produce a positive environmental and indeed social bottom line at the same time as a positive economic bottom line. It is thus the positive contribution to conservation, either directly or through local communities, which makes ecotourism worth worrying about. These bottom line contributions, therefore, are the key defining feature.

> (Buckley, 2003b, p. 81)

Of course, it is important to recognize that all three elements of the triple bottom line are not only interlinked but also co-dependent. Queensland's Ecotourism Plan 2003–2008, for example, describes how 'Ecologically sustainable practices in waste minimization can reduce operating costs, resulting in a more profitable business that will have greater capacity to contribute to conservation, provide stable employment opportunities and purchase more goods and services from local suppliers' (State of Queensland, 2002).

The financial bottom line

As Butler (1998) describes, economic sustainability has implicitly been the driving force behind tourism development, witnessed by the economic impact analyses that have been undertaken for decades. If marine ecotourism operations are not financially viable, there is the clear danger that entrepreneurs may turn to other, less sustainable, options. The previous project manager of Chumbe Island Coral Park, Zanzibar, voiced her concern over this potential scenario:

> Ecotourism ... is still an industry under the same market pressures as any other ... market disincentives ... make potential entrepreneurs look towards other more financially advantageous investments which (due to the higher turnover possible with reduced consideration of impacts ecologically and/or culturally) ultimately outcompete this corner of the market.
>
> (Carter, 2002)

As the title of a book on strategies for creating profitable and environmentally sound businesses puts it in a nutshell: 'The bottom line of green is black' (Saunders *et al.*, 1993).

This critical role of financial sustainability is graphically illustrated by the economic role played by marine park tourist operators in the Cairn–Port Douglas region of Queensland, Australia. A consultancy report conducted in 2001 highlighted that the region's economic health was closely linked to the Great Barrier Reef and the activities of reef operators, estimating that a 10% decline in marine park tour operator activity and visitation could result in an annual decline of Aus$52 million in regional output (Hassall and Associates, 2001).

However, Mules (2004) suggests that the Hassall report not only underestimated the truly public benefit, as the industry operators spent some Aus$19m (2004 prices) on activities such as access, infrastructure, interpretation and research, but also failed to address flows of taxation from tourism expenditure, as well as global non-use values associated with World Heritage listing.

He also examines the contribution that the marine tourism industry makes to management of the reef. This is a pertinent illustration of the 'bottom line of green being black' hypothesis: if the operators were not spending an estimated Aus$16.9 m on the management activities of marketing, education and stewardship, 'then it is arguable that the Federal Government would have to do so, under its responsibilities for World Heritage listing' (Mules, 2004). Indeed, this would be the case because the World Heritage Convention, as Hall (2003) describes it, is 'hard' law insofar as it carries obligations to signatory states to implement the convention correctly.

The question of economic viability of marine ecotourism operations is therefore a crucial one. While the picture of marine tour operators in the GBRMP may appear a rosy one, it must be remembered that theirs may be a boat that is easily rocked. Cater (2004) highlights the outside economic, socio-political and environmental threats to visitation levels. Any change to fiscal policies would have a significant impact. The Association of Marine Park Tourism Operators (AMPTO) put up a strong defence against possible withdrawal of the Diesel Fuel Rebate Scheme (AMPTO, 2002), as well as effectively lobbying for removal of the General Sales Tax levied on the GBRMP Environmental Management Charge (AMPTO, 2005). Both of these would have had considerable adverse effects on the industry's profitability and consequent knock-on effects on environmental performance and social benefits.

It is important to recognize that the current membership of AMPTO of 130 across all categories of the industry can present a significant collective voice in influencing policy. As discussed in Chapter 11, such industry collaboration also performs an important role in marketing, as frequently marine ecotourism businesses are small, isolated and lack the financial resources to reach the marketplace effectively. Most frequently, the start-up finance for ecotourism has come from the pockets of the owners. One entrepreneur lamented that his situation was that of being 'five years and two family savings accounts later' (Shores, 2002). While the operating costs and the environmental education programme of Chumbe Island Coral Park (see Fig. 8.1), are covered by income from tourists, it is unlikely that the initial capitalization of the project of US$1.2 million – the largest proportion of which came from the private funds of its initiator, Sibylle Reidmiller – will ever be recovered (Warth, 2004).

Individual altruism cannot be depended upon to save the day, and the failure rate of small ecotourism businesses is high. As Hillel (2002) describes: 'In Brazil, 80% of small and medium sized enterprises ... close doors within their first two years. Why should ecotourism be different? Entrepreneurship at SME level is risky.' Epler-Wood (2003) concurs with this view, citing a study of French GEF-funded ecotourism projects, which found that some 90% of projects that had received funds did not succeed. It has to be the case that sound environmental practice in marine ecotourism makes business sense.

The environmental bottom line

Over the last two decades, increasing awareness and concern about the relationship between tourism and the environment has given rise to the recognition that: 'The environment must become an economic good on which the users will be economizing: that is the environment must be given a price' (Mihalic, 2003). While previously environmental costs were externalized, it has become increasingly recognized that there is a

Fig. 8.1. Tourist bungalows, Chumbe Island, Zanzibar, Tanzania (photograph courtesy of CHICOP).

need to internalize environmental effects. This is because not only do they affect tourism firms and tourists – for example through marine pollution affecting the quality of bathing – but also non-tourism subjects, for example hotel sewage piped into the sea can reduce fish catch.

There is therefore a strong argument for the marine tourism industry to improve its environmental performance to avoid or reduce environmental taxes that may be introduced in an attempt to internalize these costs. There are further, powerful arguments for greater environmental integrity on the part of the industry. Such engagement is likely to be precipitated by the prospects of enhanced profitability arising through outcomes such as reduced operating costs, improved business image, marketability and competitive edge. Whilst the first will be covered in more detail below, the last three potential advantages are substantiated by the findings of a recent survey, which found that 54 million adult American travellers are inclined to book with travel companies that strive to protect and preserve the local environment, 17 million of whom place the environment as a top priority when deciding which companies to patronize (Travel Industry Association of America, 2003).

As long ago as 1990, Gray (1990) drew attention to not only the pressures from green consumerism, but also, increasingly, green shareholders and green employees. As Fennell (2003, p. 16) states:

> The public must demand accountability of tourism products, and tourism service providers must demonstrate an adherence to an appropriate vision in

striving for meritorious achievements in the area of sustainable development. In doing so, it is those that achieve such lofty levels who may ultimately prosper financially.

While Buckley (2003a) questions whether Couran Cove Resort on South Stradbroke Island, Queensland, Australia, can legitimately lay claim to the title of ecotourism, the 2000-capacity resort has taken significant steps to reduce its ecological footprint. Couran Cove introduces the visitor to marine and coastal ecology (and even the wider universe through astronomic observation) through an interpretation centre, walking trails and kayaking through the mangroves.

As well as an extensive revegetation and rehabilitation programme to help restore and preserve a wide range of plant species (including those of the coastal dune ecosystem), the resort also features impressive environmental design features and technologies. Re-use, recycling and appropriate disposal of waste minimize the impact of waste on the environment. Organic waste, for example, is sorted, pureed, aerated, composted and finally goes into a vermiculture processing plant, the by-product being used as soil conditioner and fertilizer in the resort's landscaping and revegetation projects (Lim, 2002).

Other environmentally sound practices at Couran Cove include those of pest control. The mosquito population, for example, is controlled by battery-operated, solar-rechargeable light traps that use carbon dioxide, a suction fan and a net to catch the insects (see Fig. 8.2). The type and likely breeding ground can thus be identified, so that the appropriate

Fig. 8.2. Mosquito trap, Couran Cove, South Stradbroke Island, Queensland, Australia (photograph courtesy of E. Cater).

bio-organic or natural predator can be used to counter the eggs or larvae (Couran Cove Island Resort, 2004a).

It is Couran Cove's energy policy, however, that presents the most pertinent illustration of a win-win scenario whereby environmental integrity makes sound business sense. The resort's energy supply comes from LPG power generators that operate at 10% of the emissions of diesel counterparts (see Fig. 8.3). The capital and recurrent costs associated with this more environmentally benign alternative have, at the same time, been significantly reduced. An independent diesel power station would have cost Aus$3 million more to install, as well as costing Aus$650,000 more per year to run. Connecting to the mainland power grid would also have cost Au$3 million. The latter option would also have been more detrimental to the environment, as a trench would have had to be dug across a Ramsar[1]-protected wetland (Couran Cove Island Resort, 2004b).

Fig. 8.3. Features of gas-fired power station, Couran Cove, Stradbroke Island, Queensland, Australia (photograph courtesy of C. Cater).

[1]Ramsar Convention on Wetlands, Iran, 1971.

Additionally, hot water in the eco-cabins and some of the resort's vehicles are solar powered. Visitors who stay at the resort can monitor their water and energy usage via their unit's TV screen, where it is displayed in graph form over a 24-h period (see Fig. 8.4). The resort's computers update these graphs every 10 min. Through these measures and other energy-saving practices, power demand has been slashed to one-third of that of similar-sized resorts.

While the efforts of individual operators may be commendable, as described in Chapter 2, they are, inevitably, set in an overall context that may jeopardize their successful operation, if not their very existence. An example of where marine ecotourism operators' interests were being compromised by the adverse environmental impacts of other marine resource stakeholders is furnished by the case of Bunaken National Park in North Sulawesi, Indonesia.

Here, the USAID-funded Natural Resources Management Program (NRM) was involved with management planning in the early 1990s but, due to ineffective management and enforcement, the National Park suffered a slow but continuous degradation of its marine resources. This was attributable to anchor damage from the ever-increasing number of tourism boats visiting the park, as well as to destructive fishing practices. While individual operators may not have been able to make a stand against such irresponsible practices that were threatening the viability of their operations, by clubbing together to form the North Sulawesi Watersports Association (NSWA) in mid-1998, they gained enough influence to succeed in the official banning of anchoring in the park.

As well as developing a self-reporting scheme whereby violators of the ban faced the threat of being exposed in the local newspaper, they

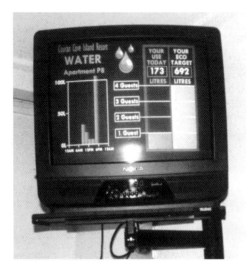

Fig. 8.4. Guest water consumption displayed on TV monitor, Couran Cove, Stradbroke Island, Queensland, Australia (photograph courtesy of E. Cater).

contributed fuel and boat time to local water police and park rangers to help with patrol activities against reef-destructive practices. The NSWA also instituted a one-off fee of US$5 per diver to support a Bunaken preservation fund (Erdman, 2001). This was formalized in 2003 in the form of a daily entrance fee to the National Park of US$5, or an annual fee of US$15, 80% of which goes back to the Bunaken National Park Management Board and is allocated to conservation programmes in the park, including environmentally friendly village development (NSWA, 2002).

Not only have divers commented on their increased satisfaction with the number of fish in the park, but also scientists have recorded an increase in live coral cover, and village fishers have reported increase in fish catches since the bombing and cyaniding have stopped. Bunaken has been chosen as the International Coral Reef Action Network (ICRAN) for its Asian demonstration site as a result of its success (Erdman, 2003).

International guidance on good environmental practice in marine recreation at large has come from a coalition of the Centre for Environmental Leadership in Business (CELB), the Tour Operators Initiative (TOI) and The Coral Reef Alliance (CORAL), who have published *A Practical Guide to Good Practice* (CELB, TOI and CORAL, undated). This covers eight key topics associated with marine recreation: (i) anchoring; (ii) boat operation; (iii) boat maintenance; (iv) boat sewage and garbage disposal; (v) snorkelling, diving and scuba; (vi) seafood consumption and souvenir purchasing; (vii) recreational fishing; and (viii) marine wildlife viewing.

The guide offers a brief summary of potential impacts, the rationale for good practice and suggestions for reducing these impacts. Along with the guide comes a self-assessment checklist to assist suppliers in understanding the issues considered by companies that are attempting to source more sustainable service providers. The 13 core questions on the checklist enquire whether the company:

- Abides by all local, regional, national and international environmental laws and regulations.
- Provides trainings, briefings or literature for employees and tourists regarding good environmental practices for snorkelling, diving, kayaking, various types of boat tours and other marine recreation activities.
- Provides information for employees and tourists regarding the potential impacts of motorized vessels and poor boating practices on coral reefs and other marine environments.
- Actively uses, and supports the use of, mooring buoys as an alternative to anchoring around coral reef ecosystems.
- Has an environmental code of conduct to guide the actions of motorized and non-motorized boat operators and tour guides when they come into contact with, or viewing distance of, marine wildlife such as turtles, manatees, dolphins and whales.

- Takes action to prevent accidental discharge of toxic substances or other waste into the environment.
- Has taken action to reduce use and ensure proper disposal of toxic antifouling bottom paints, fuels, cleaning agents and other hazardous materials.
- Uses alternative, clean-burning technology such as four-stroke outboards for smaller boats or biodiesel fuel for larger vessels with in-board propulsion systems (if applicable).
- Takes steps to minimize discharge of untreated sewage and wastewater from boats.
- Takes actions to prevent the introduction of garbage or solid waste into the marine environment.
- Supports good environmental practices to avoid catching and serving rare, threatened or endangered marine species for seafood consumption.
- Supports good environmental practices and educates customers about the negative environmental impacts of harvesting marine species from coral reefs and other marine environments to sell as ornamental souvenirs.
- Contributes to biodiversity protection and conservation projects in the local region of its operations.

It can be seen that environmental sustainability has moved towards a more centre-stage position in marine ecotourism, not only because of a need to conserve its resource base, but also because sound environmental and business practice frequently coincide. We are left with our third component of the triple bottom line, that of social sustainability, which for so long has been the Cinderella of the trinity.

The social bottom line

Following the 1992 Earth Summit in Rio, Brazil, which identified the triple bottom line of environmental, economic and social sustainability, there has been a major emphasis by the tourism industry on environmental sustainability (Ashley *et al.*, 2001). This is hardly surprising, because the Earth Summit echoed the recommendations of the Brundtland Commission Report *Our Common Future* (WCED, 1987) which, although it considered the human environment, had as its main thrust 'a concern for the physical environment and its capacity to absorb the demands made on it by various forms of economic activity, including tourism' (Butler, 1998). When this is coupled with the obvious concern of the industry with financial sustainability outlined above, we can begin to understand why social sustainability was the last to arrive on the stage.

However, mirroring the trend towards corporate social responsibility in industry at large, the tourism sector has become increasingly engaged with this dimension in recent years. Tourism Concern's International Fair Trade in Tourism Network, launched in 1999 (Tourism Concern, 1999), pointed to the need 'to strengthen the bargaining position of local destination interest groups, facilitate equitable market access for small stakeholders, raise awareness amongst consumers and influence international trade policy'.

There have been some moves towards these aims from the tourism industry at the international level. The World Tourism Organisation (now UNWTO), the UN agency responsible for tourism, in collaboration with UNCTAD, launched the Sustainable Tourism–Eliminating Poverty (ST–EP) initiative to develop sustainable tourism as a force for poverty elimination at the World Summit on Sustainable Development in Johannesburg, South Africa, in 2002.

UNEP houses the secretariat of the Tour Operators Initiative for Sustainable Tourism Development, a voluntary initiative of leading tour operators supported by UNEP, UNWTO and UNESCO, which was launched in 2000. Amongst the key operating areas identified by the Tour Operators Initiative (TOI) are: 'relations with destinations, by supporting destination stakeholders' efforts to address sustainability and proactively contributing to conservation and development projects.' The TOI has collected from individual members examples of good practice where tour operators have integrated the principles of sustainability into its various areas of operations, which are published in its report *Sustainable Tourism: The Tour Operators' Contribution* (TOI, 2003).

However, the focus of such good practice remains environmental sustainability. One case study in the publication that explicitly focuses on the marine ecosystem is the environmental awareness-raising exercise for tourists conducted in the Red Sea by the French hotel chain, Accor. Another that includes responsible behaviour in the marine environment, is that of TUI Nederland's promotion of responsible travel in Curaçao and Bonaire, discussed further below.

The Life Cycle Assessment undertaken by British Airways in St Lucia (British Airways, 1998), also cited in the publication, addresses issues such as coastal water quality but, while it claims to include sociocultural issues, the examination of these is cursory and is confined to tokenist gestures by the island's All Inclusives (British Airways, 1998, p. 78). However, this report preceded the airline's more dedicated commitment to corporate social responsibility reflected by the change in the name of its annual Environmental report to the Annual Social and Environmental Report, in 2000.

Another international industry initiative that voices an explicit commitment to the social sustainability of destinations is that of Business Enterprises for Sustainable Tourism (BEST). This is an initiative of The Conference Board, in association with the World Travel and Tourism Council. Its mission is to serve as 'a leading source of knowledge on innovative travel industry practices that advance community, business and travellers' interests'. One of the examples highlighted in their publication *Best Practices* is Turtle Island Resort, Fiji, which supports community healthcare, education and employment projects. The latter includes working with three villages as a 'social entrepreneur' to create an association of local budget and backpacker operators. Members of the association have adopted their own Code of Conduct for Responsible Tourism and have agreed to implement and be bound by its principles in their resort operations (BEST, 2002).

Turtle Island was the subject of a cultural audit undertaken by David Harrison in 1998, which 'provided a holistic view of the resort and its organization, including the context in which it operated and its major stakeholders, as well as to describe its social, economic and cultural impacts in the region'. While the audit commented favourably on many of the resort's initiatives, including the fact that it closed to guests for 1 week per year in order that volunteer specialists could run eye clinics and carry out cataract operations, it did raise three fundamental questions (Harrison, 1998):

- For whom was the resort to be a community resource?
- How far could control be replaced by partnership?
- Who should set out the policies towards neighbouring communities?

The immediacy of these questions was pertinently illustrated by the events of the Fiji coup in 2000. A total of 45 tourists had to be evacuated from the island when islanders from Naisisili and small settlements close to Turtle Island – who claimed to be landowners of the freehold island – invaded it.

It is clear that stakeholder involvement may often extend beyond initial perceptions. Many islands in Fiji that were declared freehold during the 1800s were sold without the knowledge of their original landowners. Understandably, widespread resentment follows when these islands are subsequently sold on to further outside interests. This was also exemplified in 2004 by the sale of Mago Island to the Hollywood actor, Mel Gibson, for around US$15 million dollars, an act that was condemned by a group of villagers claiming to be the original owners, who had been struggling for years to reclaim their ancestral home (Parliament of Fiji Islands, 2005).

Amongst other initiatives aimed at assisting the tourism industry towards greater social responsibility are recently established not-for-profit organizations such as the UK's The Travel Foundation and The Responsible Tourism Partnership and the Netherlands' RETOUR foundation. The Pro-Poor Tourism Partnership (a collaborative research initiative between The International Centre for Responsible Tourism, the International Institute for Environment and Development and the Overseas Development Institute) has been working with the Travel Foundation and the Dominican Republic Hotel Association, as well as with a range of other project partners in the Dominican Republic, to provide practical guidance and training for tourism providers on how they can enhance their local development impact (propoortourism, 2005). Since helping to establish and disseminate good practice is very much a focus of these initiatives, it will be instructive to see how their involvement with, and guidance on, socially sustainable marine ecotourism unfolds.

Industry Self-regulation

It is evident from the above discussion that the tourism industry is becoming increasingly proactive in its approach to sustainability. The reasons for this are many and various. Mowforth and Munt (2003) suggest that a cynical interpretation would be that a major driving force is that the industry may be trying to avoid the inevitable in terms of outside regulation. However, they point out that, in the light of the fragmented nature of the industry, it would be almost impossible to regulate for all related practices, as well as to enforce legislation. They also suggest that an alternative interpretation could be that it is 'a genuine attempt to help the industry adapt to what may become environmentally essential regulation' (p. 185).

Whether or not, at the end of the day, industry self-regulation may help to perpetuate unevenness and inequality in the pursuit of profits remains to be seen, but it is instructive to examine how the industry has been involved in the evolution and implementation of guidelines, codes of conduct, eco-labelling and certification in marine ecotourism.

Guidelines and codes of conduct

In 1999, The International Ecotourism Society (TIES) conducted an international survey of 200 small-scale, coastal-based marine tourism operators. The survey was designed to collect each operator's understanding of what guidelines were, whether they thought guidelines would be useful in their region of work and what kinds of best practices they had already implemented in their businesses. The ultimate aim of the project was to give small-scale coastal tourism operators a better idea of the resources available to make their businesses more sustainable (Halpenny, 2002).

Together with an annotated bibliography compiled by TIES and the findings from three stakeholder meetings held in the Caribbean to identify best practice, the results of the survey have been compiled by Elizabeth Halpenny into an authoritative and indispensable publication: *Marine Ecotourism: Impacts, International Guidelines and Best Practice Case Studies* (Halpenny, 2002). The reader is referred to this for a much more comprehensive account of guidelines and good practices that marine ecotourism operations should adopt. Some general observations, as well as a few examples of initiatives, follow.

Holden (2000) describes how codes of conduct have been developed by a variety of organizations, including governments and national tourist boards, the tourism industry and trade associations, and non-governmental organizations such as Tourism Concern and WWF. Their primary aims are to influence attitudes and modify behaviour among stakeholders, primarily the tourism industry, local communities involved with tourism, and tourists.

It is instructive to examine codes that have been evolved by the industry and for the industry. Scheyvens (2002, p. 186) draws attention to the role of industry, citing Cheong and Miller's description of industry stakeholders as 'tourism brokers' who 'compel the tourist to function in a certain way' as they 'are prominent in the control of tourism development and tourist conduct'. There are a number of examples of codes of conduct for marine ecotourism developed by the industry or industry associations drawing upon the advice of key scientific experts and organizations.

Examples of that ilk are: the International Association of Antarctica Tour Operators' (IAATO) guidelines; the Code of Ethics for Whale Watchers developed by marine tour operators in the Bay of Fundy (Canada/USA); the Scottish Marine Wildlife Operators Association (SMWOA) code of practice – 'Navigate with Nature'; the Sea Kayak Operators Association of New Zealand's (SKOANZ) code of practice for commercial sea kayaking; and the Whale Watch Operators Association North West Best Practice Guidelines. These associations are also referred to in Chapter 11, this volume.

Parsons and Woods-Ballard (2003) found that the SMWOA code of conduct was the most popular code utilized by whale watching operators surveyed in the west of Scotland, utilized by 47% of respondents. They suggest that its appeal lies in the facts that it is easy to use and has been produced by tour operators. In contrast, only 27% of respondents were aware of the UK Government (Department of the Environment, Transport and Regions) guidelines and none of the respondents referred to these when watching whales. While these guidelines conventionally consist of voluntary measures, the SKOANZ code of practice, mentioned in Chapter 4, reminds sea kayaking operators of the key acts and regulations that may have a bearing on their legal operation, listing 16 acts covering safety of operation, 11 acts and regulations covering environmental care and three acts relating to customer service.

As voluntary adherence to the codes of practice is the norm, there are usually no direct financial penalties used to enforce rules. Peer pressure and having a bad reputation act as effective penalties for non-compliance (Meinhold, 2003). There is also the omnipresent threat that membership of the organization can be revoked if the marine ecotourism operator does not comply. Of course this presupposes that this, in turn, will constitute a commercial threat to the operator. Also, the extent to which participants will be discerning in their choice of operator is dependent on consumer awareness.

The owner-operator of the Seaprobe Atlantis, the seagoing vessel with specially constructed underwater viewing galleries operating out of Kyle of Lochalsh, Scotland, and discussed in Chapter 4, was somewhat sceptical of the efficacy of the identity conferred by membership of the Skye and Lochalsh Marine Tourism Association. He observed that tourists were just as likely to book a trip with an operator who did not belong to the Association and who thus did not adhere to its code of practice (N. Smith, Kyle of Lochalsh, 1999, personal communication).

While the above codes of practice have been developed by the industry for the industry, there is the implicit fact that they act as a guide for the general public as well as providing a clear message to visitors that the operators are working to minimize their impacts on wildlife, and that they encourage others to do likewise.

In certain instances, industry or industry associations have also developed codes of conduct specifically aimed at the tourists themselves. The International Association of Antarctica Tour Operators, for example, has formulated specific guidance for visitors to the Antarctic outlining how to respect Antarctic wildlife, respect protected areas, respect scientific research and how to keep Antarctica pristine, as well as essential safety measures (IAATO, 2005).

It is, however, probably in the field of scuba-diving that tourists receive the most explicit guidelines. Conscientious dive operators inform clients of responsible behaviour; for example, at Apo island in the Philippines, a noticeboard requires that gloves should not be worn so that divers are deterred from touching coral. TUI Nederland, which is part of the World of TUI (which reaches 80% of European holidaymakers under its member tour operators, accounting for 18 million customers in 2004), under its 'Environmentally Aware Tourism' project, provides customers with information on responsible travel and sustainable products at various stages in their holiday to promote choices for more sustainable island holidays. Their diving guidelines for Bonaire and Curaçao, in the Netherlands Antilles, require that guests must receive an orientation and explanation of eco-diving standards as well as recommending that educational materials, such as identification of marine life, should be available (TOI, 2003).

This emphasis on explanation and education is all-important, as marine tourists need to appreciate the whys and wherefores to encourage them to actively embrace sustainable behaviour. Moscardo (2002) reports that visitors to the Great Barrier Reef who were likely to have been exposed to some educational activities knew more about tourist behaviours likely to threaten the reef environment, to rate these more seriously and to describe the reef using words related to its World Heritage status. A content analysis of 40 tourism codes of conduct conducted by Malloy and Fennell, however, revealed that 77% failed to provide the client with the rationale for abiding by the code (Fennell, 2003). Again, however, perhaps the diving industry performs better on this aspect, probably because of more active physical engagement on behalf of the participant.

The world's largest diving organization, the Professional Association of Diving Instructors (PADI), initiated their project AWARE (Aquatic

World Awareness, Responsibility and Education) in 1992. Project AWARE, also discussed in Chapter 4, aims to 'conserve underwater environments through education, advocacy and action' and achieves this by developing and disseminating educational materials and creating public awareness campaigns amongst its many activities (Nimb, 2003). However, another of Malloy and Fennell's findings holds true in the majority of diving codes of conduct and guidelines, insofar as the focus of such codes is overwhelmingly ecologically based. It is the rare exception, such as Paul's Community Diving School on Apo Island in the Philippines, that recognizes the local significance of marine resources to local livelihoods (see Fig. 8.5). As the web site declares (direct quotation): 'Often overlooked is the symbyotic relationship of people and their enviroment; this fragile ecology is as important to Apo's future as the interactions of fish and marine life are' (Apo Island, 2004).

Adherence to guidelines may provide a sustainable tourism experience but, as Halpenny (2002) suggests, will not in itself constitute an ecotourism experience unless there is an element of interpretation during the visit, as she outlines:

Fig. 8.5. Raising awareness of the significance of marine resources to local livelihoods, Apo Island, Philippines (photograph courtesy of E. Cater).

An interpretation program will help clients understand the environment they are visiting, and provide a richer, more fulfilling experience, thus increasing their enjoyment and encouraging repeat visits and positive reviews to other potential customers. It will also create a new group of environmental and social advocates who know more about the destination and their impact on the earth.

(Halpenny, 2002, p. 25)

The five key mantras for interpretation outlined by Newsome *et al.* (2002) were outlined in Chapter 6, this volume. Halpenny (2002) summarizes the key qualities of effective interpretation as including learning, behavioural and emotional aspects, also outlined by Fennell (2003), who goes on to describe Forestell's model of interpretation and environmental education developed with respect to whale watching. Forestell suggests that the combination of hard scientific facts with unscientific experiential and practical observation will result in an empowering ecotourism experience. Halpenny (2002, p. 27) presents a useful table provided by Richard Murphy, which gives examples of poor versus good interpretation of coral reefs according to the six principles of interpretation developed by Tilden, which address relevance, revelation, the art of interpretation, provocation, holism and type of audience.

There is, as will have been gathered from the earlier chapters in this book, a tremendous breadth and depth of topics in the marine context that lend themselves to effective interpretation, including biological, sociological, cultural, economic, geological, archaeological, historical, mythical, oceanographic and meteorological aspects.

While the latter topic might not spring readily to mind, it is interesting to note that the last 5 years have witnessed the growing popularity of storm tourism on the west coast of Vancouver Island, Canada, where hotels offer winter storm-watching packages. What could be more empowering than witnessing the might of the powerful winter storms around Tofino whipping the sea into 20-foot waves, armed with the knowledge that they are a product of the turbulent frontal zone between subtropical air masses and the vast, persistent Arctic low-pressure system, which establishes itself from October onwards in the Bay of Alaska.

While it is obvious that the tourism industry is not the only agent acting to shape marine ecotourists' learning, behaviour and emotions, it is not only a powerful intermediary but is also quite likely to be the one that tourists rely on. Hockings' survey of marine tour operators at the Great Barrier Reef Marine Park in Australia found three-quarters of the sample offered interpretation as part of their programme (Hockings, 1994).

Of course, the chief interface between the tourists and the marine ecotourism experience will be the marine ecoguide. Newsome *et al.* (2002) cite Weiler and Ham's advocacy of the importance of staff training in interpretation so that visitor satisfaction is improved and impacts are reduced. They suggest that the Ecotourism Association of Australia

Ecoguide Certification programme, which is part of its development of accreditation systems for tour operators, is an important step towards supporting other forms of management and reducing impacts on coral reefs and other ecosytems. The whole issue of certification and accreditation in the industry is one that has commanded much recent attention, to the extent that a special workshop was convened on the topic at the International Year of Ecotourism Summit in Quebec, Canada, in 2002.

Certification and eco-labels

As Honey and Rome (2001) describe – in their seminal work on certification and eco-labelling – tourism labelling, awards and certification on environmentally and socially responsible standards are relatively recent phenomena. Honey and Rome define certification as 'a voluntary procedure which assesses, monitors, and gives written assurance that a business, product, process, service, or management system conforms to specific requirements. It awards a marketable logo or seal to those who meet or exceed baseline standards' (Honey and Rome, p. 5).

They examined several examples of mass (such as Green Globe), sustainable (such as Costa Rica's Certification in Sustainable Tourism) and ecotourism certification (such as Australia's Nature and Ecotourism Accreditation Programme). The reader is directed towards their incisive discussion of a number of outstanding issues of uncertainty and debate (Honey and Rome, 2001, pp. 65–74).

In the light of the proliferation of tourism certification programmes across the globe, a 2-year study was undertaken by the Rainforest Alliance to examine the feasibility of establishing an international accreditation programme to grant certifying powers, in effect to certify that the certifiers are doing their job correctly (Rainforest Alliance, 2002; Font *et al.*, 2003). The proposed Sustainable Tourism Stewardship Council, an international partnership of the Rainforest Alliance, the World Tourism Organisation, The International Ecotourism Society and the United Nations Environment Program, would thus assess and help standardize certification programmes for the sustainable and ecotourism markets. One outcome of the study was the launch in 2003 of the Sustainable Tourism Certification Network of the Americas.

Australia's Nature and Ecotourism Accreditation Program (NEAP), as one of the first designed expressedly for ecotourism and rapidly becoming a model for similar initiatives around the world, is the best known and most widely documented certification programme (see, for example, Font and Buckley, 2001; Honey and Rome, 2001; Fennell, 2003). By 2005, over 80 audits had been conducted of marine tourism operators in the Great Barrier Reef Marine Protected Area (GBRMPA), most operators demonstrating compliance with the best practice standards. The rigour of the certification procedure is illustrated by the fact that one operator had its certification suspended and 11 were requested to address minor breaches. Furthermore, the process is continually monitored, with a commitment by Ecotourism Australia to audit each certified operation within the subsequent 3 years.

There are three categories of accreditation: nature tourism, ecotourism and advanced ecotourism, with the main criterion distinguishing the last two being that, in the advanced ecotourism category, the provision of opportunities to experience nature in ways that lead to greater under-standing, appreciation and enjoyment is the core element of the experience (Font and Buckley, 2001).

Amongst the GBRMPA operators to receive advanced ecotourism certification in the GBRMPA are Sea Kayaking Whitsundays, Calypso Reef Charters and Wavelength Eco-Snorkelling. While it is beyond the expertise of the authors to appraise the validity of such certification, it is none the less interesting to note that, while the latter operation uses trained marine biologists as guides, visitors are promised that: 'You can pick up and touch many different creatures and plants' (queenslandholidays, undated): a core experential element maybe, but sustainable?

We must, therefore, for many reasons, detailed and general, be cautious about what seems to be the 'steamrollering' (Mader, undated) of global certification and accreditation schemes. Detractors from the process are many and various. Ron Mader, for example, in introducing the online Ecotourism Certification Workshop 2000–2003, declared that: 'Prioritizing certification first is akin to putting a band-aid on a deep wound' and drew attention to the lack of consumer awareness and thus questionable tourist demand for certification.

He cited a survey conducted in 2003 of 100 customers of tourism operations having NEAP accreditation, where not one respondent gave accreditation of the product as their reason for choosing the tour (Mader, undated). Similar experience in West Clare, Ireland, was attributed to the demise of the IRRUS[2] branding of marine ecotourism operations. The IRRUS group set out to develop its set of marine ecotourism principles into what would effectively be a system of operator certification. Compliance would be encouraged by access to an increasingly well-known brand name as well as by the negative effect of possible exclusion if a suitable level of commitment was not demonstrated (Garrod and Wilson, 2004). However, the low level of consumer awareness, with obvious marketing implications – coupled with lack of funding and committed individuals – led to the demise of the scheme, as discussed in Chapter 11, this volume (Berrow, personal communication, 2004). Interestingly, the NatureQuest Centre in West Clare has sought certification of its marine ecotourism operations by The International Ecotourism Society (Garrod and Wilson, 2004).

---

[2]Brand name for marine ecotourism in Ireland, introduced 2000.

More fundamentally, the certification and accreditation process has been criticised as constituting 'a method to exclude, to cartelise and to club so that the weak lose their autonomy and come under the hegemony of the strong' (Rao, 2001). Pleumaron (2001) calls for certification to be seen 'in the context of the parallel push for self-regulation by transnational tourism companies and big business associations such as WTTC and PATA'.

Conclusions

This chapter has sought to explore the role of the industry towards ensuring the sustainability of marine ecotourism. While it would be naïve to pretend that the increasingly proactive stance of marine tourism operators is down to philanthropy, we need to recognize that they are key stakeholders with a strong interest, albeit commercially driven, in the future of marine ecotourism. As Fennell and Dowling (2003, p. 340) suggest, there is a need to move beyond the view of operators and service providers as a stakeholder group that must adhere only to policy and guidelines. They must be regarded as 'not only active players in the operationalisation of policy but also shapers of policy'. Assistance for the industry from initiatives such as the TOI and The Travel Foundation, particularly in disseminating best practice, will undoubtedly result in better-informed planning and implementation.

Myrdal's theory of circular and cumulative causation outlined at the beginning of this chapter recognizes the potential for upward as well as downward spirals, as he puts it: 'Nothing succeeds like success' (Myrdal, 1957, p. 12). While there is a danger of drawing the analogy too far, as Myrdal's work highlights essentially what are structural inequalities at play (where not only are unevenness and inequality perpetuated but also exacerbated), a push in the right direction, by whoever, for whatever reason, may induce the momentum for more positive and lasting change in marine ecotourism.

As Myrdal (1957, p. 85) himself declares: 'A policy of purposive interference … promises results much bigger than the efforts implied – if the efforts succeed in starting a cumulative process upwards.' The prospects for marine ecotourism are surely better than they were when there was a failure to even recognize the complex interactions, inter- and co-dependencies at work.

III Regulation, Facilitation and Collaboration

9 Planning Agencies

A Complex Scenario

As outlined in Chapter 2, this volume, planning for sustainable marine tourism is arguably considerably more complicated than that for the terrestrial environment. Not only are we faced with conflicting sectoral interests but, also, with the complicating issues of: open access; common property; the connectivity between land and sea; and differing jurisdictions. In particular, the latter apply not only to often highly mobile resources but also to 'footloose' resource utilization.

Hall (2001, p. 605), for example, cites Wood's description of cruise tourism as 'globalization at sea', with the corresponding phenomenon of deterritorialization. Tourism has received only slight and incidental attention in the literature of marine policy as a whole. This can be attributed, in part, to the fact that tourism

> has been dominantly driven by private sector interests, rather than government regulatory policies, and that much tourism takes place on the *land* of the coastal zone. Furthermore, the problems of tourism do not fall squarely within a single subdomain of marine affairs, or within the purview of a single discipline ... tourism transcends the realm of environmental pollution and protection. It is also pertinent to the policies of ports authorities and local governments, and to those of fishery management, national park, and coastal management agencies; not to mention the recreational practices of individuals.
>
> (Miller and Auyong, 1991, pp. 75–76)

It is vital, however, that we try to ground (!) marine tourism by examining the rules and regulations within which it takes place by attempting to negotiate the complex web of agencies, jurisdictions, protocols and laws that will condition its prospects for sustainability. As Hall (2001, p. 602) suggests: 'There is a clear need to gain a better understanding of the institutional and policy dimensions of integrated coastal and marine management in order to better incorporate the significance of tourism as a component of coastal and ocean development.'

The Role of Government

It may seem paradoxical, in an economic climate driven by neo-liberalist, market dictates that advocate a minimalist role for the state (Scheyvens, 2002, p. 165), to examine the role of government in the planning, regulation and management of marine tourism, but it is undeniable that all levels of governance have become increasingly engaged with the health of marine environments in recent years. While not all engage explicitly with marine tourism, there are obvious implicit implications for sustainable outcomes, given that such initiatives will shape the overall context of the seas and oceans in which it is set as a process.

International marine governance

International conventions and organizations

There are a bewildering array of international conventions and organizations governing, or attempting to govern, ocean use. Kimball (2001, p. 5) views oceans agreements as an interlocking web, exerting 'push and pull' effects on one another as 'each new development influences and leverages subsequent developments in other fora' by serving as a model. There is also the 'drag' effect, where 'more specific and binding obligations in one convention leverage the achievement of goals in another'. Here, she cites the case of the UN Convention on the Law of the Sea (UNCLOS) Article 194 (5), requiring states to take pollution control measures which 'include those necessary to protect and preserve rare or fragile ecosystems as well as the habitat of depleted, threatened or endangered species and other forms of marine life', which will obviously reinforce area and species protections established under other conventions. This has important ramifications for marine ecotourism resources.

Kimball (2001, pp. 81–82) lists the important roles of conventions as being those: (i) providing information and assessment initiatives; (ii) influencing sustainable ocean development initiatives and international support; and (iii) promoting accountability. UNCLOS is the first comprehensive, enforceable international environmental law. As such, it is held to be the most important international achievement since the approval of the UN Charter itself in 1945 (UN, 2002). Promulgated in 1982, it entered into force in 1994. UNCLOS serves as an umbrella for numerous other existing international agreements covering the oceans, including international fisheries agreements and regional initiatives. Belarus was the 150th country to ratify the convention in August 2006. Although the USA was expected to do so in 2004, being one of the last industrialized nations to act, their ratification in the near future seems unlikely following intensive conservative lobbying on the grounds of risk to national security.

The Law of the Sea Convention sets down the rights and obligations of states and provides the international basis upon which to pursue the protection and sustainable development of the marine and coastal environment. It defines five offshore zones (Kimball, 2001): (i) *internal waters* that are landward of the baseline (normally the low water line), forming part of a state's territory; (ii) *a territorial sea* of up to 12 nautical miles (nm) in which the state exercises full sovereignty; (iii) *a contiguous zone* that extends up to 24 nm miles from the baseline, in which the coastal state may prevent and punish infringements of its laws and regulations (such as customs); (iv) *an exclusive economic zone (EEZ)*, which may not extend beyond 200 nm, in which the state has sovereign rights over natural resources and other economic uses as well as jurisdiction over marine scientific research and marine environmental protection; and (v) *the continental shelf*, which may extend up to 350 nm from the baseline, where the state exercises sovereign rights over natural resources and jurisdiction over marine scientific research.

All states have the same rights and obligations on the high seas beyond these zones. UNCLOS lays down strong and binding obligations for marine environmental protection and preservation, including rare or fragile ecosystems, marine species' habitats and conservation of living marine resources. It endorses a marine ecosystems approach to marine biodiversity conservation, again exerting a strong 'drag' effect on other conventions and agreements.

Another major international marine environmental initiative is the Global Programme of Action on Protection of the Marine Environment from Land-Based Activities (GPA). As mentioned in Chapter 2, it is estimated that run-off and land-based discharges contribute 44% of all marine pollution. Concern over the costs at the national level of deterioration in coastal environments led to the promotion of the GPA by UNCED in 1995. Although it is in itself non-binding, the role of the GPA is to push for global, legally binding instruments for the reduction and/or elimination of deleterious emissions and discharges (Kimball, 2001).

The Convention on Biological Diversity also has the potential for an important role in the conservation and sustainable use of marine and coastal biodiversity. It calls upon states to conserve and sustainably manage biodiversity, taking necessary measures to protect threatened species, including the establishment of marine and coastal protected areas. It is significant, as Kimball (2001) suggests, for its emphasis on sustainable use, thus recognizing the role of socio-economic values in conservation (including indigenous knowledge), as well as acknowledging local and national concerns. It provides the key international framework on the ecosystem approach, incorporating and entailing a number of key principles. These include decentralization of resource management – incorporating stakeholder engagement – and a need to understand and manage the ecosystem in an economic context that is compatible with conservation and sustainable development.

There are also various conventions governing protected species, which obviously include marine species. These include the Convention on International Trade in Endangered Species of Wild Fauna and Flora (CITES), which aims to avoid unsustainable harvesting and commerce in wild species, as well as the Convention on the Conservation of Migratory Species of Wild Animals. As far as marine ecotourism is concerned, the role of CITES in controlling trade of coral and tropical fish is significant, as depletion in these species has obvious ramifications for destination attractiveness. Amongst other activities, the latter convention has obvious significance for marine mammal viewing, as well as for turtle watching and the observation of migratory sea birds.

There are three global instruments that define geographic areas for special protection, all of which relate to the territorial sea zone (Kimball,

2001). The Wetlands or Ramsar Convention aims to develop and maintain an international network of wetlands important for global biodiversity conservation and sustainable livelihoods. Nearly one-third of the 1000 wetlands designated by Ramsar have a marine or coastal component, including mangroves, seagrass beds, coral reefs, intertidal zones and estuaries, all of which have considerable marine ecotourism potential. The World Heritage Convention covers both natural and cultural areas of outstanding value, which again include marine and coastal areas. Over 30 natural sites thus designated have a marine or coastal component; they include the Great Barrier Reef of Australia, as well as Belize's Barrier Reef, both of which are significant tourist attractions. The Man and the Biosphere Reserve Programme (MAB) of UNESCO, although not a legally binding convention, identifies national and international priorities and provides guidance. Approximately one-third of MAB Reserves globally have a marine/coastal component.

Another international convention that has a significant bearing on marine ecotourism is that of the International Convention for the Regulation of Whaling of 1946. This convention established the International Whaling Commission (IWC), with membership open to any country that formally adheres to the convention. In 1975, a new management policy for whales was adopted by the IWC, designed to bring all stocks to the levels providing the greatest long-term harvests by setting catch limits for individual stocks below their sustainable yields. However, because of uncertainties in the scientific analyses, the IWC decided that there should be a moratorium in commercial whaling on all whale stocks, effective from 1986. This pause in commercial whaling does not affect aboriginal subsistence whaling, which is permitted from Denmark (Greenland fin and minke whales), the Russian Federation (Siberia grey whales), St Vincent and the Grenadines (humpback whales) and the USA (Alaska bowhead and, occasionally off Washington, grey whales). Since the moratorium came into effect, Japan, Norway and Iceland have issued scientific permits as part of what they declare to be research programmes.

There have been accusations that such permits have been issued merely as a way around the moratorium decision; these have been countered by claims that the catches are essential to obtain information necessary for rational management and other important research needs. All proposed permits have to be submitted for review by the Scientific Committee following guidelines issued by the Commission (IWC, 2004.) However, the ultimate responsibility for their issuance lies with the member nation and much adverse publicity surrounded Iceland's catch of 36 minke whales in the summer of 2003 (Parsons and Rawles, 2003).

Given that there is also lack of international consensus as to whether the moratorium covers small cetaceans, with many states maintaining that they are subject to national jurisdiction within the EEZ (Kimball, 2001), its efficacy must be questioned. This is all the more surprising in the light of the fact that the revenue from whale watching is worth many times that from commercial whaling. The Icelandic economy benefited by US$13.8 million from 60,000 whale watchers in 2001 (Cetacean Society International, 2003), anticipated to increase to over US$20 million by 2006 (Parsons and Rawles, 2003).

Of the international initiatives specifically aimed at consumers of marine resources examined by Kimball, the World Bank's Marine Market Transformation Initiative (MMTI) has the most relevance for marine tourism, as one of its four areas of concern is specifically to link marine tourism with coral reef conservation. The MMTI will 'support changes largely in private sector operations through policy reforms, alternative technologies, economic instruments, targeted investments, consumer education, and eco-labelling and marketing' (Kimball 2001, p. 60).

The UN Commission on Sustainable Development (CSD7) endorsed a work programme on tourism in 1999, and the secretariat will collaborate with the World Tourism Organisation in establishing a working group to promote sustainable tourism development. It invited the parties to the Convention on Biological Diversity to contribute to international guidelines for sustainable tourism development, including those in vulnerable marine and coastal ecosystems, protected areas and habitats of major importance for biodiversity (Kimball, 2001, p. 77).

There are bound to be gaps in the international agencies involved in oceans governance described above but, to add to the list, the IUCN, which was accorded status of Observer at the UN General Assembly in 1999, together with the WWF, developed a global marine policy, *Creating a Sea Change*, with the following goals: (i) maintaining the biodiversity and ecological processes of marine and coastal ecosystems; (ii) ensuring that any use of marine resources is both sustainable and equitable; and (iii) restoring marine and coastal ecosystems where their functioning has been impaired (IUCN/WWF, 1998).

Multilateral and bilateral funding

It is interesting to reflect that, until the early 1990s, tourism was seen as an inappropriate avenue for donor finance. With increasing recognition of the conservation/development nexus, and a growing engagement with the need to enhance local livelihoods through sustainable resource utilization, ecotourism captured the attention of international funding bodies as a funding avenue.

In 1992, for example, the International Resources Group prepared a report for USAID on ecotourism as a viable alternative for the sustainable management of natural resources in Africa (IRG, 1992). Since then, both multilateral and bilateral funding have been increasingly directed towards ecotourism projects. The Global Environmental Facility (GEF) of the World Bank is a financial mechanism that provides grants and concessional funds to recipients from developing and countries in transition for projects and activities that aim to protect the global environment.

There have been a number of GEF-funded projects that have a marine tourism component, ranging from the global through to the local. For example, GEF is developing a global project on best practices for integrating biodiversity considerations into the tourism sector (Kimball, 2001, p. 77); it has supported a Marine Resource Management Project in the Egyptian Red Sea that aimed to address coastal marine-related tourism and conservation; and its small grants programme has promoted marine tour guide training in five coastal communities in Belize (GEFSGP, 2004).

Amongst the underlying problems with the GEF are: (i) the fact that the World Bank manages the fund (it is implemented by UNDP and UNEP), and yet the World Bank itself is simultaneously a massive promoter of energy and forest projects and operates without adequate environmental safeguards effectively implemented in its lending; (ii) that it fails to address the macro root of many global environmental problems; and (iii) that the GEF has been used to mitigate environmental problems arising from new projects funded by the World Bank and other institutions, as well as reducing existing environmental problems (Down to Earth, 2001).

In Pakistan, the building of dams and barrages under the Indus Basin Project, funded by contributions from the World Bank and other donors – as well as necessitating the wholesale relocation of a considerable number of settlements – disrupted the distinctive livelihoods of the Indus boat people. GEF Small Grants Projects funds have been allocated to an ecotourism initiative at Taunsa barrage to create alternative livelihoods for these boat people in a sanctuary for the Indus River dolphin (GEFSGP, undated).

The European Union's European Regional Development Fund part-funded the Marine Ecotourism for the Atlantic Area (META) project, which was a collaborative exercise between Torbay Council (UK); the Marine Institute, Dublin; MBA Escuela, Gran Canaria; and the University of the West of England, Bristol (META-Project, 2000). Bilateral funding has also been increasingly directed towards marine conservation and marine tourism. The Canadian International Development Agency (CIDA) assists developing countries with the protection of their ocean environment for sustainable trade, shipping and tourism. Amongst projects supported by the German overseas development agency, GTZ, are the Chumbe Island Coral Park, Zanzibar, global winners of the 2001 British Airways Tourism for Tomorrow Award, and the establishment of marine protected areas in Negros Oriental, Philippines. The New Zealand Official Development Assistance Programme has provided technical and financial assistance to develop ecotourism accommodation and activities at Marovo Lagoon in the Solomon Islands, which provide alternative sources of livelihood and resource use to the local people as well as securing a World Heritage listing for the lagoon (Halpenny, 2000).

Effectiveness of international marine governance

It is not surprising, given the plethora of international agencies involved in some way or another with oceans governance, that their effectiveness is characterized – and thus seriously compromised – by competition and duplication of effort. Valencia (1996), for example, lists the multiplicity of UN (UNEP and UNDP) and other specialized agencies and organizations of the UN participating in the GPA (ranging from FAO to the World Health Organization) as a prime illustration of this fact. Yankov and Ruivo (1994) point to the fact that, despite the large number of global and regional institutions with competence in marine issues, and the number of legal instruments dealing with various aspects of ocean affairs, the absence of an appropriate coordinating global forum acts as a serious impediment to the identification of issues, priorities and strategic planning needs. Such a forum could also promote intra- and interregional cooperation and mobilize funding.

Given the potential of UNCLOS as a comprehensive, enforceable, international environmental law, it is disappointing that not only is the USA conspicuous by its absence as a signatory, but also that its uptake has been selective across the globe. Nicol (undated), for example, describes the situation in the Caribbean, where the weaknesses of existing environmental law and policy frameworks, lack of resources and political will – together with the problem of overlapping maritime zones – hamper its effective implementation. Furthermore, UNCLOS proceeds on the clear premise that competent international organizations have vital roles to play in the implementation of its provisions in many crucial areas.

However, as Mensah (1994) suggests, the effective discharge of these roles will entail institutional and procedural changes both within and without these organizations, as well as implications for resource allocation and a readiness to forge cooperative relationships with states and other organizations.

A further barrier to effective planning and implementation is the absence of adequate baseline information, as well as of a well-organized system of data bases on potential and actual impacts of activities, *inter alia* tourism, in different types of marine ecosystems. Kimball (2001, pp. 66–77) suggests that:

> Emerging information resources are just beginning to establish baselines against which to judge progress. Evaluating progress in the coastal/marine realm will require not only information on the incidence of introductions but also an assessment of their distribution and impacts in socio-economic and ecological terms.

Once developed, such an inventory 'may point to the need for further elaboration or harmonization at regional or global levels or in relation to particular activities'. Voluntary compliance with such harmonization could be reinforced if it were endorsed pursuant to one or more relevant conventions (e.g. regional marine, wetlands). Certain measures may even be adopted as binding rules. In the Arctic, Principles and Codes of Conduct for Arctic Tourism, developed through a WWF project, helped change operational procedures in certain tourism enterprises cooperating in pilot projects, for example, through recycling and more intensive education of clients.

However, there are a number of weak links that hamper the realization of a comprehensive inventory. The weakest, Kimball suggests, is the ability to collect, organize and disseminate knowledge and experience across the globe in order to solve site-specific problems. Secondly, is the need to strengthen knowledge and capabilities at local, national and regional levels, and thirdly is the need to foster a collective understanding of the causes, impacts, and solutions of shared oceans problems. She describes how these weak links have been compounded by the late realization of the fact that extension of the EEZ to 200 nm offshore spread impacts to ever-larger segments of society and coastal/marine ecosystems that transcended national boundaries.

Added to the above problems are those of the imposition of external agendas on local societies, particularly the case when donor funding is added into the picture. Mowforth and Munt (2003, p. 60) voice this concern, suggesting that environmental conditions and caveats placed on Western loans and grants promote a greening of social relations, which may be viewed as 'a kind of eco-structural adjustment where Third World people and places must fall in line with First World thinking'.

Regional marine governance

It is evident from the above discussion on international governance that there is a considerable problem of collaboration and coordination of efforts at that level. However, while it is essential to recognize the international dimensions of the marine environment, it is clear that there is a need to reconcile both the needs of human society as a whole with those of communities dependent on marine ecosystems as well as to reconcile the sector-specific thread of international legal instruments with the more comprehensive, ecosystem-based approach necessary to diagnose complex problems.

Kimball (2001, p. 81) suggests that it is at the subregional and regional levels that logical ecosystem-based units of ocean management converge with international institutional arrangements. This is because the international dimensions of the marine environment mean that local and national knowledge needs to be assembled at the regional level to improve understanding and effective responses.

Launched in 1974, the Regional Seas Programme of UNEP was revitalized by the adoption of the GPA in 1995. More than 140 countries participate in the 13 regional programmes in the Black Sea, Caribbean, East Africa, East Asia, the Kuwait Convention region, Mediterranean,

North-east Pacific, North-west Pacific, Red Sea and Gulf of Aden, South Asia, South-east Pacific, South Pacific and West and Central Africa (Adler, 2003). Each programme is tailored to the specific needs of its constituent states, but contains: (i) an action plan for cooperation on the management, protection, rehabilitation, development, monitoring and research of coastal and marine resources; (ii) an intergovernmental agreement of framework convention (not necessarily legally binding as, although the conventions are presented under the UNEP Regional Seas Programme umbrella, they are independent, separate juridical entities); and (iii) detailed protocols dealing with particular environmental issues such as protected areas.

In addition to the participating regions, there are five partner programmes for the Antarctic, Arctic, Baltic Sea, Caspian Sea and North-east Atlantic (OSPAR). A global effort is also underway by IUCN, the Intergovernmental Oceanographic Commission of UNESCO (IOC), other UN agencies and the US National Oceanic and Atmospheric Administration (NOAA) to improve the long-term sustainability of resources and environments of the world's large marine ecosystems and linked watersheds. Recognizing the transboundary implications of marine resources, pollution and critical habitats, the Large Marine Ecosystems Strategy defines relatively large regions of the order of 200,000 km^2. Sixty-four large marine ecosystems have been designated to date, many of which are receiving GEF support.

Individual regional marine programmes may include specific tourism-related measures, for example, three training manuals – on water and solid waste management for the tourism industry, integrated coastal area management and tourism, and siting and design of tourist facilities – are being developed through the Caribbean regional marine programme for use by educational and training institutions and individuals involved in the tourism industry (Kimball, 2001, p. 77).

Effectiveness of regional marine governance

While there have been several positive outcomes of the Regional Seas Programme, in particular increasing developing countries' capacity to participate in regional marine environmental protection by the transfer of marine science technology and knowledge, the approach has many criticisms, general and specific, levelled at it. These point to the need for restructuring and a new perspective. It is particularly criticised for its failure to involve the private sector, unions and general public, as well as to address those agencies responsible for pollution such as energy and tourism (Valencia, 1996).

Furthermore, particular concern has been voiced regarding the enactment of UNCLOS embodied in the Regional Seas Programme, particularly with respect to developing nations. For example, in the Caribbean, Nicol (undated) highlights the challenge of increasing poverty and environmental degradation among the developing countries of the region. She points to the difficulty of applying international law in the Caribbean because of the balkanized nature of marine contexts, lack of funds among the mostly developing nations, the increasing role of tourism in national economies, the special vulnerability of the region to natural hazards and the legacy of colonialism, which has left many modern Caribbean nations with outdated political and legal infrastructures.

Many of the regional decision makers are thus rejecting UNEP's regional seas programme for the Caribbean (the Cartagena Convention) based upon UNCLOS and its regime of conventions. They criticise it as a fragmented application that cross-cuts the region and relies upon extra-territorial organization and structure for implementation. For these reasons, regional institutions within the Caribbean have thus defined the Caribbean Sea as a Patrimonial Sea, or common source of sustenance and identity for all regions. They call for the region to be designated, instead of a regional sea, as 'A Special Area in Context of Sustainable Development' (a regionally organized conservation regime that relies upon existing capacity for implementation). This geographical basis defines functional space and a common identity that cross-cuts linguistic, cultural and political divisions. It is argued that such Special Area designation will be more effective in arriving at a consensus on environmental agendas, as it acts as a unifying concept as well as being a powerful metaphor.

National marine governance

As seen above, there have been a considerable number of environmental policies and regulations promoted for the marine environment in the last 20 years. However, these have mostly been reactive responses to specific issues and generally derive from outside the nation state. In the light of increasing realization of the value of the marine environment and of the accelerating pressures upon it, national governments are at last waking up to the need for a strategic, coordinated, approach that provides proactive mechanisms to manage marine biodiversity (DEFRA, 2002b). As Borgese (1994) describes: 'At the national level, the incorporation of integrated ocean policy into national development plans is gradually taking place, altering traditional approaches to social and economic development.'

As will be seen presently, the overall picture with regard to national ocean affairs is that of a fragmented, haphazard approach. However, some governments have considered the advantages of more stable and efficient mechanisms on an intersectoral basis (Yankov and Ruivo, 1994). Australia's Oceans Policy, launched in 1998, has several objectives, including the protection of Australia's marine biodiversity and the ocean environment, and ensuring that the use of oceanic resources is ecologically sustainable within its Exclusive Economic Zone. In 1999, the National Oceans Office was formed as an Executive Agency to coordinate the overall implementation and further development of Australia's Oceans Policy, which is to be implemented through Regional Marine

Plans. The 1997 Oceans Act of Canada establishes obligations for the Minister for Fisheries and Oceans for the management and conservation of Canadian waters. It also establishes the legal framework for a national strategy for the management of estuarine, coastal and marine waters within Canadian jurisdiction. India established its Department of Ocean Development as early as 1981.

In the UK, despite the fact that DEFRA (2002c, p. 15) does not believe that 'a wider, overarching stakeholder body is needed to cover all marine and coastal policies in the UK', claiming that: 'Such a large body would inevitably lack focus and duplicate much of the work that is already being taken forward in other groups', the very creation of DEFRA in the UK in 2001 brought together into one government department interests in marine science to support conservation, environmental protection, fisheries and coastal management objectives (DEFRA, 2002b). This has led the UK government to adopt an ecosystems-based approach for marine management to better integrate marine protection objectives with sustainable social and economic goals so that all those who manage or influence the marine environment work together at all levels with a common understanding. (DEFRA, 2002b).

So, what forms can government intervention take with regard to sustainable coastal and marine tourism? Hall (2001) identifies a range of five policy measures aimed at the development of coastal and marine tourism: (i) regulatory instruments (regulations, permits and licences that have a legal basis and which require monitoring and enforcement); (ii) voluntary instruments actions or mechanisms that do not require substantial public expenditure – for example, the development of information and interpretive programmes; (iii) direct government expenditure to achieve policy outcomes, including the establishment of protected areas such as marine and national parks; (iv) financial incentives, including taxes, subsidies, grants and loans, which are incentives to undertake certain activities or behaviours and which require minimal enforcement; and (v) non-intervention, where the government deliberately avoids intervention, especially with respect to allowing market forces to determine policy outcomes (however, Hall (2000a) suggests that this is relatively amoral as it allows individuals to be immoral).

Hall (2001, p. 613) stresses that there is 'no universal "best way": each region or locale needs to select the appropriate policy mix for its own development requirements'. However, he laments the fact that little research has been done into how to achieve the ideal, place-specific mix and that there is often minimal monitoring and evaluation of policy measures.

Effectiveness of national marine governance

It remains a lamentable fact that the general approach to marine conservation has been one of non-intervention in comparison with the active management framework for conservation increasingly promoted on land. In the UK, despite DEFRA's call for an ecosystems-based approach, there remains a fundamental concern that: 'Proper marine governance needs to be coupled with comprehensive and detailed reforms to the law to protect the UK's diverse marine life and cultural heritage, while providing sustainable solutions for our marine industries and activities' (Wildlife and Countryside Link, 2004). Not surprisingly, a similar scenario exists for coastal and marine tourism, which is heavily dependent on a healthy marine environment As Hall, 2001, p. 614 describes:

> Unfortunately there is usually little or no coordination between programmes that promote and market tourism and those that aim to manage coastal and marine areas ... Implementation strategies often fail to recognize the interconnections that exist between agencies in trying to manage environmental issues, particularly when, as in the case of the relationship between tourism and the environment, responsibilities may cut across more traditional lines of authority ... one of the greatest challenges facing coastal managers is how to integrate tourism development within the ambit of coastal management, and thus increase the likelihood of long-term sustainability of the coast as a whole.

Why has government involvement in coastal and marine tourism been relatively unsuccessful to date? First, it has been characterized by a fragmented, and thus often uncoordinated, approach, hampered by intersectoral competition for resources. As Timothy (2002, p. 162) describes with regard to tourism planning in general: 'Sectoral planning traditions, wherein each agency, or service provider, is most interested in achieving its own goals without discussing actions with other agencies and stakeholders who may have related interests, are common.'

Unfortunately, this traditional sectoral approach continues to dominate national administration of ocean affairs, despite increasing and intensive multiple use of the oceans and growing difficulties of management (Yankov and Ruivo, 1994). Vallejo (1994) describes the general situation, where:

> Policy-making takes place at the sectoral level, is primarily reactive and is, therefore, formulated on a piecemeal basis without interagency consultation. As a result, marine related policies have conflicting (or at best unrelated) objectives, resulting in environmental damage or simply ineffective implementation. As a consequence, decision-making procedures are highly fragmented, suffer from internal duplication and overlap and reveal competition between agencies.

This is the most common scenario across the globe. Saharuddin (2001) describes the situation in Malaysia, where the organizational structures governing the ocean for policy implementation are present, but are fragmented and uncoordinated. As a result, sectoral and intersectoral management problems have been created, such as multiple-use conflicts, overlapping of jurisdiction and duplication of efforts. Inevitably, the manifest results are that ocean management is, as

Lubchenco *et al.* (2002) described for the USA, 'haphazard, piecemeal and ineffective in the face of declining ocean conditions'.

Secondly, as Vallejo (1994) also suggests, in the majority of cases:

> Ocean affairs do not represent a central concept but are a matter subsidiary to other activities having higher priority. Their political stature is generally low. This is immediately translated, among other things, into the location of the activity being at a low level within the government hierarchy, into administrative linkages with more powerful agencies whose authority/ functions are not traditionally associated with marine affairs (for example fisheries under the Ministry of Agriculture), as well as into certain patterns of resource allocation (limited personnel and low levels of funding) ... Within the national planning process, the marine component is either one of the least developed or simply non-existent.

Thirdly, largely as a result of the above, government decision-making is consequently *ad hoc* and characterized by reactive rather than proactive decision making (Hall, 2001). Fourthly, at the implementation level, the major problem is the absence of coordination between the planning and operational levels (Vallejo, 1994). This occurs not only horizontally, between sectors and agencies, but also vertically, between different levels. Scheyvens (2002) describes how the Costa Rica Government collects tourist taxes and entrance revenues at the sea turtle nesting site in the Ostional Wildlife Refuge. However, it has not been proactive in enhancing the capacity of the local community to benefit from the increasing numbers of tourists visiting the site. Similarly, in Baja California, Mexico, Young (1999, p. 609) describes how:

> While two main federal agencies are legally empowered to both monitor tourism activities around gray whales and enforce laws that restrict such activities, there are numerous obstacles to effective government management of both. The agencies are overcentralized, and government decision makers (based in Mexico City) are unfamiliar with local ecological and social conditions. Insufficient funding for field personnel, facilities and equipment impede effective regulation of local activities in both areas.

It follows, from the above considerations, that an improved understanding of the policy process and institutional arrangements by which coastal and ocean areas are managed is essential in order that a better integration of tourism development in coastal communities and marine ecosystems may be achieved without due negative impacts (Hall, 2001).

Provincial marine governance

Although not dedicated to marine tourism, the fact that there is increasing insitutionalization of coastal management at the provincial level has obvious implications for improved integration of tourism development within coastal communities and ecosystems, while mitigating adverse impacts. In Australia, the Queensland State Government Environmental Protection Agency is preparing a Coastal Management Plan and Regional Coastal Management Plans that focus on integrated coastal zone planning and management and incorporate ecologically sustainable use and development.

In the USA, several states have advanced oceans programmes, for example Oregon's Territorial Sea Plan and Hawaii's Ocean Resource Management Plan. Under the auspices of the former, the community at Cape Arago has formulated policies to strike a balance between growing recreational and tourist use of the rocky shore environment, with the protection of marine life and habitats (Hershman, 1999). Massachusetts established its Ocean Management Initiative in 2003, to establish a more proactive process for managing oceans resources within state waters (Massachusetts Government, 2004).

Effectiveness of provincial marine governance

As at other levels of governance, provincial initiatives are vulnerable to political and leadership changes. Of four US initiatives examined by Hershman (1999), only Oregon maintained steady progress, as it was firmly established in a respected programme activity of the executive branch. A further complication arises when there are conflicts over jurisdiction between different levels of governance.

Meinhold (2003, pp. 29–31), for example, cites the case of whale-watching management in the Robson Bight Ecological Reserve, British Columbia, where the Canadian federal government has jurisdiction over its marine waters, whereas BC Parks has jurisdiction over the land portion, rubbing beaches and seabed. BC Parks lacks the mandate to legally enforce the Marine Mammal Protection Regulations, and thus depends on the Canadian Department of Fisheries and Oceans for effective enforcement.

Local marine governance

While the overall picture regarding local marine governance is that of a top-down process, beset with now-familiar problems of being reactive rather than proactive; of fragmentation; and of competition for financial resources and expertise and competition, there are some examples across the globe where the initiative has been from the bottom up.

At Ulugan Bay, in the Philippines, the councils of the five local barangays (together with ancestral domains) proposed their own community-based sustainable tourism initiatives, which were integrated with broader conservation and development issues as well as with long-term strategic planning in the wider municipality, within which Ulugan Bay is located. The draft plan was submitted to wider stakeholders before being submitted as a final draft to the municipal authority and back to the local authorities for endorsement. Once endorsed, the implementation of the action plan commenced, which included both training and capital works initiatives prioritized for implementation in each community area. These activities are supported by a rolling programme of community consultation and participation, which functions as a monitoring mechanism (Felstead, undated).

In China, in theory, local coastal governments should be in a position to play an important role in protecting the marine environment. This is because decentralization has granted local governments jurisdictional rights in handling local political and social problems, including environmental problems, together with local financial autonomy and better information than held by central government agencies. However, faced with the constraints of limited finance, lack of institutional and technical capacity and the dilemma of reconciling economic development with environmental protection, it is suggested that the international community should develop partnerships at the local level to enhance technical, financial and institutional capacity (Chen and Uitto, 2004).

Effectiveness of local marine governance

As Vodden (2002, p. 2) suggests, local capacity is a crucial factor in determining the success of local marine governance:

> Local actors and actor networks often have limited human financial and organizational resources … Despite increasing complexity, varying and often limited local capabilities have rarely been measured or taken into account when planning responsibility transfer. Nor have adequate financial resources been put into place to facilitate the transition and build capacity where it is needed.

To redress this shortfall, major international non-governmental organizations (INGOs) are increasingly becoming engaged in the types of partnership suggested by Chen and Uitto (2004), above. This is particularly so because they are often brought in as the implementation partners in international donor agency-funded projects.

Non-governmental Organizations

International NGOs

In the same way that marine conservation and, in turn, marine ecotourism, have become increasingly popular targets for multilateral and bilateral funding from supra-national and national donor agencies, so, too, have international NGOs focused on projects that promote the conservation of the marine environment whilst simultaneously enhancing coastal livelihoods. Frequently, as described above, these INGOs may be the channels through which donor funding is channelled.

The WWF is purportedly the world's premier conservation organization. Thematically, the WWF has chosen to work on: (i) oceans and coasts as one of its three target biomes; (ii) marine turtles and great whales as two from the list of flagship species that it is concentrating on; and (iii) the spread of toxic chemicals and the threats of climate change. It is clear, therefore, that the work of the WWF has relevance for marine ecotourism, and several of its projects have a declared marine ecotourism component.

For example, WWF has facilitated the production of a shared management plan for the Sulu Sulawesi Marine Ecoregion (SSME) by the three nations of the Philippines, Indonesia and Malaysia. Home to around 35 million people who are directly or indirectly dependent on coastal and marine areas for their livelihoods, a major objective is to develop operational, sustainable and conservation-linked livelihood systems. Towards this end, immediate actions include the development of model marine ecotourism sites (WWF, 2004).

Conservation International (CI), a very influential non-profit organization based in Washington, DC, USA, operates in more than 30 countries worldwide. CI has strong links with the World Bank, and its corporate partners include Bank of America, Ford Motor Company, McDonalds Corporation and ExxonMobil. CI's activities in marine ecotourism include the creation of a new marine protected area in Southern Belize to protect the whale sharks that congregate in the area and to generate revenue for local communities through ecotourism (Conservation International, 2003). CI's Marine Rapid Assessment Programs, which establish baseline biodiversity information on selected coral reef areas and analyse this information in tandem with social, environmental and other ecosystem information to produce appropriate and realistic conservation recommendations, are undertaken 'in a time frame suited to managers and decision-makers' (Conservation International, 2004).

The world's richest environmental group, with assets of US$3 billion, The Nature Conservancy (TNC) is a not-for-profit organization boasting 1 million members worldwide. Members of its corporate forum, the International Leadership Council, include Boeing, Delta Airlines, ExxonMobil, Monsanto and Proctor and Gamble. TNC's Global Marine Initiative complements the over 100 marine projects that the Conservancy has around the world. In Komodo National Park, Indonesia, TNC is working with fishermen using destructive practices, such as cyanide, to divert them to sustainable fishing and marine ecotourism (Kirkpatrick and Cook, undated).

An INGO with a specific ecotourism remit is that of The International Ecotourism Society (TIES), which changed its name from The Ecotourism Society in 2000. TIES is a much smaller INGO in terms of both membership and assets. None the less, its influence is considerable around the world in disseminating information on how to do ecotourism right (albeit set in existing power relationships, as Mowforth and Munt (2003) suggest). Amongst TIES' marine ecotourism initiatives is the publication of Marine Ecotourism: Impacts, International Guidelines and Best Practice Case Studies (Halpenny, 2003), discussed in Chapters 1 and 5, as well as guidelines on how to be a marine ecotourist (TIES, undated).

National and local NGOs

As with most of the INGO examples above, conservation may be the primary mandate of many national and local NGOs, but many have adopted ecotourism as a form of development that is complementary to the goals of conservation (Halpenny, 2003). Countering the criticism that NGOs tend to have narrow, specialist, frequently Western-centric views and ignore the public good, Halpenny suggests that this phenomenon is becoming less evident with mounting levels of professionalism, and points to the positive roles that NGOs perform in marine ecotourism in terms of financing conservation, establishing tourism and ecotourism standards, education and research.

A number of environmental, educational and scientific organizations offer nature, adventure, study and service tours to their members; these, increasingly, also incorporate ecotourism principles. The Whale and Dolphin Conservation Society's 'Out of the Blue' holidays, for example, 'give people the opportunity to see and learn about whales and dolphins and their conservation', with all profits going back into whale and dolphin conservation.

Some non-profit organizations are specifically geared to recruiting paying volunteers to work on conservation projects. The non-profit organization, Coral Cay Conservation (CCC), recruits paying volunteers to survey tropical reefs in several locations across the globe. The data and information collected on reef ecosystems not only enhance local knowledge and understanding of the fragility of such systems, but also furnish an all-important baseline to inform future decision making by facilitating the identification of zones of particular vulnerability and pointing towards those areas where tourism and other forms of economic activity in the future will do least damage.

The data furnished by Coral Cay were instrumental in the designation of the Belize Barrier Reef as a World Heritage Site in 1996, and in its subsequent management. The conferral of that status has had an undeniable impact on enhancing the image of Belize as an ecotourism destination. In the Philippines, 3 years after CCC joined forces with the Philippine Reef and Rainforest Conservation Foundation to survey the coral reefs of Danjugan Island, Negros, the island became a world-class marine reserve. Active community involvement and outreach in these volunteer programmes has meant that they epitomize bottom-up tourism planning, with broad stakeholder involvement. For example, the organization recognizes the importance of including all resource users of a region within an environmental education and awareness programme.

CCC targets a diverse range of audiences, including local schoolchildren, village community leaders, resort guests, dive instructors and tourism guides. This ensures that the knowledge gained throughout the project phase is actively put into communities, rather than staying purely within the policy realm.

The Role of Research Institutes

The role of research institutes in supporting the development of sustainable marine ecotourism is not inconsiderable. The primary mission of the world-renowned Woods Hole Oceanographic Institution at Cape Cod, USA, is 'to develop and effectively communicate a fundamental understanding of the processes and characteristics governing how the oceans function and how they interact with the Earth as a whole' (Woods Hole Oceanographic Institution, undated). Its Arctic group acts as a coordinating body for Arctic expeditions, while its coastal group seeks to 'increase understanding of natural processes and human impact in coastal areas'.

The Smithsonian Tropical Research Institute (STRI) undertakes marine environmental monitoring at the Galeta Marine Laboratory, Panama, which also acts as an educational site for local and international visitors. A management plan for the use of the adjacent area for research, education and ecotourism is being developed to allow joint use by STRI, local universities, members of the local community and visitors. The Irish Marine Institute produced a Marine Research, Technology, Development and Innovation Strategy for Ireland in 1998 that provided an economic profile of the marine tourism sector and identified prioritized R & D requirements. These priorities have since been addressed via the implementation of various activities that have included developing a framework for the development of special-interest marine tourism in the West Clare Peninsula (which was to provide the foundation for the inclusion of that area in the META-project, as discussed above and in Chapter 11).

Clearing the Turbidity

From the above analysis it would appear that, for a multitude of reasons, marine policy and, in turn, the context for planning for sustainable marine ecotourism, can be regarded as a prime – if not the most glaring – example of a meta-problem (Hall, 2000a), as discussed in Chapter 1, this volume. This is hardly surprising, given the fact that each of its components – sustainability, the marine environment and tourism – are, in themselves, meta-problems. Hall (2000a, p. 145), citing Ackoff, describes the tourism meta-problem as being characterized by highly interconnected planning and policy 'messes' which 'cut across fields of expertise and administrative boundaries and, seemingly, become connected with almost everything else'.

Equally, sustainability and the health of the marine environment are set in this enormously complicated, and confusing, scenario. The essential dilemma is how to make sense of this conundrum. The call must be to develop a coordinated approach. As Hall (2000a, p. 147) suggests, this might occur through the creation of new organizations or the allocation of new responsibilities to existing ones. Given the plethora of already existing organizations and conventions, and their problems when translated to place-specific contexts (for example, the Regional Seas programme in the Caribbean as described above) such a response would not 'by itself solve the problem of bringing various stakeholders and interests together' (Hall, 2000a, p. 147). Hall endorses the shift towards the implementation of an 'ecosystem management' approach among US government natural resource management agencies, whereby it may be possible for 'separate, partisan interests to discover a common or public interest'.

It is encouraging that a marine ecosystems approach is now being advocated at many levels by different agencies across the globe: for example by: UNCLOS; the IUCN, other UN bodies and agencies and the US NOAA in the worldwide Large Marine Ecosystems Strategy; the Community Marine Strategy of the European Community; WWF UK in its Living Seas programme; in the regional marine ecosystems of Australia's Ocean Policy; and as declared by DEFRA for the UK (DEFRA, 2002c). Concern still remains, however, as to whether such a holistic, process-based, approach will be adequately backed by effective legislation in order to achieve sustainable outcomes.

10 Management Structures

Approaches to Marine Ecotourism Management

The previous chapter examined the complex web of agencies, jurisdictions, protocols and laws with and within which marine ecotourism must operate. How these are translated and transposed on the sea in terms of marine management will, of course, be highly variable, contingent upon social, economic, institutional and political contexts that will condition its prospects for sustainable outcomes.

Approaches to marine management are typically defined as either: (i) community based, characterized by a 'bottom-up' or 'grass roots' approach; (ii) centralized, utilizing top-down or command-and-control methods; or (iii) co-management, whereby all stakeholder needs are recognized and management and responsibility is shared across local, provincial and national levels (WRI, 2004a).

Three principal marine management structures can be distinguished across the globe: (i) Community Based Coastal Resource Management (CBCRM); (ii) Marine Protected Areas (MPAs); and (iii) Integrated Coastal Zone Management (ICZM).

Each of these should play facilitative and integrative roles in order to reconcile conflicting interests and represent the various stakeholders' interests fairly and evenly. Thus, as will be seen, these structures are not necessarily mutually exclusive, and will incorporate varying degrees of collaboration. The degree to which this happens, of course, varies case by case, but the drive towards establishing integrated coastal and marine management in so many locations around the world is illustrative of widespread recognition of the need to achieve greater collaboration between levels, sectors and interests in order to ensure sustainable coastal and marine resource management.

Community-based Coastal Resource Management

One of the most effective ways in which tourism can both conserve nature and improve local livelihoods is through community approaches to natural resource management. Under Community-Based Natural Resource Management (CBNRM) 'a community may identify tourism as just one strategy for development utilizing their natural resources, while agriculture, craft production and hunting are concurrently pursued in a sustainable manner' (Scheyvens, 2002, p. 55).

Local participation in natural resource management can not only provide indigenous knowledge to assist in planning, implementation and monitoring, but also assist in more effective regulation and enforcement through community institutions and social practices to use marine resources more sustainably.

Not surprisingly, countries with extensive coastlines and a high proportion of their population living in coastal areas – for example across much of South-east Asia – have focused on Community-Based

Coastal Resource Management (CBCRM). The prime emphasis has been on fisheries resource management in the face of over-exploitation. However, as Pomeroy (1995, pp. 146–147) suggests, community-based resource management and community participation are 'not only seen as ways to improve resource management but as ways to alleviate poverty'.

The creation of community marine sanctuaries, such as that discussed below at Apo Island in the Philippines, not only increases fish abundance and diversity, but also offers the opportunity to improve livelihoods through income generated from tourist visitation. On the island of Balicasag, the Philippine Tourism Authority initiated its first 'backyard tourism' pilot project. This includes a small-scale beach hotel for scuba-divers. Villagers are employed in the resort and involved in running it: the profits are directed at the maintenance of the adjacent marine park and divers are charged extra to dive in the sanctuary area of the park. Overall, there has been a significant net contribution of marine tourism in terms of environmental quality, raising community awareness and increasing local incomes, although the distributional effects are not wholly equitable (White and Dobias, 1990).

In somewhat colder climes, a pilot community-based coastal management scheme has been instigated in the Chupa Inlet area on the Karelian coast of the Russian White Sea, where a Coastal Council has been established. Amongst the key priorities for the Council are how to protect the coast from the impact of visitors and to involve more local people in providing services and obtaining benefits from tourism (Spiridonov and Tzetlin, 2004).

Community-based management systems have the advantage of being highly adaptable to site-specific socio-economic, biological and physical characteristics. They are not without their problems however, both exogenous and endogenous. Outside factors include a different array of stakeholders in an increasingly globalized world, new technologies, unprecedented population growth and a shift from subsistence to cash economies. Within the communities, there is often a lack of legal, financial and technical resources. As a result, a collaborative approach has been advocated that recognizes all stakeholder needs, and shares management authority and responsibility across local, provincial and national levels (WRI, 2004b, c). Co-management of marine protected areas, the second of our management structures, is a step towards this. However, such a holistic approach achieves its ultimate expression in the third structure examined, that of integrated coastal management.

Marine Protected Areas

Tourist uses of the marine environment, such as scuba-diving, snorkelling, wildlife watching, boating and surfing rely on healthy marine environments. MPAs can help ensure that marine resources survive and continue to draw the recreational users that are critical to many coastal economies. Berrow (2003, p. 68), for example, describes how MPAs 'are increasingly being considered as a framework for managing whalewatching' and cites the example of Stellwagen Bank, off the North-east coast of the USA, which is one of the most important whale-watching sites in the world. A marine protected area is an area of sea especially dedicated to the protection and maintenance of biodiversity and of natural and associated cultural resources, and managed through legal or other effective means (Australian Government, 2003).

Many social and economic benefits of MPAs derive from the resource protection and high-quality environment that effective MPAs can afford.

Marine parks, nature reserves and other marine protected areas can include: reefs, seagrass beds, shipwrecks, archaeological sites, tidal lagoons, mudflats, saltmarshes, mangroves, rock platforms, underwater areas on the coast and seabed in deep water (Australian Government, 2003). While the regulation and management of individual marine activities – in particular fisheries restrictions – has been in place for many decades, effective marine conservation requires a more coordinated approach between the relevant agencies through the establishment of protected areas (IUCN, 1991). The IUCN defines a marine protected area as: 'any area of intertidal or subtidal terrain, together with its overlying water and associated flora, fauna, historical and cultural features, which has been reserved by law or other effective means to protect part or all of the enclosed environment' (IUCN, 1988).

While MPAs constitute a popular venue for ecotourism in most parts of the world, it is important to stress that marine ecotourism should not be viewed as being confined to such areas. Indeed, while there has been a proliferation of marine protected areas across the globe over the past two decades, there is still the lamentable situation where under 1% of the marine environment is within protected areas, compared with about 12% of the land surface (Hoyt, 2005).

The picture is even bleaker in the case of the high seas, which constitute an estimated 64% of the world's oceans, particularly when it is considered that 79% of all cetacean species have a strong high seas presence (Hoyt, 2005). Nearly all of the existing marine and coastal protected areas lie within national jurisdictions, and there are currently no marine and coastal protected areas outside national jurisdiction that provide effective protection to a wide range of biodiversity (CBD, 2003).

Recognition of this deficiency was made at the fifth World Parks Congress held in Durban, South Africa, in September 2003, where a declaration was made to aim towards at least five ecologically significant and globally representative high seas MPAs by 2008 (Hoyt, 2005). Marine protected areas across the globe vary considerably in terms of their size, geographical spread, biogeographical representativeness, management and effectiveness, which are discussed, in turn, below.

Size

Kelleher *et al.* (1995) identified a total of 1306 MPAs around the world in 1995. While the mean size of those inventorized (there was no information for 315 of these areas) was 100,000 ha, they suggest the median measure of 1584 ha to be a more accurate reflection of the global scenario, which is one of the dominance of many, small MPAs (the mean is distorted by a few, very large, MPAs such as the Great Barrier Reef with 34.4 million ha and the Galapagos Islands Marine Reserve at 8 million ha).

Size is an important consideration in the designation of MPAs. As a consequence of the large scale of marine ecosystems, it follows that the creation of large MPAs covering complete marine ecosystems is more likely to embrace the complex interrelationships between their constituent components. More recently, large, multiple-use protected areas have been advocated that are zoned to reflect varying levels of protection. Networks of MPAs that are 'linked together in an ecologically meaningful way' are also advocated to overcome the 'postage-stamp nature of many MPAs' (Hoyt, 2005, p. 31) in order to help deliver effective ecosystem management.

As discussed in Chapter 9, there is also a need to recognize that large marine ecosystems transcend national boundaries and thus may come under several jurisdictions. Consequently, a global effort to improve the long-term sustainability of resources and environments of the world's large marine ecosystems and linked watersheds is being made by IUCN, the Intergovernmental Oceanographic Commission of UNESCO (IOC), other UN agencies and the US National Oceanic and Atmospheric Administration (NOAA). The Large Marine Ecosystems Strategy defines relatively large regions of the order of 200,000 km^2 and has designated 64 Large Marine Ecosystems to date.

Geographical spread

The geographical spread of marine protected areas is characterized by an uneven distribution across the globe, with four marine regions (the Wider Caribbean, North-east Pacific, North-west Pacific and Australia/New Zealand) accounting for over 55%, each with over 100 MPAs (Australia/New Zealand heading the list with 260). Six marine regions (the Antarctic, Arctic, South Atlantic, Central Indian Ocean, Arabian Seas and South-east Pacific) all have under 20 MPAs and, together, account for less than 10% of the world total (Kelleher *et al.*, 1995).

Biogeographical representativeness

It is important to consider how well the major biogeographic types are represented in marine protected areas across the globe. The 'marine regions' approach used by Parks Canada guides the development of a system of marine national parks representative of the full range of biological and oceanographic variation found around the coast of Canada. Each marine region is relatively homogenous regarding climate, seabed geology, ocean currents, water mass characteristics, sea ice distribution, coastal landforms, marine plants, sea birds and marine mammals. Twenty-nine marine regions have been defined around the coast of Canada (ten on the Atlantic coast alone).

The aim then, is to designate National Marine Conservation Areas such that each of these marine regions will be represented. For example, on the Atlantic coast, one of the marine regions, the St Lawrence River Estuary, is represented by the Saguenay St Lawrence Marine Park. However, as at June 2003, only two of Canada's marine regions had representative National Marine Conservation Areas.

Of course, in common with terrestrial regions, the larger the unit to be regionalized, the larger the resultant regions. Consequently, at the global level, a total of 18 marine regions have been defined. The extent to which they represent the biogeographic zones contained within these macro-regions also varies considerably, but Australia/New Zealand is the best represented overall with 17, each with at least one marine protected area out of 19 biogeographic zones (Kelleher *et al.*, 1995).

A hierarchical approach towards representativeness can be envisaged, such as in Australia where, for example, the South Australian marine bioregions will be used as a framework for planning the South Australian Representative System of MPAs that will contribute to Australia's National Representative System of Marine Protected Areas. This, in turn, will feed into the Global Representative System of Marine Protected Areas (GRSMPA) proposed by the parties to the Convention on Biological Diversity in the Jakarta Mandate in 1995 and reviewed and updated in 2004.

The ideal of the GRSMPA is to aim towards a worldwide network that would ultimately protect 10% of all marine and coastal areas. Of course, this is easier said than done. Amongst the factors militating against such a designation are the problems of defining the biogeographical regions to be represented and delineating their boundaries in the first place. As Hamilton and Cocks (1994) describe: 'All biogeographical zones change geographically with time, marine zones more rapidly than zones on land, because faunal response to change in current patterns and temperatures is immediate ... their boundaries may well shift considerably over periods of a few years.'

They also draw attention to the fact that the designation of regions is contingent, and thus variable, upon the data set that is utilized in their delimitation and also to the highly imperfect information concerning deep water areas where, as Hamilton and Cocks (1994) suggest because there is little or no knowledge of what is to be managed: 'The concept of regionalising to define marine management units falls over.' Added to these scientific considerations are, of course, enormous political, legal and management obstacles to surmount in arriving at the GRSMPA.

Management

Responsible agency

Font *et al.* (2004) list a variety of agencies responsible for protected area management: government departments or agencies; parastatal agencies (such as Kenya Wildlife Service); NGOs; community organizations; the private sector; and a combination of two or more of these. The great majority of marine protected areas across the globe are publicly operated, with government oversight of planning and management (*MPA News*, 2003b).

More than one national agency may be responsible according to the primary purpose of the designated MPA. In the Philippines, which probably has the greatest number of marine protected areas in South-east Asia, for example, there are three responsible government departments (although the situation has been complicated somewhat since 1991 with the devolution of responsibility over the environment and natural resources to local government units, whereby municipal legislative bodies are empowered to establish marine protected areas). The Department of Environment and Natural Resources (DENR) is responsible largely for those protected areas designated on the grounds of biodiversity conservation. As a result, the MPAs for which it is responsible are usually large (over 10,000 ha) and multiple use. The Department of Tourism bears responsibility for protected areas whose primary purpose is tourism and recreation, the 58 Tourism Zones and Marine Reserves concerned being generally medium-sized (usually 100–50,000 ha). The Department of Agriculture's Bureau of Fisheries and Aquatic Resources, as would be expected, is responsible for protected areas whose prime remit is that of fisheries enhancement (at least 168 marine fisheries reserves of usually small size (2–500 ha). Due to a failure to integrate management with the livelihoods of those living within the protected area, the MPAs under DENR have been found not to be proportionally effective in the field (Uychiaoco *et al.*, 2002). A ratings exercise undertaken in Belize by the Coastal Zone Management Authority also found that the administration of government-managed reserves was 'minimally satisfactory' (*San Pedro Sun*, 2000).

In Kenya, the parastatal Kenya Wildlife Service is the mandated authority in charge of protected areas. A government department under the Ministry of Agriculture, it includes a management and paramilitary arm responsible for marine as well as terrestrial protected areas. All

MPAs have management plans produced by the KWS in collaboration with key stakeholders, including the local communities, through a consultative and participatory process that takes into account the interests and concerns of all concerned (Muthiga, 2003).

In some countries, when government agencies lack the human, technical or financial capacity to carry out this task, NGOs are delegated responsibility for the day to day management of MPAs. As Kelleher *et al.* (1995, p. 22) suggest, they frequently 'have strong links to local communities and where practicable should be closely consulted and involved in management planning and implementation and in promoting environmental awareness'.

International conservation organizations such as WWF, Conservation International and The Nature Conservancy (TNC) have been very active around the world facilitating the designation and management of MPAs and promoting community involvement. At Palmyra Atoll, south of Hawaii, after TNC initially acquired the land, the US federal government designated it a national wildlife refuge managed by the US Fish and Wildlife Service. Amongst the economic opportunites being explored for the atoll are small-scale ecotourism opportunities (*MPA News*, 2003b).

In the UK one national NGO, The National Trust, owns more than 524 km² of coastal lands in England, Wales and Northern Ireland. The Trust views its main role in local communities as being the facilitator and protector of recreational opportunities. However, while public access to the coast is considered paramount, it must be balanced with the needs of conservation (*MPA News*, 2003b). NGOs can perform a very important facilitative role in not only raising local capacity to manage and benefit from MPAs, but also in their initial designation. As described in the previous chapter, the work of the non-profit organization Coral Cay Conservation (CCC) was instrumental in the designation of MPAs in Belize and the Philippines.

Community-managed MPAs have been more prevalent in South-east Asia, in particular the Philippines and Indonesia, where there is a strong ethos of community-based coastal resource management as mentioned above. One of the classic examples in the Philippines is that of Apo Island, Negros Oriental. Following a resource management plan under Silliman University, commencing in 1978, which introduced the idea of a community-based coral reef conservation programme to the Apo Islanders, a set of marine reserve guidelines were endorsed by the island's barangay (village) council and the local municipal council in 1980.

In 1985, all of Apo Island's coral reefs were declared a marine reserve and a 'no-take' fish sanctuary, covering a 0.45km stretch of reef designated on the south-east of the island. A Marine Management Committee (MMC), composed solely of local residents, was set up to maintain and enforce the regulations of the sanctuary and reserve (Raymundo, 2002). This community-run system thus relied on the strong local support of the reserve to exert peer pressure on any potential violators. The ensuing economic benefits from diver fees and from improved fishing in areas surrounding the 'no-take' zone were estimated at more than US$126,000 (Sochaczewski, 2001).

However, with the declaration of the island as a nationally protected seascape by the National Government in 1994, Apo was placed within the National Integrated Protected Areas System. This meant that the island then came under the management of a Protected Area Management Board (PAMB). As is discussed below, although it has resulted in stronger reinforcement, this collaborative regime has not been without its problems as it is no longer a purely community-based participatory scheme (Raymundo, 2002).

The private sector may well offer the best means of protection for MPAs where both funding and management skills are in short supply. Colwell (1998) suggests that, in certain instances, small-scale, commercially supported, entrepreneurial MPAs may provide the best form of protection and that such support may come from dive resorts or similar commercial entities. Such entrepreneurs can, in certain circumstances, act as the primary stewards of coral reef resources as managers of small-scale MPAs, using tourism to achieve long-term economic and environmental sustainability.

Amongst the essential features of truly successful entrepreneurial MPAs are the inclusion of local stakeholders, together with the provision of necessary training and consultation to increase local capacity. One such example of an entrepreneurial MPA is The Chumbe Island Coral Park Project (CHICOP) in Zanzibar, Tanzania (see Box 10.1).

Collaborative or co-management of MPAs in theory can address the shortcomings of both centralized and community-based management regimes (WRI, 2004c). However, the balance of power needs to be carefully considered. On Apo island, the shift from a totally community-run marine reserve to a joint management regime where only four out of the nine members were local residents has meant an inevitable reduction in the decision-making capacity of Apo residents. Whereas the Marine Management Committee had a total say over the allocation of tourism revenue from user fees, this is now decided by the joint PAMB. Not only has there been a delay in the receipt of tourist income as fees are now channelled through the national treasury (Villegas, 2002), but also certain services previously paid for with tourism revenue – such as a monthly health care clinic, as discussed in Chapter 5, this volume – have stopped.

Clearly, the streamlining of the release of funds – as well as increased community participation – are issues that need to be addressed. This is particularly important as the increase in tourism to the island has created tensions between those who benefit, such as outside boat owners, dive operators (according to Sochaczewski (2001), the number of dive operators coming to Apo increased from 23 in 1998 to 40 by 2001) and resort owners; and those who lose out, such as local fishers, who claim that tourist divers drive away fish in their fishing grounds and damage fish traps (Raymundo, 2002). Concern regarding the

Box 10.1. Chumbe Island Coral Park Project (CHICOP), Zanzibar, Tanzania.

CHICOP faced a long, uphill struggle against bureaucratic and legislative constraints from the inception of the project in 1991 through to the arrival of the first marine ecotourists on Chumbe in 1997. After commissioning ecological baseline surveys on the flora and fauna to establish the conservation value of Chumbe Island and its fringing reef, the reef sanctuary was gazetted as a protected area in 1994. It became the first functioning marine park in Tanzania. The seven visitors' bungalows and the visitors' centre were all constructed according to state-of-the-art eco-architecture (see Fig. 10.1) (rainwater catchment, greywater recycling, compost toilets and solar power generation).

Former fishermen from adjacent villages have been employed and trained as park rangers by volunteer marine biologists and educationists (Reidmiller, 1999). The educational component of CHICOP is also important. Capacity building and the raising of local awareness have occurred via the training of the rangers and their ongoing interaction with other local fishers. Free excursions are offered to local schoolchildren during the off-season, and a visitors' centre provides information and guidelines for both day and overnight visitors.

There have, however, been a number of problems. Substantial bureaucratic delays tripled project implementation from 2 to 7 years. There is also the question of economic sustainability. Operating in an environmentally sound manner requires additional planning and may increase start-up costs. At Chumbe, the innovative eco-architecture, coupled with considerable logistical problems, extended building operations from an initially envisaged 1 year to 4. These delays caused initial cost estimates to quadruple (Reidmiller, 1999).

There is also the cost of marketing, which is a catch-22 scenario: the initial promotional costs may take up to a year to recover, but without marketing the attraction cannot attract enough visitors to cover costs. Cost recovery is therefore an undoubted problem. Projects such as Chumbe are placed in the invidious position of having to attempt to market themselves as upmarket locations. As such, they may be confronted with what is suggested to be 'unfair competition' from unmanaged nature destinations, where no management costs occur, or from donor-funded projects which effectively subsidise the tourists and tour operators, with little or no management costs being passed on (Reidmiller, 1999).

need to restrict the number of outside dive operators visiting Apo was voiced by the barangay captain (M. Pascabello, Apo, 2000, personal communication). All important cooperation from the local population regarding effective enforcement – as well as an acceptance of regulatory measures – relies on a sense of resource ownership.

The need to develop mechanisms to more directly and actively involve local communities in decision making in MPA management has also been identified in Belize, where the co-management of MPAs consists mainly of devolving government responsibility to local NGOs. McConney *et al.* (2005) examine two MPAs in the southern coastal zone of Placencia, where tourism is very significant in the local economy, which are co-managed by Friends of Nature and the Forest and Fisheries Departments of the Belize Government. They find there that: 'The dominant understanding of community participation seems to involve appointing a representative from the community, regardless of whether that individual in fact represents the many interests of that community.'

Fig. 10.1. Tourist bungalow. Chumbe Island, Zanzibar, Tanzania (photograph courtesy of CHICOP).

It is clear that relationships of power must be scrutinized when we are assessing the degree of local involvement. Walley (2004, pp. 64–66) describes the situation regarding local residents' antipathy towards the Mafia Island Marine Park being caused by the fact that participation within the marine park grossly failed to provide accountability to residents or to transform underlying power relationships in relation to national and international institutions. She concludes that:

> It is all too clear that participation does not necessarily entail democratization. In sum this social drama has pointed to the ongoing exclusion of residents within the Mafia Island Marine Park and to the deep lines of conflict existing among park actors. The efforts of planners to paper over these differences have not obscured the power hierarchies that have emerged in this drama.

(Walley, 2004)

Financing

While there are a number of alternative methods of financing protected areas, the principal ways are through government support or through revenues relating to activities within the protected area.

Font *et al.* (2004) describe the main mechanisms used by protected areas to raise funds from tourism under six headings: (i) entrance fees; (ii) user fees (such as dive fees); (iii) concessions and leases that involve payment for permission to operate within the protected area (such as licences for dive boat or kayaking operations); (iv) direct operations by the protected area management themselves; (v) taxes, such as a dedicated conservation tax or a room tax, part of which is earmarked for conservation; and (vi) volunteers offering their services for free or for basic living expenses as well as donations given to support the protected area.

Entrance fees or user fees set at an appropriate level are the most commonly utilized mechanisms for capturing a larger share of the economic value of tourism in protected areas. Although, in theory, they are one of the best ways of generating income that can constitute a substantial proportion of operational costs, in practice only a minority of marine protected areas levy such charges and, even if they do, the fee level is set below that which users would be willing to pay. This is particularly so in the case of the less economically developed countries. Green and Donnelly (2003) describe how only 25% of MPAs in the Caribbean and Central America containing coral reefs charge divers an entrance or user fee, which is most usually US$2–3 per dive or diver. As surveys conducted in Curaçao, Jamaica and Bonaire indicate a willingness-to-pay of around US$25 per person, it is clear that the potential revenue is not being realized.

Green and Donnelly point out that, if the 3.75 million divers visiting MPAs in the Caribbean region (excluding Florida) annually were to pay this higher amount, 78% of the financial shortfall currently faced could theoretically be raised. While they recognize the practical constraints of introducing and maintaining a fee collection system as well as the political and socio-economic factors that may militate against it, they point to successful implementation elsewhere in the Caribbean. At Bonaire Marine Park in the Netherlands Antilles, revenue generated by the US$10 fee per diver per year now finances a large share of management costs (Green and Donnelly, 2003).

The entrance fee of US$17 a year, or US$5.50 per day, system at the award-winning Bunaken National Marine Park in Indonesia, modelled on Bonaire's diver fee system, succeeded in doubling revenues in 1 year and collected US$11,000 in 2002 (Spergel and Moye, 2004). The history of this initiative is described in more detail in Chapter 8, this volume. Of course, the earmarking of fees is a crucial factor. In Bunaken, when the nature reserve was upgraded to the status of a marine national park in the late 1980s, control over the park, including the authority to collect fees, passed to the central government. The instigation of the multi-stakeholder Bunaken National Park Management Advisory Board (BNPMAB) to manage the protected area has, however, resulted in a remarkable turnaround that serves as a model not only for Indonesia but also globally.

BNPMAB has adopted a participatory and consultative approach to managing the entrance fee system, inaugurated in 2001. Instead of all user fees passing directly to central government, 80% of revenues are retained by the park management board, with 20% divided between local, provincial and national government (*MPA News*, 2004). A small grants programme implemented by the board ensures that, of the funds retained by the board, 30% are returned to the community in the form of small-scale conservation and community development projects, which they propose and implement themselves. The International Coral Reef Action Network (ICRAN) has chosen Bunaken as its Asian demonstration site for sustainable reef tourism.

The largest MPA in the world, the Great Barrier Reef Marine Park (GBRMP), levies an Environmental Management Charge of Aus$5 per tourist per day (see Chapter 3, this volume). In 2002/2003 the total income of Aus$6.7 million from the charge covered approximately 20% of the budget of the GBRMP Authority (Spergel and Moye, 2004), with the bulk of management costs met by the Australian taxpayer (Buckley, 2003a). However, it is estimated that marine park tourism generates Aus$2 billion per annum for the Queensland State regional economy.

A few, high profile, charismatic sites around the world are able to command much higher fees. Visitors to the Galapagos Islands National Park are willing to pay the US$100 entry fee because of its uniqueness. Another world class location is that of the Tubbataha Reefs National Marine Park in the Philippines, a World Heritage site, where foreign scuba-divers pay a US$50 reef conservation fee (Spergel and Moye, 2004). Lindberg and Halpenny (2001) present a country-by-country review of protected area visitor fees, which includes those of a number of marine protected areas across the globe.

Zoning

Zoning of marine protected areas is essential wherever the designated area embraces more than one type of activity. It is vital that where there is a multiplicity of activities, such as fishing and tourism, they are managed sensitively to prevent adverse disturbance to the natural attributes of the marine protected area. Zoning also helps to separate incompatible activities, such as marine ecotourism and commercial fishing. Australia's Great Barrier Reef Marine Park and the Florida Keys National Marine Sanctuary are regarded as good examples of zoning.

However, zoning of marine protected areas has frequently met with widespread opposition and resentment. The proposal to designate one-third of the GBRMP as a no-fishing zone met with such resistance from the fishing industry (CNN, 2003). Similar opposition from recreational fishers, together with limited scientific understanding of implications, resulted in a compromise sanctuary zone scheme being adopted for the 1989–1999 management plan for Ningaloo Marine Park in Western Australia (Department of Conservation and Land Management, 2003).

Walley (2004, p. 258) reports that the root cause of most residents' anger concerning Mafia Island Marine Park was the zoning proposals, over which they felt they had not been adequately consulted. They feared that zoning changes would make historically crucial fishing grounds inaccessible, destroying their ability to generate a livelihood. Interestingly, no-take zones, in which fishing is either temporarily or permanently off-limits, have in the past been a feature of traditional fishing cultures around the world, for example the designation of tabu areas in Fiji. It has been suggested that the acceptance of recently designated MPAs, which are no-take areas, such as Ulunikoro, by local Fijians is attributable to this cultural heritage (*MPA News*, 2001/2002).

Recognition of human activity through multiple-use zoning allows integrated management regimes to be established for continued human use while achieving conservation objectives. This is all important if local hostility towards the creation of MPAs is to be avoided, as the exclusion of traditional human activities may jeopardize the physical or economic survival of local people (Kelleher *et al.*, 1995).

The biosphere reserve concept, in which human activity is specifically provided for within buffer and transition zones surrounding highly protected areas, may be viewed as a particular variant of large, multiple-use, protected areas particularly suited to marine applications (Kelleher and Kenchington, 1991), as the concept requires integrated and sustainable management of the land/sea interface. Also, because the geographical arrangement of the core area and other zones is adaptable, it is flexible enough to accommodate seasonal or annual changes in marine areas through movable zones (Hoyt, 2005, p. 28). There are currently 90 biosphere reserves with a marine (including subtidal features) or coastal (coastal intertidal or terrestrial features) component out of a total of 314 biosphere reserves (Kelleher *et al.*, 1995, p. 11).

Enforcement

In Kenya, overlapping mandates between KWS and the Fisheries department in the marine reserves; the Forestry department in the mangrove forests within marine reserves; and the Tourism department who license all tourist activities, regardless of location, complicate the issue of enforcement. Rangers and wardens are trained by KWS not only in wildlife management but, more recently, in marine ecology, integrated coastal management and scuba. They also receive paramilitary training.

Although no formal programme has been implemented to involve communities in enforcement, the development of the Community

Wildlife department within KWS has increased consultation with local communities and hence compliance (Muthiga, 2003). Muthiga, however, suggests that compliance differs among stakeholder groups. Stakeholders depending mostly on tourism are highly compliant, because they understand the benefits of a managed system and improved habitats to their business.

As Erdmannn (2001) suggests, with reference to Bunaken, enforcement must be an integral part of National Park management if illegal and destructive practices, such as cyanide fishing, are to be curbed. As described in Chapter 8, this volume, the North Sulawesi Watersports Association, which was started in 1998 by a group of environmentally concerned marine tour operators, helps with patrol activities by contributing fuel and boat time. An initial voluntary fee of US$5 fee per diver to support a Bunaken preservation fund to step up patrols, particularly at night, has been replaced by the entrance fee that everyone has to pay to enter the marine park, but the top priority of the management board has been the development of a joint villager/ranger/ police patrol team to stop destructive fishing practices and other illegal activities such as mangrove cutting and the capture of endangered wildlife such as turtles and dugongs.

Effectiveness

Although the number of marine protected areas has grown rapidly in recent years, their performance remains highly variable. Kelleher *et al.* (1995) assessed the management level of 383 out of the 1306 MPAs they inventorized across the globe. They concluded that 31% could be classified as having a high management level (generally achieving their management objectives), 40% as moderate and 29% at a low level.

The reasons for MPAs failing to achieve their management effectiveness are many and various, but recurrent factors were: insufficient financial and technical resources; lack of data; lack of public support and unwillingness of users to follow management rules; inadequate commitment to enforce management; unsustainable use of resources occurring within MPAs; impacts of activities in land and sea areas outside the boundaries of MPAs; and lack of clear organizational responsibilities for management and lack of coordination between agencies with responsibilities relevant to MPAs (Kelleher *et al.*, 1995, p. 17).

Burke and Maidens (2004) analysed the effectiveness of MPAs in the Caribbean using expert assessment. They generated a simple measure of management effectiveness using only four broad criteria: (i) existence of management activity; (ii) existence of a management plan; (iii) availability of resources; and (iv) extent of enforcement. Of the 285 parks examined in this way, only 6% were rated as effectively managed, 13% partially effectively managed and nearly 50% judged to have an inadequate level of management.

They suggested two major reasons for such a high level of failure. The first is that of lack of long-term financial support. Kelleher *et al.* (1995) suggested that a critical issue in financing marine protected areas was the assessment and publication of the economic benefits of MPAs, which often exceed those of any alternative use. They suggested that wider regional benefits, particularly in tourism, are ignored despite the fact that these extend beyond direct financial flows from entry fees to include improved overall fish catches; there is also revenue from the external tourism industry and employment in these industries. The identification and establishment of facilities to promote ecotourism in MPAs by management agencies in cooperation with local communities and other groups is advocated.

The second major reason for failure of MPAs, as suggested by Burke and Maidens (2004), is the critical issue of a lack of support from the local community. This is usually attributable to a lack of local involvement in planning and a failure to share financial or other benefits. It is this human dimension that has been increasingly recognized as being paramount in determining the success or failure of MPAs. Mascia (2003) suggests that, rather than biological or physical variables, social factors are the primary determinants. The local acceptance of regulatory measures is a crucial factor in the establishment of an effective MPA. In general, the ownership of responsibility and compliance to rules increases as more and more users of resources are directly included in the management decisions and the responsibility becomes local.

The most important predictors of success determined by a study of 45 community-based marine protected areas in the Philippines by Pollnac *et al.* (2001) included: (i) population size of the community; (ii) a perceived crisis in terms of reduced fish populations; (iii) successful alternative income projects; (iv) high levels of participation in community decision making; and (v) continuing advice from the implementing organization along with inputs from local government.

In Kimbe Bay, West New Britain province, Papua New Guinea, the Mahonia Na Dari (Guardians of the Sea) conservation and research centre has implemented a network of Locally Managed Marine Areas (LMMAs) that are managed by the community for the community. This has been an effective grassroots approach that has contrasted with the failure of previous efforts, which failed to maintain local solutions and control.

It is not as easy as declaring that one management type is better than another. Mascia (2001) suggests that both locally and privately administered MPAs are particularly vulnerable to changes in leadership that diminish their ability or willingness to manage sites. Collaborative management systems are therefore advocated as a means of overcoming many of the weaknesses of community-based and centrally managed MPAs, as they can merge national capacity with local interest and knowledge. Such collaboration, however, must extend beyond vertical integration to embrace cross-sectoral interests.

Kelleher *et al.* (1995, p. 19) call for the integrated management of all uses of sea and land areas adjacent to MPAs, identifying land-based activities such as forest clearance, agriculture and urban development as particular threats to marine biodiversity through marine pollution. As they argue, MPAs cannot tackle such issues in isolation and therefore must be linked in with wider coastal zone management programmes. The need for an holistic, integrative approach to coastal management has been recognized for some time, but Integrated Coastal Zone Management (ICZM) as a tool for achieving sustainable levels of economic and social activity in coastal areas, while protecting the coastal environment, has recently been the focus of an unprecedented level of interest from multilateral agencies as well as from inter-governmental and individual governments.

Integrated Coastal Zone Management

The World Bank (1996, p. 1) describes ICZM as:

> a process of governance and consists of the legal and institutional framework necessary to ensure that development and management plans for coastal zones are integrated with environmental (including social) goals and are made with the participation of those affected. The purpose of ICZM is to maximise the benefits provided by the coastal zone and to minimise the conflicts and harmful effects of activities upon each other, on resources and on the environment.

UNEP advocates ICZM in its Tourism in Sensitive Areas programme, recognizing the deleterious effects of competing activities on the attraction of the coastal zone to visitors. ICZM focuses on three operational objectives:

- Strengthening sectoral management, for instance through training, legislation and staffing.
- Preserving and protecting the productivity and biological diversity of coastal ecosystems, mainly through prevention of habitat destruction, pollution and overexploitation.
- Promotion of rational development and sustainable utilization of coastal resources.

At an international level, several of the organizations and specialized agencies of the United Nations (UNDP, UNEP, UNESCO, FAO, GEF), as well as IUCN, have been actively engaged in the concept of integrating coastal management over the past decade. While this is encouraging, it also raises concern about fragmentation and duplication. There are various acronyms used in conjunction with coastal management. As well as the commonly used ICZM, there is ICM (Integrated Coastal Management) and ICAM (Integrated Coastal Area Management), which is used by UNCED, UNEP and UNESCO. The latter's Intergovernmental

Oceanographic Commission scientific programme defines ICAM as 'an interdisciplinary activity where natural and social scientists, coastal managers and policy makers, in the long term, focus on how to manage the diverse problems of coastal areas' (IOC, 2002).

Policy makers at the regional level have also recognized the need for integrated coastal management. The European Union, for example, adopted a recommendation on implementing ICZM in Europe in May, 2002. This asks member states to undertake a national stocktaking of legislation, institutions and stakeholders involved in the management of the coastal zone and, based on this, to develop national strategies to deliver ICZM over the subsequent 45 months. As a result, in the UK, in March 2003 DEFRA commissioned a national stocktaking exercise to investigate the difference between ICZM in theory and practice using a case study approach of 18 sites: five in England, four in Wales, five in Scotland and four in Northern Ireland. Simultaneously, it increased publication of its newsletter on government initiatives in the coastal and marine environment *Wavelength* to two issues per year (DEFRA, 2003b).

The Scottish Coastal Forum (SCF) is also developing a national strategy for the management of the Scottish Coast to provide an integrated coastal zone management framework that will deliver sustainable use of Scotland's coastal and inshore resources. A study of the effectiveness of the voluntary local coastal management partnership as one of the main existing delivery mechanisms of ICZM concluded that: 'It is unlikely that any other mechanism could have achieved the stakeholder involvement and strategy planning as effectively. The partnerships have also achieved this on limited funding and the support of a core of dedicated partners' (Scottish Executive, 2002, p. 1).

Elsewhere in the world, one of the longest-standing coastal zone management schemes is in the Central American country of Belize. The beginning of coastal zone management in Belize dates back to a workshop in San Pedro in 1989, where it was recognized that an integrated, holistic approach to management of coastal resources was necessary to ensure their use and protection in the long term. By 1990, a small unit was functioning and, in 1993, the GEF/UNDP CZM Project 'Sustainable Development and Management of Biologically Diverse Coastal Regions' provided the necessary financial assistance. Belize's Coastal Zone Management Authority and Institute (CZMAI) is an autonomous public statutory body mandated to implement and monitor Belize's coastal zone management and development policies.

As tourism to Belize increased by 139% between 1998 and 2001, and 84% of these tourists are accommodated in coastal communities, one of the key objectives of the CZMAI is to promote low-density levels of development that are economically, socially and ecologically acceptable. Towards this end they have published a handbook on Tourism and Recreation Best Practice for Coastal Areas in Belize (CZMAI, 2001). Barbados and Guyana are further examples of countries in the region with autonomous Coastal Zone Management Units.

Conclusions

As discussed above, there may be, indeed there should be, a certain degree of overlap between the management structures examined. This is not only a reflection of the fact that collaboration should be a feature of effective management structures, but also that there are symbiotic relationships between all three structures with, for example, CBCRM serving as a catalyst for action in ICZM.

While both ICZM and CBCRM embrace the land/sea interface, and MPAs focus on the underwater environment (tidal and subtidal), it is evident that the interconnectedness of terrestrial and aquatic ecosystems, as well as the fact that there are stakeholders common to both, requires that effective management should transcend such delineations. Each of these management structures inform, and are informed by, the others. Ecotourism activity must therefore be thought of in the context of these different scales if it is to be managed effectively.

This chapter has also highlighted the increasing recognition of the merits of an ecosystem-based approach, as discussed in the previous chapter, to protect and maintain coastal and marine ecosystem integrity. Hoyt (2005, p. 4) describes this as a management regime that addresses 'the uses and values of ecosystems with all stakeholders to maintain ecological integrity in the face of the uncertain and ever-changing nature of ecosystems'. He cites Cortner and Moote's observation that: 'Ecosystem management breaks new ground in resource management by making the social and political basis of natural resource goals explicit ... Given the recognized complexity and dynamic nature of ecological and social systems, ecosystem management is adaptive management.'

Ecosystem-based management is central to Australia's Oceans Policy (Hoyt, 2005, p. 73). Arrangements for coastal resources management are complex and affected by various factors. Torell and Salamanca (undated) argue that some of these are intractable and entrenched in the politics and economy of the country, and that there is neither a single, nor a broad-based, solution to the institutional problems affecting coastal resources management. Location-specific solutions 'must take into consideration the capabilities of those who will be responsible for implementation and must provide for material benefits to the poor and marginalized'. This reemphasizes the points made in Chapter 5, that marine ecotourism must be developed with close regard to all the existing types of capital that constitute human and non-human livelihood assets, if benefits are to accrue across the board.

11 Networks and Initiatives

Bridging Troubled Waters

As argued earlier, it is vitally important that marine ecotourism is not considered in isolation: it cannot stand alone, and it is not a universal panacea for unsustainable marine practices. Circumstances will dictate its success or failure in terms of sustainable outcomes. These, of course, will be place-specific, but the message for collaboration is clear, both within the activity (intra-sectoral) and between different sectors and interests (inter-sectoral). As Bramwell and Lane (2000, p. 4) describe, collaboration 'involves relationships between stakeholders when those parties interact with each other in relation to a common issue or "problem domain"'.

They go on to point out that resource dependency and stakeholder interdependence mean that there are potential mutual or collective benefits arising from stakeholders collaborating with each other, particularly given the complexity of issues concerning marine environments. As Wilson (2003, p. 60) states:

> Problems associated with marine ecotourism can be so complex that it is beyond the capability of any single individual or organization to resolve them. Collaboration between stakeholders in the problem domain is therefore essential, if marine ecotourism is to be developed to be genuinely sustainable.

Marine ecotourism is highly dependent on a healthy marine environment but, as seen in Chapter 2, it is only one of the myriad of activities that are affected by, and affect, the quality of the seas and oceans. Chapter 10 described the need for an integrated approach to coastal management. This need for integration extends, and is indeed connected, to the wider seas where collaboration involves not only stakeholders from different sectors but also different jurisdictions working together to achieve a common goal.

The protection of species or habitats that constitute marine ecotourism resources cannot be considered without paying regard to activities such as commercial fisheries and shipping, as well as pollution and other degradation from various land-based activities. It is also dependent upon collaboration between government agencies at different levels and between nations. There are a number of important networks and initiatives concerned with the marine environment at various scales.

Typology of Partnerships relating to Marine Ecotourism

In developing a typology of sustainable tourism partnerships in general, Selin (2000, p. 137) maps partnerships along axes according to their organizational diversity and size against geographical scale. The organizational diversity and size range from homogenous (within one sector or intra-sectoral) and small size, to multi-sector (or inter-sectoral) and large size. Selin defines homogenous as the situation where there are relatively few partners from either the commercial, non-profit or government sectors, whereas, at the other end of the spectrum, a diverse organization will frequently embrace a larger number of partners from all three sectors.

However, such a range in diversity would also be likely to reflect a wider variation in stakeholder interests. The geographical scale described by Selin ranges from community to national, but this can be usefully extended to the international arena. This is a useful framework for examining the various networks and initiatives that have relevance to marine ecotourism, because these range from small, local, dedicated initiatives, such as the Skye and Lochalsh Marine Tourism Association in Scotland, to large, international, inter-sectoral networks that are concerned with the sustainable management of the marine environment, such as the International Coral Reef Initiative, ICRI, which mobilizes governments as well as a wide range of other stakeholders in an effort to improve management practices for coral reefs and associated ecosystems (ICRAN, 2002).

While the latter category covers a whole range of activities, it is manifest that marine ecotourism can be informed by, and inform, such large-scale initiatives. As the Stakeholder Forum prior to the 2002 Earth Summit suggested, partnerships 'need to comprise big initiatives impacting on a global scale, as much as small, concrete ones which have proven to often deliver change in a more tangible manner' (Stakeholder Forum, 2002). Figure 11.1 adapts Selin's framework in order to categorize collaborative ventures in marine ecotourism; the case studies mapped accordingly are examined below in more detail.

Intra-sectoral collaboration

In terms of intra-sectoral (or within sector) collaboration, a variety of new marine ecotourism operator networks have emerged. These can perform important roles in: (i) marketing (frequently, marine ecotourism businesses are small, isolated and lack the financial resources and marketing expertise to reach the marketplace effectively); (ii) developing codes of practice; and (iii) having a collective voice to influence policy.

At the *local*, or *community*, level the impetus for the inception of such networks usually arises from concerned individuals. On the west coast of Scotland, the operators of Bella Jane Boat Trips, an award-winning boat trip to Loch Coruisk, Isle of Skye, in association with other local marine operators and with financial assistance from the local enterprise company (Skye and Lochalsh Enterprise), instigated the Skye and Lochalsh Marine Tourism Association (SLMTA) in 2000. This association was established 'to provide members with a mechanism for sharing good practice and to promote members' services to interested parties' (SLMTA, 2000). While members of the association were strongly

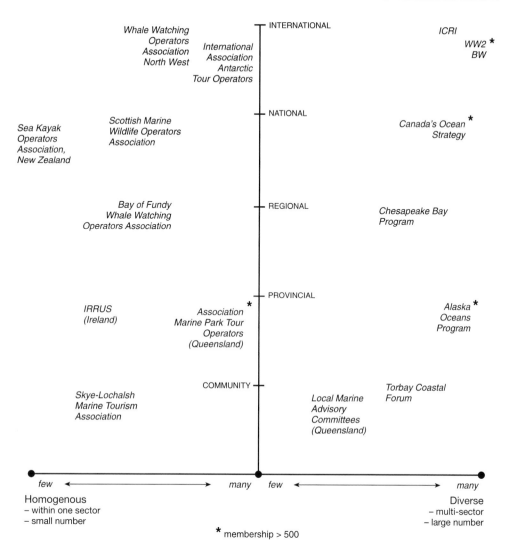

Fig. 11.1. Marine environmental networks and initiatives by organizational diversity, size and scale of operation (adapted from Selin, 2000).

encouraged to adopt the Scottish Marine Wildlife Operators Association (SMWOA) Code of Practice, its primary function was to act as a marketing umbrella in an economic environment characterized by seasonality of tourist visitation that is also highly vulnerable to perturbations such as the foot and mouth disease outbreak of 2002.

At present the SLMTA is, unfortunately, largely dormant, with at least two of its twelve members no longer operating. While Skye and Lochalsh Enterprise provided the essential start-up funding and much-appreciated advice and support from the very outset, the absence of recurrent funding for the initiative may well lead to its demise. This situation is all the more lamentable given the fact that a collective voice is likely to become even more essential as Scottish Natural Heritage is in the process of setting up statutory regulatory measures – as opposed to voluntary compliance – with the widely respected Navigate with Nature code of practice of the SMWOA (D. MacKinnon, Elgol, Scotland, 2004, personal communication).

At the *provincial* level, the Association of Marine Park Tour Operators in Queensland, Australia, represents the interests of operators who provide tourism services throughout the Great Barrier Reef Marine Park. AMPTO's members are responsible for major investments in the industry and include operators involved in day tours, extended cruising, diving, charters, aviation and visits to resort islands. The association is a not-for-profit limited company, funded by members' contributions, whose role it is to represent its members' interests in all forums and to further the development of best practice within the Great Barrier Reef Marine Park (AMPTO, 2003).

Also at the provincial level, on the west coast of Ireland, West Clare, a group of marine ecotourism providers developed a unique ecotourism brand, IRRUS, together with brand criteria, to promote sustainable marine ecotourism. The way in which the IRRUS marketing group was formed, and its subsequent fortunes, is instructive. In 1998, the Irish Marine Institute was approached by Shannon Development Ltd., the regional development authority for the Shannon region, to examine West Clare as a potential region for marine tourism development. As a result, a study report, *Special Interest Tourism in the West Clare Peninsula*, was published in 1999 by the Marine Institute, Shannon Development and Clare County Council. The Marine Study Implementation Group (a local public, private and voluntary partnership) was set up to implement the report's recommendations.

Subsequently, the Marine Institute, as one of the European partners involved in the Marine Ecotourism for the Atlantic Area (META-project) funded under the European Union's Community Initiative Interreg IIC Atlantic Area Programme, selected West Clare as the case study area for the Irish META project. A core cluster group was selected, which consisted of tour operators, accommodation providers and local community members. This META-cluster group was initially facilitated by the META-project manager to undertake the following activities:

- Development of an ecotourism brand image for West Clare.
- Development of a website and marketing literature for the promotion of ecotourism in West Clare.
- Development of ecotourism criteria for inclusion under brand marketing, i.e. codes of best practice.
- Development of a 'package' of ecotourism activities.

As the project progressed and the cluster group became more active, the project manager stepped into the role of facilitator and the cluster group became independent, establishing the IRRUS (old Irish for the Loop Head peninsula in West Clare) group in February 2000, with its own elected chairperson, secretary and committee. The group, via the META-project, was represented, together with the Shannon Dolphin and Wildlife Foundation (SDWF), on the Marine Study Implementation Group, which acted as an overall umbrella to integrate the stakeholders involved in the West Clare marine tourism product.

The IRRUS group website went live in February 2001. The site apparently registered a significant number of hits in the first 9 weeks of its existence (Hoctor, 2001; West Clare META-Project, 2001, unpublished final draft report). However, not one booking for any tourism provider was received through the website (S.D. Berrow, Kilrush, Ireland, 2004, personal communication), and the site went off-line during the summer of 2003. The Marine Study Implementation Group ceased to meet in 2002, but the implementation of the code of conduct that had been developed by SDWF in collaboration with the operators and adopted by the Implementation Group continues to be implemented with regard to dolphin watching in the Shannon estuary via the ongoing efforts of SDWF.

There are a number of factors why the initiative has not continued. The most important is lack of funding. While the META-project received considerable EU financial backing at the outset, it was not recurrent. When the project finished, local businesses did not have sufficient resources to employ even a part-time marketing officer. A smaller amount of money spent over a longer time frame would probably have had more lasting and significant results. The second factor is the top-down imposition of IRRUS from outside. Although marine ecotourism products – in particular dolphin watching – were available prior to IRRUS, local tourism providers not did not latch onto the idea of group marketing and an identifiable image in West Clare. Furthermore, the local population did not identify with the brand name IRRUS, being unaware of the origin of the name. Thirdly, there are too few products and services in West Clare to reach a critical mass, and inevitably it is the same few people who are involved in all these initiatives (S.D. Berrow, Kilrush, Ireland, 2004, personal communication).

At the *regional* level, at the Bay of Fundy, which lies between the East Canadian maritime provinces of New Brunswick and Nova Scotia, marine tour operators have developed a code of ethics for whale watchers. This code of ethics, which is re-assessed on an annual basis, aims to foster cooperation between marine tour operators for the protection of whales and other marine life, as well as the safety and understanding of their passengers by laying down criteria for vessels to adhere to, such as minimum approach distance and maximum viewing time (Adventure Nova Scotia, 2003).

At the *national* level, the Scottish Marine Wildlife Operators Association (SMWOA) was set up in 1998 by a group of Scottish marine wildlife operators in association with the Minch Project and the Scottish Tourist Board. It is a unique association made up of businesses that are dedicated to introducing their customers to the marine wildlife of Scotland in an environmentally sustainable way for their mutual benefit and to safeguard the wildlife they depend upon.

SMWOA performs several important roles. First, it acts as a point of contact, enabling businesses to voice their concerns to the statutory agencies as well as to conservation groups, who may wish to influence the way they operate, as well as acting as a point of contact for the Scottish Tourist Board. Secondly, it provides quality assurance because of the high standards set by the SMWOA in drawing up their code of conduct, 'Navigate with Nature', which was drawn up with the advice of key scientific experts and organizations, including Scottish Natural Heritage, the Royal Society for the Protection of Birds and The Sea Watch Foundation. Thirdly, it gives product identity. The code of practice for all member operators, as well as acting as a guide for the general public, provides a clear message to visitors that the operators are working to minimize their impacts on wildlife and that they encourage others to do likewise. It gives a 'comfort factor' to the visitor who will perceive care for the environment.

Fourthly, there is a clear marketing advantage, as the STB can promote members' businesses with confidence in the quality of the product. Another initiative at the national level, discussed in Chapter 4, is the Sea Kayak Operators Association of New Zealand, which set up a code of practice for commercial sea kayaking in the country in 1997. The code contains four components: safety, legislation, the environment and customer service. Some of the actions and principles are mandatory, while other levels of operation are strongly recommended (SKOANZ, 1999).

At the *international* level, the Whale Watch Operators Association North West (WWOANW) represents commercial whale watchers operating in Canada and the USA in the Pacific North-west waters of Juan de Fuca, Haro and Georgia Straights, the waters of Puget Sound and the waters surrounding the Gulf and San Juan Islands. Original guidelines developed in the early 1990s have now been developed into a series of best practice guidelines, the objectives of which are two-fold: first, to minimize potential negative impacts on marine wildlife populations by maintaining normal daily and seasonal activity patterns in the short and long terms; secondly, to provide the best viewing opportunities such that watchers have the opportunity to enjoy and learn about wildlife through observation.

The conservation management model employed by WWOANW is one of the most comprehensive self-management frameworks in the world, and its framework is being applied in the conservation management of other species elsewhere in the world (WWOANW, 2003). There are no direct financial penalties used in enforcing rules, but peer pressure and having a bad reputation seem to be effective penalties for non-compliance (Meinhold, 2003).

Another important collaborative venture at the international level is the International Association of Antarctica Tour Operators (IAATO).

Stonehouse (2001) describes how an absence of legislation in Antarctic marine tourism led to principles for management being developed by the tour operators themselves. As Antarctic tourism, described in Chapter 3, grew, cruise operators formed the IAATO coalition. The association's guidelines and codes of conduct for both its members and clients set the precedent for subsequent recommendations for visitors by the Antarctic Treaty, which also set its own guidelines. Interestingly, the industry, while working within the framework of the Treaty, takes its responsibility seriously enough as to continue to practise self-regulation as well as exercising environmental awareness. At the 2003 annual meeting of IAATO, the members of the organization with operations in the Arctic (seasonal complementarity) discussed the possibility of establishing an Arctic chapter of IAATO, and an informal subgroup was to start dialogue with the Arctic Council in recognition of the fact that IAATO represents best practice in the tourism industry (WWF, 2003c).

Inter-sectoral collaboration

Inter- or cross-sectoral partnerships are 'engaged in developing policies and planning that go beyond basic tourism questions: they also deal with broader economic, social and environmental issues' (Bramwell and Lane, 2000). As Timothy (1998) describes, they include collaboration between private and public sectors, as well as cooperation between government agencies involving different levels of administration (for example, national and provincial), as well as cross-border cooperation between same-level polities (for example, state and state). The latter is of particular relevance to marine ecotourism because of the inter-connectivity of the seas and oceans discussed in Chapter 1. The migratory routes of whales, for example, transcend political boundaries: the same whales may be viewed in a multiplicity of locations both within and between nation states. It is a sad reflection, but not surprising, that the management of extraterritorial waters lags behind that of coastal waters.

There has been an increased emphasis on the role of partnerships since The Earth Summit in Johannesburg, South Africa, in 2002. The Stakeholder Forum held prior to the summit describes the potential of what is referred to as Type 2 partnerships: 'Partnerships are seen as a vehicle to improve the quality of implementation by involving those stakeholders whose activities have direct impact on sustainable development ... they need to be multi-stakeholder and equitable in nature' (Stakeholder Forum, 2002). Multi-stakeholder partnerships are defined as groupings of stakeholders from governments, IGOs, civil society groups and businesses organized at local, national, regional and global levels (RIIA, 2002).

As the Cairns workshop on an ecosystem-based approach for managing ocean activities (NOO, 2003) concluded, if the level of

coordination and cooperation between government and other stakeholders is increased, there is a greater appreciation of common goals as
well as greater transparency, acceptance and thus success of management actions.

Bramwell and Lane (2000, p. 4) describe four main ways in which
inter-sectoral collaborative approaches should help further sustainable
development:

1. Collaboration among a range of stakeholders, including non-economic
interests, might promote more consideration of the varied natural, built
and human resources that need to be sustained for future well-being.
2. By involving stakeholders from several fields of activity, with many
interests, there may be greater potential for the integrative or holistic
approaches to policy making that can help to promote sustainability ...
Partnerships can also help reflect and help safeguard the interdependence that exists between tourism and other activities and policy
fields ...
3. If multiple stakeholders affected by tourism development were
involved in the policy-making process, then this might lead to a more
equitable distribution of the resulting benefits and costs. Participation
should raise awareness of tourism impacts on all stakeholders, and this
heightened awareness should lead to policies that are fairer in their
outcomes.
4. Broad participation in policy making could help democratize decision
making, empower participants and lead to capacity building and skill
acquisition amongst participants and those whom they represent.

In contrast to the intra-sectoral initiatives described above which
have been largely industry-driven, the inter-sectoral approaches, as will
be seen, are generally initiated by the public sector, NGOs or INGOs but,
once again, range from the local to the international.

At the *local* or *community* level, the Great Barrier Reef Marine Park
Authority has established a network of ten local marine advisory
committees (LMACs) at regional centres along the Queensland coast. Their
purpose is to involve the community in the management and ecologically
sustainable development of the Marine Park, and their principal function
is to provide a community forum for representative stakeholder groups in
the community. They also provide a communication link between
stakeholder groups and Government agencies. The LMACs comprise, on
average, 15 voluntary members from the local community and, while their
composition varies, representatives from stakeholder groups include the
tourism industry, recreational and ports fishing, commercial fishing,
specific-interest groups (e.g. recreational diving), Aboriginal interests,
conservation interests, local associations and local groups involved in
management of local resources (GBRMP, 2002).

Also at the local level, another of the partners in the EU Interreg IIc
transnational research project, Marine Ecotourism for the Atlantic Area
(META), Torbay Council (UK), established the Torbay Coastal Forum to

derive a model approach for the co-management of the natural environment and genuinely sustainable marine ecotourism. The Forum was made up of members from: (i) enforcement agencies (e.g. The Environment Agency); (ii) local and regional pressure/interest groups; (iii) the local authority; (iv) ecotourism initiative traders; (v) the fishing, angling and diving sectors; (vi) recreational craft users; (vii) general tourism operators; (viii) general public representatives; and (ix) local experts in related fields (Torbay Council, 2001, unpublished final draft report).

However, in the same way that IRRUS foundered once EU financial support ceased, the Torbay Coastal Forum also ceased to exist in 2002. Financial support from Torbay Council was not forthcoming, largely because political support waned, and because of the difficulty of getting different groups to work together. However, it could be said that the initiative was the essential precursor to the subsequent formation of a conservation partnership that has produced the Marine Biodiversity Action Plan for Torbay (D. Acland, Torquay, UK, 2004, personal communication; Torbay Coast and Countryside Trust *et al.*, 2004).

Also in the south-west of England, a vibrant local initiative, the Helford Voluntary Marine Conservation Area Group, consists of sailors, landowners, fishermen, councillors, students, marine biologists and representatives of statutory and non-statutory organizations, working together to raise awareness of the sensitivity of the intertidal area and the marine environment and to promote its sustainable use (Helford VMCA, 2003).

At the *provincial* level, the Alaska Oceans Program fosters the functioning of the Alaska Oceans Network, which is a voluntary association of conservation, fishing and Alaska Native organizations with a mission to restore and maintain healthy marine ecosystems in Alaska (Alaska Oceans Program, 2004). With an estimated 76,700 whale-watching visitors, who have a direct expenditure of US$89.1 million annually (Hoyt, 2001), as well as the burgeoning cruise market, the significance of a pristine marine environment to marine tourism in Alaska is self-evident.

In Australia, the state of South Australia released Our Seas and Coasts in 1998, a marine and estuarine strategy aimed at the conservation and ecologically sustainable use of the state's marine and estuarine environment through partnerships between community and government. Collaboration will arrive at an agreed strategic framework that will not only improve water quality and conserve and restore coastal and estuarine habitat, biodiversity and ecological processes but also, simultaneously, protect the economic base of coastal and marine areas, particularly fisheries and tourism (Moroney, 2003).

In the UK, there are a number of coastal and estuarine forums (Dorset Coast Forum, Severn Estuary Strategy, Firth of Clyde Forum, Moray Firth Partnership, Essex Estuaries Initiative, etc.), all of which promote sustainable management, use and development of these zones. The

Moray Firth Partnership, for example, is a voluntary organization made up of representatives from industry, local authorities, conservation bodies, recreational users, local residents and many others. The Essex Estuaries Initiative is a proactive network facilitating coordination and cooperation between organizations responsible for coastal management. As a European Marine Site, recognized both nationally and internationally as an important winter feeding area and summer breeding ground for migratory birds, it is part of the EU Natura 2000 network (Essex Estuary Initiative, 2002).

The Chesapeake Bay Program in the USA is a unique regional partnership that has led and directed the restoration of Chesapeake Bay since 1983. There was increased awareness during the 1970s that the Bay was experiencing considerable environmental degradation due to nutrient over-enrichment, dwindling underwater Bay grasses and toxic pollution. This was clearly jeopardizing finfish and shellfish (the bay has considerable oyster fisheries), as well as its natural attraction. Being an estuary, with varying salinity levels, the Bay tourism experience includes all types of coastal ecosystems as well as distinct natural communities.

The Chesapeake Bay Program partners include the states of Maryland, Pennsylvania and Virginia, the District of Colombia, the Chesapeake Bay Commission (a tri-state legislative body), the Environmental Protection Agency (representing the federal government) and participating citizen advisory groups. At the start of the new millennium these partners signed the new Chesapeake 2000 Agreement, which commits to protecting and restoring living resources, vital habitats and water quality of the Bay and its watershed (Chesapeake Bay Program, 2001).

One of the most proactive inter-sectoral initiatives at a *national* level is Canada's Oceans Strategy. This strategy is a response to the Canadian Government's legal obligation under the Oceans Act of 1997, which requires the Minister of Fisheries and Oceans Canada to lead and facilitate the development and implementation of a national strategy for the management of Canada's estuarine, coastal and marine ecosystems.

The Government worked closely with provincial and territorial governments, industry, academics, aboriginal and community groups, NGOs and other Canadians on over 30 Integrated Management and Marine Protected Area initiatives on all three coasts, developing the strategy as a result of the feedback and lessons learned during this process. It is anticipated that the strategy will position Canada as a world leader in oceans management, and it also aims to promote national and international collaboration as well as international oceans governance, sharing experience, promoting compliance and building capacity (Government of Canada, 2002).

At the *international* level, The White Water to Blue Water (WW2BW) Initiative is underway in the Caribbean region. WW2BW was launched, following the World Summit on Sustainable Development in

Johannesburg in 2002, in order to stimulate dynamic partnerships between public and private entities and funding agencies to promote integrated watershed and marine-based ecosystems management within the wider Caribbean region. It focuses on enhancing integrated approaches in areas such as wastewater and sanitation, sustainable agricultural practices, integrated coastal management, sustainable tourism and environmentally sound marine transportation (Leeds Tourism Group, 2004; Stakeholder Forum, 2004).

Also at the international level, The International Coral Reef Initiative (ICRI) is an informal network of governments and international agencies working with scientific and conservation institutions. It is a unique environmental partnership that brings all the stakeholders together with the objective of sustainable use and conservation of coral reefs and associated ecosystems (i.e. mangroves and seagrasses) for future generations (ICRI, 2003). ICRI is an informal mechanism that allows representatives of developing countries with coral reefs to sit in equal partnership with major donor countries and development banks, international environmental and development agencies, scientific associations, the private sector and NGOs to decide on the best strategies to conserve the world's coral reef resources.

There is a formidable list of core members and networks that constitute ICRI. Apart from the obvious government agencies and national committees, there are: INGOs (CORAL, IUCN, Marine Aquarium Council, Reef Check, WWF), International Programmes and Conventions (CBD, CITES, RAMSAR etc.), multilateral organizations (IOC, FAO, UNDP, UNEP, World Bank), research institutions (The WorldFish Centre (previously ICLARM) and WRI) as well as a number of foundations and societies (including the International Society for Reef Studies). They are linked by a rotating global secretariat, run and funded by the government of one country, but often with the assistance of others (ICRI, 2003).

ICRI's strength lies in the fact that it is a voluntary body with basic operational objectives, the agenda of which has been set by over 80 countries and states with coral reefs set at two ICRI International Workshops (1995 and 1998) – as well as at regional workshops. It does not develop and fund proposals, but ensures that the needs of the developing world concerning their coral reefs are conveyed to operational and funding organizations.

ICRI, together with UNEP, launched five communications tools in January 2002 to help the tourist industry explain to their customers the importance of protecting coral reefs. Available in five languages, these are free of charge as electronic files that can be used to print attractive and informative materials for distribution with travel documents, in-flight magazines, in hotel lobbies and rooms or at travel agencies, airport lounges, visitor information centres, reception areas and recreation centres (UNEP, 2002b).

ICRI also developed a call to action that eventually led to the creation of the International Coral Reef Action Network (ICRAN), which can be viewed as the action arm of ICRI. Launched in June 2001, and receiving its initial funding from the United Nations Foundation, it is a global partnership among coral reef conservation groups and scientists working to halt and reverse the decline in the health of the world's coral reefs, by developing a collective coral reef conservation and research programme that is multi-faceted and complementary, combining scientific, cultural, social and economic perspectives.

The various partners in ICRAN are: (i) CORAL, the Coral Reef Alliance, a member-supported non-profit organization dedicated to keeping coral reefs alive around the world, which supports ICRAN through local coral reef initiatives by raising public awareness about coral reefs and using the power of coral reef tourism to keep coral reefs alive; (ii) the Global Coral Reef Monitoring Network (GCRMN), which is an operational unit of ICRI and supports ICRAN through its activities to assess how, where and why coral reef damage is occurring and the effectiveness of management; (iii) the ICRI secretariat; (iv) UNEP's Regional Seas Program; (v) the United Nations Foundation, which provided the initial financial support and leverage, and continues to provide ongoing communication support; (vi) UNEP World Conservation Monitoring Centre, which provides database and research products with an emphasis on mapping coral reefs and associated ecosystems and protected areas; (vii) The WorldFish Centre, which also supports ICRAN through database and information systems (notably ReefBase, which was first initiated in 1993), as well as fisheries research products and socio-economic assessment with an emphasis on the needs of coastal communities; (viii) the World Resources Institute by analysing threats to coral reefs, provides valuation of ecosystem goods and services and determines priority areas for management; and (ix) the World Wildlife Fund USA, which supports ICRAN through a network of management site activities in coral reef and associated ecosystems.

ICRAN focuses on site-based solutions to reverse the decline of coral reefs, through organizations working together at the international, national and local level around the world. There are three main interlinked components of ICRAN:

- Reef management, which concentrates on site-specific strategies (local outreach and management).
- Global coral reef monitoring and assessment (continuing to develop ReefBase, which is the official database of the Global Coral Reef Monitoring Network and ICRAN; expanding the global Reefs at Risk report, etc.).
- Communications and knowledge dissemination (ICRIN, the International Coral Reef Information Network, works closely with ICRAN partners to collect and disseminate coral reef information and resources (The Coral Reef Alliance, 2002).

ICRAN has a list of demonstration and target sites that include those that specifically address tourism. These include: the Hol Chan Marine

Reserve in Belize, which is a multiple-use MPA; Bonaire Marine Park in the Netherlands Antilles; Sian Ka'an Biosphere Reserve in Mexico; and Soufriere Marine Management Area in St Lucia. Certain demonstration sites specifically address marine ecotourism, notably Bunaken in Indonesia, which was the global winner of the 2003 British Airways Tourism for Tomorrow Award. The Gili islands in Indonesia, as well as Nha Trang in Vietnam, are also two ecotourism target sites (ICRAN, 2002).

Showcasing sustainability

Added to the initiatives described above, there have been several global events to raise across-the-board awareness of the state of marine environments in recent years. The year 1997 was designated as the International Year of the Reef (IYOR) by a coalition of governments, NGOs, business associations and scientists. Endorsed by ICRI, and designed to support its activities, IYOR was intended to be a coordinated international outreach campaign, providing a global context for national and regional efforts to save coral reefs and promoting collaboration among organizations and programmes with common interests in reef management and research.

Established in 1996, and still operating, ReefCheck, a volunteer, community-based monitoring protocol designed to measure the health of coral reefs globally, became an official IYOR activity. ReefCheck 1997 involved collaboration between recreational divers and marine scientists who undertook 1-day rapid surveys of 250 reef sites across the world over an 11-week period in the summer of 1997. The surveys utilized basic techniques such as counting indicator species, measuring coral cover, and the ratio between live and dead coral (UNESCO Indonesia, 2004). All the sites studied showed signs of human impact. IYOR received extensive publicity, for example the South Pacific Regional Environment Program celebrated the 'Pacific Year of the Reef', with media materials and programmes on the theme.

In the face of growing recognition of the importance of the ocean, the marine environment and its resources for life on earth and for sustainable development, the United Nations declared 1998 as the International Year of the Ocean (IYO). Running with the slogan 'One Earth, One Ocean, One Life', the overall objective of IYO was to focus and reinforce the attention of the public, governments and decision makers on the importance of the oceans and the marine environment as resources for sustainable development. While UNESCO was the leading agency in implementing IYO, through its ocean research, monitoring, educational and assistance programme, the Intergovermental Oceanographic Commission (IOC), it was emphasized that IYO should not be considered as an event lying purely within IOC interests.

Other international organizations involved were FAO, IAEA (international Atomic Energy Association), IMO (International Maritime

Organisation), UNEP and WMO (World Meteorological Organisation). Inter-agency cooperation included joint meetings, regional assessments, joint scientific programmes and joint activities at the regional level, such as the Pan-African Coastal Zone Conference. Such cooperation was designed to generate an increased dialogue between the communities, as well as inter-sectoral communication (UNESCO, 1998).

A third global event, The International Year of Ecotourism 2002, declared by the UN General Assembly in December 1998, had as its objectives to:

- Generate greater awareness among public authorities, the private sector, the civil society and consumers regarding ecotourism's capacity to contribute to the conservation of the natural and cultural heritage in natural and rural areas, and the improvement of standards of living in those areas.
- Disseminate methods and techniques for the planning, management, regulation and monitoring of ecotourism to guarantee its long-term sustainability.
- Promote exchanges of successful experiences in the field of ecotourism.
- Increase opportunities for the efficient marketing and promotion of ecotourism destinations and products on international markets (UNEP, 2001).

Whilst not specific to the marine environment, the message for the incorporation of multi-stakeholder dialogue processes into policies, guidelines and projects at the global, regional and national levels was clearly expressed in The Quebec Declaration on Ecotourism, which was the outcome of the World Ecotourism Summit in May 2002 (UNEP/WTO, 2002).

It is difficult to draw conclusions as to the success, or otherwise, of these global exercises. Of the three, the latter has drawn most criticism, most notably from Southern NGOs and indigenous peoples' groups (Third World Network, 2001), in particular for its seemingly wholesale, uncritical promotion of ecotourism. Vivanco (2002), for example, writes of 'IYE's universalistic and self-serving vision', as described in Chapter 5.

Problems with collaboration

It is obvious from this, and the two preceding chapters, that there is a plethora of initiatives at varying scale levels. Some are dedicated to marine ecotourism, others with a much wider remit, all concerned with sustainable marine environments that obviously provide the wider context. What is evident, from the examples of networks and initiatives examined above, is that collaborative ventures have a mixed record of success. It is perhaps not surprising that dedicated marine tourism partnerships are relatively thin on the ground, as this is typical of tourism partnerships as a whole. As Selin (2000, p. 140) states, such partnerships 'are still underdeveloped due to many geographic, organizational, and political constraints'.

We must add economic constraints into this picture. As noted earlier (for example the cases of SLMTA, Torbay Coastal Forum and IRRUS), recurrent funding for collaborative efforts is notably deficient. Sharpley and Telfer (2002, p. 163) note that: 'It is typical throughout the world for the more populated and industrial interiors to be favoured, which leads to a lack of administrative support and funding for economic development, including tourism, in peripheral areas.' While their observation is obviously directed at land-based differentials, it is interesting to reflect that the marine environment presents perhaps the most extreme example of peripherality, particularly when the cross-jurisdictional factor is built in.

It is at the local or provincial level that the experience of collaborative ventures is at its most patchy, not for the lack of trying by a few, seriously committed, stakeholders but precisely because of that: the administrative and financial burden falls on the shoulders of those few. Consequently, we find that those networks and initiatives that are based on a sound financial footing with guaranteed recurrent funding, and an extensive membership base which is galvanized by strong political support – such as the Great Barrier Reef LMACs and the Chesapeake Bay Program – are those which are successful. Conversely, initiatives that have stagnated or ceased have faced problems of withdrawal of finance, too few members pulling together and waning political support.

At the international level, it is inevitable that such a proliferation of institutions and initiatives, let alone the veritable minefield of acronyms, gives an overall impression of disarray and duplication of effort regarding management of the marine environment. As Duda and Sherman (2002, p. 797) declare, there is 'fragmentation among institutions, international agencies, and disciplines, lack of cooperation among nations sharing marine ecosystems, and weak national policies, legislation and enforcement'. They call for drastic reforms to address the imperative for collaboration between 'competing global programs, competing interests of donors, competing priorities of international finance institutions' (p. 828).

Not surprisingly, faced with different jurisdictions with frequently divergent priorities, the picture is one of unevenness and variability when we examine the success, or otherwise, of global or regional initiatives. ICRI (1999), for example, laments the lack of national level commitments to coral reef programmes in some countries that has hindered the implementation of global and regional achievements. While UNEP and several of its Regional Seas Programmes have been productive partners, ICRI argues that the ongoing role of UNEP and the function of regional coordination need to be identified more clearly and strengthened.

12 Conclusion

Between the Devil and the Deep Blue Sea

The title to this book reflects the positioning of marine ecotourism as a process and as a principle in the overall context of coastal and marine environments in their widest sense. This wider context is vital for our understanding of how, and why, marine ecotourism is positioned between the 'devil' – in the form of the myriad of factors that may militate against sustainable outcomes – and the prospects for tourism use of the 'deep blue sea'. In the same way that Gordon and Goodall (2000, p. 292) call for a need 'to understand, in a theoretically informed way, *how* the processes of interaction between tourism and sets of place characteristics operate, and develop over time, in different contexts', we have aimed to highlight not only the characteristics of marine ecotourism but also the enormous complexities of the interchanges and interdependencies involved in its coastal and marine setting.

It is essential to recognize that contingencies of place (Williams and Shaw, 1998) both shape and are shaped by economic, sociocultural, political, ecological, institutional and technical forces that are exogenous and endogenous as well as dynamic. These forces may have enabling or constraining effects (Hall and Page, 1999) and are dictated by scale and circumstance (Lew and Hall, 1998). There are seemingly limitless combinations and permutations of these forces that either make for or militate against sustainable outcomes for marine ecotourism because of place and time specificity.

However, certain general, recurrent, themes have emerged throughout the book. One of the most significant is the need to converge the debate on sustainability with those in political economy (Williams and Shaw, 1998). As they suggest, citing Harvey: 'Ecological arguments are never socially neutral any more than sociopolitical arguments are ecologically neutral' (p. 59).

The Political Economy of Sustainable Marine Ecotourism

We examined the confrontations and co-dependencies between marine ecotourism and other economic activities, tourism and otherwise, in Chapter 2. It is an unfortunate fact that other tourism activities – including eco-opportunist marine nature tourism frequently masquerading under the title of ecotourism – may compromise the success, if not the very existence, of marine ecotourism. It is even more evident that other economic sectors may have a potentially deleterious effect on coastal and marine environments and, in turn, upon the prospects for sustainable marine ecotourism. These are not just marine-based (such as aquaculture, oil extraction, underwater dredging and mining) but also land-based (such as destructive logging and unsustainable agricultural practices resulting in coastal siltation and eutrophication of coastal waters). The significance of land-based sources of marine pollution such as sewage, industrial pollution and agricultural run-off is recognized by The White Water to Blue Water Partnership (WW2BW), examined in Chapter 1.

We also considered the setting of marine ecotourism in the global political economy in Chapter 2, recognizing that centre–periphery relationships are framed by political and economic relationships of power. This is particularly significant in the developing countries, where three of the largest non-profit organizations in the world – the World Wildlife Fund (WWF), Conservation International (CI) and The Nature Conservancy (TNC) wield very considerable influence. We described how these BINGOs (Big International Non-governmental Organizations) have strong links with bilateral and multilateral funding agencies in Chapter 9, which serves to consolidate their influence still further. When it is considered that their combined revenues for work in the developing countries accounted for over 50% of the approximately US$1.5 billion available for conservation in 2002, it is obvious that their agendas will predominate (Chapin, 2004).

As Hartwick and Peet (2003, p. 189) describe, environmental concern has been 'ideologically and institutionally incorporated into the global neoliberal hegemony of the late 20th century' such that 'the global capitalist economy can grow, if not with clear environmental conscience, then with one effectively assuaged'. Walley (2004, pp. 244–248) describes the situation of Mafia Island, Tanzania, where WWF was very instrumental in the setting up of Mafia Island Marine Park and declares that:

> Despite the seeming promise of 'participation', the institutional frameworks in which participation is embedded easily leaves existing social inequalities unchanged … It became apparent that people now believed that the park intended, not to encourage 'participation', but to impose its decisions upon residents for the benefit of park officials or rich tourists, demonstrating in their view a callous disregard for residents' well-being.

In a later article, she expresses concern that, given the low wages, the seasonal work and the relatively small number of jobs created by the tourist industry, most families would see little benefit from this alternative income strategy and yet 'such distorted assumptions continued to drive the organization's "global" agenda as well as its plans for Mafia Island Marine Park' (Walley, 2004/5, p. 6). She concludes that:

> Nearly all those dynamics conceptualised as 'new' about the Mafia Island Marine Park, including the merging of conservation and development agendas, the isolation of ecotourism as a development strategy, and the role of participation and transnational bureaucracies, are not ruptures, but rather build upon and work through existing and historical institutional structures and power relationships.

(Walley, 2004, pp. 262–264).

A drop in the ocean?

We discussed in Chapter 2 the potential spread effects from ecotourism, disseminating knowledge and awareness of sustainable practices. To what extent can marine ecotourism offer an economic incentive to divert away from unsustainable activities? This is not an easy question to answer, faced with the harsh realities of the marketplace and, once more, is likely to be place- and time-specific. It is undeniable that the phenomenal growth of whale watching at many locations across the globe over recent years (detailed in Chapter 4) has given considerable impetus, and economic rationale, to whale watching as opposed to whale hunting as a commercial activity.

However, Topelko and Dearden (2005, p. 123) examine the potential for the same scenario with regard to the shark-watching industry and conclude that:

> For areas involved in shark fishing and shark watching, a conservation strategy for sharks involving tourism could facilitate progression along the continuum from Situation 3 (there is no shark watching and local sharks are fished) to Situation 1 (shark watching is flourishing and there is no, or mimimal, consumptive use of sharks).

Nevertheless, they point out that, as we discussed in Chapter 3, despite the potential of the industry:

> to generate considerable income and contribute to the conservation of some shark species in some locations, the economic incentives do not appear large enough to encourage a reduction in fishing pressure appropriate to the scale of threat now facing sharks. With an estimated 100 million sharks caught *each year* [authors' italics], the scale of threat to sharks is enormous.

> (Topelko and Dearden, 2005, p. 123)

So, once again, we turn to the consideration of scale. Despite our contestation of the tendency to confine ecotourism to small-scale participation, the fact remains that most marine ecotourism operators are small and medium-sized enterprises, and this raises our next issue: the question of economic viability.

Economic viability of marine ecotourism

We need to consider the economic viability of marine ecotourism, not only if it is to be a serious contender for the title of sustainable operations but also because it inevitably attaches a financial value to nature. Regarding the first point, we examined in Chapter 8 the need for financial sustainability as a crucial component of the triple bottom line: the bottom line of green is black. Hillel (2002) describes how entrepreneurship at SME level is risky, declaring how 'Unsuccessful ecolodges and unemployed professionals unfortunately are a reality in many cases'.

The question of finance and support for ecotourism marketing, particularly given the relatively small size of the market and the burgeoning number of ecotourism enterprises, is also acute. There is a considerable problem of understanding the market: Wight (2002, p. 230) describes how, for Alberta, Canada:

> The biggest challenge was to obtain national and international ecotourism market information, to determine market needs, characteristics, trip and product preferences, changing demand, destinations of interest, and information to assist in marketing appropriately. This was known to be a costly and ambitious endeavour.

Mader (2002) notes that: 'Too many noble eco-friendly projects have failed because there has been no investment in marketing ... How many ecotourism projects funded by the international development banks or agencies still exist?' Andrews (1998) critically appraises the development of Mafia Island Marine Park, where tourism was intended to provide long-term social and economic benefits to the community. He argues that:

> Tourist projection figures were highly exaggerated. When it was clear that tourism was never going to be in a position to fund the park in a sustainable manner, no redress was made. This put enormous pressure on the fledgling and struggling tourist operators on Mafia Island who were major stakeholders but ... were rarely consulted.

(Andrews, 1998, p. 278)

The dilemma of supply outstripping demand was addressed by the Third World Network (TWN) and Tourism Investigation Monitoring (TIM) team regarding the International Year of Ecotourism (IYE) 2002, declaring that:

> If the IYE is to suggest that all UN member countries should encourage ecotourism projects in rural and natural areas, the danger of an oversupply of ecotourism facilities is very real. What happens if thousands of communities around the world compete with each other for a share of the ecotourism market? And who will take the responsibility, when ecotourism initiatives make investments based on miscalculated demand and later face decline, local businesses go bankrupt and entire communities are pushed into crisis? We need to be honest about the high degree of failure.

(TWN et al., 2000)

Ironically, because ecotourism strategies are being endorsed, and even financed, by multilateral agencies, donor funding may even 'crowd out conservation-oriented investors who cannot compete in a climate where park management is funded by external grants that sometimes tolerate the high overheads of state-run institutions' (Reidmiller, 2003). Furthermore, concern has been expressed that such artificial buoying up of tourism enterprises by donor finance is no guarantee of success. Dixey (2005, p. 65), for example, expresses concern that much community-based tourism has been inappropriately donor-driven, not market-led, and attributes a high rate of failure to:

a lack of market research, weak linkages to the tourism industry, small market profile, low product quality and development levels in communities, internal community disputes and poor local governance, and a lack of information dissemination, coordination and planning and sharing of common lessons and good practice.

Andrews (1998, p. 275) describes how there were few problems raising large amounts of donor funding for Mafia Island Marine Park, but that: 'There were no mechanisms for the individual donors to communicate or make funding decisions as a coordinated body ... This situation was ruthlessly exploited with many elements of the project receiving dual funding with conflicting objectives.'

There are also many examples of where ecotourism has to be supported by financial handouts, through either public sector subsidies or individual altruism. Wilkie and Carpenter (1998) are sceptical of the prospects for a viable tourist industry in more isolated, less well-endowed protected areas in the Congo Basin, when even the most well-established and accessible sites, with abundant and charismatic wildlife, have marginal revenue-generating capacity. Consequently, ecotourism in the Congo Basin constitutes a net financial cost to protected area management. In Jamaica, Gaymans (1996) describes how the government is creating and maintaining costly trails, allowing visitors to walk through for free with the rationale that tourist expenditure will boost local and national economies. He argues, however, that this strategy 'reinforces the absurd notion that nature itself has no economic value'.

The potential pitfalls of individual altruism are exemplified by the problems of cost recovery in the case of Chumbe Island, Zanzibar – as discussed in Chapter 8 – together with the pointed illustration of the small-scale ecotourism operator who summed up his situation as being 'five years and two family savings accounts' later (Shores, 2002). One of the key findings of a study of Australian nature-based tourism ventures was that new entrants need to ensure that they have sufficient resources to protect themselves in the initial years of operation, because growth is likely to be slower than expected, and costs are likely to be higher (McKercher and Robbins, 1998).

Our second concern – that marine ecotourism commodifies marine nature – is also discussed in Chapters 7 and 8. Should it present an unattractive investment prospect because of market disincentives, or even fail because of unfair competitive advantage, there is the clear danger that marine ecotourism entrepreneurs will look towards other, more financially advantageous, investment options. Without policy intervention, these alternatives will ultimately outcompete ecotourism, due to the higher turnover possible with reduced consideration of environmental and cultural impacts. There are also ethical dimensions to this commodification, through the misappropriation of nature (and culture) as we discuss in Chapter 5 and in more detail below, as well as the need for a conservation ethic to guide use of common-pool resources (CPR) underlined by the economic dependency on CPRs in many regions of the world (Holden, 2005).

Buckley (2005), however, highlights the difficulties of incorporating an ethical test into the operational criteria for any practical application of ecotourism as advocated by Fennell (2004), as certain instances may be far from straightforward. Buckley (2005) examines the case of Baffin Island, Canada, where local Inuit shuttle seakayakers board a speedboat to view narwhal and then go on to hunt this endangered species in the vicinity. Marine ecotourism, logistically and financially (the revenue helps pay for fuel and maintenance of the high-speed vessels), is therefore complicit in this activity. The Canadian Government regulates harvesting of narwhal by the Inuit for traditional cultural purposes, but this does not extend to the sale of narwhal tusks for cash sales to visiting cruise tourists, which seems to be a covert activity in the area, as this is strictly prohibited under CITES. Buckley (2005, p. 134) points out that the dilemma is one of where 'ethical concerns relating to an endangered species conflict with ethical concerns relating to indigenous or impoverished peoples, as is quite often the case'.

An equally vexatious example is given by Evans (2005), who examines how the loss of whale meat produced for domestic consumption by indigenous Tongan whalers – who were not, in themselves, a significant contributor to the drastic decline in humpback whale stocks (caused by international commercial operators) – has had significant consequences for both the national economy and the health of individual Tongans. He argues that:

> Whale-watching tourism is frequently presented as the economic and moral antithesis of whaling, and thus whale-watching advocates systematically preclude development options that include the consumptive use of whales … whaling is a moral, not economic or ecological issue … the suppression of any serious debate of this issue is a product of western ethnocentrism and a contemporary form of cultural imperialism.
>
> (Evans, 2005, p. 49)

Furthermore, he questions the viability of whale-watching tourism in terms of an economic development strategy for Tonga, given the competition from more accessible and more firmly established sites in New Zealand. Once again, we return to the considerations of political economy, as discussed in Chapters 2 and 5. Paying regard to the overall context means that, as with any other economic activity, we cannot escape from the fact that ecotourism is both shaped by and shapes the markedly inequitable structure, both internationally and intra-nationally, in which it is cast as a process.

Structural inequalities

Amongst the many concerns voiced by critics of the IYE was that it did not 'confront the structural inequalities that characterize ecotourism's origins and practice' (Vivanco, 2002). There is no substantiation with hard facts to guarantee the claim that ecotourism generally contributes to a more equitable distribution of tourism income and a reduction in poverty. Indeed, it has been argued that ecotourism may even exacerbate, or even create, divisions, as we examined in Chapter 5. Clifton (2004, p. 157) describes how, in the Wakotobi Marine National Park, Indonesia, the financial benefits from a dive ecotourism operation are essentially limited to local staff employed by the outfit. He suggests that resentment might be generated from more distant communities against both the ecotour operator and more proximate communities who enjoy a greater share of the benefits.

Bianchi (2004, p. 499) describes how, even where macro-economic indicators of tourism for many of the regions in southern Europe may look impressive, they often disguise underlying structural inequalities and weaknesses in their political economy, with growth occuring 'at the price of economic dependency, heightened class and regional inequalities, environmental degradation, particularly in coastal and marine areas, and radical changes to regional cultural practices and social relations'.

Collective thought: collective action

The question of intra-generational equity highlights the significance of social considerations in appraising the sustainability of marine ecotourism. As Williams and Shaw (1998, p. 51) suggest: 'The neglect of intra-generational equity considerations is ... critical given that this underlies, usually implicitly rather than explicitly, much of the discussion of such issues as partnership, community participation and the distribution of economic and environmental benefits.'

It is therefore essential that the ramifications of changes to more ecologically sustainable forms of production, such as marine ecotourism, are considered in relation to social conditions and implications for economic and social sustainability (Hudson, cited in Williams and Shaw, 1998). Sustainable development 'must be viewed as an evolving complex system' in which 'the alteration or disturbance of one component from within or without, may affect a hundred others' (Farrell and Twining-Ward, 2005, p. 110).

The essential dilemma is to reconcile different, sometimes polarized, often conflicting, viewpoints and values while recognizing that nothing is fixed or static: 'Sustainability concepts are themselves forever evolving, adapting to site and regionally specific conditions, and they can never be cast as universal' (Farrell and Twining-Ward, 2005, p. 110). How do we begin to appreciate, and respond to, the vast complexity of interactions and interchanges involved in marine ecotourism? It is obvious that the viewpoint of any one stakeholder, researcher or facilitator will constitute only a partial insight, so the central message – which has been reiterated throughout this book – is one for a concerted, collective approach, conceptually and practically.

All Hands on Deck

Throughout the book it has become manifest that we are, indeed, dealing with a meta-problem, as described by Hall (2000a) and discussed in Chapters 1 and 9. Hall examines how both tourism and the environment constitute meta-problems, as they are characterized by highly interconnected planning and policy issues. Indeed, for a multitude of reasons, marine tourism policy and, in turn, the context for planning for sustainable marine ecotourism, can be regarded as a prime, if not glaring, example of a meta-problem. As we discuss in Chapter 9, this is hardly surprising, given the fact that each of its components: sustainability, the marine environment and tourism are, in themselves, meta-problems. The vast extent and open nature of the marine environment is characterized by a high degree of connectivity not only within the sea but also at air/sea and land/sea interfaces, as examined in Chapter 1.

When we add the complicating factors of open access, common-pool resources, global environmental change, multiple jurisdictions and competing sectors, we can see that policy and planning issues for marine ecotourism are far from simple, since they (as already quoted in Chapter 9) 'cut across fields of expertise and administrative boundaries and, seemingly, become connected with almost everything else' (Ackoff, cited in Hall, 2000a). As Miller and Auyong (1991) declare: 'The problems of tourism do not fall squarely within a single subdomain of marine affairs, or within the purview of a single discipline.' Furthermore, planning for marine ecotourism is inevitably cast in the overall state of affairs of ocean management, which has been described as haphazard, piecemeal and ineffective (Lubchenco *et al.*, 2002).

Despite, or indeed perhaps because of, increasing and intensive multiple use of the oceans, policy making has tended to be dominated by a sectoral approach, which is primarily reactive and formulated on a piecemeal basis without inter-agency consultation, resulting in policies which often have conflicting objectives, resulting in turn in environmental damage or ineffective implementation. Decision making is thus highly fragmented and characterized by internal duplication and overlap, reflecting competition within and between sectors (Vallejo, 1994).

Given the almost unparalleled complexities involved, it is obvious that – as described in Chapter 1 – we need to draw on a range of disciplines in order to better understand the multiple contexts, issues and viewpoints implicated in marine ecotourism across the globe. The essential challenge, however, is to move towards a holistic, integrated approach, rather than the piecemeal, disjointed, approaches which, as described in Chapter 9, have characterized coastal and marine tourism to date.

To throw light on the complexities of the interlinkages and interchanges that exist within and between the diversity of processes which operate in the marine realm and, in turn, dictate the variability, viability and vulnerability – as well as the validity and value of marine ecotourism – we have drawn upon a wide range of disciplines in this book, including politics, economics, anthropology, sociology, biology, geography, oceanography, geology, climatology, psychology and philosophy.

The innumerable sub-disciplines that have assisted our exploration range from institutional economics to animal geographies. That articles on marine tourism in general are published in journals as diverse as *Ecological Economics* and *The Journal of Environmental Psychology* is a fair reflection of the relevance of diverse branches of learning to our quest. However, while these varying perspectives are invaluable in, for example, embracing different scale levels as in political ecology, or throwing light on tourist motivation and experience through humanistic psychology, they are only part of the whole. Furthermore, the emergence of narrow sub-disciplines may be a reflection of scholars retreating 'into the safety of their home domain which, in turn, can lead to further specialisation' (Adger *et al.*, 2003, p. 1096). As they go on to argue: 'Monodisciplinary analyses of environmental decisions are unable to reflect the nature of decisionmaking adequately, leading to "thin" explanations' (p. 1097).

It could be argued that a *multidisciplinary* approach is a step in the right direction insofar as it involves a number of disciplines coming together, with specialists working alongside one another. However, while it enables issues and problems to be examined from different perspectives, each disciplinary group will be working within its own field on a specific aspect of the same issue, and the end product of this exercise will just be a juxtaposition of disciplinary outputs. Visser (2004) suggests that we need to avoid this outcome, as there will be no systematic attempt at integration. Farrell and Twining-Ward (2004, p. 286) reiterate Norgaard's call for a 'transformation from disciplinary to interdisciplinary or even transdisciplinary thinking'.

Visser (2004, p. 29), in making recommendations for coastal zone research, recognizes that *interdisciplinarity* 'has been on the policy agenda for almost two decades, as the public awareness and the recognition of the intricate relationships between natural and social phenomena have become widespread'. It involves specialists working interactively on a problem, contributing their experience and disciplinary knowledge by transferring concepts and methods from one discipline to another. Adger *et al.* (2003) advocate an interdisciplinary approach to environmental decision making because it enables a more holistic or 'thick' understanding of environmental decisions, accommodating plural methodologies and methods. While interdisciplinarity provides for cross-fertilization of ideas between disciplines, however, merely to appreciate the interlinkages and interchanges is not enough: a move towards greater coherence (Laffoley *et al.*, 2004) is necessary.

Recognizing that the confines of interdisciplinarity mean that: 'There is still an enormous gap between recognition of complex interfaces and the implementation of an integrative approach to the kind, size and contents of these interelationships', Visser goes on to advocate a *transdisciplinary* approach for coastal zone research (Visser, 2004, p. 29). The main assumption of transdisciplinarity is that it transcends disciplinary divisions and boundaries, recognizing that the real world and its problems are not neatly ordered into confined disciplines. Consequently, transdisciplinarity is problem focused: starting from real world problems and drawing from many disciplines to build knowledge around these.

Visser (2004, pp. 27–29) outlines what she considers to be four distinguishing, advantageous, features of transdisciplinarity. First she identifies an essential paradox: because transdisciplinary research challenges existing assumptions and concepts, it forces reflexivity within individual disciplines, with members questioning their own premises and theories. Secondly, it is transparent insofar as it identifies conflicts and complementarities between disciplines. Thirdly, it is realistic, as it accommodates disjunctures, recognizing that diverse disciplines will attach differing values to certain concepts. Visser gives the example of the concept of the system that appeals to marine ecologists because it embraces the relationship between individual species, but is viewed by anthropologists as being too functional and deterministic. Finally, transdisciplinarity aims at advancing the research agenda by identifying 'new research questions and concepts that *move beyond* the partner disciplines' (2004, p. 29).

Farrell and Twining-Ward also advocate transdisciplinarity, arguing that: 'The wider, more versatile, research oriented transdisciplinary approach allows for better understanding of the integration of natural and social systems' (2004, p. 286). Visser (2004, p. 30) reasons that:

> The relevance of a transdisciplinary, and thus necessarily a trans-sectoral, approach is that it tries to move beyond the boundaries, knowledge, and assumptions of government institutions. Such an approach necessarily involves other segments and groups of society, with different and not sectorally determined bodies of knowledge, ranging from coastal communities and fishers' unions, to NGOs together with central and decentralized government institutions and international organizations.

The moves towards ecosystem-based approaches to coastal and marine management across the globe signify international recognition of the need to maintain systems in a comprehensive manner to ensure the achievement of global sustainability.

The Marine Ecosystem Approach

The diversity of marine resources that can be utilized for marine ecotourism has been a theme apparent throughout the book. In Chapter 3, we concluded that comprehensive resource management was central to sustainable tourism use. The concept of an ecosystem-based approach to natural resource management gained currency at the Earth Summit in Rio, Brazil, in 1992 and, as described at the Cairns Workshop on Ecosystem Based Management of Ocean Activities in 2003 (National Oceans Office, 2003), became an underpinning concept of the Convention on Biological Diversity, which describes the approach as 'a strategy for the integrated management of land, water and living resources that promotes conservation and sustainable use in an equitable way'.

The ecosystem approach is defined by the EU as:

> The comprehensive integrated management of human activities, based on best scientific knowledge about the ecosystem and its dynamics, in order to identify and take action on influences which are critical to the health of the marine ecosystems, thereby achieving sustainable use of ecosystem goods and services and maintenance of ecosystem integrity.

> (European Commission Joint Research Centre, 2006)

As discussed in Chapter 9, Hall (2000a, p. 147) endorses the shift towards the implementation of an 'ecosystem management' approach among natural resource management agencies, whereby it may be possible for 'separate, partisan interests to discover a common or public interest ... '.

However, as indicated earlier, mere integration of concepts and actions may not go far enough towards ensuring a holistic approach. A report for English Nature (Laffoley *et al.*, 2004) outlines how the ecosystem approach to marine and coastal environments should move beyond solely the requirement for integration to embody the distinguishing features of transdisciplinarity described above. In the report, the need for coherence is stressed, reflecting 'the need to go beyond simply integrating existing measures, to achieve more fundamental reorientations of perspectives, relationships and actions within and across sectors' (p. 21).

It distinguishes between *integration*, which they argue 'alone ... can potentially incur the cost of being reductionist, or attempts to create new structures that may be politically impracticable' (the difficulty of applying UNEP's Regional Seas Programme for the Caribbean via the Cartagena Convention, as described in Chapter 9, is a case in point), and *coherence*. In contrast, the latter 'potentially delivers the *benefit* of the sum of the parts exceeding the whole', arguing that without such a fundamental cross-sectoral reassessment it is 'unlikely that the adoption of the Ecosystems Approach will be radical or effective enough to make real and lasting changes in the long-term decline in ecosystems, the biodiversity they contain, and the social and economic benefits that they can provide' (2004, p. 21).

The English Nature report suggests a new framework consisting of 'seven areas of coherence', which are useful in conceptualizing the broad scope of the approach and enabling prioritization of required actions. The first three, environmental coherence, economic coherence and social coherence, are the classic trinity of sustainability; the next two, spatial coherence and temporal coherence, address the fact that ecosystems operate at different scales and change over time; the penultimate, scientific coherence, recognizes the need to furnish the management process with the best available information; and the last, institutional coherence, reflects the need to work beyond traditional societal boundaries. It is, of course, recognized that these seven areas of coherence are not mutually exclusive.

The sustainability transition

The requirements for spatial and temporal coherence, in particular, highlight the fact that the situation is far from fixed or static. Farrell and Twining-Ward (2004, p. 288) describe how: 'Understanding of sustainability has shifted from the notion of a stable achievable goal, to the concept of transition based on multiple spatial and temporal scales in a dynamic landscape of human values.' As they later go on to argue:

> Varying temporal and spatial scales involved in the interaction of subsystems within tourism systems, and the evolving aspirations and values of local people and their representative stakeholders involved in co-management, together with the probability of surprise from within or outside the system, will always prevent the uniform achievement of permanence.
>
> (Farrell and Twining-Ward, 2004)

There is a need to recognize that wherever, whenever, 'continual change and evolution prevents the attainment of simultaneous sustainability' (Farrell and Twining-Ward, 2005, pp. 111, 119). Awareness of this inescapable reality led to the emergence during the 1990s of the concept of the sustainability transition which, as Farrell and Twining-Ward describe:

> incorporates a 'place-based' understanding of the interactions between environment and society, and it adopts a systems approach using adaptive management and social learning', indicating that there is no one management endpoint but 'continual development towards biophysical and human well-being'.
>
> (Farrell and Twining-Ward, 2005, p. 118)

Spatial coherence

The place-based understanding, or spatial coherence as referred to by Laffoley *et al.* (2004, pp. 43–44), involves a recognition that:

> Marine and coastal ecosystems encompass a continuum from small-scale features within habitats to oceans and the wider sea. Applying the Ecosystem Approach in marine and coastal environments requires recognition of the need to operate across such a range of spatial scales ... human activities need to be managed in the context of functioning

ecosystems at the appropriate scale. The scales may vary, depending on the nature of the activity or indeed with the nature of an institutional regulatory process ... A hierarchy of scales will be needed, ranging from a national level planning framework, co-ordination at a regional seas level, through to the flexibility to produce local plans where required.

Indeed, it is at the local scale that the myriad of factors conditioning the prospects for sustainable marine ecotourism are perhaps expressed most cogently. As Clark and Dickson (2003, p. 8059) argue:

Agenda setting at the global, continental, and even national scale will miss a lot of the most important needs ... The transcendent challenge is to help promote the relatively 'local' (place- or enterprise-based) dialogues from which meaningful priorities can emerge, and to put in place the local support systems that will allow those priorities to be implemented ... Where such systems exist, the production of usable, place-based knowledge for promoting sustainability research has been impressive indeed.

However, place specificity dictates that: 'Because a set of interacting variables behave in a particularly successful way in one place does not mean that they will behave similarly elsewhere' (Farrell and Twining-Ward, 2005). As described in Chapter 9, Hall (2001, p. 613) also stresses that there is 'no universal "best way": each region or locale needs to select the appropriate policy mix for its own development requirements'. However, he laments the fact that little research has been done into how to achieve the ideal, place-specific mix and that there is often minimal monitoring and evaluation of policy measures.

What is clear is that:

The imposition of a universal blueprint for tourism development, a set of 'meta-principles' founded on mainstream planning and designation processes, is inappropriate given the diverse developmental contexts and needs of tourism destinations, particularly in less developed countries.

(Southgate and Sharpley, 2002, p. 261)

Andrews (1998, p. 278) picks up on this latter point by stating that his hope is that: 'Experiences on Mafia Island will encourage institutions and agencies to closely evaluate the advantages and disadvantages of applying sophisticated developed-world paradigms in developing countries.'

Temporal coherence

The time dimension is a crucial factor in marine ecotourism: we have described above when discussing problems of cost recovery, and elsewhere in the book (for example, in describing the length of time that it took to achieve community-based coastal resource management on Apo Island, the Philippines, in Chapter 10), how success cannot be achieved overnight. Cast in an overall context where, traditionally, 'many commercial operators adopt a short-term perspective on tourism, and are essentially driven by the motive of profit more than any altruistic (or indeed commercial) concern for future generations of the environment upon which they depend' (Southgate and Sharpley, 2002, p. 257), a call for a much longer time perspective may appear to be swimming against the tide.

However, it is a crucial requirement of the sustainability transition: continually evolving, adaptive management of marine ecotourism is likely to be compromised if it is couched in the short term, trying to achieve unrealistic indicators of success set against timescales that are far too short (Laffoley et al., 2004). In addition to the pragmatic reasons just outlined, we must recognize that the co-evolution of social and natural systems, in particular manifested in global environmental change, means that: 'Much longer timescales need to be considered if management is to make a difference in the face of such changes' (Laffoley et al., 2004, p. 47). This requires long-term political commitment, which Laffoley et al. (2004) suggest needs to be enshrined in a legal framework in order to ensure that longer-term and wider benefits are not sacrificed for short-term gains.

Nevertheless, adaptive management in marine tourism also needs to respond to the following facts: not only are we witnessing a formidable 'speeding up' of changes (consider, for example the significant growth in scuba-diving over recent decades, as described in Chapters 4 and 6, and recent changes in human/nature relationships as described in Chapters 5 and 7), but also the intensity of such changes is increasing, with a increasing number of tourists wanting to engage with coastal and marine environments, even in hitherto remote, peripheral locations such as the Maldives.

It will also have to respond to sudden perturbations as described in Chapter 2, such as the impact of international terrorism, witnessed by the abduction of marine tourists from Sipadan, Malaysia, in 2000 and from Palawan, the Philippines, in 2001, or of natural disasters such as the South Asian Tsunami of 2004 and tropical cyclones such as Hurricane Wilma in Mexico in 2005.

Institutional coherence

The requirement of institutional coherence has particular resonance for coastal and marine ecotourism faced with the challenges of different, frequently conflicting, interests and values; with the frequently convoluted issues of open-access, common-pool resources, the connectivity between land and sea, and differing jurisdictions as described above and in earlier chapters; and with the complicated considerations of multiple spatial and temporal scales.

It follows that no one institutional framework is sufficient on its own to be able to cope with such multidimensionality, and that we will be looking at 'multilayered governance architecture', as described by Hall (2005, p. 133), ranging and incorporating all levels from supranational to local. Hall (2003, p. 31) cites the example of the Shark Bay region in

Western Australia, a World Heritage site renowned for its dolphin watching, where 'visitors and operations are subject to a range of institutional influences which interact with each other'. The activities of the Shark Bay Shire Council are governed by the constitution of Western Australia; it is subject to federal law in relation to its World Heritage designation; and Australia itself is subject to its international treaty organizations.

It is important, therefore, to situate the planning and management of coastal and marine ecotourism within the various institutional arrangements at multiple levels and scales, as described in Chapters 9, 10 and 11. So, large marine ecosystems (LMEs), despite their detractors who criticize them as being 'top-down' solutions which are 'high off the ground' (Chapin, 2004) global approaches, should have a role to play in taking on the huge global threats to marine ecosystems and species that constitute major resource for marine ecotourism.

At the other end of the scale, however, there is a need to recognize the relevance of appropriate local governance structures which, until recently, have received little attention, and to adopt the 'new institutionalist' perspective which recognizes the value of 'endogenously created (rather than imposed) institutional arrangements that generate levels of mutual trust and assurance amongst resource users, and which provide the necessary incentives and constraints to maintain cooperation' (Southgate and Sharpley, 2002, p. 252).

Andrews (1998) suggests that building capacity in existing institutions with local communities is more appropriate and cost effective than developing new ones. The fundamental challenge, however, is how to achieve 'cross-scale' governance by articulating 'local-level, bottom-up, participatory approaches … with international and national top-down regulatory strategies' (Adger *et al.*, 2003, p. 1101).

Scientific coherence

Institutional coherence, as described above, will depend very heavily on enhanced dialogue, greater transparency and opportunities for greater exchanges between all stakeholders, at all scale levels, recognizing that the flow of information should be two-way. As Visser (2004, p. 42) argues: 'An appropriate governance of the coast should be supported by and profit from the kind of integrative research that is able to improve our understanding of the complexity and diversity of social action and biodiversity in coastal areas around the world'. One key issue in meeting the requirement of temporal coherence described above is, as Laffoley *et al.* (2004) outline, that of overcoming 'the concept of "shifting baselines" where managers and decision makers fail to see the scale of changes that have occurred'.

A major problem in the case of marine ecotourism, very much related to the requirement for scientific coherence that calls for, amongst other criteria, improved access to data, is the lack of baseline data

against which to monitor change, as discussed in Chapter 9. Boon *et al.*
(2002, pp. 100–101) describe the need for feedback models to service
adaptive management regimes, but point out that: 'This can only be
achieved if information is generated early in the development phase of
the tourism development programme thereby providing input for the
design phase and baseline data for spatial and temporal considerations.'

There are, of course, a number of constraints that militate against
this desirable state of affairs. As Strain *et al.* (2006) outline, the dynamic
and multidimensional nature of the marine environment mean that not
only is data collection and updating a formidable task, but also that data
are usually collected on a project-based approach, and rarely shared
between organizations. This scenario is particularly evident in the
developing countries where, as the Chief Executive Officer of Coral Cay
Conservation describes:

> Insufficient financial and national human resources often limit the ability for
> the timely acquisition of basic data essential for effective resource
> assessment, monitoring and management. In cases where time-bound
> discrete project funding is made available (such as Eritrea, where US$5m
> was made available through UNDP-GEF for coastal marine resource
> assessment initiatives) it is often the case that what in-country technical
> competence is available is exported overseas for higher educational training,
> thus effectively depleting the already limited available technical human
> resources for periods of years.

> (P. Raines, London, 2006, personal communication)

Also, inevitably, there are considerable problems in separating out the
net changes attributable to coastal and marine ecotourism set in the
enormously complex context, which we have spelt out throughout the
book. As Southgate and Sharpley, (2002, p. 256) declare: 'It is often difficult
to differentiate between environmental changes caused by tourism from
those associated with changing biophysical conditions or those related to
other social or economic factors.' Numerous examples within this book also
demonstrate little coherence in 'scientific' management of ecotourism
experiences across borders. Contrast the small example of Australia and
New Zealand, with largely similar societies, tourism products and
environmental challenges. The former permits managed swimming with
whales, but not dolphins, whilst the latter is the very opposite.

Adaptive management

The challenge of a multiplicity of spatial and temporal scales, as well as
changing human activity, inevitably demands flexibility, striking an
appropriate balance across social, economic and environmental
boundaries (Laffoley *et al.*, 2004, p. 58). As Farrell and Twining-Ward
(2004, p. 278) argue, there is a need for tourism researchers to venture
outside the core tourism system:

to explore the other connections and interactions that extend as far as tourism significantly affects the ways of life, the economic wellbeing of the system, and the people involved, either directly or indirectly. This comprehensive tourism system encompasses multiple system levels from the core, to the global or Earth system, all inter-related, open and hierarchical.

Adding in the question of environmental integrity, it is obvious that two-way relationships are implicit, with coastal and marine ecotourism being not only instrumental in shaping, but also being shaped by, multiple system components and levels. Farrell and Twining-Ward go on to identify the existence of complex adaptive tourism systems (CATS), which require adaptive management concepts such as *adaptive carrying capacity* that factor in 'new scientific knowledge, locality, seasonality, tourist behaviour and local preferences' (284).

Such adaptive management would adjust to the diverse, different and continually evolving situations in coastal and marine environments in order to effect a sustainability transition. This is likely to involve compromises that will be site-specific. Outcomes may well prove to be suboptimal from the viewpoints of some or all concerned but, in the circumstances, more acceptable, feasible and practicable than hitherto unrealistic, unattainable end goals, thus resulting in more sustainable marine ecotourism than previously.

A Voyage of Discovery

Reflecting back on our observations in the book it is evident that, in attempting to situate or 'ground' marine ecotourism in the overall context, the complexity of issues raised may well present as a veritable 'can of worms', as we describe for one particular scenario in Chapter 2. However, this should encourage and not deter further investigation. As Walley (2004, pp. 262–264) suggests, we should embrace rather than shy away from 'a recognition of the "patchwork" complexity of human experience as well as human–environmental relations' and while, as she argues, this will not solve everything, the actual *search* for greater understanding is vitally important in itself.

Our quest to advance the conceptual and practical understanding of marine ecotourism and the physical, technological, ecological, economic, cultural, social, political and institutional contexts at varying scales, and from different stakeholder perspectives in which it is cast as a process, has undeniably led us into what, for us, were previously uncharted waters. However, our exploration now means that we feel that we can reflect back on the sustainability of marine ecotourism with greater insight. To embrace the words of T.S. Eliot (1942):

> We shall not cease from exploration,
> And the end of all our exploring,
> Will be to arrive where we started,
> And know the place for the first time.

References

ABC (2004) *Vanuatu – Saving Nemo.* Broadcast 9 November 2004; reporter, Mark Corcoran.

Adger, W.N., Brown, K., Fairbrass, J., Jordan, A., Paavola,J., Rosendo, S. and Seyfang, G. (2003) Governance for sustainability: towards a 'thick' analysis of environmental decisionmaking. *Environment and Planning A* 35, 1095–1110.

Adler, E. (2003) *A World of Neighbours: UNEP's Regional Seas Programme* (http://www.unep.ch/seas/main/hhist.html, accessed 6 May 2004).

Adler, J. (1989) Travel as performed art. *American Journal of Sociology* 94 (6), 1366–1391.

Adventure Nova Scotia (2003) http://www.whatasite.com.adventure/whale_ethics.html (accessed 28 August 2003).

afrol (2000) *Mangroves of Western Africa Threatened by Global Warming.* http://www.afrol.com/Categories/Environment/env019_mangroves_threatened.htm (accessed 1 February 2006).

Ala'ilima, F. and Ala'ilima, L. (2002) Manono: an experiment with community-based ecotourism. In: *Sixth International Permaculture Conference Proceedings*, Chapter 6 (http://www.rosneath.com.au/ipc6/ch06/alailima, accessed 5 May 2005).

Alaska Oceans Program (2004) *Save Alaska's Oceans* (http://www.alaskaoceans.net/, accessed 5 February 2004).

Allen, L. (2004) Hotels find a friend in Nemo. *The Weekend Australian Financial Review*, 23–24 January, p. 16.

Allen, M.C. and Read, A.J. (2000) Habitat selection of foraging bottlenose dolphins in relation to boat density near Clearwater, Florida. *Marine Mammal Science* 16, 815–824.

Almagor, U. (1985) A tourist's 'vision quest' in an African game reserve. *Annals of Tourism Research* 12 (1), 31–48.

AMPTO (2002) *Fuel Taxation Inquiry Industry Submissions: AMPTO* (http://fueltaxinquiry.treasury.gov.au/content/Submission/Industry/downloads/AMPTO_226.asp, accessed 3 June 2005).

AMPTO (2003) *About Us* (http://www.ampto.com.au/aboutus.htm, accessed 22 January 2004).

AMPTO (2005) *AMPTO Business Plan 2005* (http://wwwampto.com.au/business_plan.html, accessed 6 June 2005).

Anderson, B. (1991) *Imagined Communities.* Verso, London.

Anderson, D.M. (2003) Testimony of Dr Donald M. Anderson. *Hearing on the Harmful Bloom and Hypoxia Research Amendments Act of 2003.* Committee on Science Subcommittee on Environment, Technology and Standards, US House of Representatives (http://www.house.gov/science/hearings/ets03/mar13/anderson.pdf, accessed 23 August 2005).

Andersson-Cederholm, E. and Hultman, J. (2006) Tourists and global environmental change: a possible scenario in relation to nature and authenticity. In: Gössling, S. and Hall, C.M. (eds) *Tourism and Global Environmental Change.* Routledge, Abingdon, UK and New York, pp. 293–304.

Andrews, G. (1998) *Mafia Island Marine Park, Tanzania: Implications of Applying a Marine Park Paradigm in a Developing Country* (http://iodeweb1.vliz.be/odin/bitstream/1834/905/1/Mafia+Island+marine+park.pdf, accessed 30 June 2006).

Anheuser-Busch (2005) http://www.anheuser-busch.com/ (accessed 15 June 2005).

Antonioli, C. and Reveley, M.A. (2005) Randomised controlled trial of animal facilitated therapy with dolphins in the treatment of depression. *British Medical Journal* 331, 26.

Apo Island (2004) http://www.apoisland.com (accessed 2 March 2004).

Ashley, C. (2000) *The Impacts of Tourism on Rural Livelihoods: Namibia's Experience.* Working Paper 128, Overseas Development Institute, London.

Ashley, C., Roe, D. and Goodwin, H. (2001) *Pro-Poor Tourism Strategies: Making Tourism Work for the Poor.* Pro-Poor Tourism Report No 1, ODI, IIED, CRT, London.

Associated Press (2006) Whales kill prey in front of shocked tourists. *The Guardian*, 6 July 2006, p. 22.

Atlantis Submarines (2005) http://www.atlantisadventures.com (accessed 1 June 2005).

Australian Government (2003) *Marine Protected Areas* (http://www.ea.gov.au/coasts/mpa, accessed 30 January 2003).

Barker, N.H.L. and Roberts, C.M. (2004) Scuba diver behaviour and the management of diving impacts on coral reefs. *Biological Conservation* 120, 481–489.

Barker, T. and Ross, A. (2003) Exploring cultural constructs: the case of sea mullet management in Moreton Bay, South East Queensland, Australia. In: Haggan, N., Brignall, C. and Wood, L. (eds) *Putting Fishers' Knowledge to Work.* Fisheries Centre Research Report 11 (1), University of British Columbia, Vancouver, Canada, pp. 290–306.

Barnes, R.S.K. and Mann, K.H. (eds) (1980) *Fundamentals of Aquatic Ecology.* Blackwell, Oxford, UK.

Barros, F. (2001) Ghost crabs as a tool for rapid assessment of human impacts on exposed sandy beaches. *Biological Conservation* 97, 339–404.

Baxter, A.S. and Donoghue, M. (1995) *Management of Cetacean Watching in New Zealand.* Department of Conservation, Auckland, New Zealand (http://www.physics.helsinki.fi/whale/newzeala/manage/html, accessed 25 June 1999).

BBC News (2005a) *Elephant Explosion Triggers Cull Row.* 6 November 2005 (http://news.bbc.co.uk/2/hi/africa/4392800.stm, accessed 12 February 2006).

BBC News (2005) *Man Relives Shark Attack Escape.* 26 March 2005 (accessed 26 May 2006).

Beard, J. and Ragheb, M. (1983) Measuring leisure motivation. *Journal of Leisure Research* 15 (3), 219–228.

Beardsworth, A. and Bryman, A.E. (2001) The wild animal in late modernity: the case of the Disneyization of zoos. *Tourist Studies* 1, 83–104.

Bellos, A. (2000) Galapagos turmoil: tortoise dragged into fishing war. *The Guardian*, 30 December 2000.

Berrow, S. (2003) An assessment of the framework, legislation and monitoring required to develop genuinely sustainable whalewatching. In: Garrod, B. and Wilson, J.C. (eds) *Marine Ecotourism: Issues and Experiences*. Channel View, Clevedon, UK, pp. 66–78.

Berry, C. and Davison, A. (2001) *Bitterharvest: a Call for Reform in Scottish Aquaculture*. Report for WWF, Perth, UK.

Besio, K., Johnston, L. and Longhurst, R. (2003) Why look at animals when you can swim with dolphins? *Tourism at the Limits Conference*, University of Waikato, Hamilton, New Zealand, December 2003.

BEST (Business Enterprises for Sustainable Tourism) (2002) Turtle Island Resort. *BEST Practices* 3 (1).

Bianchi, R.V. (2004) Tourism restructuring and the politics of sustainability: a critical view from the European periphery (the Canary Islands). *Journal of Sustainable Tourism* 12 (6), 495–529.

BirdLife International (2005) *Seabirds in the North Sea: Victims of Climate Change?* (http://www.birdlife.org/news/features/2005/01/north_sea_seabirds.html, accessed 31 January 2006).

Blaikie, P. (2000) Development, post-, anti-, and populist: a critical review. *Environment and Planning A* 32, 1033–1050.

Bloch, C. (2000) Flow: beyond fluidity and rigidity. A phenomenological investigation. *Human Studies* 23, 43–61.

Blue Flag (undated) *Blue Flag Campaign* (http://www.blueflag.org, accessed 2 February 2006).

Blue Oceans (2004) http://www.blue-oceans.com/scuba/fiji/divereports.html (accessed 15 June 2005).

Boon, P.I., Burridge, T.R. and Fluker, M. (2002) A case for supply-led nature-based tourism within the marine and coastal temperate systems of South-Eastern Australia. *Journal of Ecotourism* 1 (2/3), 93–103.

Borgese, E.M. (1994) Global governance and the four problem areas. In: Payoyo, P.B. (ed.) *Ocean Governance: Sustainable Development of the Seas*. UN University Press, Tokyo (http://www.unu.edu/unupress/unupbooks/uu15oeuu15oe0r.htm, accessed 6 May 2004).

Borrini-Feyerabend, G. (1996) *Collaborative Management of Protected Areas: Taking the Approach to the Context in Issues in Social Policy*. IUCN, Gland, Switzerland.

Bramwell, B. and Lane, B. (2000) Collaboration and partnerships in tourism planning. In: Bramwell, B. and Lane, B. (eds) *Tourism Collaboration and Partnerships*. Channel View, Clevedon, UK, pp. 1–19.

Bramwell, B., Henry, I., Jackson, G., Prat, A.G., Richards, G. and van der Straaten, J. (1996) *Sustainable Tourism Management: Principles and Practice*. Tilburg University Press, Tilburg, Netherlands.

Brandon, K. and Margoluis, L. (1996) Structuring ecotourism success: framework for analysis. Plenary Paper, *The Ecotourism Equation: Measuring the Impacts*. International Society of Tropical Foresters, Yale University, New Haven, Connecticut.

British Airways (1998) *An Assessment of the Environmental Impacts of Tourism in St Lucia*. Report May 1998 prepared by UK CEED for British Airways and British Airways Holidays.

Brosnan, D.M. and Crumrine, L.L. (1994) Effects of human trampling on marine rocky shore communities. *Journal of Experimental Marine Biology and Ecology* 177, 79–97.

BTR (2003) *Assessment of Tourism Activity in the Great Barrier Reef Marine Park region*. Bureau of Tourism Research, Canberra, Australia.

Buckley, R.C. (2002a) Surf tourism and sustainable development in Indo-Pacific Islands. I. The industry and the islands. *Journal of Sustainable Tourism* 10, 405–424.

Buckley, R.C. (2002b) Surf tourism and sustainable development in Indo-Pacific Islands. II. Recreational capacity management and case study. *Journal of Sustainable Tourism* 10, 425–442.

Buckley, R. (2003a) *Case Studies in Ecotourism*. CABI, Wallingford, UK.

Buckley, R. (2003b) Environmental inputs and outputs in ecotourism: geotourism with a positive triple bottom line? *Journal of Ecotourism* 2 (1), 76–82.

Buckley, R.C. (2004) Environmental impacts of motorised off-highway vehicles. In: Buckley, R.C. (ed.) *Environmental Impacts of Ecotourism*. CABI, Wallingford, UK, pp. 83–97.

Buckley, R. (2005) In search of the narwhal: ethical dilemmas in ecotourism. *Journal of Ecotourism* 4 (2), 129–134.

Buddemeier, A. and Fautin, B. (1993) Coral bleaching as an adaptive mechanism: a testable hypothesis. *BioScience* 43, 320–326.

Bulbeck, C. (2005) *Facing the Wild: Ecotourism, Conservation and Animal Encounters*. Earthscan, London.

Burgess, G.H. (1998) Diving with elasmobranchs: a call for restraint. *Shark News* 11, July 1998, IUCN/SSC Shark Specialist Group.

Burke, L. and Maidens, J. (2004) *Reefs at Risk in the Caribbean*. Research report, World Resources Institute, Washington, DC.

Burkey, S. (1993) *People First*. Zed Books, London.

Burns, P.M. (2004) Tourism planning: a third way? *Annals of Tourism Research* 31 (1), 24–43.

Butler, R. (1998) Sustainable tourism – looking backwards to progress? In: Hall, C.M. and Lew, A.A. (eds) *Sustainable Tourism: a Geographical Perspective*. Longman, Harlow, UK, pp. 25–34.

Byrnes, T. and Warnken, J. (2003) Establishing best-practice environmental management: lessons from the Australian tour-boat industry. In: Buckley, R., Pickering, C. and Weaver, D.B. (eds) *Nature-based Tourism, Environment and Land Management*. CABI, Wallingford, UK, pp. 111–122.

Cahn, M. (2002) Sustainable livelihoods approach: concept and practice. Paper presented at *Development Studies of New Zealand Conference, 2002* (http://devnet.massey.ac.nz/papers/Cahn,Miranda.pdf, accessed 10 May 2005).

CALM (2004a) *Draft Revised Zoning Scheme for the Ningaloo Marine Park and Proposed Additions to the Marine Reserve System*. Conservation and Land Management, Western Australia.

CALM (2004b) *Snorkelling at Turquoise Bay. Park Notes Cape Range National Park and Ningaloo Marine Park*. Conservation and Land Management, Western Australia.

Calumpong, H. (2000) *Community Based Coastal Resources Management in Apo Island*. Silliman University, Philippines.

Carney, D. (1999) *Livelihood Approaches Compared*. DFID, London.

Carter, E. (2002) *From Chumbe* (e-mail to E. Cater, 24 June 2002).

Carter, M. (2005) *The Illegal Killing of Scotland's Seals: Further Eyewitness Accounts* (http://www.salmonfarmmonitor.org/guest.html, accessed 30 January 2006).

Cassini, M.H. (2001) Behavioural responses of South American fur seals to approach by tourists – a brief report. *Applied Animal Behaviour Science* 71, 341–346.

Cater, C. (2004) *Marine Tourism Industry Review*. Queensland Tourism Industry Council, Brisbane, Australia.

Cater, C. (2005) Book review. Lück, M. and Kirstges, T.: Global ecotourism policies and case studies: perspectives and constraints. *Journal of Ecotourism* 3 (3), 214–216.

Cater, C. (2006) Adventure tourism: will to power? In: Church, A. and Coles, T. (eds) *Tourism, Power and Space*. Chapter 4, Routledge, London.

278 *References*

Cater, C. and Cater, E. (2001) Marine environments. In: Weaver, D.B. (ed.) *The Encyclopedia of Ecotourism*. CABI, Wallingford, UK, pp. 265–285.

Cater, E. (2003) Between the devil and the deep blue sea: dilemmas for marine ecotourism. In: Garrod, B. and Wilson, J. (eds) *Marine Ecotourism: Issues and Experiences*. Channel View, Clevedon, UK, pp. 37–47.

CBD (Convention on Biological Diversity) (2003) *Status and Trends of and Threats to Protected areas*. UNEP/CBD, Montreal, Canada.

CDNN (2002) Shark feeding fanatic Erich Ritter in stable condition after shark attack at Walker's Cay Bahamas feeding site. *CYBER DIVER News Network*, 25 April 2002.

CDNN (2005) A SCUBA diver was swallowed by white shark says witness. *CYBER DIVER News Network*, 5 June 2005.

CELB, TOI and CORAL (undated) *A Practical Guide to Good Practice* (http://www.coralreefalliance.org/programs/tourismhandbook.html, accessed 9 June 2005).

Cessford, G.R. (1998) *Sea-kayaker Satisfactions, Impact Perceptions, and Attitudes toward Management Options in Abel Tasman National Park*. Department of Conservation Wellington, New Zealand.

Cetacean Society International (2003) It's a wonder the International Whaling Commission survives. *Whales Alive* 12 (2) (http://csiwhalesalive.org/csi03204.html, accessed 1 July 2004).

Chapin, M. (2004) A challenge to conservationists. *World Watch*, November/December, 17–31.

Chatwin, B. (1987) *The Songlines*. Jonathan Cape, London.

Chen, S. and Uitto, J.I. (2004) Governing marine and coastal environment in China: building local government capacity through international cooperation. *China Environment Series* 6, 67–80 (http://wwics.si/edu/topics/pubs/6-feature_5.pdf, accessed 1 July 2004).

Chesapeake Bay Program (2001) *Overview of the Bay Program* (http://www.chesapeakebay.net, accessed 5 February 2004).

Church, A. and Coles, T. (2006) *Tourism, Power and Space*. Routledge, London.

Clark, W.C. and Dickson, N.M. (2003) Sustainability science: the emerging research program. *Proceedings of the National Academy of Sciences of the United States of America* 100 (14), 8059–8061.

Clifton, J. (2004) Evaluating contrasting approaches to marine ecotourism: 'dive tourism' and 'research tourism' in the Wakatobi Marine National Park, Indonesia. In: Boissevain, J. and Selwyn, T. (eds) *Contesting the Foreshore: Tourism, Society and Politics on the Coast*. Amsterdam University Press, Amsterdam.

Cloke, P. and Perkins, H.C. (1997) Cracking the canyon with the awesome foursome: representations of adventure tourism in New Zealand. *Environment and Planning D: Society and Space* 16, 185–218.

Cloke, P. and Perkins, H.C. (2002) Commodification and adventure in New Zealand tourism. *Current Issues in Tourism* 5 (6), 521–549.

Club Marine (2005) Whale ahoy! *Club Marine* 20 (4), 146–154. Edgecliff, New South Wales, Australia.

CNN (2003) Barrier Reef eco-plan unveiled. *CNN*, 3 December 2003 (http://www.cnn.com/2003/WORLD/asiapcf/auspac/12/03/australia.reef/index.html, accessed 6 September 2004).

Cochrane, C. (1998) Sipadan's last chance? *Action Asia* 7 (1), 17–19.

Cohen, J. (2001) Ecotourism in the inter-sectoral context. In: Weaver, D.B. (ed.) *The Encyclopedia of Ecotourism*. CABI, Wallingford, UK, pp. 497–508.

Collinsa, L.B., Zhua, Z.R., Wyrwollb, K. and Eisenhauerc, A. (2003) Late Quaternary structure and development of the northern Ningaloo Reef, Australia. *Sedimentary Geology* 159, 81–94.

Colman, J.G. (1997) A review of the biology and ecology of the whale shark. *Journal of Fish Biology* 51, 1219–1234.

Colwell, S. (1998) Entrepreneurial marine protected areas: small-scale, commercially supported coral reef protected areas. In: Hatziolos, M.E., Hooten, A.J. and Fodor, M. (eds) *Coral Reefs: Challenges and Opportunities for Sustainable Management.* World Bank, Washington, DC.

Commonwealth of Australia (2002) *White Shark* (Carcharodon carcharias) *Recovery Plan July 2002.* Environment Australia, Commonwealth of Australia, Canberra, Australia.

Connelly, C. (2004) *Attention all Shipping: a Journey around the Shipping Forecast.* Little, Brown, London.

Conservation International (2003) *New Marine Protected Area to Safeguard World's Largest Fish* (http://www.conservation.org/xp/news/press_releases/2003/071403.xml, accessed 24 March 2004).

Conservation International (2004) *Homepage* (http://www.conservation.org/xp/CIWEB/home, accessed 27 June 2004).

Constantine, R. (1999) Effects of tourism on marine mammals in New Zealand. *Science For Conservation: 106.* Department of Conservation, Wellington, New Zealand.

Constantine, R., Brunton, D.H. and Dennis, T. (2004) Dolphin-watching tour boats change bottlenose dolphin (*Tursiops truncatus*) behaviour. *Biological Conservation* 117, 299–307.

Cooper, C., Gilbert, D., Fletcher, J. and Wanhill, S. (1993) *Tourism: Principles and Practice.* Longman, Harlow, UK.

Coral Princess Cruises (2005) http://www.coralprincesscruises.com (accessed 22 June 2005).

Cordell, K. (2004) *Outdoor Recreation for 21st Century America. A report to the nation: the National Survey on Recreation and the Environment.* Venture Publishing, Pennsylvania.

Corkeron, P.J. (1995) Humpback whales (*Megaptera novaeangliae*) in Hervey Bay, Queensland: behaviour and responses to whale-watching vessels. *Canadian Journal of Zoology* 73, 1290–1299.

Couran Cove Island Resort (2004a) *Pest Management: a Holistic Approach.* Factsheet.

Couran Cove Island Resort (2004b) *Energy Management.* Factsheet.

Cousteau, J.Y. (1953) *The Silent World.* Hamish Hamilton, London.

Craig-Smith, S.J., Tapper, R. and Font, X. (2006) The coastal and marine environment. In: Gössling, S. and Hall, C.M. (eds) *Tourism and Global Environmental Change.* Routledge, Abingdon, UK and New York, pp. 107–127.

Crang, P. (1997) Performing the tourist product. In: Rojek, C. and Urry, J. (eds) *Touring Cultures: Transformations of Travel and Theory.* Routledge, London, pp. 137–154.

CRC Reef (2001) Crown-of-thorns Starfish on the Great Barrier Reef. *Current State of Knowledge,* April 2001. CRC Reef, Townsville, Australia.

CRC Reef (2003) *Marine Tourism on the Great Barrier Reef: Current State of Knowledge June 2003.* CRC Reef, Townsville, Australia.

CRC Reef (2005) *Seagrasses* (http://www.reef.edu.au/asp_pages/secb.asp?FormNo=12, accessed 12 January 2005).

Creel, L. (2003) *Ripple Effects: Population and Coastal Regions.* Population Reference Bureau (http://www.prb.org/pdf/RippleEffects_Eng.pdf, accessed 3 March 2004).

Cresswell, T. (1999) Embodiment, power and the politics of mobility: the case of female tramps and hobos. *Transactions of the Institute of British Geographers* NS24, 175–192.

Csikszentmihalyi, M. (1975) *Beyond Boredom and Anxiety*. Jossey-Bass, San Francisco, California.

CZMAI (2001) *Tourism and Recreation Best Practice for Coastal Areas in Belize* (http://www.coastalzonebelize.org, accessed 2 February 2005).

Dale, C. (2000) Contested territories: an exploration of the notion of quiet enjoyment in National Park policy and practice. *North West Geographer: Journal of the Manchester Geographical Society* 3 (2), 21–31.

Davenport, J. and Davenport, J.L. (2006) The impact of tourism and personal leisure transport on coastal environments. *Estuarine, Coastal and Shelf Science* 67 (1/2), 280–292.

Davis, D. and Gartside, D.F. (2001) Challenges for economic policy in sustainable management of marine natural resources. *Ecological Economics* 36, 223–236.

Davis, D., Banks, S., Birtles, A., Valentine, P. and Cuthill, M. (1997) Whale sharks in Ningaloo Marine Park: managing tourism in an Australian marine protected area. *Tourism Management* 18 (5), 259–271.

DEFRA (2002a) Taking to the water with English Heritage. *Wavelength* 7, Autumn 2002.

DEFRA (2002b) *Safeguarding our Seas: a Strategy for the Conservation and Sustainable Development of our Marine Environment*. DEFRA, London.

DEFRA (2002c) *Seas of Change*. DEFRA, London.

DEFRA (2003) *Integrated Coastal Zone Management* (http://www.defra.gov.uk/ environment/marine/iczm., accessed 27 August 2003).

DEH (1993) The role of indigenous people. *Resource Assessment Commission Coastal Zone Inquiry Final Report, Chapter 10*. Department of the Environment and Heritage, Canberra, Australia.

De Haas, H.C. (2002) Sustainability of small-scale ecotourism: the case of Niue, South Pacific. *Current Issues in Tourism* 5 (3/4), 319–337.

Department of Conservation (2005a) *Review of Abel Tasman National Park Management Plan*. Nelson/Marlborough Conservancy Fact Sheet 152, March 2005, Department of Conservation, Wellington, New Zealand.

Department of Conservation (2005b) *Nelson/Marlborough Visitor Statistics 1 July 2003–30 June 2004*. Nelson/Marlborough Conservancy Fact Sheet 153, January 2005, Department of Conservation, Wellington, New Zealand.

Department of Conservation and Land Management (2003) *Proposed Zoning Scheme for Ningaloo Marine Park and the Proposed Additions to the Marine Conservation Reserve System*. Department of Conservation and Land Management, Western Australia.

Desmond, J. (1999) *Staging Tourism: Bodies on Display from Waikiki to Sea World*. University of Chicago Press, Chicago, Illinois.

DETR (2000) The Welsh–Irish Seascapes Project. *Wavelength* 5, Autumn 2000. Development Policy (http://www.btr.gov.au/service/confproc/ecotourism99/Section_3.pdf).

Ditton, R.B., Osburn, R.H., Baker, T.L. and Thailing, C.E. (2002) Demographics, attitudes, and reef management preferences of sport divers in offshore Texas waters. *Journal of Marine Science* 59, 186–191.

Dixey, L. (2005) *Inventory and Analysis of Community-based Tourism in Zambia*. USAID Production, Finance and Technology Programme (PROFIT), Lusaka, Zambia.

Dixon, J.A., Scura, L.F. and van't Hof, T. (1993) Meeting ecological and economic goals: marine parks in the Caribbean. *Ambio* 22 (2/3), 117–125.

DOE (2005) Deep Ocean Expeditions (http://www.deepoceanexpeditions.com/, accessed 5 October 2006).

Dolnicar, S. and Fluker, M. (2003) Behavioural market segments among surf tourists – investigating past destination choice. *Journal of Sports Tourism* 8 (3), 186–196.

Douglas, N. and Douglas, N. (2004) *The Cruise Experience: Global and Regional Issues in Cruising*. Pearson, Harlow, UK.

Dowdeswell, J.A. (2004) Oceans. In: Pile, S. and Thrift, N. (eds) *Patterned Ground*. Reaktion, London, pp. 113–115.

Down to Earth (2001) *The Global Environmental Facility*. Down to Earth IFI factsheet 18 (http://dte.gn.apc.org/Af18.htm, accessed 1 March 2004).

Duda, A.M. and Sherman, K. (2002) A new imperative for improving management of large marine ecosystems. *Ocean and Coastal Management* 45, 797–833.

Duffus, D.A. and Dearden, P. (1993) Recreational use, valuation, and management of killer whales on Canada's Pacific coast. *Environmental Conservation* 20 (2), 149–156.

Eagles, P. and Higgins, B. (1998) Ecotourism market and industry structure. In: Lindberg, K., Epler-Wood, M. and Engeldrum, D. (eds) *Ecotourism: a Guide for Planners and Managers*. Vol. 2, The Ecotourism Society, Vermont, pp. 11–43.

Eliot, T.S. (1942) *Little Gidding*. Faber and Faber, London.

Elliot, J. (2003) Invasion of the yellow ducks. *Sunday Times*, 13 July 2003, p. 11.

Ellis, F. and Allison, E. (2004) *Livelihood Diversification and Natural Resource Access*. FAO Livelihood Support Programme (LSP) working paper 9, FAO, Rome.

Emerton, L. and Tessema, Y. (2001) *Economic Constraints to the Management of Marine Protected areas: the Case of Kisite Marine National Park and Mpunguti Marine National Reserve, Kenya*. IUCN Eastern Africa Regional Office, Nairobi.

Entus, S. (2002) *Re: Participative (Business) Community Development*. Discussion list (trinet@hawaii.edu).

Enzenbacher, D.J. (1995) The regulation of Antarctic tourism. In: Hall, C.M. and Johnston, M.E. (eds) *Polar Tourism: Tourism in the Arctic and Antarctic regions*. Wiley, Chichester, UK, pp. 179–216.

EPA (2005a) *Great Sandy Region Management Plan 1994–2010, September 2005*. Queensland Government, Brisbane, Queensland, Australia.

EPA (2005b) *Sink the Brisbane* (http://www.epa.qld.gov.au/about_the_epa/coming_events/sink_the_brisbane/, accessed 9 June 2006).

Epler-Wood, M. (2002) *Ecotourism: Principles, Practices and Policies for Sustainability*. UNEP and The International Ecotourism Society, Paris and Burlington, Vermont.

Epler-Wood, M. (2003) The Ecoclub interview. *Ecoclub International Ecotourism Monthly*, 54 (http://ecoclub.com/news/054/interview.html, accessed 3 June 2005).

Erdmann, M.V. (2001) Saving Bunaken. *Inside Indonesia* January–March 2001 (http://www.insideindonesia.org/edit65/bunaken.htm, accessed 13 November 2002).

Erdmann, M.V. (2003) *The Bunaken Entrance Fee: Your Money Making a Difference*. North Sulawesi Tourism Promotion Board (http://www.north-sulawesi.org/bunaken.html, accessed 13 November 2002).

Essex Estuaries Initiative (2002) *Essex Estuaries Initiative* (http://www.essexestuaries.org.uk, accessed 16 January 2004).

E turbo news (2005) *Is Dining Better under the Sea?* 21 April 2005.

European Commission Joint Research Centre (2006) *Action 2121: Monitoring and Assessment of Marine Ecosystems* (http://ies.jrc.cec.eu.int/ecomar.html, accessed 19 October 2006).

Evans, M. (2005) *Whale-Watching and the Compromise of Tongan Interests through Tourism* (http://www.sicri.org/assets/downloads/SICRI05_PDF/SICRI2005_Evans.pdf, accessed 23 August 2006).

Farrell, B.H. and Twining-Ward, L. (2004) Reconceptualizing tourism. *Annals of Tourism Research* 31 (2), 274–295.

Farrell, B.H. and Twining-Ward, L. (2005) Seven steps towards sustainability: tourism in the context of new knowledge. *Journal of Sustainable Tourism* 13 (2),109–122.

Felstead, M.L. (undated) *Coastal Resources Management, Ulugan Bay, Palawan Island, The Philippines* (http://www_unesco.org/csi/act/ulugan/ulugan4.htm, accessed 24 August 2004).

Fennell, D. (1999) *Ecotourism.* Routledge, London.

Fennell, D. (2000) Ecotourism on trial – the case of billfish angling as ecotourism. *Journal of Sustainable Tourism* 8 (4), 341–345.

Fennell, D. (2003) *Ecotourism,* 2nd edn. Routledge, London and New York.

Fennell, D. (2004) Deep ecotourism: seeking theoretical and practical reverence. In: Singh, T.V. (ed.) *New Horizons in Tourism: Strange Experiences and Stranger Practices.* CABI, Wallingford, UK, pp. 109–120.

Fennell, D.A. and Dowling, R.K. (2003) Ecotourism policy and planning: stakeholders, management and governance. In: Fennell, D.A. and Dowling, R.K. (eds) *Ecotourism Policy and Planning.* CABI, Wallingford, UK, pp. 331–344.

Fisheries and Oceans Canada (2006) *Ocean Tourism* (http://www.mar.dfo-mpo.gc.ca/pande/ecn/ns/e/ns11-e.asp, accessed 5 May 2006).

Flintan, F. (2002) *Flip-flops and Turtles – Women's Participation in the Kiunga National Marine Reserve ICDP, Kenya.* Working paper No. 5, Engendering Eden Project, International Famine Centre, University College, Cork, Ireland.

Flintan, F. (2003) *'Engendering' Eden Volume 1: Women, Gender and ICDPs: Lessons Learnt and Ways Forward.* IIED Wildlife and Development Series No. 16, IIED, London.

Flores, M. (undated) *Six Steps in the Making of the Olango Birds and Seascape Tour* (http://www.oneocean.org/ambassadors/migratory_birds/obst/six_steps_in_the_making.html, accessed 28 April 2005).

Fluker, M. (2003) Riding the wave: defining surf tourism. *Proceedings of the 13th International Research Conference of the Council for Australian University Tourism and Hospitality (CAUTHE), Coffs Harbour, Australia, 5–8 February* (CD-ROM).

Font, X. and Buckley, R. (2001) *Tourism Ecolabelling.* CABI, Wallingford, UK.

Font, X., Sanabria, R. and Skinner, E. (2003) Sustainable tourism and ecotourism certification: raising standards and benefits. *Journal of Ecotourism* 2 (3), 213–218.

Font, X., Cochrane, J. and Tapper, R. (2004) *Tourism for Protected Area Financing: Understanding Tourism Revenues for Effective Management Plans.* Leeds Metropolitan University, Leeds, UK.

Forest, A.M. (2001). The Hawai'ian spinner dolphin, *Stenella longirostris*: effects of tourism. MSc thesis, Texas A&M University, College Station, Texas.

Forestell, P.H. and Kaufman, G.D. (1990) The history of whale watching in Hawaii and its role in enhancing visitor appreciation for endangered species. *Congress on Coastal and Marine Tourism: a Symposium and Workshop on Balancing Conservation and Economic Development.* National Coastal Resources Research and Development Institute, Newport, Oregon.

Frangialli, F. (2005) *Climate Change Poses Risk to Tourism WTO Warns* (http://www.travelwirenews.com/cgi-script/csArticles/articles/000064/006432.htm, accessed 8 November 2005).

Franklin, A. (2003) *Tourism: an Introduction.* Sage, London.

Galapagos Conservation Trust (2005a) *Artisanal Fishing as a Cultural Experience, a Novel Alternative* (http://www.gct.org/aug05_1.html, accessed 5 October 2005).

Galapagos Conservation Trust (2005b) *Frequently Asked Questions* (http://www.gct.org/faq.html, accessed 25 May 2005).

Garrod, B. and Wilson, J. (2004) Nature on the edge? Marine ecotourism in peripheral coastal areas. *Journal of Sustainable Tourism* 12 (2), 95–120.

Garrod, B., Wilson, J. and Bruce, D. (2001) *Planning for Marine Ecotourism in the EU Atlantic Area: Good Practice Guidance.* University of the West of England, Bristol, UK.

Gartside, D. (2001) *Fishing Tourism: Charter Boat Fishing.* Wildlife Tourism Publication No. 12. CRC for Sustainable Tourism, Queensland, Australia.

Gaymans, H. (1996) Five parameters of ecotourism. In: *The Ecotourism Equation: Measuring the Impacts.* Bulletin 99, Yale School of Forestry and Environmental Studies, New Haven, Connecticut.

GBRMPA (Great Barrier Reef Marine Park Authority) (2002) *Local Marine Advisory Committees* (http://www.gbrmpa.gov.au/corp_site/management/lmac/index.html, accessed 6 May 2003).

GBRMPA (2003) *GBRMPA Joins Disney To Tell Reef Story* (http://www.gbrmpa.gov.au/corp_site/info_services/media/2003/2003-03-12.html, accessed 3 September 2004).

GBRMPA (2004) *Tourism and Recreation* (http://www.gbrmpa.gov.au/corp_site/key_issues/tourism, accessed 1 September 2004).

GBRMPA (2005) Reef Walking Guidelines (http://www.gbrmpa.gov.au/corp_site/key_issues/tourism/reef_walking.html, accessed 22 June 2006).

GEFSGP (Global Environment Facility Small Grants Programme) (2004) *Promoting Marine Tour Guide Training in Communities that Impact the Belize Barrier Reef Reserve System* (http://www.gefsgp.org/2.html, accessed 13 May 2004).

GEFSGP (undated) Profiles of GEF/SGP Funded Projects in Pakistan during Operational Phase (http://www.un.org.pk/profilesgefsgpprojects.htm, accessed 1 March 2004).

George, P.S. (2004) *Passage to the New Eden: Tourism in Florida. Myths and Dreams: Exploring the Cultural Legacies of Florida and the Caribbean* (http://www.jayikislakfoundation.org/millennium-exhibit/george1.htm, accessed 31 May 2005).

Giblettt, R. (1992) Philosophy (and sociology) in the wetlands: the s(ub)lime and the uncanny. *New Formations* 18, 142–159.

Gidwitz, T. (2002) *The Deadly Tides* (http://www.tomgidwitz.com/main/tides.htm, accessed 23 July 2005).

Gjerdrum, C., Vallee, A.M.J., StClair, C.C., Bertram, D.F., Ryder, J.L. and Blackburn, G.S. (2003) Tufted puffin reproduction reveals ocean climate variability. *Proceedings of the National Academy of Sciences of the United States of America* 100 (16), 9377–9382.

Glavovic, B., Scheyvens, R. and Overton, J. (2002) Waves of adversity, layers of resilience: exploring the sustainable livelihoods approach. Paper given at the *Development Studies of New Zealand Conference,* 2002 (http://devnet.massey.ac.nz/papers/Glasovic,%20Overton%20&%20Scheyvens.pdf, accessed 10 May 2005).

Gordon, I. and Goodall, B. (2000) Localities and Tourism. *Tourism Geographies* 2 (3), 290–311.

Gössling, S. and Hall, C.M. (eds) (2006) *Tourism and Global Environmental Change: Ecological, Economic, Social and Political Interrelationships.* Routledge, New York and London.

Gössling, S., Kunkel, T., Schumacher, K. and Zilger, M. (2004) Use of molluscs, fish, and other marine taxa by tourism in Zanzibar, Tanzania. *Biodiversity and Conservation* 13, 2623–2639.

Government of Canada (2002) *Canada's Ocean Strategy* (http://www.cos-soc.gc.ca, accessed 27 January 2004).

Gray, J. (1998a) SeaCanoe Thailand – lessons and observations. In: Miller, M.L. and Auyong, J. (eds) *Proceedings of the 1996 World Congress on Coastal and Marine Tourism,* University of Washington, Seattle and Oregon Sea Grant Program, Oregon State University, Corvallis, Oregon, pp. 139–144.

Gray, J. (1998b) *Update on SeaCanoe Wars.* Trinet (http://www.trinet.com, accessed 2 December 1998).

Gray, R.H. (1990) *The Greening of Accountancy.* Certified Accountants Publications, London.

Green, E. and Donnelly, R. (2003) Recreational scuba diving in Caribbean Marine Protected Areas: do the users pay? *Ambio* 32 (3), 140–144.

Green, E.P. and Short, F.T. (2003) *World Atlas of Seagrasses.* UNEP/WCMC and University of California Press, Berkeley, California.

Greenpeace (undated) *From Fish to Fodder* (http://archive.greenpeace.org/comms/cbio/fodder.html, accessed 31 January 2006).

Hall, C.M. (2000a) Rethinking collaboration and partnership: a public policy perspective. In: Bramwell, B. and Lane, B. (eds) *Tourism Collaboration and Partnerships: Politics, Practice and Sustainability.* Channel View, Clevedon, UK, pp. 143–158.

Hall, C.M. (2000b) *Tourism Planning; Policies, Processes and Relationships.* Prentice Hall, Harlow, UK.

Hall, C.M. (2001) Trends in ocean and coastal tourism: the end of the last frontier? *Ocean & Coastal Management* 44, 601–618.

Hall, C.M. (2003) Institutional arrangements for ecotourism policy. In: Fennell, D.A. and Dowling, R.K. (eds) *Ecotourism Policy and Planning.* CABI, Wallingford, UK, pp. 21–38.

Hall, C.M. (2005) *Tourism: Rethinking the Social Science of Mobility.* Pearson Education, Harlow, UK.

Hall, C.M. and Johnston, M.E. (eds) (1995) *Polar Tourism: Tourism in the Arctic and Antarctic Regions.* Wiley, Chichester, UK.

Hall, C.M. and Page, S.J. (1999) *The Geography of Tourism and Recreation.* Routledge, London.

Halpenny, E. (2000) The state and critical issues relating to international ecotourism. In: McArthur, S. and Dowling, R. (eds) *Australia – the World's Natural Theme Park: Proceedings of the Ecotourism Association of Australia, National Conference 1999,* Fraser Island, Queensland, Australia. Ecotourism Association of Australia, Brisbane, pp. 45–52.

Halpenny, E.A. (2001) Islands and coasts. In: Weaver, D.B. (ed.) *The Encyclopedia of Ecotourism.* CABI, Wallingford, UK, pp. 235–250.

Halpenny, E. (2002) *Marine Ecotourism: Impacts, International Guidelines and Best Practice Case Studies.* The International Ecotourism Society, Burlington, Vermont.

Halpenny, E. (2003) NGOs as conservation agents: achieving conservation through marine education. In: Garrod, B. and Wilson, J. (eds) *Marine Ecotourism: Issues and Experiences.* Channel View, Clevedon, UK.

Hamilton, N.T.M. and Cocks, K.D. (1994) The application of marine biogeographic techniques to the oceanic environment. *Proceedings of a Workshop Towards a Marine Regionalisation for Australia,* Sydney, 4–6 March 1994 (http://www.deh.gov.au/coasts/mpa/nrsmpa/regionalsation/study1.html, accessed 20 February 2005).

Hammitt, W. (1984) Cognitive processes involved in environmental interpretation. *Journal of Environmental Education* 15 (4), 11–15.

Hansen, L. (2004) *Testimony for Senate Committee on Commerce, Science and Transportation on the Impacts of Climate Change* (http://commerce.senate.gov/hearings/testimony.cfm?id=1080&wit_id=3054, accessed 5 May 2006).

Harriott, V.J. (2002) *Marine Tourism Impacts and their Management on the Great Barrier Reef.* CRC Reef Research Centre technical report No. 46, CRC Reef Research Centre, Townsville, Australia.

Harrison, D. (1998) *Working with the Tourism Industry: a Case Study from Fiji* (http://www.devstud.org.uk/studygroups/tourism/resources/harrison.pdf, accessed 4 June 2005).

Hartwick, E. and Peet, R. (2003) Neoliberalism and nature: the case of the WTO. *Annals of the American Academy of Political and Social Science* 590, 188–211.

Harzen, S. (1998) Habitat use by the bottlenose dolphin (*Tursiops truncatus*) in the Sado Estuary, Portugal. *Aquatic Mammals* 24, 117–128.

Hassall & Associates (2001) *Socio Economic Impact Assessment of the Contribution of Marine Tourism Operators to the Cairns–Douglas Region.* Undertaken for the Association of Marine Tourism Operators, Queensland, Australia.

Hawkins, J.P. and Roberts, C.M. (1992) Effects of recreational SCUBA diving on fore-reef slope communities of coral reefs. *Biological Conservation* 62, 171–178.

Healy, R. (1994) Tourist merchandise as a means of generating local benefits from ecotourism. *Journal of Sustainable Tourism* 2 (3), 137–151.

Helford VCMA (2003) *Community, Commerce and Conservation* (http://www.helfordmarineconservation.co.uk/conserve.htm, accessed 16 January 2004).

Henry, E. and Hammill, M.O. (2001) Impact of small boats on the haulout activity of harbour seals (*Phoca vitulina*) in Metis Bay, Saint Lawrence Estuary, Quebec, Canada. *Aquatic Mammals* 27, 140–148.

Hershman, M.J. (1999) *Building Capacity for Ocean Management: Recent Developments in US West Coast States* (http://www.oceanservice.noaa.gov/websites/retiredsites/natdia_pdf/19hershman.pdf, accessed 27 August 2004).

Hervey Bay City Council (2005) (http://www.herveybay.qld.gov.au/, accessed 5 October 2006).

Higham, J. and Lück, M. (2007) *Marine Wildlife Tourism Management.* CABI, Wallingford, UK. (in press)

Hillel, O. (2002) *Re [iye 2002] Ecotourism and Guides.* Discussion list (iye2002@yahoo groups.com, accessed 8 July, 2002).

Hinch, T. (2001) Indigenous territories. In: Weaver, D. (ed.) *The Encyclopedia of Ecotourism.* CABI, Wallingford, UK, pp. 345–357.

Hockings, M. (1994) A survey of the tour operator's role in marine park interpretation. *The Journal of Tourism Studies* 5 (1), 16–28.

Hoctor, Z. (2001) *Marine Ecotourism: a Marketing Initiative in West Clare.* The Marine Institute, Dublin.

Hoctor, Z. (2003) Community participation in marine ecotourism development in West Clare, Ireland. In: Garrod, B. and Wilson, J.C. (eds) *Marine Ecotourism: Issues and Experiences.* Channel View, Clevedon, UK.

Holden, A. (2000) *Environment and Tourism.* Routledge, London.

Holden, A. (2005) Tourism, CPRs and environmental ethics. *Annals of Tourism Research* 32 (3), 805–807.

Holland, S.M., Ditton, R.B. and Graefe, A.R. (1998) An ecotourism perspective on billfish fisheries. *Journal of Sustainable Tourism* 6 (2), 97–115.

Holmes, A. (2004) *Pearls of Wisdom.* Emirates Diving Association, December 2004 (http://www.emiratesdiving.com/images/EDA%20Dec%202004.pdf, accessed 25 January 2006).

Holy, N. (2004) Tangled in the food web. *Earth Island Journal* 19 (1) (http://www.earthisland.org/eijournal/new_articles.cfm?articleID=866&journalID=77, accessed 24 January 2006).

Honey, M. (1999) *Ecotourism and Sustainable Development: Who Owns Paradise?* Island Press, Washington, DC.

Honey, M. and Rome, A. (2001) Protecting Paradise: Certification Programs for Sustainable Tourism and Ecotourism. Institute for Policy Studies, Washington, DC.

Hoogvelt, A. (1985) *The Third World in Global Development.* Macmillan, London.

Horizon (1999) Volcanoes of the deep. 18 November 1999 (http://www.bbc.co.uk/science/horizon/1999/vents.shtml, accessed 5 February 2006).

Horn, C., Simmons, D.G. and Fairweather, J.R. (1998) *Evolution and Change in Kaikoura: Responses to Tourism Development.* Tourism Research and Education Centre Report No. 6, University of Lincoln, Lincoln, New Zealand.

Hou, J.-S., Lin, C.-H. and Morais, D.B. (2005) Antecedents of attachment to a cultural tourism destination: the case of Hakka and Non-Hakka Taiwanese visitors to Pei-Pu, Taiwan. *Journal of Travel Research* 44 (2), 221–233.

Howden, D. (2005) Whale and dolphins threatened by naval sonar devices, says UN report. *The Independent,* 25 January 2005.

Hoyt, E. (2001) *Whale Watching 2001: Worldwide Tourism Numbers, Expenditures, and Expanding Socioeconomic Benefits.* International Fund for Animal Welfare, Yarmouth Port, Massachusetts.

Hoyt, E. (2005) *Marine Protected Areas for Whales, Dolphins and Porpoises: a World Handbook for Cetacean Habitat Protection.* Earthscan, London.

Hughes, P. (2001) Animals, values and tourism: structural shifts in UK dolphin tourism provision. *Tourism Management* 22, 321–329.

Hydropolis Hotel (2005) http://hydropolis.com (accessed 15 June 2005).

Hylgaard, T. and Liddle, M.J. (1981) The effect of human trampling on a sand dune ecosystem dominated by *Empetrum nigrum. Journal of Applied Ecology* 18, 559–569.

IAATO (2005) *IAATO Overview of Antarctic Tourism 2004–2005 Antarctic Season.* IAATO, Basalt, Colorado.

ICRAN (2002) *Coral Reef Action: Sustaining Communities Worldwide.* ICRAN/WCMC, Cambridge, UK.

ICRI (1999) *ICRI Achievements 1995–1998* (http://www.icriforum.org/secretariat/achievements.html, accessed 7 May 2003).

ICRI (2003) *What is the International Coral Reef Initiative?* (http://www.icriforum.org, accessed 7 May 2003).

IFEES (2003) *Activities Project Development: Zanzibar* (http://www.ifees.org/act_pro_zanzibar.htm, accessed 15 January 2004).

Ingram, S.N. (2000) The ecology and conservation of bottlenose dolphins in the Shannon Estuary, Ireland. PhD thesis, University College Cork, Cork, Ireland.

IOC (2002) *Integrated Coastal Area Management* (http://ioc.unesco.org/icam, accessed 29 August 2003).

IRG (1992) IRG. *Ecotourism: a Viable Alternative for Sustainable Management of Natural Resources in Africa.* Agency for International Development Bureau for Africa, Washington, DC.

Iso-Ahola, S. (1982) Towards a social psychology of tourism motivation: a rejoinder. *Annals of Tourism Research* 9, 256–261.

IUCN (1988) *Proceedings of the 17th Session of the General Assembly of IUCN and 17th Technical Meeting,* San José, Costa Rica, 1–10 February 1988. IUCN, Gland, Switzerland.

IUCN (1991) *Guidelines for Establishing Marine Protected Areas.* IUCN, Gland, Switzerland.

IUCN (2006) *IUCN Red List of Threatened Species* (http://www.iucnredlist.org/, accessed 20 October 2006).

IUCN/WWF (1998) *Creating a Sea Change: a WWF/IUCN Vision for our Blue Planet* (http://www.iucn.org/themes/marine/pdf/seachang.pdf, accessed 13 May 2004).

IWC (2004) *IWC Information* (http://www.iwcoffice.org/commission/iwcmain.htm, accessed 1 July 2004).

Jamal, T. and Getz, D. (2000) Community roundtables for tourism-related conflicts: the dialectics of consensus and process structures. In: Bramwell, B. and Lane, B. (eds) *Tourism Collaboration and Partnerships: Politics, Practice and Sustainability.* Channel View, Clevedon, UK, pp. 159–182.

Jarvis, C.H. (2000) If Descartes swam with dolphins: the framing and consumption of marine animals in contemporary Australian tourism. Doctoral dissertation, Department of geography and environmental studies, University of Melbourne, Melbourne, Australia.

Jelinski, D.E., Krueger, C.C. and Duffus, D.A. (2002) Geostatistical analyses of interactions between killer whales (*Orcinus orca*) and recreational whale-watching boats. *Applied Geography* 22, 393–411.

Jennings, G. (2006) *Water-Based Tourism, Sport, Leisure, and Recreation Experiences* Elsevier, Burlington, Massachusetts.

Johns, G.M., Leeworthy, V.R., Bell, F.W. and Bonn, M.A. (2001) *Socioeconomic Study of Reefs in Southeast Florida.* Final report, 19 October 2001, Hazen and Sawyer, P.C. Hollywood, Florida.

Jules Undersea Lodge (2005) http://www.jul.com (accessed 15 June 2006).

Katz, C. (1998) Whose nature, whose culture? Private productions of space and the preservation of nature. In: Braun, B. and Castree, N. (eds) *Remaking Reality: Nature at the End of the Millennium.* Routledge, London, pp. 46–63.

Kay, A.M. and Liddle, M.J. (1984) *Tourist Impact on Reef Corals.* 1984 report to Great Barrier Reef Marine Park Authority. Great Barrier Reef Marine Park Authority, Townsville, Australia.

Kelleher, G. (1999) *Guidelines for Marine Protected Areas.* IUCN, Gland, Switzerland.

Kelleher, G. and Kenchington, R. (1991) *Guidelines for Establishing Marine Protected Areas.* IUCN, Gland, Switzerland.

Kelleher, G., Bleakley, C. and Wells, S. (1995) *A Global Representative System of Marine Protected Areas.* The Great Barrier Reef Marine Park Authority, The World Bank, The World Conservation Union (IUCN), Washington, DC.

Kelpwatch (2004) http://www.geol.utas.edu.au/kelpwatch/ (accessed 29 September 2006).

Khalid, F.M. (2004) Islamic basis for environmental protection. In: Taylor, B. and Kaplan, J. (eds) *Encyclopedia of Religion and Nature.* Continuum International, London.

Kimball, L.A. (2001) *International Ocean Governance: Using International Law and Organizations to Manage Marine Resources Sustainably.* IUCN, Gland, Switzerland.

Kinver, M. (2005) Healthy mangrove forests helped save lives in the Asia tsunami disaster, a new report has said (http://news.bbc.co.uk/2/hi/science/nature/4547032.stm, accessed 1 February 2006).

Kirkpatrick, H. and Cook, C. (undated) *The Nature Conservancy Programme* (http://www.spc.int/coastfish/News?LRF/2/8TNC.htm, accessed 26 July 2004).

Kovacs, K.M. and Innes, S. (1990) The impact of tourism on harp seals (*Phoca groenlandica*) in the Gulf of St Lawrence, Canada. *Applied Animal Behaviour Science* 26, 15–26.

Kroese, I. (1998) Shark cage diving in South Africa – sustainable recreational utilisation? *Shark News* 12, July 1998. IUCN/SSC Shark Specialist Group.

Kubodera, T. and Mori, K. (2005) First-ever observations of a live giant squid in the wild. *Proceedings of the Royal Society B* 272 (1581), 2583–2954.

Laffoley, D.d'A., Maltby, E., Vincent, M.A., Mee, L., Dunn, E., Gilliland, P., Hamer, J.P., Mortimer, D. and Pound, D. (2004) *The Ecosystem Approach. Coherent actions for Marine and Coastal Environments. A Report to the UK Government.* English Nature, Peterborough, UK.

Lan, T.D. (undated) *Marine Protected Areas as an Initiative for Sustainable Development in the Coastal Zone of Vietnam: Hon Mun Marine Protected Area Pilot Project* (http://www.rabbitgraph.de/cdg/p_lan.htm, accessed 26 May 2005).

Lash, S. and Urry, J. (1994) *Economies of Signs and Space.* Sage, London.

Lean, G. (2005) Global warming causing massive die off of fish and birds on the West Coast. *The Independent,* 13 November 2005.

Leeds Tourism Group (2004) *Sustainable Tourism and Coastal Marine Management in the Wider Caribbean*. Leeds Metropolitan University, Leeds, UK.

Lencek, L. and Bosker, G. (1998) *The Beach: the History of Paradise on Earth*. Pimlico, London.

Lew, A.A. and Hall, C.M. (1998) The geography of sustainable tourism: lessons and prospects. In: Hall, C.M. and Lew, A.A. (eds) *Sustainable Tourism: a Geographical Perspective*. Longman, Harlow, UK, pp. 199–203.

Lim, C. (2002) The socioeconomic importance of eco-resort management practices. In: Rizzoli, A.E. and Jakeman, A.J. (eds) *Integrated Assessment and Decision Support: Proceedings of the First Biennial Meeting of the Environmental Modelling and Software Society*, Vol. 2, pp. 496–501.

Lindberg, K. and Halpenny, E. (2001) *Protected Area Visitor Fees Country Review* (http://www.ecotourism.org/pdf/protareasfeesoverview.pdf, accessed 28 October 2004).

Lofoten-info (undated) *The Norwegian Fishing Village Museum* (http://www.lofoten-info.no/fiskmus.htm, accessed 10 May 2005).

Lourie, S.A. and Vincent, A.C.J. (2004) Using biogeography to help set priorities in marine conservation. *Conservation Biology* 18 (4), 1004–1020.

Lowe, C. (2006) *Wild Profusion: Biodiversity Conservation in an Indonesian Archipelago*. Princeton University Press, Princeton, New Jersey.

Lubchenco, J., Davis-Born, R. and Simler, B. (2002) The Need for a New Ocean Ethic. *Open Spaces* 5 (1).

Lück, M. (2003a) Environmentalism and on-tour experiences of tourists on wildlife watch tours in New Zealand: a study of visitors watching and/or swimming with wild dolphins. PhD thesis, The University of Otago, Dunedin, New Zealand.

Lück, M. (2003b) Large-scale ecotourism – a contradiction in itself? In: Lück, M. and Kirstges, T. (eds) *Global Ecotourism Policies and Case Studies*. Channel View, Clevedon, UK.

Lück, M. (2003c) *Marine Tourism* (http://www.pearsoned.com.au/elearning/hall/files/lueck.pdf_, accessed 2 April 2004).

Lück, M. (2003d) Education on marine mammal tours as agent for conservation – but do tourists want to be educated? *Ocean & Coastal Management* 46 (9/10), 943–956.

Lück, M. (2007) *Encyclopedia of Tourism and Recreation in Marine Environments*. CABI, Wallingford, UK. (in press)

Lundberg, M. (undated) *Magic Weapons and the Art of Scrimshaw* (http://www.explorenorth.com/library/yafeatures/bl-scrimshaw.htm, accessed 10 May 2005).

Lusseau, D. (2003). How do tour boats affect the behavioural state of bottlenose dolphins (*Tursiops* spp.)? Applying Markov chain modelling to the field study of behavior. *Conservation Biology* 17, 1785–1793.

Lusseau, D. and Higham, J. (2004) Managing the impacts of dolphin-based tourism through the definition of critical habitats: the case of bottlenose dolphins (*Tursiops* spp.) in Doubtful Sound, New Zealand. *Tourism Management* 25, 657–667.

Lynch, O.J. (1999) *Promoting Legal Recognition of Community-based Property Rights, Including the Commons: Some Theoretical Considerations* (http://www.ciel.org/Publications/promotinglegalrecog.pdf, accessed 2 May 2006).

Macnaghten, P. and Urry, J. (1998) *Contested Natures*. Sage, London.

Mader, R. (2002) [iye2002] *Marketing and Development*. Discussion list (iye2002@yahoo groups.com).

Mader, R. (undated) *Rethinking Ecotourism Certification* (http://www.planeta.com/ecotravel/tour/certification.html, accessed 17 August 2005).

Mani, D. (undated) *Culture as a Key Element of Human Security* (http://www.uncrd.or.jp/hs/doc/02a_mani_culture.pdf, accessed 10 May 2005).

Markwell, K. (2001) An intimate rendezvous with nature? Mediating the tourist–nature experience at three tourist sites in Borneo. *Tourist Studies* 1, 39–57.

Mascia, M.B. (2001) Designing effective coral reef marine protected areas: a synthesis report based on presentations at the *9th International Coral Reef Symposium*. Special report to: World Commission on Protected Areas–Marine, April 2001, IUCN, Washington, DC.

Mascia, M.B. (2003) The human dimension of Coral Reef Marine Protected areas: recent social science research and its policy implications. *The Journal of the Society for Conservation Biology* 17 (2), 630–632.

Maslow, A. (1973) *The Farther Reaches of Human Nature.* Pelican, London.

Maslow, A. (1987) *Motivation and Personality*, 3rd edn. Harper and Row, New York.

Massachusetts Government (2004) *Massachusetts Ocean Management Initiative* (http://www.state.ma.us/czm/oceanmgtinitiative.htm, accessed 12 May 2004).

May, J. (1996) In search of authenticity off and on the beaten track. *Environment and Planning D: Society and Space* 14, 709–736.

McAloon, J., Simmons, D.G. and Fairweather, J.R. (1998) *Kaikoura: Historical Background.* Tourism Research and Education Centre Report No. 1. University of Lincoln, Lincoln, New Zealand.

McCarthy, M. (2004) Disaster at sea: global warming hits UK birds. *The Independent*, 30 July 2004.

McConney, P., Mahon, R. and Pomeroy, R. (2005) *Moving Beyond the Critiques of Co-Management: Theory and Practice of Adaptive Co-Management* (http://www.omm.ca/documents/McConney%20et%20al.pdf, accessed 26 January 2005).

McKercher, B. and Robbins, B. (1998) Business development issues affecting nature-based tourism operators in Australia. *Journal of Sustainable Tourism* 16 (2), 173–188.

McKie, R. (2005) Puffins being wiped out as shrub chokes nesting sites. *The Observer*, 18 December 2005.

McMinn, S. and Cater, E. (1998) Tourist typology: observations from Belize. *Annals of Tourism Research* 25 (3), 675–699.

McNeil, B.I., Matear, R.J. and Barnes, D.J. (2004) Coral reef calcification and climate change: the effect of ocean warming. *Geophysical Research Letters* 32, 10.1029/2004GL021541.

Medio, D., Ormonda, R.F.G. and Pearson, M. (1997) Effect of briefings on rates of damage to corals by scuba divers. *Biological Conservation* 79, 91–95.

Meinhold, S.L. (2003) Designing an education program to manage the undesirable effects of whale watching. MA thesis, Royal Roads University, Victoria, British Columbia, Canada.

Mendoza, M. (2002) *Whale Watching – What Effects?* The Associated Press, Moss Landing, California, 25 February 2006.

Mensah, T.M. (1994) The competent international organizations: internal and external changes. In: Payoyo, P.B. (ed.) *Ocean Governance: Sustainable Development of the Seas.* UN University Press, Tokyo (http://www.unu.edu/unupress/unupbooks/uu15oe/uu15oe0r.htm, accessed 6 May 2004).

META-Project (2000) *Marine Ecotourism for the Atlantic Area (META-): Baseline Report.* University of the West of England, Bristol, UK.

Mihalic, T. (2003) Economics and environmental tourism policy. In: Fennell, D.A. and Dowling, R.K. (eds) *Ecotourism Policy and Planning*, CABI, Wallingford, UK, pp. 99–120.

Miller, M.L. (1993) The rise of coastal and marine tourism. *Ocean & Coastal Management* 20 (3), 181–199.

Miller, M.L. and Auyong, J. (1991) Coastal zone tourism: a potent force affecting environment and society. *Marine Policy* 15 (1), 75–99.

Milne, S.S. (1998) Tourism and sustainable development: the global–local nexus. In: Hall, C.M. and Lew, A.A. (eds) *Sustainable Tourism.* Addison Wesley, London, pp. 35–48.

Moeran, B. (1993) The language of Japanese tourism. *Annals of Tourism Research* 10, 93–108.

Monbiot, G. (1995) Monbiot. *The Guardian,* 3 March 1995.

Morgan, D.J. (1998) The adventure tourism experience on water: perceptions of risk and competence and the role of the operator. MA thesis, Lincoln University, Lincoln, New Zealand.

Moroney, D. (2003) Coasts and seas and Natural Resource Management planning in SA *The Marine & Coastal Community Network* (http://ww.mccn.org.au/sa/default.asp?page=projectitem&projectid=22, accessed 5 February 2004).

Morton, B. (2003) Editorial: Ningaloo. *Marine Pollution Bulletin* 46, 1213–1214.

Moscardo, G. (2002) Don't know, don't care: the importance of information for visitors to the Great Barrier Reef. In: Laws, E. (ed.) *Tourism Marketing: Quality and Service Management Perspectives.* Continuum, London, pp. 159–168.

Moscardo, G. (2004) East versus West: a useful distinction or misleading myth. *Journal of Tourism* 52 (1), 7–20.

Mosedale, S. (undated) What is stakeholder analysis. In: *Enterprise Development Impact Assessment Information Service, Frequently Asked Questions* (http://www.enterprise-impact.org.uk/FAQs/index.shtml#StakeAnalysis, accessed 4 February 2005).

Mowforth, M. and Munt, I. (1998) *Tourism and Sustainablity. New Tourism in the Third World.* Routledge, London.

Mowforth, M. and Munt, I. (2003) *Tourism and Sustainability: Development and New Tourism in the Third World,* 2nd edn. Routledge, London.

MPA News (2001) Paper parks: why they happen, and what can be done to change them. *MPA News* 2 (11), 1–4.

MPA News (2001/2) Insights on MPAs and indigenous peoples. *MPA News* 3 (6), 3–6.

MPA News (2002) Financial support for fishermen who are affected by Marine Reserves: examining the merits. *MPA News* 3 (11), 1–3.

MPA News (2003a) Using locals in enforcement, some MPA managers see improved compliance as a result. *MPA News* 5 (1), 1–3.

MPA News (2003b) Private-sector ownership of MPAs: cases illustrate challenges and opportunities. *MPA News* 4 (10), 1–4.

MPA News (2004) Tools and strategies for financial sustainability: how managers are building secure utures for their MPAs. *MPA News* 5 (5), 1–4.

Mules, T. (2004) *The Economic Contribution of Tourism to the Management of the Great Barrier Reef Marine Park: a Review.* Prepared for Queensland Tourism Industry Council, Australia.

Mundet, L. and Ribera, L. (2001) Characteristics of divers at a Spanish resort. *Tourism Management* 22, 501–510.

Musa, G. (2003) Sipadan: an over-exploited scuba diving paradise? An analysis of tourist impact, diver satisfaction and management priorities. In: Garrod, B. and Wilson, J.C. (eds) *Marine Ecotourism Issues and Experiences.* Channel View, Clevedon, UK, pp. 122–137.

Mustapa, S.A.H.B.S. (2005) Showcasing maritime heritage artefacts for the benefit of the tourist industry in Malaysia. *International Journal of Nautical Archaeology* 34, 211.

Muthiga, N. (2003) Enforcement in Kenya's Marine Protected Area network: *Proceedings of International Marine Ecosystems Management Symposium,* Manila, Philippines (http://www.icriforum.org/itmems/presentations/T12_NMuthiga.doc, accessed 18 August 2003).

Muthiga, N., Maina, J. and McClanahan, T. (2003) The effectiveness of management of Marine Protected Areas in Kenya. *Proceedings of International Marine Ecosystems Management Symposium*, Manila, Philippines (http://www.icriforum.org/itmems/presentations/T14_Kenya.pdf , accessed 18 August 2003).

Myers, G.A. (2002) Local communities and the new environmental planning: a case study from Zanzibar. *Area* 34 (2), 149–159.

Myrdal, G. (1957) *Economic Theory and Underdeveloped Regions*. Methuen, London.

NASA (2005) *The Ocean and the Carbon Cycle* (http://science.hq.nasa.gov/oceans/system/carbon.html, accessed 23 August 2006).

National Oceans Office (NOO) (2003) Developing an ecosystem-based approach for managing ocean activities. Outcomes from the *Workshop on Ecosystem-Based Management of Ocean Activities*, Cairns, Australia, June 2003 (http://www.oceans.gov.au/pdf/EBM/Cairns, accessed 2 May 2004).

National Trust for Scotland (2005) *Mixed Breeding Results on St Kilda* (http://www.nts-seabirds.org.uk/kildasep05.aspx, accessed 25 January 2006).

Neil, D.T. and Brieze, I. (1996) Wild dolphin provisioning at Tangalooma, Moreton Island: an evaluation. *Moreton Bay and Catchment Conference*, 13–14 December 1996, University of Queensland, Australia.

NERC (2005) *Ocean Drilling* (http://www.nerc.ac.uk/publications/odp, accessed 5 May 2006).

Newbery, B. (1997) In league with Captain Nemo. *Geographical* 69 (2), 35–41.

Newsome, D., Moore, S.A. and Dowling, R.K. (2002) *Natural Area Tourism: Ecology, Impacts and Management*. Channel View, Clevedon, UK.

Nicol, H.N. (undated) *The Caribbean as an Environmentally Sensitive Area: are New Regimes Required?* (http://www.kun.nl/ncbcr/CommunicatingBorders/bio/nicol-paper.doc, accessed 27 May 2004).

Nimb, H. (2003) PADI and Project AWARE. *UNESCO Asia–Pacific Regional Workshop on the 2001 Convention on the Protection of Underwater Cultural Heritage* (http://www.unescobk.org/fileadmin/user_upload/culture/Underwater/HK_presenta tions/Day%20One%20-%20Henrik%20Nimb.pdf, accessed 13 June 2005).

NMFS (National Marine Fisheries Service) (1999) *Code of Angling Ethics*. National Oceanic and Atmospheric Administration, Department of Commerce, Washington, DC (http://www.nmfs.noaa.gov/irf/ethics.html, accessed 2 May 2006).

NOAA (2004) *White Water to Blue Water Initiative*. US Department of State and National Oceanic and Atmospheric Administration Fact Sheet, Washington, DC (http://www.state.gov/g/oes/rls/fs2002/15624.htm, accessed 20 May 2006).

Norton, A. (1996) Experiencing nature: the reproduction of environmental discourse through safari tourism in Africa, *Geoforum* 27 (3), 355–373.

Norton, T. (2005) *Under Water to Get out of the Rain*. Century, London.

NSWA (2002) *The Bunaken Entrance Fee: Your Money Making a Difference* (http://www.north.sulawesi.org/bunaken.html, accessed 18 August 2003).

oneocean (1999) At Olango challenge spells opportunity. *Overseas: the Online Magazine for Sustainable Seas* 2 (2) (http://www.oneocean.org.oversear/feb99/at_olango_challenge_spells_opportunity.html, accessed 28 April 2005).

Orams, M.B. (1995) Managing interaction between wild dolphins and tourists at a dolphin feeding program, Tangalooma, Australia. The development and application of an education program for tourists, and an assessment of 'pushy' dolphin behaviour. PhD thesis, The University of Queensland, Brisbane, Australia.

Orams, M. (1997) 1996 World Congress on Coastal and Marine Tourism. *Tourism Management* 18 (2), 115–110.

Orams, M.B. (1999) *Marine Tourism: Development, Impacts and Management*. Routledge, London.

Orri, D. (1995) A case study in Patagonian whale watching. *Encounters with Whales Conference*, Hervey Bay, Australia (http://www.physics.helsinki.fi/whale/argentina/orri/cas.html, accessed 19 June 1999).

Osbourne, P.L. (2000) *Tropical Ecosystems and Ecological Concepts*. Cambridge University Press, Cambridge, UK.

Ostrom, E. (2000) Private and common property rights. In: *Encyclopedia of Law and Economics. Vol. II, Civil Law and Economics* (http://encyclo.findlaw.com/2000book.pdf, accessed 23 May 2006).

PADI (2005) *PADI Certification Statistics*. PADI, Santa Ana, California.

Page, S.J. and Dowling, R.K. (2002) *Ecotourism*. Prentice Hall, Harlow, UK.

Park, T., Bowker, J.M. and Leeworthy, V.R. (2002) Valuing snorkeling visits to the Florida Keys with stated and revealed preference models. *Journal of Environmental Management* 65, 301–312.

Parker, S. (2001) The place of ecotourism in public policy and planning. In: Weaver, D.B. (ed.) *The Encyclopedia of Ecotourism*. CABI, Wallingford, UK, pp. 509–520.

Parliament of Fiji Islands (2005) *Hansard Report*, 7 March 2005 (http://www.parliament.gov.fj/hansard/viewhansard.aspx?hansardID=330&viewtype=full, accessed 16 June 2005).

Parsons, E.C.M. and Rawles, C. (2003) The resumption of whaling by Iceland and the potential negative impact in the Icelandic whale-watching market. *Current Issues in Tourism* 6 (5), 444–448.

Parsons, E.C.M. and Woods-Ballard, A. (2003) Acceptance of voluntary whalewatching codes of conduct in West Scotland: the effectiveness of governmental versus industry-led guidelines. *Current Issues in Tourism* 6 (2), 172–182.

Parsons, E.C.M., Birks, I., Evans, P.G.H., Gordon, J.C.D., Shrimpton, J.H. and Pooley, S. (2000) The possible impacts of military activity on cetaceans in West Scotland. *European Research on Cetaceans* 14, 185–191.

Pearce, P.L. (1982) *The Social Psychology of Tourist Behaviour*. Pergamon Press, Oxford, UK.

Pettersson-Löfquist, P. (1995) The development of open water algae farming in Zanzibar: reflections on the socio-economic impact. *Ambio* 24 (7/8), 487–491.

Pirsig, R.M. (1974) *Zen and the Art of Motorcycle Maintenance: an Inquiry into Values*. Vintage, London.

Place, S. (1991) Nature tourism and rural development in Tortuguero. *Annals of Tourism Research* 18, 186–201.

Pleumaron, A. (2001) *Message 171. Ecotourism Certification Discussion* (http://groups.yahoo.com/group/ecotourism_certification/message/171, accessed 19 January 2001).

Plog, S.C. (1977) Why destination areas rise and fall in popularity. In: Kelly, E.M. (ed.) *Domestic and International Tourism*. Institute of Certified Travel Agents, Wellesley, Massachusetts, pp. 26–28.

Plog, S.C. (1991) *Leisure Travel: Making it a Growth Market ... Again!* Wiley, New York.

Pollnac, R.B., Crawford, B.R. and Gorospe, M.L.G. (2001) Discovering factors that influence the success of community-based marine protected areas in the Philippines. *Ocean and Coastal Management* 44 (11/12), 683–710.

Pomeroy, R.S. (1995) Community-based and co-management institutions for sustainable coastal fisheries management in Southeast Asia. *Ocean and Coastal Management* 27 (3), 143–162.

Ponting, J. (2001) Managing the Mentawais: an examination of sustainable tourism management and the surfing tourism industry in the Mentawai Archipelago, Indonesia. MA thesis, University of Technology, Sydney, Australia.

Poon, A. (1993) *Tourism, Technology and Competitive Strategies.* CABI, Wallingford, UK.

Poseidon Resorts (2005) http://www.poseidonresorts.com/ (accessed 3 December, 2005).

Potter, R., Binns, T., Elliot, J.A. and Smith, D. (2004) *Geographies of Development*, 2nd edn. Pearson/Prentice Hall, Harlow, UK.

Pretty, J. (1995) The many interpretations of participation. *In Focus* 16, 4–5.

propoortourism (2005) *Pro-Poor Tourism* (http://www.propoortourism.org.uk, accessed 7 January 2001).

Queensland Government (2003) http://www.tq.com.au/media/corporate-news/archive/nemo-to-hook-great-barrier-reef-visitors.cfm (accessed 8 October 2004).

Queenlandholidays (undated) *Wavelength Eco Snorkel Reef Tour* (http://www.queenslandholidays.com.au/tropical_north_queensland/502694/svc_50480, accessed 1 July 2005).

Radley, A. (1995) The elusory body and social constructivist theory. *Body and Society* 1 (2), 3–23.

Rainforest Alliance (2003) Sustainable Tourism Stewardship Council: Raising the Standards and Benefits of Sustainable Tourism and Ecotourism Certification. Rainforest Alliance, New York.

Rao, N. (2001) *Message 14. Ecotourism Certification Discussion* (http://groups.yahoo.com/group/ecotourism_certification/message/14, accessed 17 January 2001).

Raymundo, L.J. (2002) *Community-Based Coastal Resources Management of Apo Island, Negros Oriental, Philippines: History and Lessons Learned* (http://www.icran.org/SITES/doc/ws_apo.pdf, accessed 23 May 2005).

Reidmiller, S. (1999) *The Chumbe Island Coral Park Project* (http://www.chumbe.island@raha.com, accessed 30 April 1999).

Reidmiller, S. (2003) How can the private sector benefit from investing in marine conservation? Some experiences of the Chumbe Project in Zanzibar/Tanzania. *Fifth World Parks Congress: Sustainable Finance Stream.* Durban, South Africa (http://www.conservationfinance.org/WPC/WPC.documents/Apps_07_Reidmiller_P1 v1.pdf, accessed 27 January 2004).

Richter, L. (1989) *The Politics of Tourism in Asia.* University of Hawaii Press, Honolulu, Hawaii.

RIIA (Royal Institute of International Affairs) (2002) *What will it take to make 'Type 2' Partnerships for Implementation work?* Discussion paper – draft for comment (http://www.worldsummit2002.org/texts/RIIA2BaliPaper.pdf, accessed 28 January 2004).

Riley, R. (1995) Prestige-worthy tourism behaviour. *Annals of Tourism Research* 22, 630–649.

Ritter, F. (2003) *Interactions of Cetaceans with Whale Watching Boats – Implications for the Management of Whale Watching Tourism.* M.E.E.R. e.V., Berlin.

Robards, M.D., Willson, M.F., Armstrong, R.H. and Piatt, J.F. (1999) *Sand Lance: a Review of Biology and Predator Relations and Annotated Bibliography.* Research paper PNW-RP 521, United States Department of Agriculture Forest Service, Pacific Northwest Research Station, Portland, Oregon.

Roberts, P. and Trow, S. (2002) *Taking to the Water: English Heritage's Initial Policy for the Management of Maritime Archeology in England.* English Heritage, London.

Romero, L.M. and Wikelski, M. (2002) Exposure to tourism reduces stress-induced corticosterone levels in Galapagos marine iguanas. *Biological Conservation* 108 (3), 371–374.

Ross, G.L. (2001) Response of Hawaiian spinner dolphins to boat presence in Midway Atoll. MA thesis, San Francisco State University, San Francisco, USA.

Rouphael, A.B. and Inglis, G.J. (2001) 'Take only photographs and leave only footprints?': an experimental study of the impacts of underwater photographers on coral reef dive sites. *Biological Conservation* 100, 281–287.

RSPB (2005) *Fears of Poor Seabird Breeding Season Confirmed* (http://www.rspb.org.uk/birds/seabirdfailure.asp, accessed 25 January 2006).

RSPB (2006) *North Sea Birds under Threat from Industrial Fishing* (http://www.rspb.org.uk/policy/marine/news/threat.asp, accessed 31 January 2006).

RTSC Europe (1997) *Facts and Figures*. RTSC, Switzerland.

Rudkin, B. and Hall, C.M. (1996) Unable to see the forest for the trees: ecotourism development in Solomon Islands. In: Butler, R. and Hinch, T. (eds) *Tourism and Indigenous Peoples*. Thomson, London, pp. 203–226.

Ryan, C. (ed.) (1997) *The Tourist Experience*. Cassell, London.

Ryan, C., Hughes, K. and Chirgwin, S. (2000) The gaze, spectacle and ecotourism. *Annals of Tourism Research* 27(1), 148–163.

Saharuddin, A.H. (2001) National ocean policy – new opportunities for Malaysian ocean development. *Marine Policy* 25 (6), 427–436.

Saltzer, R. (2001) *Understanding Visitor Wildlife Interactions: Sea World Visitor Survey.* Data Summary Report, CRC for Sustainable Tourism, Queensland, Australia.

Saltzer, R. (2002) *Understanding Great Barrier Reef Visitors: Preliminary Results.* CRC Reef Research Project B2.1.1, Data Summary Report 1, CRC Reef Research Centre, Townsville, Australia.

San Pedro Sun (2000) Fisheries-CZMA/I differ on management of MPAs. *San Pedro Sun* 10 (44), 30 November 2000.

Sanson, L. (1994) An ecotourism case study in sub-Antarctic islands. *Annals of Tourism Research* 21 (2), 344–354.

Sathiendrakumar, R. and Tisdell, C. (1989) Tourism and the economic development of The Maldives. *Annals of Tourism Research* 16, 254–269.

Saunders, T., McGovern, I. and Kerry, J.F. (1993) *The Bottom Line of Green is Black: Strategies for Creating Profitable and Environmentally Sound Businesses.* Harper Collins, San Francisco, California.

Scheyvens, R. (2002) Growth and benefits of Budget Beach *Fale* tourism in Samoa. Paper given at *Development Studies of New Zealand Conference*, 2002 (http://www.devnet.org.nz/conf2002/papers/Scheyvens_Regina.pdf, accessed 25 May 2005).

Schiebe, K. (1986) Self-narratives and adventure. In: Sarbin, T. (ed.) *Narrative Psychology: the Storied Nature of Human Conduct*. Praeger, New York, pp. 129–151.

Schiel, D.R. and Taylor, D.I. (1999) Effects of trampling on a rocky intertidal assemblage in southern New Zealand. *Journal of Experimental Marine Biology and Ecology* 235, 213–235.

Schrope, M. (2005) The Deep. *New Scientist* November 2005, 36–51.

Schuler, S., Calavan, K., Esim, S., Gambill, D. and Monsod, T. (1998) *Assessment of Gender Integration in the USAID/Philippines Strategic Objectives*. USAID Women in Development Project, Washington, DC.

Schulman, A. (2005) *A Warm Unwelcome* (http://www.grist.org/news/maindish/2005/01/25/schulman-seabirds, accessed 25 January 2006).

Schuster, B.K. (1992) What puts the eco in ecotourism? *The Undersea Journal* 1, 45–46.

Scottish Executive (2002) *Assessment of the Effectiveness of Local Coastal Management Partnerships as a Delivery Mechanism for Integrated Coastal Zone Management*. Scottish Executive Social Research, Edinburgh, UK.

SeaCanoe (1999) *'Eco' Development Thailand: SeaCanoe* (http//seacanoe.com/seamore2.html, accessed 13 May 1999).

Sea Kayaker Magazine (2005) http://www.seakayakermag.com/ (accessed 20 June 2005).

Selin, S. (2000) Developing a typology of sustainable tourism partnerships. In: Bramwell, B. and Lane, B. (eds) *Tourism Collaboration and Partnership: Politics, Practice and Sustainability*. Channel View, Clevedon, UK, pp. 129–142.

Shackley, M. (1998) 'Stingray City' – managing the impact of underwater tourism in the Cayman Islands. *Journal Of Sustainable Tourism* 6 (4), 328–338.

Shackley, M. (1992) Manatees and tourism in southern Florida: opportunity or threat? *Journal of Environmental Management* 34, 257–265.

Shah, K. and Gupta, V. (2000) *Tourism, the Poor and Other Stakeholders: Experience in Asia.* Fair Trade in Tourism Project, ODI, London.

Sharpley, R. and Telfer, D.J. (2002) *Tourism and Development: Concepts and Issues* Channel View, Clevedon, UK.

Shepherd, N. (2003) How ecotourism can go wrong: the case of SeaCanoe and Siam Safari, Thailand. In: Lück, M. and Kirstges, T. (eds) *Global Ecotourism Policies and Case Studies: Perspectives and Constraints.* Channel View, Clevedon, UK, pp. 137–146.

Shields, R. (1991) *Places on the Margin. Alternative Geographies of Modernity.* Routledge, London.

Shores, J. (2002) *Ecotourism Financing*, intro. John Shores. Discussion list (ecotourism_financing@yahoogroups.com, accessed 1 August 2002).

Simmons, D.G. and Fairweather, J.R. (1998) *Towards a Tourism Plan for Kaikoura.* Tourism Research and Education Centre Report No. 10, University of Lincoln, Lincoln, New Zealand.

Simons, P. (2001) How ducks quacked it. *The Guardian*, 29 November 2001.

SKOANZ (1999) *Code of Practice May 1999* (http://www.seakayak.org.nz/seakayak/code.html, accessed 13 June 2003).

Slavin, T. (1998) *Ethical Business* (http://wordspy.com/words/triplebottomline.asp, accessed 3 June 2005).

SLMTA (2000) *Introduction* (http://www.slmta.co.uk/pages/intro.html, accessed 20 January 2004).

Sloan, K. (1987) Valuing Heron Island: preliminary report. Paper presented to the *16th Conference of Economists*, Surfers Paradise, Australia, August.

Smith, N. (2005) *Marine Harvest Slaughter Scotland's Seals: an Eye Witness Account* (http://www_salmonfammonitor.org/guestdecember2005.shtml, accessed 30 January 2006).

Sochaczewski, P.S. (2001) Conservation experiment in Philippines provides benefits and frustrations. *Geographical* October 2001.

Sofield, T. (1994) Tourism in the South Pacific review essay: tourism: a serpent in paradise? And oceans of dreams: currents of change. *Annals of Tourism Research* 21, 207–219.

Sofield, T. (1996) Anuha Island Resort: a case study of failure. In: Butler, R. and Hinch, T. (eds) *Tourism and Indigenous Peoples.* Thomson, London, pp. 176–202.

Sofield, T. (2005) Sustainable ecotourism: getting the balance right. *International Ecotourism Forum and Symposium*, Zhejiang Forestry University, Lin'an City, Zhejiang Province, China, 15–16 November 2005.

Sofield, T. and Li, F.M. (2001) *Cultural Factors Affecting Wildlife Tourism in China* (http://www.wildlifetourism.org.au/ppts/swtc_sofield_trevor.pdf, accessed 2 November 2005).

South African Collaborative White Shark Research Programme (2005) http://www.sharkresearch.org/pages/index.html_ (accessed 20 June 2005).

Southgate, C. and Sharpley, R. (2002) Tourism, development and the environment. In: Sharpley, R. and Telfer, D.J. (eds) *Tourism and Development.* Channel View, Clevedon, UK, pp. 231–262.

Spalding, M.D., Green, E.P. and Ravilious, C. (2001) *World Atlas of Coral Reefs.* University of California Press, Berkeley, California.

Spergel, B. and Moye, M. (2004) *Financing Marine Conservation: a Menu of Options.* WWF Center for Conservation Finance, Washington, DC.

Spiridonov, V. and Tzetlin, A. (2004) White Sea hope. *Arctic Bulletin* 4.04, 11.

Spooner, S.Q. (2003) How tourism benefits from the 'ADMAT Model' for the preservation of underwater cultural heritage. Paper presented to *5th Annual Caribbean Conference on Sustainable Tourism Development*, St Kitts, September 2003.

Sri Lanka Tourism (2005) Tourism 'Bounce Back' Campaign to reach out worldwide. *Sri Lanka News*, 11, 13 January 2005 (http://www.contactsrilanka.org, accessed 20 January 2005).

Stakeholder Forum (2002) *Network 2002.* Vol. III, Issue II, June 2002 (http://www.earthsummit2002.org, accessed 23 August 2002).

Stakeholder Forum (2004) *Network 2005, March 2004* (http://www.stakeholderforum.org, accessed 13 May 2004).

State of Queensland (2002) *Queensland Ecotourism Plan 2003–2008.* Tourism Queensland, Queensland Government, Australia.

Stolk, P., Markwell, K. and Jenkins, J. (2005) Perceptions of artificial reefs as scuba diving resources: a study of Australian recreational scuba divers. *Annals of Leisure Research* 8 (2/3), 153–173.

Stonehouse, B. (2001) Polar environments. In: Weaver, D. (ed.) *The Encyclopedia of Ecotourism.* CABI, Wallingford, UK, pp. 219–234.

Stonehouse, B. and Crosbie, K. (1995) Tourist impacts and management in the Antarctic Peninsula area. In: Hall, C.M. and Johnston, M.E. (eds) *Polar Tourism: Tourism in the Arctic and Antarctic regions.* Wiley, Chichester, UK.

Stonich, S., Sorensen, J.H. and Hundt, A. (1995) Ethnicity, class, and gender in tourism development: the case of the Bay Islands, Honduras. *Journal of Sustainable Tourism* 3 (1), 1–28.

Strain, L., Rajabifard, A. and Williamson, I. (2006) Marine administration and spatial data infrastructure. *Marine Policy* 30 (4), 431–441.

Sulaiman, Y. (2005) Malaysian government fears impact of tourism on island marine life. *.travelwirenews*, 10 October 2005 (http://www.travelwirenews.com/cgi-script/csArticles/articles/000057/005795-p.htm, accessed 12 October 2005).

Surfrider (undated) *Cruise Ship Pollution* (http://www.surfrider.org/a-z/cruise.asp, accessed 2 May 2006).

Sustaining Livelihoods in Southern Africa (2002) Social Capital and Sustainable Livelihoods, Issue 5 March 2002 (http://www.cbnrm.net/pdf/khanya_002_slsa_issue05_sc.pdf, accessed 10 May 2005).

Swarbrooke, J., Beard, C., Leckie, S. and Pomfret, G. (2003) *Adventure Tourism: the New Frontier.* Butterworth Heinemann, Oxford, UK.

SWT/WWF (2005) News release. E-mail from Cheales, N. (NCheales@swt.org.uk), 25 February 2005. Re: enquiry from web site. E-mail to E.A. Cater (e.a.cater@reading.ac.uk).

Sydney Morning Herald (2004) Migaloo thrills tourists. 22 June 2004.

Tangalooma Wild Dolphin Resort (2005) http://www.tangalooma.com (accessed 4 April 2004).

Taylor, G. (1995) The community approach: does it really work? *Tourism Management* 16 (7), 487–489.

Teo, P. (2002) Striking a balance for sustainable tourism: implications of the discourse on globalisation. *Journal of Sustainable Tourism* 10 (6), 459–474.

The Chief Engineer (2006) *Dubai Invests In Artificial Resort Islands* (http://www.chiefengineer.org/content/content_display.cfm/seqnumber-content/2318.htm, accessed 25 January 2006).

The Coral Reef Alliance (2002) *International Coral Reef Information Network* (http://www.coralreef.org/about, accessed 11 April 2002).

The Economist (2005) Special report: The Everglades. *The Economist*, 8 October 2005.

The International Ecotourism Society (undated) *Marine Ecotourism: How to be a Marine Ecotourist* (http://www.eco-tour.org/info/w_10040_en.html, accessed 5 April 2006).

The Observer (2006) Secrets of nature still enthral us. *The Observer* 5 March 2006.

The Wildlife Trusts (2005) *The Wildlife Trusts' Basking Shark Survey* (http://basking sharks.wildlifetrusts.org, accessed 2 June 2006).

Third World Network (2001) An open letter to UN Secretary Kofi Annan. *Earth Island Journal* 16 (3) (http://www.earthisland.org/eijournal/new_articles.cfm?articleID= 237&journalID=48, accessed 6 December 2002).

Thomas, L. (2002) Fish-hooks in the case for reserves. *New Zealand Herald* 31 January 2002.

Thrift, N.J. (1999) Steps to an ecology of place. In: Massey, D., Allen, J. and Sarre, P. (eds) *Human Geography Today.* Polity, Cambridge, UK, pp. 295–322.

Thrift, N. (2001) Still life in nearly present time: the object of nature. In: McNaghten, P. and Urry, J. (eds) *Bodies of Nature.* Sage, London.

Timothy, D.J. (1998) Cooperative tourism planning in a developing destination. *Journal of Sustainable Tourism* 6 (1), 52–68.

Timothy, D.J. (2002) Tourism and community development. In: Sharpley, R. and Telfer, D.J. (eds) *Tourism and Development.* Channel View, Clevedon, UK, pp. 149–164.

TOI (2003) *Sustainable Tourism: the Tour Operators' Contribution.* Tour Operators Initiative Secretariat, UNEP, Paris.

Topelko, K.N. and Dearden, P. (2005) The shark watching industry and its potential contribution to shark conservation. *Journal of Ecotourism* 4 (2), 108–128.

Torbay Coast and Countryside Trust, Devon Bird Watching and Preservation Society, Devon Sea Fisheries, Devon Wildlife Trust, English Nature and The Seahorse Trust (2004) *Tor Bay Marine Biodiversity Action Plan.* Torbay Coast and Countryside Trust, Torquay, UK.

Torell, M. and Salamanca, A.M. (undated) Navigating the Institutional Landscape: Introduction and Overview (http://www.worldfishcenter.org/Pubs/institutional_sea/ pub_insea2.pdf_, accessed 26 January 2005).

Tourism Concern (1999) Update and action: fair trade in tourism. *In Focus* 31.

Tourism Concern (2005) *Post Tsunami Reconstruction and Tourism: a Second Disaster?* Tourism Concern, London.

Travel Industry Association of America (2003) *Geotourism: the New Trend in Travel.* Travel Industry Association of America, Washington, DC.

Turner, B. (1996) *The Body and Society*, 2nd edn. Sage, London.

UN (2002) *Oceans and Law of the Sea* (http://www.un.org/Depts/los/index.htm, accessed 29 April 2004).

UNDP (2001) *Projects in Maldives: Importance of the Marine Biodiversity of Maldives* (http://www.mv.undp.org/projects/environment_living2.htm, accessed 8 May 2006).

UNEP (2001) *About the International Year of Ecotourism (IYE) 2002* (http://www.uneptie.org/pc/tourism/ecotourism/wes_portfolio/about/iye.htm, accessed 1 March 2004).

UNEP (2002a) *State of Environment, Maldives 2002* (http://www.rrcap.unep.org/reports/ soe/maldives_climate.pdf, accessed 8 May 2006).

UNEP (2002b) *Coral or no Coral? It is my Choice* (http://www.unep.org/Documents/ Default.asp?DocumentID=233&ArticleID=2993, accessed 7 May 2003).

UNEP/WTO (2002) *Quebec Declaration on Ecotourism* (http://www.world-tourism.org/ sustainable/IYE/quebec/anglais/declaration.html, accessed 22 October 2002).

UNESCO (1998) *1998 International Year of the Ocean Web Site* (http:ioc.unesco.org/ iyo/introduction.htm, accessed 9 February 2004).

UNESCO (2001a) *United Nations Urged to Include Oceans and Coasts at World Summit on Sustainable Development* (http://www.unesco.org/bpi/eng/unescopress/2001/ 01-133e.shtml, accessed 9 February 2004).

UNESCO (2001b) *Indigenous People and Parks: The Surin Islands Project.* Coastal and small islands papers 8, UNESCO, Paris.

UNESCO (2002a) *Australian National Periodic Report Section II: Report on the State of Conservation of Great Barrier Reef.* UNESCO, Paris.

UNESCO (2002b) *State of Conservation of World Heritage Properties. Administrative Committee of Mount Huangshan Scenic Site, October 2002* (http://whc.unesco.org/ archive/periodicreporting/cycle01/section2/547.pdf, accessed 3 December 2005).

UNESCO Indonesia (2004) http://www.unesco.or.id/prog/science/cms/coral.htm (accessed 6 August 2005).

Urry, J. (1990) *The Tourist Gaze.* Sage, London.

Urry, J. (1995) *Consuming Places.* Routledge, London.

US Submarines (2003) *The Tourist Submarine Business.* US Submarines, Inc., Fort Lauderdale, Florida.

Uychiaoco, A.J., Alino, P.M. and White, A.T. (2002) Marine Protected Areas in the Philippines: towards harmonizing goals and strategies. *Proceedings of IUCN/WCPA-EA-4 Taipei Conference*, T'aipei, Taiwan, March 2002.

Valencia, M.J. (1996) *A Maritime Regime for Northeast Asia.* Oxford University Press, Hong Kong.

Valentine, P.S., Birtles, A., Curnock, M., Arnold, P. and Dunstan, A. (2004) Getting closer to whales: passenger expectations and experiences, and the management of swim with dwarf minke whale interactions in the Great Barrier Reef. *Tourism Management* 25, 647–655.

Vallejo, S.M. (1994) New structures for decision making in integrated ocean policy: introduction. In: Payoyo, P.B. (ed.) *Ocean Governance: Sustainable Development of the Seas.* UN University Press, Tokyo (http:www.unu.edu/unupress/unupbooks/ uu15oe/uu15oe0b.htm, accessed 6 May 2004).

Veijola, S. and Jokinen, E. (1994) The body in tourism. *Theory, Culture and Society* 11, 125–151.

Viders, H. (1997) *Marine Conservation in the 21st Century.* AZ Publishing, Flagstaff, Arizona.

Villegas, M.J. (2002) *Protecting the People of the Protected Area* (http://mobilemediaph. com/projectE/ApoIsland/ApoIsland_community.html, accessed 11 October 2004).

Villena, M. and Spash, C.L. (2000) *Exploring the Approach of Institutional Economics to the Environment.* Environment Discussion Paper Series 11, Cambridge Research for the Environment, Department of Land Economy, University of Cambridge, UK.

Visser, L.E. (2004) Reflections on transdisciplinarity, integrated coastal development, and governance. In: Visser, L.E. (ed.) *Challenging Coasts. Transdisciplinary Excursions into Integrated Coastal Zone Development.* Amsterdam University Press, Amsterdam, pp. 23–47.

Vivanco, L. (2002) Seeing the dangers lurking behind the International Year of Ecotourism. *The Ecologist* 32 (2), 26.

Vodden, K. (2002) *Governance for Sustainability – Lessons from Canada* (http://www.sfu. ca/coastalstudies/voddenparis.doc, accessed 1 July 2004).

Walker, P.A. (2003) Reconsidering 'regional' political ecologies: toward a political ecology of the rural American West. *Progress in Human Geography* 27 (1), 7–24.

Walley, C.J. (2004) *Rough Waters: Nature and Development in an East African Marine Park.* Princeton University Press, Princeton, New Jersey and Oxford, UK.

Walley, C.J. (2004/2005) *Best Intentions: the Story of Tanzania's People's Park* (http://www.bostonreview.net/BR29.6/Walley.html, accessed 30 June 2006).

Wardlow, J. (2004) *Will Puffins Disappear?* (http://www.ch4.org.uk/eduarticle.php/Will+Puffins+Disappear%3F, accessed 25 January 2006).

Warnken, J., Dunn, R.J.K. and Teasdale, P.R. (2004) Investigation of recreational boats as a source of copper at anchorage sites using time-integrated diffusive gradients in thin film and sediment measurements. *Marine Pollution Bulletin* 49, 833–843.

Warth, H. (2004) *Rationale for the Award TO DO! 2004 Award Winner Chumbe Island Coral Park Ltd* (http://www.studienkreis.org.engl/wettbewerbe/todo/04tanzania.html, accessed 25 May 2005).

WCED (World Commission on Environment and Development) (1987) *Our Common Future*. United Nations, New York.

Wearing, S. and McDonald, M. (2002) The development of community-based tourism: rethinking the relationship between tour operators and development agents as intermediaries in rural and isolated area communities. *Journal of Sustainable Tourism* 10 (3), 191–206.

Weaver, D.B. (1998) *Ecotourism in the Less Developed World*. CABI, Wallingford, UK.

Weaver, D.B. (2001) Ecotourism in the context of other tourism types. In: Weaver, D.B. (ed.) *The Encyclopedia of Ecotourism*. CABI, Wallingford, UK, pp. 73–83.

Weaver, D.B. (2002) Asian ecotourism: patterns and themes. *Tourism Geographies* 4 (2), 153–172.

Weaver, D.B. and Schlüter, R. (2001) Latin America and the Caribbean. In: Weaver, D.B. (ed.) *The Encyclopedia of Ecotourism*. CABI, Wallingford, UK, pp. 173–188.

Weiler, B. and Hall, C.M. (eds) (1992) *Special Interest Tourism*. Belhaven, London.

Wells, R.S. (1993) The marine mammals of Sarasota Bay. In: *Sarasota Bay: 1992 Framework for Action*, Sarasota Bay National Estuary Program, Sarasota, Florida, pp. 9.1–9.23.

Westera, M. (2003) The effect of recreational fishing on targeted fishes and trophic structure, in a coral reef marine park. PhD thesis, Edith Cowan University, Perth, Western Australia.

Whale Watch (1999) *Company Profile*. Whale Watch, Kaikoura, New Zealand.

Wheeller, B. (1994) Egotourism, sustainable tourism and the environment – a symbiotic, symbolic or shambolic relationship? In: Seaton, A.V., Jenkins, C.L., Wood, R.C., Dieke, P.U.C., Bennett, M.M., MacLellan, L.R. and Smith, R. (eds) *Tourism: the State of the Art*. Wiley, Chichester, UK, pp. 647–654.

White, A.T. and Dobias, R.J. (1990) Community marine tourism in the Philippines and Thailand: a boon or bane to conservation? In: Miller, M.L. and Auyong, J. (eds) *Proceedings of the 1990 Congress on Coastal and Marine Tourism*. National Coastal Resources Research and Development Institute, Newport, Oregon.

White Shark Diving Company (2006) *Cage diving in South Africa* (http://www.sharkcagediving.co.za, accessed 26 January 2006).

Whitmore, M. (2003) Limits of the nature-based tourism experience: a sociological analysis. In: *Tourism at the Limits Conference*, University of Waikato, Hamilton, New Zealand, December 2003.

Wildlife and Countryside Link (2004) *A Future for our Seas* (http://www.wcl.org.uk/downloads/2004/WCL01_Governance_BP5_19Apr04.pdf, accessed 27 August 2004).

Wight, P.A. (2002) Supporting the principles of sustainable development in tourism and ecotourism: government's potential role. *Current Issues in Tourism* 5 (3/4), 222–244.

Wilkie, D.S. and Carpenter, J.F. (1998) Bushmeat hunting in the Congo Basin: an assessment of impacts and options for mitigation. *Biodiversity and Conservation* 8 (7), 927–955.

Williams, A.M. and Shaw, G. (1998) Tourism and the environment: sustainability and economic restructuring. In: Hall, C.M. and Lew, A.A. (eds) *Sustainable Tourism: a Geographical Perspective.* Longman, Harlow, UK, pp. 49–59.

Williams, V. (2001). *Captive Orcas Dying to Entertain you: the Full Story.* WDCS, Bath, UK.

Wilson, A. (1992) *The Culture of Nature.* Blackwell, Oxford, UK.

Wilson, C. and Tisdell, C. (2001) Sea turtles as a non-consumptive tourism resource especially in Australia. *Tourism Management* 22, 279–288.

Wilson, E.O. (1993) Biophilia and the conservation ethic. In: Kellert, S. and Wilson, E.O. (eds) *The Biophilia Hypothesis.* Island Press and Shearwater Books, Washington, DC and Covelo, California.

Wilson, J. (2003) Planning policy issues for marine ecotourism. In: Garrod, B. and Wilson, J.C. (eds) *Marine Ecotourism Issues and Experiences.* Channel View, Clevedon, UK, pp. 48–65.

Wilson, J. and Garrod, B. (2003) Introduction. In: Garrod, B. and Wilson, J.C. (eds) *Marine Ecotourism Issues and Experiences.* Channel View, Clevedon, UK, pp. 1–11.

Wolch, J. (1998) Zoopolis. In: Wolch, J. and Emel, J. (eds) *Animal Geographies: Place, Politics, and Identity in the Nature–Culture Borderlands.* Verso, London.

Woodland, D.J. and Hooper, J.N.A. (1977) The effect of human trampling on coral reefs. *Biological Conservation* 11, 1–4.

Woods Hole Oceanographic Institution (undated) *Info at a Glance* (http://www.whoi.edu/home/index_about.html, accessed 17 October 2006).

World Bank (1996) *Guidelines for Integrated Coastal Zone Management* (http://www.norcoast.org/pages/iczm.htm, accessed 27 August 2003).

World Bank (2005) *Tsunami Impact and Resources Annex 8 Tourism Sector* (http://siteresources.worldbank.org/INTMALDIVES/Resources/mvna-annex-08.pdf, accessed 23 May 2006).

WRI (World Resources Institute) (1996) *Pressures on Marine Biodiversity* (http://www.wri.org/wri/wr-96-97/bi_txt5.html, accessed 27 May 2006).

WRI (2004a) *Management Approaches* (http://projects.wri.org/project_content_text.cfm?ContentID=767, accessed 26 January 2005).

WRI (2004b) *Local Management Explored in Recent Years* (http://projects.wri.org/project_content_text.cfm?ContentID=773, accessed 26 January 2005).

WRI (2004c) *Towards a Collaborative Model* (http://projects.wri.org/project_content_text.cfm?ContentID=774, accessed 26 January 2005).

WTO (2003) *Djerba Declaration on Tourism and Climate Change* (http://www.world-tourism.org/sustainable/climate/decdjerba-eng.pdf, accessed 8 November 2005).

WWF (1996) Editorial. *Arctic Bulletin* 96 (2), 3.

WWF (2001) *Clear? ... or Present Danger? Great Barrier Reef Pollution Report Card,* June 2001. WWF Australia, Sydney.

WWF (2003a) *The Implications of Climate Change for Australia's Great Barrier Reef.* WWF Australia, Sydney.

WWF (2003b) *Securing Australia's Great Barrier Reef. WWF Australia's proposal: World Class Protection for Special, Unique and Representative Areas.* WWF Australia, Sydney.

WWF (2003c) *Arctic Bulletin* 3.03, 14.

WWF (2004) *Sulu and Sulawesi Seas Conservation Results* (http://www.worldwildlife.org/wildplaces/ss/results.cfm, accessed 5 October 2004).

WWF (undated) *Conservation in the Fiji Islands* (http://www.wwfpacific.org.fj/fiji.htm, accessed 26 January 2005).

WWOANW (2003) *Best Practice Guidelines* (http://www.nwwhalewatchers.org/guidelines.html, accessed 22 January 2004).

Yáñez-Arancibia, A., Lara-Domínguez, A.L., Rojas Galaviz, J.L., Zárate Lomeli, D.J., Villalobos Zapata, G.J. and Sánchez-Gil, P. (1999) Integrating science and management on coastal marine protected areas in the Southern Gulf of Mexico. *Ocean & Coastal Management* 42, 319–344.

Yankov, A. and Ruivo, M. (1994) An ocean assembly. In: Payoyo, P.B. (ed.) *Ocean Governance: Sustainable Development of the Seas.* UN University Press, Tokyo (http://www.unu.edu/unupress/unupbooks/uu15oe/uu15oe0r.htm#v.%20conclusions, accessed 6 May 2004).

Young, E. (1999) Balancing conservation with development in small-scale fisheries: is ecotourism an empty promise? *Human Ecology* 27 (4), 581–620.

Young, E.H. (2003) Balancing conservation with development in marine-dependent communities. In: Zimmerer, K.S. and Bassett, T.J. (eds) *Political Ecology: an Integrative Approach to Geography and Environment-Development Studies.* The Guildford Press, New York and London, pp. 29–49.

Yunis, E. (2004) *Tourism, Poverty Alleviation and Microcredit: a First Glance* (http://uncdf.org/english/microfinance/newsletter/pages/july_2004/news_tourism, accessed 26 May 2005).

Zann, L.P. (2005) The social value of the coastal and marine environment to Australians. In: *Our Sea, Our Future: Major Findings of the State of Marine Environment Report for Australia* (http://www.deh.gov.au/coasts/publications/somer/chapter2.html, accessed 28 April 2005).

Zee News (2006) Dubai's delicate marine ecosystem under threat (http://www.zeenews.com/znnew/articles.asp?aid=242202&ssid=26&sid=env, accessed 25 January 2006).

Zimmerer, K.S. and Bassett, T.J. (2003) Future directions in political ecology: nature–society fusions and scales of interaction. In: Zimmerer, K.S. and Bassett, T.J. (eds) *Political Ecology: an Integrative Approach to Geography and Environment-Development Studies.* The Guildford Press, New York and London, pp. 275–295.

Zwirn, M., Pinsky, M. and Rahr, G. (2005) Angling ecotourism: issues, guidelines and experience in Kamchatka. *Journal of Ecotourism* 4 (1), 16–31.

Index

Page numbers in *italics* denote pages with photographs.